Terror in the Mind of God

Comparative Studies in Religion and Society
Mark Juergensmeyer, editor

Terror
in the Mind
of God

THE GLOBAL RISE OF
RELIGIOUS VIOLENCE

Mark Juergensmeyer

UNIVERSITY OF CALIFORNIA PRESS
Berkeley / Los Angeles / London

University of California Press

Berkeley and Los Angeles, California

University of California Press, Ltd.

London, England

© 2000 by

The Regents of the University of California

Juergensmeyer, Mark.

Terror in the mind of God : the global rise of
religious violence / Mark Juergensmeyer.

p. cm.—(Comparative studies in religion
and society; 13)

Includes bibliographical references (p.   ) and
index.

ISBN 0-520-22301-2 (alk. paper)

1. Violence—Religious aspects. I Title. II Series.
BL65.V55J84 2000

291.1'78331—dc21   99-30466

                                      CIP

Printed in the United States of America

9 8 7 6 5 4 3 2 1

The paper used in this publication meets the mini-
mum requirements of American National Standard
for Information Sciences—Permanence of Paper for
Printed Library Materials, ANSI Z39.48-1984.

to terror's victims

I will send my terror before you,
and will throw into confusion all the people . . .

Exodus 23:27

Contents

Preface and Acknowledgments

I am sometimes asked why a nice guy like me would want to study religious terrorism. Those who ask this question usually brush the intellectual explanations aside—as if my interest in the global dimensions of religion and society weren't reason enough. They search for something more personal.

One answer I give is that my work on nationalism and global conflict has led to a concern about areas of the world where social transformations have not been easy, and where peaceful options have shredded into violence. I have seen the unraveling of social order close at hand, having lived for a time in India's Punjab, a region torn apart by spiraling violence between militant Sikhs and the Indian government. With the horrors of that era of terror in mind, I have sought to understand how civil order can collapse, and I have looked for a more general explanation for the merger of religion and violence than this one example can offer.

Yet another answer is more personal still. As someone who was raised in the religious milieu of midwestern Protestantism, I know the power of religion to provide a transformative vision of the human potential. In my experience this transformative quality of religion has been a positive thing—it has been associated with images of personal wholeness and social redemption—and it has mostly been nonviolent. I say "mostly" because I can remember moments from my own religious involvement in civil rights and antiwar movements a generation ago that were dangerously confrontational and occasionally bloody. So I feel a certain kinship with present-day religious activists who take religion seriously, and I wonder if one of their motivations might be a spiritual conviction so strong that they are willing to kill and to be killed for moral reasons.

Yet my own social activism never reached such extremes, nor could I imagine a situation where even the most worthy of causes could justify taking another person's life. Thus I have looked for other motivations for those who have perpetrated acts of religious terrorism rather than simply struggling for a worthy cause. I have wondered why their views of religion and social engagement have taken such a lethal turn and why they have felt so justified in undertaking actions that have led to destruction and death, often committed in brutal and dramatic ways.

In seeking answers to these questions, I found myself looking not only at particular people and case studies, but also at the larger social and political changes that affect the globe at this moment of history and provide the context for many violent encounters. It is this theme that runs through my previous book, *The New Cold War? Religious Nationalism Confronts the Secular State*, and to some extent this work is a continuation of that interest, though here I focus on events rather than on activist movements. Thus I find myself returning to what attracted me to the subject of religious terrorism intellectually: my sense that a study of this striking phenomenon can tell us something about religion, about public violence, and about the character of contemporary society on virtually a global scale.

In this attempt to understand the recent rise of religious violence around the world, I have a number of colleagues to thank. The case studies that are the heart of this project would not have been possible without the help of those who provided both insight and contacts. In Israel I relied on Ehud Sprinzak and Gideon Aran for information on Jewish activism; Zaid Abu-Amr, Ariel Merari, and Tahir Shreipeh for insight into the Hamas movement; and the support of the Yitzhak Rabin Center for Israel Studies in Tel Aviv, the Carnegie Commission on Preventing Deadly Conflict, and the Tantur Ecumenical Institute, Jerusalem, for housing and travel arrangements. For the prison interviews in Lompoc, California, I relied on the assistance of Terry Roof, Warden David Rardin, Associate Warden Jack Atherton, and Congressman (and colleague) Walter Capps. For an introduction to the Algerian community in Paris I thank François Godement and Michelle Zimney. Regarding Christian militia and abortion activists in the United States, I am grateful to Michael Barkun, Julie Ingersoll, and

Matt Miller. In Belfast I appreciated the help of Jim Gibney and the Sinn Féin Press Office, and I learned much from Tom Buckley, Brian Murphy, and Martin O'Toole. For help in contacting Sikh activists in India and the United States and in understanding Sikh politics, I value the suggestions of Cynthia Mahmood, Gurinder Singh Mann, Hew McLeod, Harish Puri, and several Sikh colleagues who prefer to remain nameless. In Jummu and Kashmir, I appreciate the arrangements provided by Pramod Kumar and the Institute for Development and Communication. In Japan my contacts with, and understanding of, the Aum Shinrikyo movement were facilitated by Koichi Mori, Ian Reader, and Susumu Shimazono.

Specific chapters related to these case studies were read by Sprinzak, Aran, Barkun, Ingersoll, Miller, Mahmood, Mann, McLeod, Puri, Reader, Shimazono, "Takeshi Nakamura" (a pseudonym), Mahmud Abouhalima, and Michael Bray. In addition, portions of early drafts and related essays were reviewed by Karen McCarthy Brown, Jack Hawley, Roger Friedland, and Robin Wright; and the entire manuscript was read by William Brinner, Martha Crenshaw, Ainslie Embree, Bruce Lawrence, and Richard Hecht.

I have also learned much from the circle of scholars involved in terrorist research. It includes Crenshaw, Sprinzak, Bruce Hoffman, Ariel Merari, Jerrold Post, David Rapoport, Paul Wilkinson, and the helpful staff at the Centre for the Study of Terrorism and Political Violence, St. Andrews University, Scotland, which I visited in 1997. It was Rapoport who first used the quotation from Exodus that I have borrowed for the front of this book. At Santa Barbara I have appreciated the support of my colleagues, Friedland, Hecht, Richard Appelbaum, Marguerite Bouraad-Nash, Juan Campo, Benjamin J. Cohen, Don Gevirtz, Giles Gunn, Barbara Holdrege, Wade Clark Roof, Ninian Smart, Alan Wallace, David White, and the faculty associated with Global and International Studies.

I am grateful to my students, who have challenged me to present these ideas in a clear and forthright manner. I appreciate especially those in my graduate seminars in religious violence at Santa Barbara and, in 1996, at the Graduate Theological Union in Berkeley; the undergraduates in my courses in terrorism and global conflict at UCSB, and a host of research assistants over the years, beginning with the many in Berkeley whom I have seen mature in their professional careers. For this book, it was Greg Kelly who helped me in Honolulu; and at Santa Barbara Joe Bandy, Amaury Cooper, Christian Garfield, Robert Gedeon, Omar Kutty, Shawn Landres, John Nemec, Brian

Roney, Amory Starr, and consistently reliable Justin Pawl. I am especially grateful for the diligence and impertinence of several former students who worked closely with me on several of the case studies, who
wrestled with many of the ideas, and whose imprint can be found
throughout these pages. Antony Charles helped to bring South and
Southeast Asia into focus, Darrin McMahon despaired over and then
enhanced my understanding of Europe and the Enlightenment, and
Aaron Santell helped make sense out of Japan and the Middle East.

Support for my research came from a senior research fellowship
from the American Council of Learned Societies and matching funds
from the Division of Social Science at the University of California,
Santa Barbara, facilitated by Dean Donald Zimmerman. I also appreciate the patience and insight of several audiences who heard parts of this
manuscript presented as lectures, including the K. Brooke Anderson
Lecture at Brown University and the Eugene and Mary Ely Lyman
Lectures at Sweet Briar College, as well as presentations at Delta
College, Haverford College, the University of California at San Diego,
the Tantur Ecumenical Institute in Jerusalem, the Yitzhak Rabin Center
for Israel Studies in Tel Aviv, The George Washington University, the
EPIIC International Seminar of the Fletcher School of Law and
Diplomacy, the Watson Institute for International Studies at Brown, the
Center for American Religion at Princeton University, and faculty sem-
inars of the communications and sociology departments at the
University of California, Santa Barbara. Portions of some chapters were
published in articles in Mark Juergensmeyer, ed., *Violence and the
Sacred in the Modern World*; David Rapoport, ed., *Inside Terrorist
Organizations*; *Journal of Terrorism and Political Violence*; *Fletcher
Forum*; and *Annals of the American Academy of Political and Social
Science*. Portions of my article "Religion and Violence," which was
published without attribution in the *Harper Dictionary of Religion*, are
also utilized in various places in this book.

In the process of publication I was aided by the able staff of
Publication Services and the University of California Press. I am grateful especially to Doug Abrams Arava for helping to craft the manuscript, Reed Malcolm for guiding it through publication, and James
Clark for his unwavering support. For many years Doug and Reed have
helped to uphold the high standards of the Comparative Studies in
Religion and Society series of the Press, and I am pleased that this book
bears that series' imprimatur. A standard of a different sort has been set

by Sucheng Chan, my colleague and spouse, who insists on the best and whose own writing is a model of elegance and conceptual clarity.

To those activists I interviewed and who are named in the list at the end of this book, I extend my appreciation. I know that many of them, especially those who have supported acts of violence for what they regard as personal and moral reasons, will feel that I have not fully understood or sufficiently explained their views. Perhaps they are right. An effort at understanding is just that, an attempt to enter other people's worlds and recreate the moral and strategic logic of the decisions they make. The effort is always, perhaps necessarily, imperfect, for I do not inhabit their lives nor, in these cases, do I concur with their choices. I hope, however, that the subjects of this book will agree that, not just for their sakes but also for the sake of a more peaceful world in which understanding replaces anger and hate, at least I have tried.

For some people, however, whatever contribution this and the many other efforts at understanding and alleviating violence may offer will come too late. I refer to those who have been victims of terrorist attacks. As I worked on this book, I was interrupted by pictures of the tragic bombing of the American embassy in Kenya in August 1998. Shards of glass rained down from the twenty-two-story building adjacent to the embassy and the secretarial school where the bomb exploded, compounding the resulting misery. No one witnessing the images of the blinded, bandaged, and slashed Kenyans could fail to be moved by the destructive power of terrorist acts. I dedicate this book to these and the many other victims of religious violence in recent years. Their sacrifices will not be forgotten. My conviction is that the same religion that motivates such potent acts of destruction also carries an enormous capacity for healing, restoration, and hope.

Introduction

CHAPTER 1

Terror and God

When plastic explosives attached to a Hamas suicide bomber ripped through the gentrified Ben Yehuda shopping mall in Jerusalem in September 1997, the blast damaged not only lives and property but also the confidence with which most people view the world. As images of the bloodied victims were projected from the scene, the double arches of a McDonald's restaurant were visible in the background, their cheerful familiarity appearing oddly out of place with the surrounding carnage. Many who viewed these pictures saw symbols of their own ordinary lives assaulted and vicariously felt the anxiety—the terror—of those who experienced it firsthand. After all, the wounded could have included anyone who has ever visited a McDonald's—which is to say virtually anyone in the developed world. In this sense, the blast was an attack not only on Israel but also on normal life as most people know it.

This loss of innocence was keenly felt by many Americans after news of ethnic shootings in California and Illinois in 1999; the attack on American embassies in Africa in 1998; abortion clinic bombings in Alabama and Georgia in 1997; the bomb blast at the Olympics in Atlanta and the destruction of a U.S. military housing complex in Dhahran, Saudi Arabia, in 1996; the tragic destruction of the federal building at Oklahoma City in 1995; and the explosion at the World Trade Center in New York City in 1993. These incidents and a host of violent episodes associated with American religious extremists—including the Christian militia, the Christian Identity movement, and Christian anti-abortion

activists—have brought Americans into the same uneasy position occupied by many in the rest of the world. Increasingly, global society must
confront religious violence on a routine basis.

The French, for example, have dealt with subway bombs planted by
Algerian Islamic activists, the British with exploding trucks and buses
ignited by Irish Catholic nationalists, and the Japanese with nerve gas
placed in Tokyo subways by members of a Hindu-Buddhist sect. In
India residents of Delhi have experienced car bombings by both Sikh
and Kashmiri separatists, in Sri Lanka whole sections of the city of
Colombo have been destroyed both by Tamils and by Sinhalese militants, Egyptians have been forced to live with militant Islamic attacks
in coffeehouses and riverboats, Algerians have lost entire villages to
savage attacks perpetrated allegedly by supporters of the Islamic
Salvation Front, and Israelis and Palestinians have confronted the
deadly deeds of both Jewish and Muslim extremists. For many Middle
Easterners, terrorist attacks have become a way of life.

In addition to their contemporaneity, all these instances share two
striking characteristics. First, they have been violent—even vicious—in
a manner calculated to be terrifying. And, second, they have been motivated by religion.

The Meaning of Religious Terrorism

The ferocity of religious violence was brought home to me in 1998
when I received the news that a car bomb had exploded in a Belfast
neighborhood I had visited the day before. The following day firebombs ripped through several pubs and stores, apparently in protest
against the fragile peace agreement signed earlier in the year. It was an
eerie repetition of what had happened several years before. A suicide
bombing claimed by the militant wing of the Palestinian Muslim political movement, Hamas, tore apart a bus near Hebrew University in
1995, the day after I had visited the university on, I believe, the very
same bus. The pictures of the mangled bodies on the Jerusalem street
and the images of Belfast's bombed-out pub, therefore, had a direct and
immediate impact on my view of the world.

What I realized then is the same thing that all of us perceive on some
level when we view pictures of terrorist events: on a different day, at a
different time, perhaps in a different bus, one of the bodies torn to
shreds by any of these terrorist acts could have been ours. What came
to mind as I heard the news of the Belfast and Jerusalem bombings,

however, was not so much a feeling of relief for my safety as a sense of betrayal—that the personal security and order that is usually a basic assumption of public life cannot in fact be taken for granted in a world where terrorist acts exist.

That, I take it, is largely the point: terrorism is meant to terrify. The word comes from the Latin *terrere*, "to cause to tremble," and came into common usage in the political sense, as an assault on civil order, during the Reign of Terror in the French Revolution at the close of the eighteenth century. Hence the public response to the violence—the trembling that terrorism effects—is part of the meaning of the term. It is appropriate, then, that the definition of a terrorist act is provided by us, the witnesses—the ones terrified—and not by the party committing the act. It is we—or more often our public agents, the news media— who affix the label on acts of violence that makes them terrorism. These are public acts of destruction, committed without a clear military objective, that arouse a widespread sense of fear.

This fear often turns to anger when we discover the other characteristic that frequently attends these acts of public violence: their justification by religion. Most people feel that religion should provide tranquility and peace, not terror. Yet in many of these cases religion has supplied not only the ideology but also the motivation and the organizational structure for the perpetrators. It is true that some terrorist acts are committed by public officials invoking a sort of "state terrorism" in order to subjugate the populace. The pogroms of Stalin, the government-supported death squads in El Salvador, the genocidal killings of the Khmer Rouge in Cambodia, ethnic cleansing in Bosnia and Kosovo, and government-spurred violence of the Hutus and Tutsis in Central Africa all come to mind. The United States has rightfully been accused of terrorism in the atrocities committed during the Vietnam War, and there is some basis for considering the nuclear bombings of Hiroshima and Nagasaki as terrorist acts.

But the term "terrorism" has more frequently been associated with violence committed by disenfranchised groups desperately attempting to gain a shred of power or influence. Although these groups cannot kill on the scale that governments with all their military power can, their sheer numbers, their intense dedication, and their dangerous unpredictability have given them influence vastly out of proportion with their meager military resources. Some of these groups have been inspired by purely secular causes. They have been motivated by leftist ideologies, as in the cases of the Shining Path and the Tupac Amaru in Peru, and the

Red Army in Japan; and they have been propelled by a desire for ethnic or regional separatism, as in the cases of Basque militants in Spain
and the Kurdish nationalists in the Middle East.

But more often it has been religion—sometimes in combination with
these other factors, sometimes as the primary motivation—that has in-
cited terrorist acts. The common perception that there has been a rise
in religious violence around the world in the last decades of the twentieth century has been borne out by those who keep records of such
things. In 1980 the U.S. State Department roster of international terrorist groups listed scarcely a single religious organization. In 1998 U.S.
Secretary of State Madeleine Albright listed thirty of the world's most
dangerous groups; over half were religious.[1] They were Jewish,
Muslim, and Buddhist. If one added to this list other violent religious
groups around the world, including the many Christian militia and
other paramilitary organizations found domestically in the United
States, the number of religious terrorist groups would be considerable.
According to the RAND–St. Andrews Chronology of International
Terrorism, the proportion of religious groups increased from sixteen of
forty-nine terrorist groups identified in 1994 to twenty-six of the fifty-
six groups listed the following year.[2] For this reason former U.S.
Secretary of State Warren Christopher said that terrorist acts in the
name of religion and ethnic identity have become "one of the most important security challenges we face in the wake of the Cold War."[3]

Throughout this study we will be looking at this odd attraction of
religion and violence. Although some observers try to explain away religion's recent ties to violence as an aberration, a result of political ideology, or the characteristic of a mutant form of religion—fundamentalism—these are not my views. Rather, I look for explanations in the
current forces of geopolitics and in a strain of violence that may be
found at the deepest levels of religious imagination.

Within the histories of religious traditions—from biblical wars to cru-
sading ventures and great acts of martyrdom—violence has lurked as a
shadowy presence. It has colored religion's darker, more mysterious
symbols. Images of death have never been far from the heart of religion's
power to stir the imagination. One of the haunting questions asked by
some of the great scholars of religion—including Émile Durkheim,
Marcel Mauss, and Sigmund Freud—is why this is the case. Why does
religion seem to need violence, and violence religion, and why is a divine
mandate for destruction accepted with such certainty by some believers?

These are questions that have taken on a sense of urgency in recent years, when religious violence has reappeared in a form often calculated to terrify on a massive scale. These contemporary acts of violence are often justified by the historical precedent of religion's violent past. Yet the forces that combine to produce religious violence are particular to each moment of history. For this reason, I will focus on case studies of religious violence both within their own cultural contexts and within the framework of global social and political changes that are distinctive to our time.

This is a book about religious terrorism. It is about public acts of violence at the turn of the century for which religion has provided the motivation, the justification, the organization, and the world view. In this book, I have tried to get inside the mindset of those who perpetrated and supported such acts. My goal is to understand why these acts were often associated with religious causes and why they have occurred with such frequency at this juncture in history. Although it is not my purpose to be sympathetic to people who have done terrible things, I do want to understand them and their world views well enough to know how they and their supporters can morally justify what they have done.

What puzzles me is not why bad things are done by bad people, but rather why bad things are done by people who otherwise appear to be good—in cases of religious terrorism, by pious people dedicated to a moral vision of the world. Considering the high-sounding rhetoric with which their purposes are often stated, it is perhaps all the more tragic that the acts of violence meant to achieve them have caused suffering and disruption in many lives—not only those who were injured by the acts, but also those who witnessed them, even from a distance.

Because I want to understand the cultural contexts that produce these acts of violence, my focus is on the ideas and the communities of support that lie behind the acts rather than on the "terrorists" who commit them. In fact, for the purposes of this study, the word "terrorist" is problematic. For one thing, the term makes no clear distinction between the organizers of an attack, those who carry it out, and the many who support it both directly and indirectly. Are they all terrorists, or just some of them—and if the latter, which ones? Another problem with the word is that it can be taken to single out a certain limited species of people called "terrorists" who are committed to violent acts. The implication is that such terrorists are hell-bent to commit terrorism for whatever reason—sometimes choosing religion, sometimes another ideology, to justify their mischief. This logic concludes that terrorism exists because terrorists exist, and if we just got rid of them, the world would be a more pleasant place.

Although such a solution is enticing, the fact is that the line is very thin between "terrorists" and their "non-terrorist" supporters. It is also not clear that there is such a thing as a "terrorist" before someone conspires to perpetrate a terrorist act. Although every society contains sociopaths and others who sadistically enjoy killing, it is seldom such persons who are involved in the deliberate public events that we associate with terrorism, and few studies of terrorism focus exclusively on personality. The studies of the psychology of terrorism deal largely with social psychology; that is, they are concerned with the way people respond to certain group situations that make violent public acts possible.[4] I know of no study that suggests that people are terrorist by nature. Although some activists involved in religious terrorism have been troubled by mental problems, others are people who appear to be normal and socially well adjusted, but who are caught up in extraordinary communities and share extreme world views.

Most of the people involved in acts of religious terrorism are not unlike Dr. Baruch Goldstein, who killed over thirty Muslims as they were praying at the Tomb of the Patriarchs in Hebron on February 25, 1994. Goldstein was a medical doctor who grew up in a middle-class community in Brooklyn and received his professional training at Albert Einstein College of Medicine in the Bronx. His commitment to an extreme form of Zionism brought him to Israel and the Kiryat Arba settlement, and although he was politically active for many years—he was Rabbi Meir Kahane's campaign manager when he ran for the Israeli parliament— Goldstein did not appear to be an irrational or vicious person. Prior to the attack at Hebron, his most publicized political act had been a letter to the editor of the *New York Times*.[5] If Goldstein had deep and perverse personality flaws that eventually surfaced and made him a terrorist, we do not know about them. The evidence about him is to the contrary: it indicates that, like his counterparts in Hamas, he was an otherwise decent man who became overwhelmed by a great sense of dedication to a religious vision shared by many in the community of which he was a part. He became convinced that this vision and community were profoundly assaulted, and this compelled him to a desperate and tragic act. He was certainly single-minded about his religious concerns—even obsessed over them—but to label Goldstein a terrorist prior to the horrible act he committed implies that he was a terrorist by nature and that his religiosity was simply a charade. The evidence does not indicate either to be the case.

For this reason I use the term "terrorist" sparingly. When I do use it, I employ it in the same sense as the word "murderer": it applies to specific persons only after they have been found guilty of committing such a crime, or planning to commit one. Even then I am somewhat cautious about using the term, since a violent act is "terrorism" technically only in the eyes of the courts, more publicly in the eyes of the media, and ultimately only in the eyes of the beholder. The old saying "One person's terrorist is another person's freedom-fighter" has some truth to it. The designation of terrorism is a subjective judgment about the legitimacy of certain violent acts as much as it is a descriptive statement about them.

When I interviewed militant religious activists and their supporters, I found that they seldom used the term "terrorist" to describe what their groups had done. Several told me that their groups should be labeled militant rather than terrorist. A Lutheran pastor who was convicted of bombing abortion clinics was not a terrorist, he told me, since he did not enjoy violence for its own sake. He employed violence only for a purpose, and for that reason he described these events as "defensive actions" on behalf of the "unborn."[6] Activists on both sides of the struggle in Belfast described themselves as "paramilitaries." A leader in India's Sikh separatist movement said that he preferred the term "militant" and told me that "'terrorist' had replaced the term 'witch'" as an excuse to persecute those whom one dislikes.[7] One of the men convicted of bombing the World Trade Center essentially agreed with the Sikh leader, telling me that the word "terrorist" was so "messy" it could not be used without a lot of qualifications.[8] The same point of view was expressed by the political leader of the Hamas movement with whom I talked in Gaza. He described his movement's suicide attacks as "operations."[9] Like many activists who used violence, he likened his group to an army that was planning defensive maneuvers and using violence strategically as necessary acts. Never did he use the word "terrorist" or "terrorism."

This is not just a semantic issue. Whether or not one uses "terrorist" to describe violent acts depends on whether one thinks that the acts are warranted. To a large extent the use of the term depends on one's world view: if the world is perceived as peaceful, violent acts appear as terrorism. If the world is thought to be at war, violent acts may be regarded as legitimate. They may be seen as preemptive strikes, as defensive tactics in an ongoing battle, or as symbols indicating to the world that it is indeed in a state of grave and ultimate conflict.

In most cases in this book, religious language is used to characterize this conflict. When it is, what difference does religion make? Do acts of violence conducted by Hamas have different characteristics from those conducted by secular movements, such as the Kurds? The question is whether religious terrorism is different from other kinds.

In this book it will become clear that, at least in some cases, religion does make a difference. Some of these differences are readily apparent—the transcendent moralism with which such acts are justified, for instance, and the ritual intensity with which they are committed. Other differences are more profound and go to the very heart of religion. The familiar religious images of struggle and transformation—concepts of cosmic war—have been employed in this-worldly social struggles. When these cosmic battles are conceived as occurring on the human plane, they result in real acts of violence.

This leads to yet another question: when religion justifies violence, is it simply being used for political purposes? This question is not as simple as it may first appear. It is complicated largely because of the renewed role that religion plays in various parts of the world as an ideology of public order—especially in movements of religious nationalism—in which religious and political ideologies are intertwined. As the cases in this book will show, religion is not innocent. But it does not ordinarily lead to violence. That happens only with the coalescence of a peculiar set of circumstances—political, social, and ideological—when religion becomes fused with violent expressions of social aspirations, personal pride, and movements for political change.

For these reasons, questions about why religious terrorism has occurred at this moment in history have to be raised in context. By "context" I mean the historical situations, social locations, and world views related to violent incidents. To understand these, we will explore not only the mindset of religious activists who have committed violence but also the groups that have supported them and the ideologies to which they subscribe.

Seeing Inside Cultures of Violence

Terrorism is seldom a lone act. When Dr. Baruch Goldstein entered the Tomb of the Patriarchs carrying an automatic weapon, he came with the tacit approval of many of his fellow Jewish settlers in the nearby community of Kiryat Arba. When Rev. Paul Hill stepped from a side-walk in Pensacola, Florida, and shot Dr. John Britton and his security escort as they prepared to enter their clinic, he was cheered by a certain circle of militant Christian anti-abortion activists around the country. When the followers of Sheik Omar Abdul Rahman drove a rented truck to the underground garage of the World Trade Center, igniting it and its lethal cargo, they came as part of a well-orchestrated plan that involved dozens of coconspirators and thousands of sympathizers in the United States, Egypt, Palestine, and elsewhere throughout the world.

As these instances show, it takes a community of support and, in many cases, a large organizational network for an act of terrorism to succeed. It also requires an enormous amount of moral presumption for the perpetrators of these acts to justify the destruction of property on a massive scale or to condone a brutal attack on another life, especially the life of someone one scarcely knows and against whom one bears no personal enmity. And it requires a great deal of internal conviction, social acknowledgment, and the stamp of approval from a legitimizing ideology or authority one respects. Because of the moral, ideological, and organizational support necessary for such acts, most of them come as collective decisions—such as the conspiracy that led to the release of nerve gas in the Tokyo subways and the Hamas organization's carefully devised bombings.

Even those acts that appear to be solo ventures conducted by rogue activists often have networks of support and ideologies of validation behind them, whether or not these networks and ideologies are immediately apparent. Behind Yitzhak Rabin's assassin, Yigal Amir, for instance, was a large movement of Messianic Zionism in Israel and abroad. Behind convicted bomber Timothy McVeigh and Buford Furrow, the alleged attacker of a Jewish day-care center, was a subculture of militant Christian groups that extends throughout the United States. Behind Unabomber Theodore Kaczynski was the strident student activist culture of the late 1960s, in which one could easily become infected by the feeling that "terrible things" were going on.[10] Behind the two high school students who killed themselves and thirteen of their classmates in Littleton, Colorado, in 1999 was a quasi-religious "trenchcoat" culture of gothic symbolism. In all of these cases the activists thought that their acts were supported not only by other people but by a widely shared perception that the world was already violent: it was enmeshed in great struggles that gave their own violent actions moral meaning.

This is a significant feature of these cultures: the perception that their communities are already under attack—are being violated—and that their acts are therefore simply responses to the violence they have experienced. In some cases this perception is one to which sensitive people outside the movement can readily relate—the feeling of oppression held by Palestinian Muslims, for example, is one that many throughout the world consider to be an understandable though regrettable response to a situation of political control. In other instances, such as the imagined oppression of America's Christian militia or Japan's Aum Shinrikyo movement, the members' fears of black helicopters hovering over their homes at night or the allegations of collusion of international governments to deprive individuals of their freedoms are regarded by most people outside the movements as paranoid delusions. Still other cases—such as those involving Sikh militants in India, Jewish settlers on the West Bank, Muslim politicians in Algeria, Catholic and Protestant militants in Northern Ireland, and anti-abortion activists in the United States—are highly controversial. There are sober and sensitive people to argue each side.

Whether or not outsiders regard these perceptions of oppression as legitimate, they are certainly considered valid by those within the communities. It is these shared perceptions that constitute the cultures of violence that have flourished throughout the world—in neighborhoods of Jewish nationalists from Kiryat Arba to Brooklyn where the struggle to defend the Jewish nation is part of daily existence, in mountain towns in Idaho and Montana where religious and individual freedoms are thought to be imperiled by an enormous governmental conspiracy, and in pious Muslim communities around the world where Islam is felt to be at war with the surrounding secular forces of modern society. Although geographically dispersed, these cultures in some cases are fairly small: one should bear in mind that the culture of violence characterized by Hamas, for example, does not implicate all Palestinians, all Muslims, or even all Palestinian Muslims.

I could use the term "communities" or "ideologies" of terrorism rather than "cultures" of violence, but what I like about the term "culture" is that it entails both things—ideas and social groupings—that are related to terrorist acts. Needless to say, I am using the term "culture" beyond its narrow meaning as the aesthetic products of a society.[11] Rather, I employ it in a broad way to include the ethical and social values underlying the life of a particular social unit.

My way of thinking about culture is enriched by the ideas of several scholars. It encompasses the idea of "episteme" as described by Michel

Foucault: a world view, or a paradigm of thinking that "defines the conditions . . . of all knowledge."[12] It also involves the notion of a nexus of socially embedded ideas about society. Pierre Bourdieu calls this a "habitus," which he describes as "a socially constituted system of cognitive and motivating structures."[13] It is the social basis for what Clifford Geertz described as the "cultural systems" of a people: the patterns of thought, the world views, and the meanings that are attached to the activities of a particular society. In Geertz's view, such cultural systems encompass both secular ideologies and religion.[14]

The cultural approach to the study of terrorism that I have adopted has advantages and disadvantages. Although it allows me to explore more fully the distinctive world view and moral justifications of each group, it means that I tend to study less closely the political calculations of movement leaders and the international networks of activists. For these aspects of terrorism I rely on other works: historical studies such as Bernard Lewis's classic *The Assassins*; comprehensive surveys such as Walter Laqueur's *Terrorism* (revised and republished as *The Age of Terrorism*) and Bruce Hoffman's *Inside Terrorism,* which covers both historical and contemporary incidents;[15] studies in the social psychology of terrorism by Walter Reich and Jerrold Post;[16] political analyses such as Martha Crenshaw's work on the structure of terrorist organizations in Algeria and Peter Merkl's analysis of left-wing terrorism in Germany;[17] and the contributions of Paul Wilkinson and Brian Jenkins in analyzing terrorism as an instrument of political strategy.[18]

These works leave room for other scholars to develop a more cultural approach to analyzing terrorist movements—efforts at reconstructing the terrorists' world views from within. This research has led to a number of significant case studies, including analyses of the Christian militia by Jeffrey Kaplan, the Christian Identity movement by James Aho, Irish paramilitarists by Martin Dillon, Sikh militants by Cynthia Keppley Mahmood, Jewish activists by Ehud Sprinzak, and Hamas suicide bombers by Paul Steinberg and Anne Marie Oliver.[19] These and other works, along with my own case studies and some interesting reportage by international journalists, make possible an effort such as this one: a comparative cultural study of religious terrorism.

This book begins with case studies of religious activists who have used violence or who justify its use. The first half of the book contains chapters on Christians in America who supported abortion clinic bombings and militia actions such as the bombing of the Oklahoma City federal building, Catholics and Protestants who justified acts of terrorism in Northern Ireland, Muslims associated with the bombing of the World Trade Center in New York City and Hamas attacks in the Middle East, Jews who supported the assassination of Prime Minister Yitzhak Rabin and the attack in Hebron's Tomb of the Patriarchs, Sikhs identified with the killing of India's prime minister Indira Gandhi and Punjab's chief minister Beant Singh, and the Japanese Buddhists affiliated with the group accused of the nerve gas attack in Tokyo's subways.

Since these case studies are not only about those directly involved in terrorist acts but also about the world views of the cultures of violence that stand behind them, I have interviewed a number of people associated with these cultures. In the chapters that follow, however, I have chosen to focus on only a few. In some cases I have highlighted the established leaders of political organizations, such as Dr. Abdul Aziz Rantisi, Tom Hartley, and Simranjit Singh Mann. In other cases I have chosen outspoken activists who have been convicted of undertaking violent acts, such as Mahmud Abouhalima, Michael Bray, and Yoel Lerner. In yet other cases I have selected members from the lower echelons of activist movements, such as Takeshi Nakamura and Yochay Ron. The interviews that I have chosen to describe in detail are therefore diverse. But in each case—in my opinion—they best exemplify the world views of the cultures of violence of which the individuals are a part.

In the second half of the book I identify patterns—an overarching logic—found within the cultures of violence described in the first half. I try to explain why and how religion and violence are linked. In Chapter 7 I explain why acts of religious terrorism are undertaken not only to achieve a strategic target but also to accomplish a symbolic purpose. In Chapters 8 and 9, I describe how images of cosmic confrontation and warfare that are ordinarily found in the context of heaven or history are sometimes tied to this-worldly political battles, and I explain how the processes of satanization and symbolic empowerment develop in stages. In Chapter 10, I explore the way that religious violence has provided a sense of empowerment to alienated individuals, marginal groups, and visionary ideologues.

In the last chapter of this book I return to questions directly about religion: why anyone would believe that God could sanction terrorism and why the rediscovery of religion's power has appeared in recent years in such a bloody way—and what, if anything, can be done about it. I have applied what I have learned about religious terrorism to five scenarios in which violence comes to an end.

In order to respond to religious terrorism in a way that is effective and does not produce more terrorism in response, I believe it is necessary to understand why such acts occur. Behind this practical purpose in writing this book, however, is an attempt to understand the role that violence has always played in the religious imagination and how terror could be conceived in the mind of God.

These two purposes are connected. One of my conclusions is that this historical moment of global transformation has provided an occasion for religion—with all its images and ideas—to be reasserted as a public force. Lurking in the background of much of religion's unrest and the occasion for its political revival, I believe, is the devaluation of secular authority and the need for alternative ideologies of public order. It may be one of the ironies of history, graphically displayed in incidents of terrorism, that the answers to the questions of why the contemporary world still needs religion and of why it has suffered such public acts of violence, are surprisingly the same.

Cultures of Violence

CHAPTER 2

Soldiers for Christ

The shootings at a Jewish day care center in California on August 10, 1999, by a Christian Identity activist rekindled the fear and anger evoked by the 1996 bombing of the Atlanta Olympic Games, the 1995 devastation of the Oklahoma City federal building, and a rash of abortion clinic attacks throughout the decade. Like residents of Belfast and London, Americans were beginning to learn to live with acts of religious terrorism: shocking, disturbing incidents of violence laced with the passion of religion—in these cases, Christianity.

My attempt to understand contemporary religious violence around the world begins with these Christian examples. Although much of the world's attention has been riveted to incidents in the Middle East, I have chosen to initiate my search with a phenomenon that most American readers will find both familiar and strange: Christian militancy in the West. What is familiar is the setting. What is strange is the idea that religious warfare exists in the most modern of twentieth-century societies. Also surprising, at least to some, is that terrorist acts have been justified by Christian principles.

It is good to remember, however, that despite its central tenets of love and peace, Christianity—like most traditions—has always had a violent side. The bloody history of the tradition has provided images as disturbing as those provided by Islam or Sikhism, and violent conflict is vividly portrayed in both the Old and New Testaments of the Bible. This history and these biblical images have provided the raw material for theologically justifying the violence of contemporary Christian groups. Attacks on abortion clinics, for instance, have been viewed not only as assaults on a practice that some Christians regard as immoral, but also as skirmishes in a grand confrontation between forces of evil and good that has social and political implications.

The theological justifications for these acts are varied. In the United States, at least two major schools of thought lie behind Christian abortion clinic bombings, one based on Reconstruction Theology and the other on ideas associated with the Christian Identity movement. The latter also provides the ideological support for many of America's militia movements. The violence in Northern Ireland is justified by still other theological positions, Catholic and Protestant.

Why would a Christian support violent acts of terror? This is the question that brought me to an American clergyman, Rev. Michael Bray of Bowie, Maryland, who was convicted of a series of abortion clinic attacks and defends the use of lethal weapons against clinic staff. This is my attempt to understand his troubled view of the world.

Mike Bray and Abortion Clinic Bombings

It was "a cold February night" in 1984 when Rev. Michael Bray and a friend drove a yellow Honda from his home in Bowie to nearby Dover, Delaware. The trunk of the car held a cargo of ominous supplies: a cinder block to break a window, cans of gasoline to pour in and around a building, and rags and matches to ignite the flames. The road to Delaware was foggy and the bridge across the Chesapeake Bay was icy. The car skidded and a minor accident occurred, but the pair were determined to forge ahead. "Before daybreak," Bray said, "the only abortion chamber in Dover was gutted by fire and put out of the business of butchering babies."[1] The following year, Bray and two other defendants stood trial for destroying seven abortion facilities in Delaware, Maryland, Virginia, and the District of Columbia, with a total of over one million dollars in damages. He was convicted of these charges and served prison time until May 15, 1989.

When I talked with Rev. Bray in his suburban home in Bowie in 1996 and again in 1998, I found nothing sinister or intensely fanatical about him. He was a cheerful, charming, handsome man in his early 40s who liked to be called Mike. Hardly the image of an ignorant, narrow-minded fundamentalist, Mike Bray enjoyed a glass of wine before dinner and talked knowledgeably about theology and political ideas.[2]

It was a demeanor quite different from his public posture. In my interview with Bray on March 20, 1998, he had just appeared on the ABC television program *Nightline*, in a program focusing on anti-abortion acts of terrorism.[3] The host, Ted Koppel, had accused Bray of being the author of the underground manual *Army of God*, which provides detailed instructions for various forms of destruction and sabotage aimed at abortion facilities. Bray did not deny Koppel's accusation, but he did not admit to it either. When I talked with Bray a few days later and asked him about the authorship of the document, he repeated his noncommittal stance but was able to show me a copy of the manual he happened to have on file. It was written in his own characteristically jaunty and satirical style, and I suspected that Koppel's suggestion was correct. Bray's identification with the Army of God movement was established in his trial some years ago when the initials AOG were found on abortion buildings that he was accused of having torched. When I asked Bray why, if he had not written it, he would hesitate to deny his authorship of the booklet, he said that "it was good to show solidarity with anyone who is being maligned for writing such a book."[4]

Whether or not he was the author, Bray clearly sympathized with the ideas in the manual. As a leader in the Defensive Action movement, Mike Bray has justified the use of violence in anti-abortion activities, although his attacks on abortion clinics have been considered extreme even by members of the pro-life movement. The same has been said of his acknowledged writings. Bray publishes one of the country's most militant Christian newsletters, *Capitol Area Christian News*, which has focused on abortion, homosexuality, and what Bray regards as the Clinton administration's pathological abuse of government power.

Bray was the spokesman for two activists who were convicted of murderous assaults on abortion clinic staffs. On July 29, 1994, Bray's friend, Rev. Paul Hill, killed Dr. John Britton and his volunteer escort James Barrett as they drove up to The Ladies Center, an abortion clinic in Pensacola, Florida. Several years earlier another member of Bray's network of associates, Rachelle ("Shelly") Shannon, a housewife from rural Oregon, also confessed to a string of abortion clinic bombings. She was convicted of attempted murder for shooting and wounding Dr. George Tiller as he drove away from his clinic in Wichita, Kansas. Bray wrote the definitive book on the ethical justification for anti-abortion violence, *A Time to Kill,* which defended his own acts of terrorism, the murders of abortion clinic doctors, and the attempted murder by Shannon.[5] And yet in person Rev. Michael Bray is in many ways an affable and interesting man.

Mike Bray has always been active, he told me, having been raised in a family focused around sports, church activities, and military life. His father was a naval officer who served at nearby Annapolis, and Mike grew up expecting to follow in his father's military footsteps. An athletic hero in high school, he took the most popular girl in class to the senior prom. Her name was Kathie Epstein—according to Bray the Kathie Lee who later became an actress and a nationally televised talk show host with Regis Philbin. Mike's own career was marked by less obvious attributes of success. He attended Annapolis for a year and then dropped out, living what he described as a "prodigal" life. He searched for religion as a solution to his malaise and was for a time tempted by the Mormons. Then the mother of his old girlfriend, Kathie Lee, steered him toward Billy Graham and the born-again experience of evangelical Christianity. Mike was converted and went to Colorado to study in a Baptist Bible college and seminary.

Yet Bray never quite rejected the Lutheranism of his upbringing. So when he returned to Bowie, he rejoined his childhood church and became the assistant pastor. When the national Lutheran churches merged, Bray led a faction of the local church that objected to what it regarded as the national church's abandonment of the principle of scriptural literalism. Seeing himself as a crusader, Mike and his group of ten families split off and in 1984 formed the Reformation Lutheran Church, an independent group affiliated with the national Association of Free Lutheran Congregations. Over ten years later, Bray's church remained a circle of about fifty people without its own building. The church operated out of Bray's suburban home: Bray remodeled the garage into a classroom for a Christian elementary school, where he and his wife taught a small group of students.

Increasingly, Mike Bray's real occupation became social activism. Supported by his wife, members of the church, and his volunteer associate pastor, Michael Colvin—who held a Ph.D. in classics from the University of Indiana and worked in the federal health care administration—Mike and his followers launched anti-abortion crusades and tapped into a growing national network of like-minded Christian activists. They became concerned that the federal government—particularly the attorney general, whom Mike called "Janet Waco Reno"—was undermining individual freedoms and moral values. He saw American society in a state of utter depravity, over which its elected officials presided with an almost satanic disregard for truth and human life. He viewed President Clinton and other politicians as "neo-pagans," sometimes comparing them to Hitler. The Nazi image pervaded Bray's understanding of how ethically minded people should respond to such a threat. Regarding the activities that led to his prison conviction, Bray has "no regrets." "Whatever I did," he said, "it was worth it."

According to Bray, Americans live in a situation "comparable to Nazi Germany," a state of hidden warfare, and the comforts of modern society have lulled the populace into a lack of awareness of the situation. Bray is convinced that if there were some dramatic event, such as economic collapse or social chaos, the demonic role of the government would be revealed, and people would have "the strength and the zeal to take up arms" in a revolutionary struggle. What he envisions as the outcome of that struggle is the establishment of a new moral order in America, one based on biblical law and a spiritual, rather than a secular, social compact.

Until this new moral order is established, Bray said, he and others like him who are aware of what is going on and have the moral courage to resist it are compelled to take action. According to Bray, Christianity gives him the right to defend innocent "unborn children," even by use of force, whether it involves "destroying the facilities that they are regularly killed in, or taking the life of one who is murdering them." By the latter, Bray means killing doctors and other clinical staff involved in performing abortions.

Bray defends the 1994 actions of his friend, Rev. Paul Hill, in killing Dr. John Britton and his escort. Bray's theological justifications are echoed by Hill himself. "You may wonder what it is like to have killed an abortionist and his escort," Hill wrote to Bray and his other supporters after the killings.[6] "My eyes were opened to the enormous impact" such an event would have, he wrote, adding that "the effect would be incalculable." Hill said that he opened his Bible and found sustenance in Psalms 91: "You will not be afraid of the terror by night, or of the arrow that flies by day." Hill interpreted this as an affirmation that his act was biblically approved.

When I suggested to Bray that carrying out such violent actions is tantamount to acting as both judge and executioner, Bray demurred. Although he did not deny that a religious authority has the right to pronounce judgment over those who broke the moral law, he explained that attacks on abortion clinics and the killing of abortion doctors were essentially defensive rather than punitive acts. According to Bray, "there is a difference between taking a retired abortionist and executing him, and killing a practicing abortionist who is regularly killing babies." The first act is in Bray's view retributive, the second defensive. According to Bray, the attacks were aimed not so much at punishing clinics and abortionists for their actions as at preventing them from "killing babies," as Bray put it. He was careful to say that he did not advocate the use of violence, but morally approved of it in some instances. He was "pro-choice," as he put it, regarding its use.

Theological Justifications

Bray found support for his position in actions undertaken during the Nazi regime in Europe. His moral exemplar in this regard was the German theologian and Lutheran pastor, Dietrich Bonhoeffer, who abruptly terminated his privileged research position at Union Theological Seminary in New York City to return to Germany and clandestinely join a plot to assassinate Hitler. The plot was uncovered before it could be carried out, and Bonhoeffer, the brilliant young ethical theorist, was hanged by the Nazis. His image of martyrdom and his theological writings lived on, however, and Bonhoeffer has often been cited by moral theorists as an example of how Christians could undertake violent actions for a just cause and how occasionally they are constrained to break laws for a higher purpose.

These were positions also held by one of Bonhoeffer's colleagues at Union Theological Seminary, Reinhold Niebuhr, whom Bray also cited. Often touted as one of the greatest Protestant theologians of the twentieth century, Niebuhr wrestled with one of Christianity's oldest ethical problems: when it is permissible to use force—even violence—in behalf of a righteous cause. Niebuhr began his career as a pacifist, but in time he grudgingly began to accept the position that a Christian, acting for the sake of justice, could use a limited amount of violence.[7]

Niebuhr was drawing on a strain of religious activism that went back to Christianity's origins. The tradition emerged in the context of revolutionary struggles against the Roman occupation of Israel. The New Testament indicates that at least two of Jesus' disciples were members of the rebellious Jewish party, the Zealots. Scholars dispute whether or not the Jesus movement was considered antigovernment at the time, but the New Testament clearly records that the Roman colonial government charged Jesus with sedition, found him guilty, and executed him for the crime.[8]

Did Jesus in fact support the violent overthrow of the Roman occupation? The answer to that question is unclear, and the controversy over whether Christianity sanctions violence has hounded the Church from its earliest days. It can be argued that Christians were expected to follow Jesus' example of selfless love, to "love your enemies and pray for those who persecute you" (Mt 5:44). Evidence for the other side comes from such incidents as Jesus driving the moneychangers from the Temple and such enigmatic statements as Jesus' dark prophecy "Do not think that I have come to bring peace on earth; I have come not to bring peace but a sword" (Mt 10:34; see also Lk 12:51–52). The early Church fathers, including Tertullian and Origen, asserted that Christians were constrained from taking human life, a principle that prevented Christians from serving in the Roman army. Thus the early Christians were essentially pacificists.

When Christianity vaulted into the status of state religion in the fourth century C.E., Church leaders began to reject pacifism and accept the doctrine of just war, an idea first stated by Cicero and later developed by Ambrose and Augustine.[9] This idea justified the use of military force under certain conditions, including proportionality—the expectation that more lives would be saved by the use of force than would be lost—and legitimacy, the notion that the undertaking must be approved by an established authority. The abuse of the concept in justifying military adventures and violent persecutions of heretical and minority groups led Thomas Aquinas in the thirteenth century to reaffirm that war was always sinful, even if it was occasionally waged for a just cause. Remarkably, the just-war theory still stands today as the centerpiece of Christian understanding concerning the moral use of violence.[10] Some modern Christian theologians have adapted the theory of just war to liberation theology, arguing that the Church can embrace a "just revolution."[11]

Reinhold Niebuhr showed the relevance of just-war theory to social struggles in the twentieth century by relating the idea to what he regarded as the Christian requirement to fulfill social justice. Viewing the world through the lens of what he called "realism," Niebuhr concluded that moral suasion is not sufficient to combat social injustices, especially when they are buttressed by corporate and state power. For this reason, he explained in a seminal essay, "Why the Christian Church Is Not Pacifist," that it is at times necessary to abandon nonviolence in favor of a more forceful solution.[12] Building his case on

Augustine's understanding of original sin, Niebuhr argued that righteous force is sometimes necessary to extirpate injustice and subdue
evil within a sinful world, and that small strategic acts of violence are
occasionally necessary to deter large acts of violence and injustice. If
violence is to be used in such situations, Niebuhr explained, it must
be used sparingly and as swiftly and skillfully as a surgeon's knife.[13]

In addition to the "just war," however, there are other, less legitimate
examples of religious violence from Christianity's heritage, including the
Inquisitions and the Crusades. The thirteenth-century Inquisitions were
the medieval Church's attempt to root out heresy, involving torture of
the accused and sentences that included burning at the stake. The
Spanish Inquisition in the fifteenth century was aimed largely at Jews
and Muslims who had converted to Christianity but were investigated
to see if the conversions were sincere; again, torture and death were
standard features of these spurious trials. The nine Crusades—which
began in 1095 with Pope Urban II's plea for Christians to rise up and re-
take the Shrine of the Holy Sepulcher in Jerusalem, which had fallen into
Muslim hands, and ended some three centuries later—were punctuated
with the Christian battle cry *Deus volt* ("God wills it"). As the armies
moved through Europe on their way to the Holy Land, they gathered the
poor and desperate for quixotic ventures that led to virtually no military
conquests of lasting value. They did, however, lead to the deaths of thousands of innocent Muslims and Jews. Today the memory of this tragic
period in Christian history is evoked in the epithet "crusader," applied
to anyone committed to a cause with excessive zeal.

One might think of the Crusades when one considers the religious
commitment of anti-abortion activists such as Rev. Michael Bray who
turn to violence in their war with abortion clinic staff and their defenders, the secular state. Bray, however, found refuge not in the historical example of the Crusades but in the ethical justification offered
by Niebuhr, along with the example of Christian sacrifice in the assassination attempt by Bonhoeffer. These modern liberal Christian defenders of the just role of violence gave Bray the impression that
Christian theology has supported his own efforts to bring about social
change through violent acts.

But Bray radically differs from Niebuhr and Bonhoeffer theologically
and in his interpretation of the contemporary situation—comparing
America's democratic state to Nazism and advocating a biblically based
religious politics to replace the secular government. It is unlikely that
Bray's positions would be accepted by these or any other theologian

within mainstream Protestant thought. Bonhoeffer and Niebuhr, like most modern theologians, accepted the principle of the separation of church and state; they felt that separation is necessary to the integrity of both institutions. Niebuhr was especially wary of what he called "moralism"—the intrusion of religious or other ideological values into the political calculations of statecraft.

To support his ideas about religious politics, therefore, Bray had to look beyond mainstream Protestant thought. Rejecting Bonhoeffer's and Niebuhr's "affliction" with moderate neo-orthodox theology, Bray found intellectual company in a group of writers associated with the more conservative Dominion Theology, the position that Christianity must reassert the dominion of God over all things, including secular politics and society. This point of view—articulated by such right-wing Protestant spokespersons as Rev. Jerry Falwell and Pat Robertson—led to a burst of social and political activism in the Christian right in the 1980s and 1990s.

The Christian anti-abortion movement is permeated with ideas from Dominion Theology. Randall Terry, founder of the militant anti-abortion organization Operation Rescue and a writer for the Dominion magazine *Crosswinds*, signed the magazine's "Manifesto for the Christian Church." The manifesto asserted that America should "function as a Christian nation" and opposed such "social moral evils" of secular society as "abortion on demand, fornication, homosexuality, sexual entertainment, state usurpation of parental rights and God-given liberties, statist-collectivist theft from citizens through devaluation of their money and redistribution of their wealth, and evolutionism taught as a monopoly viewpoint in the public schools."[14]

At the extreme right wing of Dominion Theology is a relatively obscure theological movement that Mike Bray found particularly appealing: Reconstruction Theology, whose exponents long to create a Christian theocratic state. Bray had studied their writings extensively and possesses a shelf of books written by Reconstruction authors. The convicted anti-abortion killer Paul Hill cited Reconstruction theologians in his own writings and once studied with a founder of the movement, Greg Bahnsen, at Reformed Theological Seminary in Jackson, Mississippi.[15]

Leaders of the Reconstruction movement trace their ideas, which they sometimes called "theonomy," to Cornelius Van Til, a twentieth-century Presbyterian professor of theology at Princeton Seminary who took seriously the sixteenth-century ideas of the Reformation theologian John Calvin regarding the necessity for presupposing the authority of God in all worldly matters. Followers of Van Til, including his former students Bahnsen and Rousas John Rushdoony, and Rushdoony's son-in-law, Gary North, adopted this "presuppositionalism" as a doctrine, with all its implications for the role of religion in political life.

Reconstruction writers regard the history of Protestant politics since the early years of the Reformation as having taken a bad turn, and they are especially unhappy with the Enlightenment formulation of church-state separation. They feel it necessary to "reconstruct" Christian society by turning to the Bible as the basis for a nation's law and social order. To propagate these views, the Reconstructionists established the Institute for Christian Economics in Tyler, Texas, and the Chalcedon Foundation in Vallecito, California. They publish a journal and a steady stream of books and booklets on the theological justification for interjecting Christian ideas into economic, legal, and political life.[16]

According to the most prolific Reconstruction writer, Gary North, it is "the moral obligation of Christians to recapture every institution for Jesus Christ."[17] He feels this to be especially so in the United States, where secular law as construed by the Supreme Court and defended by liberal politicians is moving in what Rushdoony and others regard as a decidedly un-Christian direction, particularly in matters regarding abortion and homosexuality. What the Reconstructionists ultimately want, however, is more than the rejection of secularism. Like other theologians who utilize the biblical concept of "dominion," they reason that Christians, as the new chosen people of God, are destined to dominate the world.

The Reconstructionists possess a "postmillennial" view of history. That is, they believe that Christ will return to earth only after the thousand years of religious rule that characterizes the Christian idea of the millennium, and therefore Christians have an obligation to provide the political and social conditions that will make Christ's return possible. "Premillennialists," on the other hand, hold the view that the thousand years of Christendom will come only after Christ returns, an event that will occur in a cataclysmic moment of world history. Therefore they tend to be much less active politically. Followers of Reconstruction Theology such as Mike Bray, Dominion theologians such as Pat Robertson, and many leaders of the politically active Christian Coalition are postmillenialists and hence believe that a Christian kingdom must be established on earth before Christ's return. They take seriously the idea of a Christian society and a form of religious politics that will make biblical code the law of the land.

In my conversations with Mike Bray, he insisted that the idea of a society based on Christian morality was not a new one, and he emphasized the "re-" in "reconstruction." Although Bray rejects the idea of a
pope, he appreciates much of the Roman Catholic Church's social
teachings and greatly admires the tradition of canon law. Only recently
in history, he observed, has the political order in the West not been
based on biblical concepts. Since he is opposed to this disestablishment
of the political role of the Church, Bray labels himself an "antidises-
tablishmentarian."

Bray is serious about bringing Christian politics into power. He
imagines that it is possible, under the right conditions, for a Christian
revolution to sweep across the country and bring in its wake constitu-
tional changes that would allow for biblical law to be the basis of social legislation. Failing that, Bray envisages a new federalism that
would allow individual states to experiment with religious politics on
their own. When I asked Bray what state might be ready for such an experiment, he hesitated and then suggested Louisiana and Mississippi,
or, he added, "maybe one of the Dakotas."

Not all Reconstruction thinkers have endorsed the use of violence,
especially the kind that Bray and Hill have justified. As Gary North admitted, "there is a division in the theonomic camp" over violence, especially with regard to anti-abortion activities. Some months before
Paul Hill killed Dr. Britton and his escort, Hill—apparently hoping for
Gary North's approval in advance—sent a letter to North along with a
draft of an essay he had written justifying the possibility of such killings
in part on theonomic grounds. North ultimately responded, but only
after the murders had been committed. North regretted that he was too
late to deter Hill from his "terrible direction" and chastised Hill in an
open letter, published as a booklet, denouncing Hill's views as "vigi-
lante theology."[18] According to North, biblical law provides exceptions
to the commandment "Thou shalt not kill" (Ex 20:13), but in terms
similar to just-war doctrine: when one is authorized to do so by "a
covenantal agent" in wartime, to defend one's household, to execute a
convicted criminal, to avenge the death of one's kin, to save an entire
nation, or to stop moral transgressors from bringing bloodguilt on an
entire community.[19]

Hill—joined by Bray—responded to North's letter. They argued that
many of those conditions applied to the abortion situation in the United
States. Writing from his prison cell in Starke, Florida, Paul Hill said that
the biblical commandment against murder also "requires using the means

necessary to defend against murder—including lethal force."[20] He went
on to say that he regarded "the cutting edge of Satan's current attack" to
be "the abortionist's knife," and therefore his actions had ultimate theological significance.[21] Bray, in *A Time to Kill*, spoke to North's concern
about the authorization of violence by a legitimate authority or "a
covenental agent," as North put it. Bray raised the possibility of a "righteous rebellion."[22] Just as liberation theologians justify the use of unau-
thorized force for the sake of their vision of a moral order, Bray sees the
legitimacy of using violence not only to resist what he regards as murder—abortion—but also to help bring about the Christian political order
envisioned by Reconstruction thinkers such as Gary North. In Bray's
mind, a little violence is a small price to pay for the possibility of fulfill-
ing God's law and establishing His kingdom on earth.

Eric Robert Rudolph and Timothy McVeigh

A somewhat different set of theological justifications lay in the background of another anti-abortion activist, Eric Robert Rudolph. When federal agents conducted a massive and well-publicized manhunt to capture
Rudolph in 1998 and 1999, they had a long list of alleged charges to present before him, including bombing abortion clinics in Birmingham,
Alabama, and Atlanta, Georgia; blasting a lesbian bar in Atlanta; and exploding a bomb at the 1996 Atlanta Olympics. What these incidents have
in common is their relationship to what many Christian activists regard as
sexual immorality: abortion and homosexuality. According to Michael
Bray, Rudolph's anger at the Olympic organizers came in part because the
carriers of the Olympic torch, which passed through the southern United
States on its way to Atlanta, skirted one county in North Carolina that
had approved an ordinance declaring that "sodomy is not consistent with
the values of the community." Rudolph is said to have interpreted this de-
tour in the torch's journey as a pro-gay stance on the part of the Olympic
organizers.[23] In a broader sense, however, Rudolph was concerned about
the permissiveness of secular authorities in the United States and "the
atheistic internationalism" controlling one side of what Bray calls "the
culture war" in modern society.[24]

    These concerns are shared by many Christian activists, but in Ru-
dolph's case they are associated especially with a branch of Christianity
with which Rudolph became familiar in childhood: Christian Identity. At
one time he and his mother stayed at the Identity compound led by Dan

Gayman, and there are press reports that Rudolph knew the late Identity preacher Nord Davis. The theology of Christian Identity is based on racial supremacy and biblical law. It has been in the background of such movements as the Posse Comitatus, the Order, the Aryan Nations, the supporters of Randy Weaver at Ruby Ridge, Herbert Armstrong's Worldwide Church of God, the Freeman Compound, and the World Church of the Creator. It is popular in many militia movements and motivated Buford Furrow in his 1999 assault on a Jewish center in Granada Hills, California.

Christian Identity ideas were most likely part of the thinking of Timothy McVeigh, the convicted bomber of the Oklahoma City federal building. McVeigh was exposed to Identity thinking through the militia culture with which he was associated and through his awareness of the Christian Identity encampment, Elohim City, on the Oklahoma-Arkansas border. Although there is no evidence that McVeigh was ever affiliated with the commune, phone calls he made to Elohim City in the months before the bombing are a matter of record, including one made two weeks before the bombing.[25] McVeigh once received a citation for a minor traffic offense ten miles from the commune on the only access road to it. McVeigh also imbibed Identity ideas, or concepts similar to them, through such publications as *The Patriot Report*, an Arkansas-based Christian Identity newsletter that McVeigh received, and perhaps most of all from the book *The Turner Diaries*.[26] According to McVeigh's friends, this was "his favorite book"; it was "his bible," some said.[27] According to one gun collector who saw McVeigh frequently at gun shows, he hawked the book at bargain prices to anyone interested in buying it, and never let it leave his side.[28] More to the point, McVeigh's telephone records indicate that despite his denials, he talked several times directly with the author of the novel, including a conversation shortly before the Oklahoma City attack.[29]

The author is William Pierce, who received a Ph.D. from the University of Colorado. For a time Pierce taught physics at Oregon State University, and he once served as a writer for the American Nazi Party. Although he has denied affiliation with the Christian Identity movement—and in fact attacked the clubbishness of most Identity groups—Pierce's ideas are virtually indistinguishable from Identity thinking. In 1984 Pierce proclaimed himself the founder of a religious compound very similar to those associated with the Christian Identity movement. He called it the Cosmotheist Community.[30]

Pierce's novel, written under the pseudonym Andrew Macdonald, was the main vehicle for his Identity/Cosmotheist ideas. Published in 1978, it describes an apocalyptic battle between freedom fighters and a dictatorial American government. The novel soon became an underground classic, selling 200,000 copies in gun shows and through mail-order catalogues. It served as the blueprint for activists such as Robert Matthews, who was implicated in the 1984 assassination of a Jewish talk-show host in Denver. Matthews, like Timothy McVeigh, seems to have taken seriously the novel's predictions of the encroachment of government control in America and the resistance by a guerrilla band known as "the Order." Matthews called his own movement "the Order," and the modus operandi McVeigh used in destroying the Oklahoma City federal building was almost exactly the same as the one used by patriotic guerrillas to attack government buildings in Pierce's novel.

Although written almost eighteen years before the 1995 Oklahoma City blast, a section of *The Turner Diaries* reads almost like a news account of the horrifying event. It describes in chilling detail how the fictional hero blew up a federal building with a truckload of "a little under 5,000 pounds" of ammonium nitrate fertilizer and fuel oil. Timothy McVeigh's own truck carried 4,400 pounds of the same mixture, packaged and transported exactly as described in the novel. According to Pierce's story, the purpose of the bombing was to launch an attack against the perceived evils of the government and to arouse the fighting spirit of all "free men."[31] According to Pierce, such efforts were necessary because of the mindset of dictatorial secularism that had been imposed on American society as the result of an elaborate conspiracy orchestrated by Jews and liberals hell-bent on depriving Christian society of its freedom and its spiritual moorings.

Pierce and Christian Identity activists yearn for a revolution that would undo America's separation of church and state—or rather, because they disdain the organized Church, they want to merge "religion and state" in a new society governed by religious law. This is why so many Identity groups live together in theocratic societies such as Elohim City, the Freeman Compound, the Aryan Nations compound, and Pierce's Cosmotheist Community. Although these religious communalists believe in capitalism, many hold property in common. They also share an apocalyptic view of history and an even more conspiratorial view of government than the Reconstructionists. They believe that the great confrontation between freedom and a government-imposed slavery is close at hand and that their valiant, militant efforts can threaten the evil system and awaken the spirit of the freedom-loving masses. These are ideas that came to Timothy McVeigh from William Pierce and *The Turner Diaries* and indirectly from the theories of Christian Identity.

Christian Identity thought originated in the movement of British Israelism in the nineteenth century. According to Michael Barkun, who has written extensively about the movement, one of the founding fathers was John Wilson, whose central work, *Lectures on Our Israelitish Origin*, brought the message to a large British and Irish middle-class audience.[32] Wilson claimed that Jesus had been an Aryan, not a Semite; that the migrating Israelite tribes from the northern kingdom of Israel were in fact blue-eyed Aryans who somehow ended up in the British Isles; and that the "Lost Sheep of the House of Israel" were none other than present-day Englishmen.[33] According to later versions of this theory, people who claim to be Jews are imposters. Some versions of Identity thinking regard them as descendants of an illicit sexual act between Eve and Satan; other versions have them as aliens from outer space. In either case, Identity thinking claims that the people known as Jews pretend to be Jews in order to assert their superiority in a scheme to control the world. The Jews' plot is allegedly supported by the secret Protestant order of Freemasons.

British Israelism came to the United States in the early twentieth century through the teachings of the evangelist Gerald L. K. Smith and the writings of William Cameron, a publicist for the automobile magnate Henry Ford.[34] Ford himself supported many of Cameron's views and published a book of anti-Semitic essays written by Cameron but attributed to Ford, *The International Jew: The World's Foremost Problem*. Cameron conveyed such Christian Identity tenets as the necessity for the Anglo-Saxon race to retain its purity and political dominance, and the need for Western societies to establish a biblical basis for governance. The Christian Identity philosophy was promoted further by Bertram Comparet, a deputy district attorney in San Diego, and Wesley Swift, a Ku Klux Klan member who founded the Church of Jesus Christ-Christian in 1946. This church was the basis for the Christian Defense League, organized by Bill Gale at his ranch in Mariposa, California, in the 1960s, a movement that spawned both the Posse Comitatus and the Aryan Nations.[35]

British Israelism appealed to the elite of nineteenth-century British society, but by the time these ideas came to the United States, the ideology had taken a more strident and political turn. Most of the followers of Christian Identity were relatively benign, and according to Jeffrey

Kaplan, who studied contemporary Christian Identity groups in the American Midwest and Northwest, their ideas tended to be simplified in the public mind and the groups reduced to the ranks of "monsters" in America's right-wing fringe.[36] Though that may be true, the fact remains that the ideology lies behind some of the more heinous groups and actions in American society in the late twentieth century.

In the 1980s and 1990s the largest concentration of Christian Identity groups was in Idaho—centered on the Aryan Nations compound near Hayden Lake—and in the southern Midwest near the Oklahoma-Arkansas-Missouri borders. In that location a Christian Identity group called the Covenant, the Sword and the Arm of the Lord (CSA) established a 224-acre community and a paramilitary school, which it named the Endtime Overcomer Survival Training School.[37] Nearby, Christian Identity minister Robert Millar and former Nazi Party member Glenn Miller established Elohim City, whose members stockpiled weapons and prepared themselves for "a Branch Davidian–type raid" by the U.S. government's Bureau of Alcohol, Tobacco, and Firearms.[38] It was this Christian Identity encampment that Timothy McVeigh contacted shortly before the Oklahoma City federal building blast.

The American incarnation of Christian Identity incorporated many of the British movement's paranoid views, updated to suit the social anxieties of many contemporary Americans. For instance, the United Nations and the Democratic Party were alleged to be accomplices in a Jewish-Freemason conspiracy to control the world and deprive individuals of their freedom. In a 1982 Identity pamphlet, Jews were described as "parasites and vultures" who controlled the world through international banking.[39] The establishment of the International Monetary Fund, the introduction of magnetized credit cards, and the establishment of paper money not backed by gold or silver were listed as the final steps in "Satan's Plan."[40]

Gun control is also an important issue to Christian Identity supporters, since they believe that this is how the "Jewish-UN-liberal conspirators," as they call them, intend to eliminate the last possibilities of rebellion against centralized power. These "conspirators" are thought to be hell-bent on depriving individuals of the weapons they might use to defend themselves or free their countrymen from a tyrannical state. This obsession with gun control has made many Christian Identity followers natural allies with the National Rifle Association. The rhetoric of the NRA has played a significant role in legitimizing Christian Identity members' fears of the evil intentions behind gov-

ernmental gun control and has provided a public voice for their paranoid views.

By the late 1990s the Christian Identity movement had become publicly identified as one of the leading voices of America's radical right.
The dean of the movement is Richard Butler, an eighty-year-old former
Presbyterian minister often described as "the elder statesman of
American hate."[41] Waiting in the wings is Butler's designated succes-
sor, Neumann Britton of Escondido, California. Although Butler's
Aryan Nations compound in Idaho consists of only a handful of supporters on a twenty-acre farm, its web site receives over five hundred
hits daily. Moreover, the movement received an infusion of financial
support from two Silicon Valley entrepreneurs, Carl E. Story and R.
Vincent Bertollinni. Their organization, the Eleventh Hour Remnant
Messenger, is said to have spent a million dollars promoting Christian
Identity ideas as of 1999, and to have access to fifty million more. One
of the projects they funded was the mass mailing of a videotape fea-
turing Butler presenting his Christian Identity theory of "Adam's pure
blood seed-line," and the alleged global conspiracy to destroy it.[42]

At the extreme fringes of the Christian Identity movement are rogue
terrorists. Some are like Buford Furrow, who once lived in Butler's compound and married Matthews' widow, and Benjamin Smith, the 1999
Fourth of July sniper in Illinois and Indiana, who belonged to an
Identity-like church that eschews other Identity groups and, for that
matter, all of Christianity. Others are like Timothy McVeigh, whose
group was virtually an anti-organization: a nameless, close-knit cadre.

The world as envisioned by Timothy McVeigh, Buford Furrow,
Benjamin Smith, William Pierce, Richard Butler, and Michael Bray—by
followers of both Christian Identity and Reconstruction thought—is a
world at war. Identity preachers cite the biblical accounts of Michael the
Archangel destroying the offspring of evil to point to a hidden albeit
"cosmic" war between the forces of darkness and the forces of light.[43]
Reconstruction thinkers also see the world enmeshed in a great moral
struggle. "There is murder going on," Mike Bray explained, "which we
have to stop." In the Christian Identity view of the world, the struggle is
a secret war between colossal evil forces allied with the United Nations,
the United States, and other government powers, and a small band of the
enlightened few who recognize these invisible enemies for what they
are—satanic powers, in their view—and are sufficiently courageous to
battle them. Although Bray rejects much of Christian Identity's conspiratorial view of the world, and specifically decries its anti-Semitism, he does

appreciate its commitment to fight against secular forms of evil and its insistence on the need for a Christian social order.

As Mike Bray explained, his justification of violence against abortion clinics is not the result of a personal vendetta against agencies with which he and others have moral differences, but the consequence of a grand religious vision. His position is part of a great crusade conducted by a Christian subculture in America that considers itself at war with the larger society, and to some extent victimized by it. Armed with the theological explanations of Reconstruction and Christian Identity writers, this subculture sees itself justified in its violent responses to a vast and violent repression waged by secular (and, in some versions of this vision, Jewish) agents of a satanic force.

Mike Bray and his network of associates around the country see themselves engaged in violence not for its own sake but as a response to the institutional violence of what they regard as a repressive secular government. When he is said to have poured gasoline on rags and ignited fires to demolish abortion clinics, therefore, those within his culture did not view this as an assault on civil liberties or as a vengeful and hateful crime. Instead, Bray could be seen as firing the opening salvos in a great defensive Christian struggle against the secular state, a contest between the forces of spiritual truth and heathen darkness, in which the moral character of America as a righteous nation hangs in the balance.

Catholics and Protestants in Belfast

This notion of a great struggle also lies behind the thinking of at least some activists on each side of the so-called troubles of Northern Ireland, an area racked by terrorist attacks since the early 1960s. When firebombs tore through two shops and a pub in Belfast on August 2, 1998 — and an enormous car bomb two weeks later obliterated the nearby neighborhood of Omagh, killing twenty-four — it was clear that the fragile peace agreement negotiated earlier in the year by a former senator from the United States, George Mitchell, had not yet brought lasting peace to the region. On one side of the troubles are Irish nationalists who wish to absorb the six counties of Northern Ireland into the Republic of Ireland; on the other side are Protestants who have lived in Northern Ireland for generations and want to maintain the loyalty of the region to the British Union. Yet though the conflict is between Catholics and Protestants, most observers question to what degree religion is actually at the heart of the dispute.

This is the question I put to a leading member of the nationalist Sinn Féin party in Belfast two days before the firebombs exploded. The Sinn Féin leader, Tom Hartley, had been a comrade of Gerry Adams and Bobby Sands since the 1970s, and when I talked with him he was serving as the leader of the party in the Belfast city council, where he served as an elected councillor.[44] Hartley was an articulate, thoughtful man with a thick head of hair and an even thicker Irish brogue. The bluejeans and open shirt he was wearing were more in keeping with his working-class headquarters in the war zone of Belfast's Falls Road, which I had visited the day before. The building had been barricaded with large rocks to keep car bombs from exploding in front of the headquarters. Hartley's other office was in the elegant surroundings of the Belfast City Hall, which looked vaguely like a miniature version of the U.S. Capitol building. In a workroom near the gleaming marble rotunda, the Catholic activist fixed a cup of coffee and speculated about the religious aspects of the Northern Irish conflict.

Hartley said that he basically agreed with his colleague Gerry Adams that Republicans like himself were engaged in an anticolonial struggle that had nothing to do with religion.[45] They simply wanted the British out. The problem, Hartley explained, was that the conflict had been made into a religious dispute by the British a century ago when they encouraged large numbers of Protestants from Scotland and England to settle in the Northern Irish counties. The result, Hartley said, was tension between peoples with two different religious labels, and more than that, between two different ways of thinking. Hartley speculated that some of the trouble between the two communities was due to differences in what he called the "thought processes" of the religions and in the characteristics of Roman Catholic and Protestant cultures.

Catholics like himself were "hierarchical," Hartley explained, adding that it was a hallmark of Catholic thinking to assume that all Catholics in a region such as Ireland are part of a unified community, the leaders of which can generally count on the loyalty of their people. When Gerry Adams participated in peace negotiations earlier in 1998, he could do so in secret, Hartley said, knowing that his party would stand behind him even if they did not know what the terms of his agreement would be. Adams acted "like an archbishop," Hartley acknowledged, and yet his Sinn Féin comrades approved of his position.

The Irish Protestants, on the other hand, would never do such a thing. They were democratic "up their arse, if you don't mind my saying so," Hartley said. As a result, they were constantly looking for local bases of power and did not easily trust other groups or authorities. Hartley explained that even though the Protestants had been nasty to him and other Catholics, he observed with some surprise that "they were even nastier to each other." Their leadership was based not on office but on charisma, which was powerful but ephemeral. Once these leaders died or were defeated, Hartley speculated, "you'll see a dogfight" among Protestants to determine their successors. The Omagh attack by the "Real IRA" showed that Catholics were capable of holding dogfights themselves, since the extremist Catholic attack was aimed at Gerry Adams as much as at the Protestant and government opposition. Yet Hartley's point was valid. In general, Adams had much broader support within the Catholic community than did any single leader within the quarreling Protestant camp.

Perhaps none of these Protestant figures was more quarrelsome than the Reverend Ian Paisley. Hartley agreed that Paisley, perhaps more than any other figure in the Catholic-Protestant dispute, brought religion into the politics of Northern Ireland and employed religious ideas and images in legitimizing the use of violence. Paisley was a firebrand Protestant preacher who was born into a Baptist family of Scottish ancestry in Northern Ireland in 1926.[46] Eventually he broke with the established Protestant denominations and founded the Free Presbyterian Church, for which his own Martyrs Memorial Church on Ravenhill Road, Belfast, is the flagship congregation.

When I was shown around the sanctuary of the church by members of Paisley's staff, I was struck not only by the Protestant simplicity of the attractive modern building but also by the stark images of nationalism. On either side of the pulpit was a flag: the Union Jack on the preacher's right and the flag of Ulster (Northern Ireland) on his left, with a crown at its center. To the side of the podium were plaques. "For God and Ulster" read one, and another was a memorial to those Protestants who had fallen in defense of Northern Ireland's union with the United Kingdom. In a corridor outside the sanctuary were busts of the great martyrs of the Protestant tradition, including Martin Luther, John Calvin, John Wesley, and George Whitefield. In another room in the church a series of windows featured significant moments in the life of Ian Paisley himself, forever etched as images in the glass.

This was one side of Paisley, the stormy egomaniacal preacher who was so annoyed with Margaret Thatcher's peaceful overtures to the Irish Republican Army that he condemned her in a prayer during his

Sunday morning service. "O God," Paisley intoned, "in wrath take vengeance upon this wicked, treacherous, lying woman." Then, as if to goad God more quickly into action, Paisley prayed, "Grant that we shall see a demonstration of Thy Power."[47] It is open to question whether God ever assented to Paisley's requests and performed acts of vengeance on moderate British leaders; Irish Catholics; members of the IRA and officers in their political party, Sinn Féin; and anyone else whom Rev. Paisley found annoying. But it is not at all unlikely that some of the preacher's more zealous followers took up the task of divine vengeance on their own.

A second side of Paisley was that of international religious organizer, leader of a broad network of like-minded religious conservatives that gave credibility and support to his religio-political positions. For years Paisley befriended the Rev. Bob Jones, the American evangelical pastor and founder of the university in Greenville, South Carolina, to which he attached his name. Paisley and Jones preached in each other's pulpit, and together they founded the World Congress of Fundamentalists. The objective of the organization was, in part, to show their displeasure with the liberal World Council of Churches. Paisley also established the European Institute of Protestant Studies, whose stated goals were "expounding the Bible and exposing the Papacy."[48] According to a notice in the first issue of its newsletter, *The Battle Standard*, published in October 1997, the Institute, which was housed in Paisley's church, "hopes to establish correspondents throughout the world so that it can give a global view of the state of Protestantism."[49] By 1999 the denomination that he established, the Free Presbyterian Church, boasted over seventy churches and over twelve thousand followers in a dozen countries, including Australia, Germany, and the United States.

The third side—one intimately related to the other two—was Paisley the politician. In 1998 he simultaneously held three elected political positions: member of the British parliament, member of the Northern Irish assembly, and one of three Northern Irish representatives to the European parliament. Unhappy with what he regarded as the moderating impulses of the largest Protestant party in Northern Ireland, the Unionists, Paisley founded his own Democratic Unionist Party (DUP), which at one time threatened to rival its parent party in number of supporters. It was also one of the most severe critics of Northern Ireland's first minister, David Trimble.

Though David Trimble was an arch Unionist and member of the militantly loyalist Orange Order, he was not loyalist enough for Paisley.

When Trimble denounced the Orangemen's planned march through the town of Ballymoney in 1998, after three small boys had been burned alive in a terrorist act aimed at their Catholic-Protestant mixed-marriage parents, Paisley alone among Unionist leaders led the greatly diminished parade of diehard Orangemen through the town. When Trimble acceded to the peace accord brokered by George Mitchell, Paisley claimed that his former colleague had become a traitor. When Trimble—along with John Hume, a Catholic political leader—received the Nobel Prize for Peace on October 16, 1998, Paisley belittled the award as "a bit of a farce."[50]

Is there a connection between Paisley's religious views and his political position? This is the question I put to Stuart Dignan, a staff member in the Belfast office of the DUP. "No," Dignan told me, pointing out that members of the governing council came from a variety of churches, not just Paisley's own Free Presbyterian Church.[51] But Dignan did affirm that they were all active Protestant Christians and that they agreed with Paisley on political and moral issues—including opposition to abortion and homosexual rights. Moreover, Dignan said, they all agreed that in some way religion mattered in political life, a significance that was symbolized by the phrase "for God and Ulster."

Paisley has been quite specific about how one's loyalties to God and Ulster can be related. Like the adherents of Reconstruction Theology, Paisley reached into Protestant history for his vision of a religious state. Like the Reconstructionists, he found attractive the theocratic model crafted in the sixteenth century by John Calvin and revived in the eighteenth-century Calvinist ideas of George Whitefield. Like the followers of the Christian Identity movement, Paisley conceives of Christianity as being under siege by demonic forces embodied in the government and certain social groups, though in Paisley's case these groups are not Jews and other racial minorities, but Paisley's religious opponents: Irish Catholics and apostate Protestants. Utilizing the anti-Catholic writings of such Protestant figures as John Calvin and John Wesley, Paisley has branded Catholics as bearers of "satanic deception."[52] In one sermon he asked where Jesus Christ could be found today and quickly gave one answer himself: "not in the Vatican."[53]

Critics of Paisley debate whether all his talk about the satanic deception of Catholicism and the call for God's vengeance against his political enemies has simply been strident rhetoric or whether it has led to acts of violence. At one time, Paisley's DUP was closely linked with the paramilitary Ulster Resistance movement. But in 1989 Paisley publicly renounced the movement's terrorism and announced that these ties would be severed. Ever since, Stuart Dignan told me, the party has stated adamantly that it does not support violence.

Even so, Dignan admitted that in 1998 groups such as the ultramilitant Ulster Volunteer Force publicly proclaimed their support for Paisley's position. Dignan quickly pointed out that the militants' admiration for Paisley did not imply Paisley's support for them, especially for their terrorist tactics. Yet it is clear that Protestant paramilitary activists—terrorists for the Loyalist side—have received spiritual sustenance and moral encouragement from Paisley's statements. Billy Wright, a Protestant paramilitarist convicted of charges related to several terrorist incidents, told the BBC journalist Martin Dillon that Paisley was one of his heroes and that he regarded him as a great defender of the faith.[54]

When Dillon asked Wright directly whether the Irish conflict was a "religious war," Wright said that "religion is part of the equation." Elaborating, Wright explained that he not only had an obligation to defend his religious compatriots—by violence if necessary—but also that religion provided him a moral sanction to enter into violent encounters. According to Wright, he and his Protestant comrades "have the right to fight, to defend and to die for what we believe is Truth."[55]

Interestingly, some of the paramilitary activists on the Catholic side of the conflict said much the same thing about their own dedication to the struggle and their own moral justifications for killing. There was less agreement on the Catholic side, however, over whether religion is central to the dispute. Part of the issue concerned definitions. Those who thought of religion as something sanctioned by the Church would not identify the Irish Republican side as very religious. But those who thought of religion in the broadest sense, as part of a society's culture, saw the Republican position as a religious crusade.

Most of the activists in the IRA and the Sinn Féin party had a strong Catholic upbringing and shared in what the Sinn Féin leader, Tom Hartley, described to me as the "Catholic culture" of Irish tradition.[56] Several Catholic priests, and even some nuns, were quietly supportive of the Irish Republican struggle. Father Denis Faul thought that the IRA leader, Bobby Sands, had a "religious motivation" and "theological justification" for undertaking his hunger strike in prison.[57] Fr. Faul went on to say that the Catholic culture of the Irish gave them the ability to kill and be killed, since death "is a sacrifice" and "the opportunity of forgiveness" lessens the guilt involved in killing.[58] The religious nature of Irish nationalism was also asserted by Conor Cruise O'Brien, an Irishman who has written eloquently about contemporary world conflicts. O'Brien has acknowledged that in his native land religion and nationalism are "like lungs"—one could scarcely exist without both, and not at all without at least one.[59] He described the IRA offensive as "a major convergence of religion and nationalism" and termed it "a kind of Holy War."[60]

Considering the Catholic dimensions of Irish nationalism described by Sinn Féin activists such as Hartley and writers such as O'Brien, it is something of a surprise that the hierarchy of the Catholic Church publicly has taken a dim view of the IRA and Sinn Féin activities. This is all the more surprising in light of Ian Paisley's accusation that "Rome is behind the troubles—that is an indisputable fact."[61] This "fact" is indeed disputable, however, considering the antagonistic position that the Church's hierarchy has taken against the IRA and the Sinn Féin party from the very beginning of the conflict. Some leaders, such as Archbishop Cahal Daly, have been downright vitriolic. Tom Hartley related to me an incident involving a group of Catholic clergy who signed a petition mildly supporting the Republican position. When their names were published as signators, Church leaders had them quietly transferred from Northern Ireland to areas of the country with less contention.[62] Some claimed that the Catholic IRA activists were eager to divorce their paramilitary activities from their religious obligations so that they would not have to confess their sins of violence to their priests.[63]

Tom Hartley expressed bitterness that the hierarchy of the Roman Catholic Church has not been more supportive of what he and other Sinn Féin members believe is a movement in support of Catholic culture as much as Irish nationalism. Hartley gave several examples of instances where he thought that the Church was trying to interject itself in Sinn Féin's sphere of influence. According to Hartley, the Church would receive money from the British government to provide social benefits to the community, a role that Sinn Féin had played. The Church provided an ideology and political organization that competed in some ways with the Republican cause.

I asked Hartley if the reverse was not also true: hadn't Sinn Féin in many ways replaced the official Catholic Church, especially in acting as spokesperson for the community and providing a moral voice for the masses? After all, I pointed out, Sinn Féin had opened a series of Advice Centers where individuals could receive solace and support in times of crisis, just as the Church had always done. Hartley noted that these

Advice Centers were meant to deal primarily with political and social issues, not personal or spiritual ones. Still, he acknowledged, in some ways Sinn Féin had taken over the role of moral leadership that he feels the Church had abdicated. In a curious way, Sinn Féin has been pioneering in a new kind of religious community, a kind of Irish political Catholicism.

So even though Sinn Féin is not cozy with the Catholic hierarchy, it has encouraged a certain Northern Irish revival of Catholicism, or at least "Catholic culture," as Hartley calls it. In a more direct way, Ian Paisley and his political and religious organizations have spurred a revival of Protestant culture and thought within their community. On both the Irish and Protestant sides, violence is related to the renewed role that religion has come to play in Northern Ireland's public life. In that sense the Christian activists on either side of the Northern Irish struggle are not that different from one another. Nor are their roles that dissimilar from those of their politically active Christian brethren in the violent militia and anti-abortion movements in the United States, an ocean away.

CHAPTER 3

Zion Betrayed

The 1999 peace talks with Palestinians constituted a "betrayal," Jewish activists in Israel asserted, echoing remarks made after the Wye River negotiations in October 1998.[1] Members of the Council of Jewish Communities in Judea, Samaria, and Gaza described Israel's stance as a "pathetic capitulation" and proclaimed that the Israeli prime minister was "no longer our leader."[2] Intentionally or not, their strident posture in 1998 had helped to prepare a climate of hatred that justified a series of violent demonstrations against an already weakened government that toppled at the end of the year. These angry statements and outbursts of activism were not just expressions of disagreement with policy, however; they were signs of frustration with a world gone awry. The dissenters' anxiety was personal as well as political, and in a fundamental way their fears were intensely religious.

The antipeace demonstrations in 1998 and 1999, following the tragic assassination of Israel's prime minister Yitzhak Rabin in 1995 by Yigal Amir and the 1994 attack at the Tomb of the Patriarchs in Hebron by Dr. Baruch Goldstein, have shaken many Israelis' image of themselves as a tolerant and peace-loving people. Yet the perpetrators of both of these acts of terrorism justified their deeds with Jewish theology, historical precedents, and biblical examples. In the world view of Amir, Goldstein, and many of their colleagues, their people are caught up in a war with cultural, political, and military dimensions. In talking with Israel's religious activists, it became clear to me that what they were defending was not only the political entity of the state of Israel, but a vision of Jewish society that had ancient roots.

Yoel Lerner and the Assassination of Yitzhak Rabin

Yoel Lerner was one of those activists who yearned for a Jewish society in Israel. He hoped for the restoration of the ancient temple in Jerusalem, the exclusive right of Jews to settle on the West Bank of the Jordan River, and the creation of a state based on biblical law. Although he would later become deeply disappointed over Netanyahu's performance at Wye River in 1998 and the election of Ehud Barak as Israel's prime minister in 1999, when I visited him in his book-lined study in the heart of the walled city of old Jerusalem in 1998, he was still buoyed by the assassination of Rabin and the subsequent successes of the conservative Likud party candidates. He had just been to visit Rabin's assassin, Yigal Amir, in the prison cell where he languished. Or, rather, Lerner had attempted to visit Amir but was prohibited from entering. Instead, Lerner and several of his colleagues brought a cake on the occasion of Amir's twenty-seventh birthday and proceeded to sing "Happy Birthday" outside the prison walls as photographers and television cameras recorded the spectacle.

The antiterrorism laws in Israel prevented Lerner from saying anything supportive of Yigal Amir, he explained to me. Even in private conversations, "I cannot call him a hero, a patriot, or a martyr," Lerner said, his tone indicating that he would very much like to use all of these terms in describing Amir.[3]

Yoel Lerner is a large, rabbinic-looking man with thick glasses and an even thicker beard. He enjoys talking Israeli politics with his energetic American accent, and he possesses what one of Israel's foremost authorities on the religious right, Ehud Sprinzak, has described as a "discursive and logical mind."[4] This was the third interview I had had with Lerner over a ten-year period, and our conversations had often focused on another new plan or political party Lerner was about to launch that would revitalize Jewish nationalism. Though over the years many of his political schemes had fallen apart, on this occasion he seemed more optimistic. When I first talked with him in Jerusalem in 1989, he had just completed prison time for his part in an attempt to blow up the Dome of the Rock, the Muslim shrine believed to be located almost exactly on the site of the great Jewish temple that was destroyed almost two thousand years ago.

Later he had attempted to establish political parties, resisted the notion that any of the West Bank could be ceded to Arab authority, and tried to mobilize support for rebuilding the original structure on Temple Mount in Jerusalem.[5]

Several years ago Lerner and his wife moved into an apartment in Jerusalem's old walled city for political as well as religious reasons. His quarters were located next to the Treasures of the Temple exhibit, a modern tourist attraction that showed pictures of what the temple must have looked like in biblical times. Behind the tourist attraction, Lerner and his colleagues were locating candidates for a revived priesthood, re-building musical instruments and priestly robes and jewelry, and trying to assemble the necessary elements for religious sacrifices. They wanted to be ready when the temple was rebuilt. Most difficult was the task of locating the biblically prescribed "red heifer" needed for religious rites. They were assured by biologists, however, that a strain of cattle could be produced with a reddish-brown coat that could pass, with a certain amount of imagination, as biblically red.

All of this was important to Yoel Lerner, who believes in a form of Messianic Zionism. In his view the prophesied Messiah will come to earth only after the temple is rebuilt and made ready for him. Thus the issue of the temple was not only a matter of cultural nostalgia but also one of pressing religious importance. After all, Lerner pointed out, many of the laws incumbent on Jews in the Bible are related to temple ritual, and Jews can hardly obey these laws if there is no temple in which to perform them.[6] In Lerner's view the redemption of the whole world depends upon the actions of Jews in creating the conditions nec-essary for messianic salvation.

The location of the biblical temple is often described as directly be-neath the holy Muslim shrine, the Dome of the Rock. Lerner assured me, however, that his latest archeological information located the tem-ple slightly beside the Dome, between the shrine and the al-Aqsa mosque, so technically it was not necessary to completely demolish the Muslim holy place. Moreover, according to Sprinzak, Lerner was no longer "impatient for the coming of the Messiah."[7] Still, Jewish control over the sacred city was essential, Lerner said, and he regarded it as heretical to give up the least bit of biblical land—by which he meant all of the West Bank—to Arabs and their Palestinian Authority.

This is why the peace negotiations with Arab leaders were so deeply disappointing, why the Oslo Peace Accord between Rabin and Arafat had made Lerner profoundly unhappy, and why he felt that the assassination of Rabin by Yigal Amir was morally justified. In an earlier interview with Lerner, several weeks before Rabin's assassination, he told me that he thought Israel was going in a seriously wrong direction—not only for the sake of its political security, but more important, in Lerner's view, for the sake of its spiritual mission. He later told me that there had been a great deal of discussion in the months before Rabin's death about the religious justifications for the political assassination—or "execution," as Lerner called it—of Jewish leaders who were felt to be dangerously irresponsible and were de facto enemies of Judaism. Thus it was "no surprise" to Lerner that someone like Yigal Amir was successful in killing Rabin. The only thing that puzzled him, he said, was that "no one had done it earlier."[8]

On the evening of November 4, 1995, on their way to a great peace rally held in the plaza of the city hall in Tel Aviv, Israel's prime minister Yitzhak Rabin and his wife, Leah, discussed the possibility of violence and the precautions that they should take against it. What they feared were reprisals from militant members of Hamas against the peace overtures that Rabin had made. They were aware of militant Jewish opposition to the peace process as well, but "never in our wildest imaginations," Leah Rabin told me, "did we ever think he would be attacked by a Jew. We simply did not think it possible that one Jew could even think of killing another."[9]

Later that evening Rabin addressed a cheering crowd of 100,000, telling them that he thought that Israelis believed in peace and were "ready to take a risk for it."[10] Observers said that it was one of Rabin's finest hours, a high point in his political career, and a moment of great personal satisfaction. Minutes later, just after he had descended the staircase and was walking to his car beside the government building, a student from Tel Aviv's conservative Bar-Ilan University aimed his pistol and shot the prime minister at point-blank range. As Rabin lay dying on the sidewalk next to the car, the student, Yigal Amir, was apprehended by the police. He was quoted as saying that he had "no regrets" for what he had done, adding that he had "acted alone and on orders from God."[11]

Later, Amir—a former combat soldier who had studied Jewish law—said that his decision to assassinate the prime minister was not a casual one and that he had attempted to carry out the act on two previous occasions. At those times, however, the conditions had not been right. His

decision to kill the prime minister was influenced by the opinions of
militant rabbis that such an assassination would be justified by the
"pursuer's decree" of Jewish legal precedence.[12] The principle morally
obligates a Jew to halt someone who presents "a mortal danger" to
Jews. Such a danger, Amir reasoned, was created by Rabin in allowing
the Palestinian Authority to expand on the West Bank.

Actually, Yoel Lerner told me, the pursuer's decree was not a very
convincing basis for killing Rabin. To use that as a justification one
would have to prove that Rabin had intended to kill Jews. Instead,
Lerner and his friends came up with three other reasons they thought
gave even greater justification for Rabin's "execution," as Lerner put it.
One was that Rabin's government was, in his view, "illegitimate" since
it was formed by a coalition of liberal Jewish and Arab votes and had
secretly negotiated with the PLO. The second reason was the "anti-
Jewishness" of Rabin's policies that forfeited Jewish authority, and the
third was Rabin's "treason" in giving away state land. In wartime—
which certainly characterized present-day tensions, according to
Lerner—the punishment for treason should be death.

So when Lerner and his colleagues talked of Netanyahu's "treason"
in 1998, many concerned Israelis feared that the climate of hate that
culminated three years earlier in the killing of Rabin had returned.[13]
Knowing that he could be charged with incitement to violence, Lerner
was careful in choosing his words, and he spoke metaphorically in describing to me his reactions on hearing the news that Rabin had been
killed. He said he felt the same sense of relief that one might feel at having finally brought under control a "runaway train." The train, he said,
"had been stopped."[14] Someone had to do it, Lerner said, and he felt
that Yigal Amir deserved to be treated as a national patriot.

This was why Lerner and his colleague, Avigdor Eskin, went to Amir's
prison and serenaded him with birthday songs. It was also why Lerner reserved a place of honor for Yigal Amir on his wall. On one of the few
spaces in Lerner's dusty study that was not covered with bookshelves was
a collection of photographs, including one of Yigal Amir with the words,
in Hebrew, "the man who stopped the train and delivered the nation of
evils." Most of the others portrayed on his wall were dead, Lerner
pointed out. He described them as martyrs in the cause of Jewish freedom. Prominent among the pictures were the faces of Rabbi Meir
Kahane and Dr. Baruch Goldstein. In both cases, Lerner said, they were
killed not only because they were perceived as Jewish freedom fighters

but also because their opponents saw them, like Yigal Amir, as enemies of the secular state. They also saw them, I added, as Jewish terrorists.

Baruch Goldstein's Attack at the Tomb of the Patriarchs

Baruch Goldstein, like his colleague Yoel Lerner, saw the situation of Jewish people in Israel as that of victims oppressed in their own land. In his case, however, the encroaching presence of Arabs on the West Bank was not just a distant threat. Goldstein lived there, and he saw on a daily basis what he perceived to be the Arabs' arrogance in thinking that they had a right to the land on which they lived.

Goldstein had watched with mounting wrath as Palestinian Arabs increased their attacks on his fellow residents of Kiryat Arba, a settlement built primarily for religiously active Jews who wanted to live near the ancient town of Hebron, known to its almost exclusively Arab Muslim population by its Palestinian name, al Khalil. As a medical doctor raised in America, Goldstein had considerable influence in the settlement and had been elected to the town council. Military officials would notify him when a Jewish settler in the surrounding area had been attacked, and in turn he would contact the authorities when there were difficulties affecting the settlement. He complained that automobiles driven by Jewish settlers had been stoned on the major road leading to Jerusalem, and several settlers had been killed. At night he could hear noises from the loudspeaker of a mosque located just across the fence from the settlement, and occasionally he heard someone shouting the terrible words *itbah al-yahud*: "slaughter the Jews."[15]

On February 24, 1994, the night before the celebration of Purim—a holiday marking the deliverance of Jews from extinction at the hands of their oppressors—Goldstein went to the shrine at the Tomb of the Patriarchs in Hebron/al Khalil. The shrine is located above the Cave of Machpelah, the site where Abraham, Sarah, Isaac, and other biblical figures revered by the three Abrahamic faiths—Judaism, Christianity, and Islam—were said to have been entombed more than three thousand years ago. The shrine, a large fortresslike stone building, contained halls of worship for both Jews and Muslims; the mosque of Ibrahim (Abraham, in Arabic) had been standing on this site since the seventh century. Goldstein went to the Jewish side, where worshippers were gathered to listen to a reading of the Scroll of Esther, as is traditionally done on Purim eve. But his meditation was interrupted by boisterous voices outside, and again the terrible words were shouted—*itbah al-yahud*—this time by a gang of Arab youths. Goldstein turned and saw that the armed guards that the Israeli government had stationed at the site were ignoring the commotion. They did nothing. Dr. Goldstein was outraged and felt that both Judaism and the Jewish people had been deeply humiliated.

Goldstein had had enough. Before dawn the next morning, on the day of Purim, he returned to the shrine, this time entering the mosque on the Muslim side of the building, where early-rising worshippers were beginning their morning prayers. Goldstein pulled out a Galil assault rifle he had hidden in his coat and began firing indiscriminately into the crowd of men and boys who were prayerfully kneeling on the carpeted floor. After firing 111 shots and killing more than thirty worshippers, and injuring scores more, Goldstein was overwhelmed by the crowd and pummeled to death.

Ironically, minutes later, when the Israel military officials heard the first reports of shooting at the mosque, they tried to find Dr. Goldstein, as they often did when there was a crisis involving the Jewish settlers. They wanted to alert him that there was trouble. They dialed his pager and waited in vain for a response.

Some months after the awful incident, I was at the elaborate gravesite that had been constructed near Goldstein's home in Kiryat Arba, talking with the volunteer guard, Yochay Ron. "Dr. Goldstein did the right thing," said the thin young man, who was wearing blue jeans, a white t-shirt, and an embroidered skullcap, and carrying an automatic rifle.[16] At the time of Goldstein's funeral, over a thousand of the settlement's six thousand residents came to honor him during a driving rainstorm. Soon thereafter the grave had become a shrine, and the raised granite slab was surrounded by a concrete plaza and ringed by pillared lamps. Yochay Ron was one of several volunteers who took turns guarding the site and explaining its significance to strangers.

After Rabin's assassination, when public attitudes turned hostile toward zealots such as Goldstein, the Israeli government attempted to prohibit the construction of a shrine at Goldstein's gravesite by outlawing the building of memorials at the grave of any murderer. Yoel Lerner and his comrades had protested this law and claimed that it would apply to the grave of Yitzhak Rabin as well as Dr. Goldstein, since Rabin had authorized the killing of Jews in the *Altalena* incident at the time Israel was created, in 1948.[17] Lerner and his allies set up a vigil on Mount Herzl across from Rabin's grave, and although they were not allowed to display signs directly referring to the fallen leader, they cleverly displayed words from the scripture, "Thou Shalt Not Kill," to make their point.

When I visited Goldstein's gravesite in 1995, it was still a popular attraction for members of the Jewish right wing. Yochay Ron, like Yoel Lerner, regarded Goldstein as a patriot. He explained that although he would miss Goldstein's leadership in his community, he "felt good" when he heard the news of what Goldstein had done. Ron's only regret was that Goldstein's death did not have more of a strategic impact, and that it did not drive the Arabs out of Hebron/al Khalil. Even as we spoke, other Arabs were coming to the Tomb of the Patriarchs; they still arrived daily at the Ibrahim mosque to say their morning prayers. Ron felt that he and all Jews were "at war with the Arabs" and that peace would not come until all biblical lands were redeemed by Jewish occupation and the Arabs had gone.

Yochay Ron is a native son of Israel. He was born some thirty years ago in the northern part of the country in a small town near the Sea of Galilee. As a youth he was diligently religious and studied at a yeshiva, a religious school. When he heard that a new Jewish settlement was being established in the West Bank city of Hebron by messianic Zionists, Ron was eager to become a part of what he regarded as a great spiritual adventure. In 1979 a small group of Jewish women and children from Kiryat Arba crawled through the window of an abandoned hospital, occupying it and illegally establishing a Jewish settlement on the site, Beit Hadassah.[18] Ron enthusiastically joined this radical venture, and in time the settlement grew to more than fifty families, with some 450 Jews sequestered in what amounted to an armed fortress in a city of more than one hundred thousand Arab Muslims.

Virtually all of the residents of Beit Hadassah were there for religious and political reasons: they wanted to make the point that Hebron/al Khalil was still a Jewish city. The settlers in adjacent Kiryat Arba were making much the same statement, as were thousands of other settlers on the West Bank who were followers of the Gush Emunim movement and members of the Kach party, once led by the late Rabbi Meir Kahane. Not all the Jewish settlers occupied land on the West Bank, Golan Heights, and Gaza Strip for religious reasons, however; many were simply trying to find a relatively inexpensive place to live. Among the latter were recent Russian immigrants who fled to Israel not only because of religious oppression but also in search of an improved way of life.

Yochay Ron's wife was such an immigrant, an attractive blond woman who had come from the former Soviet Union several years earlier. While Ron and I were talking at Goldstein's graveside, she arrived with a busload of new Russian immigrants for whom she was serving as a sort of tour guide. She brought them to view Goldstein's shrine as if it were a major attraction, and in animated Russian she tried to instill a sense of the religious importance of his act. According to Ron, she was also explaining why it is necessary to maintain and defend Jewish outposts on the West Bank, how the Jewish faith is inextricably linked with the land, and how the liberation of the land is a prerequisite to spiritual liberation.

Yochay Ron agreed with what she was saying. He said that the biblical lands—specifically the ancient towns and sites on the West Bank— are sacred, and that Jews are under God's requirement to occupy them. Ron mentioned an incident of Arab drug dealing that he saw occurring in the alleyway behind the Beit Hadassah settlement; from Ron's perspective, this was an example of how Muslims had desecrated the land. The urgency of the mission of Yochay Ron and his fellow religious settlers was heightened by the peace process, the establishment of the Palestinian Authority, and the arrival of Arab police. When Rivka Zerbib, another Jewish settler living in Hebron, first saw the armed Palestinian policemen, it is reported that she felt "humiliation" because, she said, "it's not their place here."[19]

Though her comment may sound like a racist statement, she and other religiously active settlers claim that their views are not anti-Arab but rather pro-Jewish. They say that they simply want to defend the faith. Yochay Ron, for example, justified Dr. Goldstein's actions in killing innocent Muslim civilians while they were kneeling at prayer by stating that "all Arabs who live here are a danger to us." He went on to explain that Arabs are dangerous because "they threaten the very existence of the Jewish community on the West Bank."[20]

Meir Kahane and Jewish Justifications for Violence

The idea that the creation of a Palestinian government on the West Bank poses a danger not only to Israel as a nation but to Jews in general and to Judaism as a religion, was explained to me some years earlier by Rabbi Meir Kahane.[21] Kahane was the founder of Israel's right-wing Kach (Thus) Party. His picture graced Yoel Lerner's wall along with

Goldstein's, and his ideas greatly influenced the radical Eyal movement, with which Yigal Amir was associated. Kahane's ideas were also directly behind the thinking of Dr. Baruch Goldstein, who saw Kahane as a hero and who had been a loyal member of Kahane's political party. It was not a coincidence that Goldstein's grave was located next to Kahane Square, the locale at Kiryat Arba designated to honor the martyred radical rabbi.

When I talked with Rabbi Meir Kahane in Jerusalem on January 18, 1989, the year before his death, it was immediately following a rally in the ballroom of the Sheraton Hotel proclaiming the impending creation of a new state, Judaea. At that time the Israeli political leaders were giving the first hints of a solution to the Palestinian problem that would involve "land for peace." Much of the West Bank would be handed over to a Palestinian authority, perhaps leading to the eventual establishment of a Palestinian state. Kahane's idea was that if any land were to be relinquished by Israel, he would immediately claim sovereignty over it on behalf of this new political entity, Judaea. At the rally, which I attended with Prof. Ehud Sprinzak and several of his students, Kahane came equipped with a new flag displaying a stylized star of David on a field of blue and white, posted on a wall in the glittering surroundings of the hotel ballroom. Most of the several hundred in attendance were settlers from the West Bank associated with the Gush Emunim. Not all of them welcomed Kahane's leadership, and it was clear that the idea of such a state was more of a symbolic than a political threat. Yet the proposition had emotional appeal and allowed those present to vent their anxieties about an impending surrendering of their homes by Israeli authorities. It also allowed them to express with a vengeance their feelings about the historic and spiritual significance of the Jewish presence on the West Bank.

After the rally, I followed Rabbi Kahane through the lobby of the hotel until we found a relatively quiet place and began a conversation that was only occasionally interrupted by well-wishers. An American boy, for instance, approached the rabbi tentatively and told Kahane that he came from his area of New York City, greatly admired him, and wanted to join his movement when he grew up. Kahane, who spoke with an unmistakable Brooklyn accent, chatted with the lad for a while about American baseball and then returned to my questions about the role of religion in Israeli nationalism.

Rabbi Kahane came by his Brooklyn accent honestly. A native New Yorker with a long history of Jewish political activism, Kahane was a founder of the Jewish Defense League (JDL) in the 1960s, a movement intended to counter acts of anti-Semitism.[22] For a time he also served as an informant to the FBI, turning over information about the radical groups he joined. In 1971 he came to Israel and embraced a more messianic vision of Jewish politics, and in 1974 he created the Kach ("Thus") Party. Kahane had adopted a "get tough" stance toward Judaism's detractors, which had worked well in the liberal political atmosphere of the United States, where Jews were in the minority. There his JDL was portrayed in the mass media as a Jewish version of the Black Panthers, defending the rights of the oppressed. In Israel, however, where Jews were in power, the same belligerence often came off as racist bigotry; some called it a kind of Jewish Nazism. His statements about Arabs were compared word for word with those of Hitler about Jews and were found to be surprisingly similar.[23] In the same vein, a biography of the rabbi appearing in the mid-1980s was sardonically titled *Heil Kahane*.[24] Kahane was elected to the Knesset in 1984, but after he served a term his party was banned in 1988 because of its "racist" and "undemocratic positions."[25]

At the heart of Kahane's thinking was "catastrophic messianism," as Ehud Sprinzak has called it.[26] The idea is that the Messiah will come in a great conflict in which Jews triumph and praise God through their successes. This was Kahane's understanding of the term *kiddush ha-Shem* "the sanctification of God." Anything that humiliated the Jews was not only an embarrassment but a retrograde motion in the world's progress toward salvation. This is the reason Dr. Baruch Goldstein was so severely troubled on Purim eve, the night before he entered the mosque at the Tomb of the Patriarchs to kill innocent Muslims. Following Kahane's teachings, he felt that he—with all Jews—had been deeply humiliated by the taunts of Arab youths to "slaughter the Jews," insults that were neither countered nor halted by the Israeli guards at the site.

This line of thinking was not idiosyncratic to Kahane. Ever since the creation of the state of Israel, some Zionists have been impressed with the idea that the present-day secular Jewish state is the forerunner of the established biblical Israel.[27] According to Rabbi Avraham Yitzhak ha-Kohen Kuk (also transliterated as Kook), the chief rabbi of pre-Israel Palestine, the secular state of Israel is the avant garde for the religious Israel to come; it contains a "hidden spark" of the sacred, a Jewish mystical concept used by Kuk.[28] This messianic Zionism was greatly enhanced by Israel's successes in the 1967 Six-Day War. The military victory led to a great national euphoria, a feeling that Israel was suddenly moving in an expansive and triumphant direction. Jewish nationalists impressed with Kuk's theology felt strongly that history was quickly leading to the moment of divine redemption and the re-creation of the biblical state of Israel.

Kahane deviated from Kuk's version of messianic Zionism in that he saw nothing of religious significance in the establishment of a secular Jewish state. According to Kahane, the true creation of a religious Israel was yet to come. Unlike other Jewish conservatives who held this point of view, however, he felt that it was going to happen fairly soon and that he and his partisans could help bring about this messianic act. This is where Kahane's notion of *kiddush ha-Shem* was vital: insofar as Jews were exalted and their enemies humiliated, God was glorified and the Messiah's coming was more likely.

The enemies of Israel to be humiliated included any who came in the way of the movement toward reestablishing the biblical nation. Primarily they were Arabs, who occupied the land that the Jews had to reclaim in order to reestablish the biblical boundaries of Israel, and sec-ular Jews, who had no use for the concept of a religious Israel in the first place. Kahane told me that he did not hate the Arabs; he "re-spected them" and felt that they "should not live in disgrace in an oc-cupied land."[29] For that reason they should leave. The problem, Kahane said, was not that they were Arabs but that they were non-Jews living in a place designated by God for the Jewish people.[30]

The opposition of Kahane and the JDL to Arab political power ap-parently extended outside the Middle East. In 1985, after a leader of the American-Arab Anti-Discrimination Committee, Alex Odeh, ap-peared on the ABC television program *Nightline*, where he quarreled with a representative of the JDL, he was mysteriously murdered in his office in Santa Ana, California. The FBI's three main suspects in the crime, all of them JDL members, fled to Israel, where they have avoided prosecution ever since. The three—Robert Manning, Keith Fuchs, and Andy Green—were also involved in anti-Arab incidents in Israel. Manning joined the Kiryat Arba settlement near Hebron, and the three became active supporters of Meir Kahane.[31]

Though Kahane did not despise Arabs, he told me, what he truly de-tested was the secular Jewish state. Anticipating the hatred that would animate a religious Jew such as Yigal Amir into assassinating the prime minister of Israel, Kahane said that although he loved all Jews, "secu-lar government is the enemy."[32] For that reason, supporters of the sec-ular state must be treated as major obstacles to the coming of the

Messiah. "Miracles don't just happen," Kahane said, referring to the messianic arrival, "they are made." He believed that his own efforts and those of his followers would help to "change the course of history."[33]

If violence was necessary to achieve this remarkable alteration of the course of history, Rabbi Kahane said, so be it. As one of Kahane's colleagues explained, they had "no problem" with "using force" to achieve religious goals.[34] They reminded me that Jewish law allowed for two kinds of just war: obligatory and permissible. The former was required for defense, and the latter was allowed when it seemed prudent for a state to do so. The determination of when the conditions existed for a just war were to be made by a council of elders—the Sanhedrin—or a prophet, in the case of permissible war. In the case of obligatory war, the determination could be made by a government ruled by Jewish law: a Halakhic state. Since none of these religious entities exists in the present day, the conditions were to be determined by any authoritative interpreter of Halakha, such as a rabbi.[35] Kahane, of course, was a rabbi and therefore felt free to pass judgment on the morality of his own movement's actions.

It is true that Judaism, like most religious traditions, justifies violence to some extent, at least in cases of righteous warfare. In fact, some of the earliest images of the tradition are the most violent. "The Lord is a warrior," proclaims Exodus 15:3, and the first books of the Hebrew Bible include scenes of utter desolation caused by divine intervention.

In later years Judaism was largely nonviolent, despite militant clashes with hellenized Syreans in the Maccabean Revolt (166–164 B.C.E.) and with Romans in the revolt at Masada (73 C.E.). But at the level of statecraft, the rabbis did sanction warfare. They distinguished between "religious" war and "optional" war.[36] The former they required as a moral or spiritual obligation: to protect the faith or defeat enemies of the Lord. They contrasted these battles with wars waged primarily for reasons of political expediency. Thus Kahane's reasoning, like that of Yigal Amir following the assassination of Prime Minister Rabin, had some ties to traditional thinking.

During the rally at the Sheraton Hotel proclaiming the state of Judaea, Kahane called on the people of Israel to rise up and reclaim the West Bank as an act of "just war." He argued that defense was not the only religious basis for warfare: national pride was also a legitimate reason.[37] He reminded the Jews that their claim to the West Bank came from a two-thousand-year-old vision, when the Jews came "out of the fear and shame of exile." And now, he asked them, "what about our national

pride?" He pointed out that Jews were afraid to go to the Mount of
Olives, much less to Judaea and Samaria. He urged them to fight to retain their self-esteem and pride. Kahane also justified acts of violence as
expressions of the war that is already raging but is seldom seen—the battle for the reestablishment of a religiously Jewish state, the enemies of
which are both Arabs and secular Jews. "Every Jew who is killed has two
killers," Kahane explained, "the Arab who killed him, and the government who let it happen."[38] This logic exonerated Kahane's use of force
not only against Arabs, but also potentially against his own people.

In using violence against cosmic foes, Kahane indicated, the lives of
individuals targeted for attack were not important. "We believe in collective justice," one of Kahane's colleagues explained.[39] By that he
meant that any individual who was part of a group deemed to be the
enemy might justifiably become the object of a violent assault, even if
he or she might have been an innocent bystander. In a spiritual war
there is no such thing; all are potential soldiers. "War is war," Kahane
said.[40] One of the purposes of violence against Arabs was to "scare
them" and not let them assume that they could live in Israel peacefully
or normally.[41]

This kind of language led Kahane to be dubbed "Israel's Ayatollah."[42]
His posturing left a legacy of violence—including not only the massacre
at the Tomb of the Patriarchs and the assassination of Yitzhak Rabin, but
also his own death in 1990. Within a day of Kahane's murder, two elderly
Palestinian farmers were shot dead along the roadside near the West
Bank city of Nablus, apparently in retaliation for Kahane's killing. Thus
the spiral of violence that Kahane encouraged continued. An editorial
writer for the New York Times, who described Kahane's life as "a passionate tangle of anger and unreason," referred to his death as the product of a "legacy of hate."[43] Kahane was part of a culture of violence, one
that he himself helped to shape. He and colleagues such as Baruch
Goldstein not only responded to violence but also produced it in new acts
of death and destruction, a spiral of violence that continued long after the
zealous rabbi's death.

In a curious twist of history, Kahane's murder in downtown
Manhattan on November 5, 1990, was related to a Muslim terrorist attack, the bombing of the World Trade Center, less than three years later.
Kahane had returned to New York City, his home town, to garner
money and financial support for his radical Kach movement. When he
entered the New York Marriott Hotel at the corner of 49th Street and
Lexington Avenue, a yellow cab circled the block, waiting to pick up an

accomplice in the planned assassination. Inside the hotel one of the cab driver's colleagues, El Sayyid Nosair, a thirty-four-year-old immigrant from Egypt, waited patiently for Kahane to speak. The radical rabbi greeted the crowd of some one hundred orthodox Jews, mostly from Brooklyn. He then rambled on at some length about the need to create a Zionist Emergency Evacuation Rescue Organization that would move Jews from the United States to the new settlements in Israel, to protect them from the prophesied collapse of the American economy, which Kahane claimed would trigger a new holocaust against the Jews.[44]

After the speech, as well-wishers crowded around the rabbi, they were joined by Nosair, who had donned a black skullcap for the occasion. Just a few feet from Kahane, Nosair suddenly pulled out a gun and fatally shot him in the neck, quickly running out into the street, where he looked for the cab to make his getaway. Seeing a yellow taxi, he jumped inside. But it was the wrong cab. The driver was not Nosair's accomplice but a Hispanic from the Bronx, and his vehicle soon became caught in traffic. Fleeing the taxicab and running on foot, Nosair was apprehended by a postal police officer nearby who heard the crowd, saw Nosair running, and joined the chase.

The assassination was a shocking event for New York City and a seminal moment in the histories of three groups. It created a crisis for the assassin's colleagues, who later became involved in bombing the World Trade Center, in part to give them the clout that they thought would help in their demands for Nosair's release from prison. On the Jewish side, the death of their leader radically changed Kahane's movement: some followers sought revenge for his assassination, and this motive, along with Kahane's anti-Arab ideology, compelled his disciple, Goldstein, to attack Muslim worshippers in the shrine of the Tomb of the Patriarchs in Hebron in 1995. The assassination also indirectly affected the Palestinian movement Hamas, since the retaliatory attacks of Goldstein and other militant Jews emboldened them to escalate their own militant actions and target innocent Jewish civilians, just as Goldstein had fired on innocent Arabs. This led to a series of suicide assaults in Jerusalem and Tel Aviv throughout the 1990s. One of these suicide bombings in a Jerusalem market on July 31, 1997, was to have been followed by the bombing of public buildings in New York City, a plot that was intercepted by the FBI and New York police. The copycat bombing was planned by a Muslim group in Brooklyn said to be associated with the group involved in the World Trade Center attack—thus completing the circle of interaction among the three militant groups.

The accomplice who was said to have been driving the yellow cab intended for the man implicated in Kahane's assassination, Nosair, was Mahmud Abouhalima.[45] As we shall soon see, the role he played in the World Trade Center bombing was paradigmatic of a certain kind of militant Muslim involvement in political affairs. As Abouhalima has made clear, his alleged involvement in Kahane's killing and the World Trade Center bombing was committed not only out of a hatred of Kahane's Jewish extremism and the global American power represented by the World Trade Center, but also because of a vision of an ideal Islamic society that he hoped would be more powerful and enduring than competing versions of political order, be they militantly Jewish or aggressively secular. In a curious way, Abouhalima's vision of a religious society and the vision of a Jewish future longed for by Meir Kahane, Baruch Goldstein, and Yoel Lerner were remarkably similar. Ultimately, however, their inherent xenophobia made them incompatible, as Kahane's murder so graphically demonstrated.

CHAPTER 4

Islam's "Neglected Duty"

The selection of the American embassies in Kenya and Tanzania as tar-gets on August 7, 1998, for bombings allegedly arranged by Osama bin Laden followed a macabre tradition. Symbols of secular political power were also chosen—perhaps again by bin Laden—when an American military residence hall in Dhahran, Saudi Arabia, was bombed in 1996 and when a truckload of explosives was ignited in the parking garage of New York City's World Trade Center in 1993. Although many of the bombing sites chosen by the Lebanese Amal and Hizbollah movements in the 1980s and 1990s were military, the actions of bin Laden—along with Hamas in Palestine and the al Gamaa-i Islamiya movement in Egypt in the 1990s—were aimed more broadly. They were directed not only at symbols of political and economic power, such as embassies and trade centers, but also at other centers of secular life: residence halls, office buildings, buses, shopping malls, cruise boats, and coffeehouses. In Algeria the inhabitants of whole villages were slaughtered, allegedly by supporters of the Islamic Salvation Front. All of these incidents were assaults on society as a whole.

This series of terrifying events raises a complicated question: why have these three things—religious conviction, hatred of secular society, and the demonstration of power through acts of violence—so frequently coalesced in recent Islamic activist movements? To begin to search for answers to this question, I talked with one of the men convicted of the bombing of the World Trade Center, Mahmud Abouhalima. He was part of a group of Muslims, most of them from Egypt, who lived on the outskirts of New York City in Queens and Jersey City and came together as a paramilitary organization through their commitment to a visionary Muslim ideology articulated by a remarkable leader, Sheik Omar Abdul Rahman.

Mahmud Abouhalima and the World Trade Center Bombing

Mahmud Abouhalima is a strong, tall man whose striking red hair and beard have led some to call him "Mahmud the Red."[1] He was accused but never convicted of being the cab driver for the bungled getaway following the assassination of Rabbi Meir Kahane in 1990. His relationship with the alleged assassin, El Sayyid Nosair, is well established, however, and he is said to have admitted to an investigator that he tried to buy weapons to defend his group against the Jewish Defense League, an American organization founded by Kahane. The man from whom he allegedly attempted to buy the weapons, Wadih el Hage, was a Lebanese Muslim living in Texas who later worked for Osama bin Laden, and who was arrested in September 1998 for being part of the network involved in the bombing of the American embassies in Kenya and Tanzania.[2] Though Abouhalima's ties to bin Laden are at best obscure, he is well known for his associations with Sheik Omar Abdul Rahman and the group responsible for the bombing of the World Trade Center in 1993, an act for which Abouhalima himself was charged, tried, and convicted. When I spoke to him on two occasions in 1997, he was serving a lifetime sentence at a federal penitentiary.[3]

According to some accounts of the World Trade Center blast, Abouhalima was the "mastermind" of the event, a label of notoriety that is sometimes also given to his fellow activist, Ramzi Yousef.[4] In the trial that convicted him in 1994, Abouhalima was portrayed as crucial to the attack: evidence was presented that placed him at the site of the New Jersey warehouse where bomb materials were collected and assembled, and among the members of the group who stopped at a filling station to refuel the rental truck as it made its final trip to the World Trade Center parking lot the night before the explosion. At the time of the blast itself, at noon on February 26, 1993, some claimed that Abouhalima was across the street from the towers, looking expectantly out the window of the classical-music annex of a record store, J&R Music, disappointed that the bombing caused such little damage.[5] If the amount of explosives in the truck had been just a little larger and the truck placed slightly differently in the basement parking area, it would have brought down an entire tower—which most likely would have fallen sideways, destroying the second tower as well. Instead of six people killed, the number perished could easily have climbed to two hundred thousand. It would have included most of the fifty thousand workers and an equal number of visitors on site at the World Trade Center on that fateful day, plus another hundred thousand workers in the surrounding buildings, which would have been destroyed if both towers fell. If indeed Abouhalima had expected that sort of disaster, he must have been disappointed with the relatively modest explosion that resulted, even though its assault on the public's consciousness made it one of the most significant terrorist acts in American history.

The first of two conversations I had with Abouhalima took place in August 1997, when I met with him by special arrangement in an otherwise empty visitor's room of the maximum-security prison in Lompoc, California—which prides itself as "the new rock," a formidable and secure successor to Alcatraz. He was brought into the room handcuffed and accompanied by three guards. Dressed in green prison garb, Abouhalima's figure was indeed striking—tall, red-haired, his face freckled—and his English was fluid and colloquial. He leaned over as he spoke, often whispering, as if to reinforce the intimacy and importance of what he said.

When I talked with him, he was hoping that his conviction could still be appealed, and for this reason Abouhalima avoided discussing particulars related to the trial and to the bombing itself. He claimed to be innocent of all charges, a point that he repeated in letters to me in 1998 and 1999. Moreover, he claimed that he almost never talked with journalists or scholars for fear of being misquoted or—he said—falsely implicated in the crimes that put him in prison. He specifically denied the allegations of direct involvement in the World Trade Center bombing for which he had been convicted. Abouhalima related to me a dramatic moment in the trial when the prosecution's sole witness to his participation in the act—the New Jersey service station attendant on duty the night that the truck carrying the explosives was refueled—was asked to look around the courtroom and identify the tall, red-headed man he had seen with the truck at the time. Instead of pointing toward Abouhalima, the attendant startled the audience by pointing past him toward one of the jurors, saying "it was a person like this one."[6] Abouhalima had reasons, therefore, for thinking that the case against him was fairly slim, and it was understandable that he did not want to discuss the bombing or the events surrounding it.

Although restricted in what he felt he could say, Abouhalima was quite eloquent on the subject that I wanted to discuss with him—the public role of Islam and its increasingly political impact. He also felt free to talk about the subject of terrorism in general and terrorist incidents of which he was not accused, including the Oklahoma City federal building bombing. The trial of Terry Nichols, one of the defendants in the case, was being conducted at the time of my second interview with him, and in response to my questions, Abouhalima discussed the progress of the trial and helped me understand why such a bombing might occur.

"It was done for a very, very specific reason," Abouhalima told me, contradicting any impression I might have had that the federal building was bombed for no reason at all, or for the most general of symbolic statements. "They had some certain target, you know, a specific achievement," Abouhalima said, adding that "they wanted to reach the government with the message that we are not tolerating the way that you are dealing with our citizens."[7]

Was the bombing an act of terrorism, I asked him? Abouhalima thought for a moment and then explained that the whole concept was "messed up." The term seemed to be used only for incidents of violence that people didn't like, or rather, Abouhalima explained, for incidents that the media have labeled terrorist.

"What about the United States government?" Abouhalima asked me. "How do they justify their acts of bombings, of killing innocent people, directly or indirectly, openly or secretly? They're killing people everywhere in the world: before, today, and tomorrow. How do you define that?" Then he described what he regarded as the United States' terrorist attitude toward the world. According to Abouhalima, the United States tries to "terrorize nations," to "obliterate their power," and to tell them that they "are nothing" and that they "have to follow us." Abouhalima implied that many forms of international political or economic control could be kinds of terrorism. He also gave specific examples of cases where he felt the United States had used its power to kill people indiscriminately.

"In Japan, for instance," Abouhalima said, referring to the atomic bomb blasts, "through the bombs, you know, that killed more than two hundred thousand people." Perhaps it was just a coincidence, but the number of casualties Abouhalima cited in Hiroshima and Nagasaki was the same number that would have been killed in the World Trade Center blast, according to estimates, if the bombs had been placed differently and both towers brought down, as allegedly planned.

Was the Oklahoma City blast a terrorist response to the government's terrorism? "That's what I'm saying," Abouhalima replied. "If they believe, if these guys, whoever they are, did whatever bombing they say they did in Oklahoma City, if they believe that the government unjustifiably killed the people in Waco, then they have their own way to respond. They absolutely have their own way to respond," he repeated for emphasis, indicating that the Oklahoma City bombing "response" was morally justified.

"Yet," I said in an effort to put the event in context, "it killed a lot of innocent people, and ultimately it did not seem to change anything."

"But it's as I said," Abouhalima responded, "at least the government got the message." Moreover, he told me, the only thing that humans can do in response to great injustice is to send a message. Stressing the point that all human efforts are futile and that those who bomb buildings should not expect any immediate, tangible change in the government's policies as a result, Abouhalima said that real change—effective change—"is not in our hands," only "in God's hands."

This led to a general discussion about what he regarded as the natural connection between Islam and political order. Abouhalima said this relationship had been weakened by modern leaders of Islamic countries, such as those in his native Egypt, as a result of the influence of the West in general and the United States in particular. The president of Egypt, for example, was not really Muslim, Abouhalima implied, since he "watered down" Islamic law. Leaders such as President Hosni Mubarak "said yes" to Islamic law and principles, Abouhalima explained, but then turned around and "said yes" to secular ideas as well, especially regarding such matters as family law, education, and financial institutions, where Muslim law prohibits usery.[8] He claimed the character of many contemporary politicians was deceitful: they pretended to be Muslim but in practice followed secular—implicitly Western—codes of conduct.

Mahmud Abouhalima's religious influences began at an early age. He was raised in Kafr al-Dawar, a town in northern Egypt near Alexandria, where he attended a Muslim youth camp. It offered him the "first light for understanding what it is to be a Muslim," Abouhalima said.[9] He took courses at Alexandria University and became increasingly active in Islamic politics, especially the outlawed al Gamaa-i Islamiya, led by Sheik Omar Abdul Rahman.

In 1981, when Abouhalima was 21, he left Egypt—perhaps to escape the watchful eye of the Egyptian internal security forces—and went to Germany on a tourist visa. Egypt's president Anwar Sadat was rounding up Muslim activists at the time, and one week after Abouhalima's departure Sadat was assassinated, allegedly by Abouhalima's former colleagues, supporters of Sheik Omar Abdul Rahman. The sheik himself stood trial, accused of complicity in the act, but was never convicted. During this time Abouhalima was living in Munich, but when the German government tried to deport him in 1982, Abouhalima searched for a way to remain in the country. A rapidly arranged marriage to a somewhat emotionally unstable German nurse living in his apartment building made it possible for Abouhalima to continue his German residency.[10] In 1985 this marriage dissolved and Abouhalima married another German woman, Marianne Weber.

During his initial years in Germany, Abouhalima said, he lived a "life of corruption—girls, drugs, you name it." He went through the outward signs of Islamic reverence—daily prayers, fasting during the month of Ramadan—but he had left the real Islam behind.[11] After a while, he "got bored" with his wayward existence, began reading the Qur'an again, and returned to a committed religious life. At this time his wife, Marianne, who by her own admission had also been living a dissolute life before she married Abouhalima, became a Muslim as well. Soon afterward, in 1985, he and Marianne came to the United States. They settled in New York City, and a three-month visa turned into an extended stay. His renewed interest in Islam was nurtured by a large and active Muslim community centered on Atlantic Avenue in downtown Brooklyn.

"Islam is a mercy," Abouhalima told me, explaining that it rescued the fallen and gave meaning to one's personal life. This was something that he desperately needed when lured by the lifestyle of secular society, first in Germany and then in the United States. He told a story, a sort of parable, about a lion cub that was raised among sheep. The cub thought he was a sheep until another lion came along and showed him his reflection in a clear pond. That's what his Muslim teachers and his spiritual readings had shown him, Abouhalima said. He was "a Muslim, not a sheep."[12]

Abouhalima seized the opportunity to prove that he was not a sheep in 1988, when he joined the Muslim struggle in Afghanistan. Although he had been earning his income as a New York City taxi driver, Abouhalima was also serving as a volunteer worker at the Alkifah

Afghan Refugee Center in Brooklyn. There Afghani refugees told of the Mujahedin's heroic struggle against the Soviet-backed government of Najibullah in their homeland. The center was said to have been funded by Osama bin Laden.[13] Abouhalima admitted to me that he went to Afghanistan during that time (something he had previously denied) but that he was there solely in a nonmilitary "civil" capacity. According to some accounts, however, he was indeed involved in the military struggle and had volunteered for the suicidal task of minesweeping, going in front of the Muslim troops with a long stick to probe the earth for land mines.[14] But even if he had not been involved in any direct military way, I said to Abouhalima, it was a dangerous time to be in that country. Why would he want to risk his life for such a cause? "It is my job," Abouhalima explained, "as a Muslim." He said that he felt he had a mission "to go wherever there is oppression and injustice and fight it."[15]

When he returned, his Afghani service had earned him the admiration of many in his circle of Muslim activists, and according to some accounts he continued to wear his military fatigues and combat boots on Brooklyn's city streets.[16] He became more deeply engaged in Muslim political causes and helped arrange for the leading figure in Egypt's radical Muslim community—Sheik Omar Abdul Rahman—to become established in the United States. The sheik had also been in Afghanistan, and his arrival in July 1990 from the Sudan made significant waves in the militant Muslim community in the New York City area. In fact, he was soon at odds with the man who sponsored his immigration to the United States, Mustafa Shalabi, the leader of the Alkifah Afghan Refugee Center and a friend of Abouhalima. Eventually, however, it became clear that Abouhalima's loyalty in the emerging competition was with the sheik, and when Shalabi was murdered in 1991, Abouhalima was a suspect but was never formally charged. With Shalabi out of the way, the sheik was the unchallenged leader of the New York area's militant Muslim community.

Sheik Omar Abdul Rahman was a blind Islamic scholar who had once been a professor of theology at the prestigious Al Azhar University in Cairo and who was linked with one of Egypt's most revolutionary Islamic movements, al Gamaa-i Islamiya ("the Islamic group"). The sheik was implicated in the assassination of Anwar Sadat and in a series of violent attacks on the government in his native region, the oasis area of Fayoum—charges for which he was eventually acquitted. Suspicions of the sheik's involvement, however, remained. Followers of the sheik were also believed to be responsible for two more killings in Egypt—the murder of Parliament Speaker Rifaat Mahgoub and a secular writer, Farag Foda—and assassination attempts on Prime Minister Hosni Mubarak and the Nobel-prize-winning novelist Naguib Mahfouz. With the government closing in on his group, Sheik Abdul Rahman repaired to the Sudan and eventually made it to New Jersey. He entered the United States presumably by error; officials at the American embassy in Khartoum did not detect his name on a list of those requiring special permission—although some commentators claim that the sheik had been favored by the CIA because of his support for anticommunist rebels in the Afghanistan war and was allowed to enter the United States as a sort of reward.

In the United States, Sheik Abdul Rahman became established in a small mosque called El Salam ("the place of peace") located above a Chinese restaurant in Jersey City, New Jersey. There he preached against the evils of secular society and helped the struggling members of his flock understand why they were oppressed, both in the Middle East and in the United States. He singled out America for special condemnation because it helped to create the state of Israel, supported the secular Egyptian government, and sent its troops to Kuwait during the Gulf War, all of which the sheik deemed "un-Islamic."[17]

Listening attentively to the words of Sheik Omar Abdul Rahman was a growing circle of mostly male Islamic activists in their thirties who had immigrated to the United States from several Middle Eastern countries. It included Muhammad Salameh, an unemployed Palestianian refugee; Siddig Ali, a Sudanese organizer; Nidal Ayyad, who was trained as a chemical engineer; Ibrahim El-Gabrowny, the president of the Abu Bakr mosque in Brooklyn; his cousin, El Sayyid Nosair, who was imprisoned from charges related to the killing of Meir Kahane; and a man known by various names, including "Ramzi Ahmed Yousef," a Pakistani said to be born in Iraq and raised in Kuwait who had masterminded some of the most imaginative scenarios of recent terrorist history. It also included Abouhalima, who for a time served as the sheik's chauffeur and bodyguard.

I wanted to ask Abouhalima why Muslim activists such as Sheik Abdul Rahman would target the United States as an enemy. Although he did not respond to that question directly—and in fact praised America for its religious freedom, claiming that it was easier for him to be a good Muslim in this country than in Egypt—he did answer indirectly when he talked about how Jewish influence controlled America's news media,

financial institutions, and government. In that sense, Abouhalima explained, although the United States claimed to be secular and impartial
toward religion, "it is involved in religious politics already."[18]

Abouhalima made it clear that America's involvement in religious
politics—its support for the state of Israel and for "enemies of Islam"
such as Egypt's Mubarak—is not the result of Christianity. Rather, it
was due to America's ideology of secularism, which Abouhalima regards not as neutrality but as hostility toward religion, especially Islam.
He cited the U.S. Department of Justice, which he called the
"Department of Injustice." I asked him if the United States would be
better off if it had a Christian government. "Yes," Abouhalima replied,
"at least it would have morals."[19]

Abouhalima's bitterness toward the Justice Department was compounded by its swift prosecution of the case against him and his colleagues in a series of trials. The one that ended on March 4, 1994, focused on the anti-American motives for the assault; it convicted
four—Muhammad Salameh, Nidal Ayyad, Ahmad Muhammad Ajaj,
and Abouhalima—of bombing the Center and indicted Ramzi Ahmed
Yousef as a fugitive in the crime. The second trial, ending on January
17, 1996, convicted nine—including a life sentence for Sheik Omar
Abdul Rahman—for their part in what the judge described as a "terrorist conspiracy" of a magnitude comparable with militant fascism
and communism.[20] The prosecution offered evidence that the circle of
Muslim activists associated with the sheik had intended to blow up not
only the World Trade Center but also the United Nations buildings in
Manhattan, two New York commuter tunnels under the Hudson River,
and the Manhattan headquarters of the FBI.

A third trial, begun on May 13, 1996, focused on the fugitive, who
had been captured in Pakistan in a dramatic raid on his Karachi hotel
room in February 1995. Yousef, whose real name appeared to be
Abdul Basit Mahmoud Abdul Karim, was implicated not only in the
New York events but also in a series of terrorist plots, including one
aimed at assassinating the pope when he visited the Philippines in
1995 and the so-called Project Bojinka, which, if carried out, would
have led to the destruction of eleven large U.S. passenger airplanes
over the Pacific Ocean in one momentous day in 1995. The trial ended
on September 5, 1996, with Yousef's conviction for conspiracy in the
case of the Bojinka plot; in August 1997 Yousef again stood trial in
New York City, this time for his part in the bombing of the World
Trade Center.

After all of these trials, Abouhalima said, secular America still did not understand him and his colleagues. What, I asked him, was missing? What was it that we did not understand?

"The soul," he said, "the soul of religion, that is what is missing." Without it, Abouhalima said, Western prosecutors, journalists, and scholars like myself "will never understand who I am." He said that he understood the secular West because he had lived like a Westerner in Germany and in the United States. The seventeen years he had lived in the West, Abouhalima told me, "is a fair amount of time to understand what the hell is going on in the United States and in Europe about secularism or people, you know, who have no religion." He went on to say, "I lived their life, but they didn't live my life, so they will never understand the way I live or the way I think."

Abouhalima compared a life without religion to a pen without ink. "An ink pen," he said, "a pen worth two thousand dollars, gold and everything in it, it's useless if there's no ink in it. That's the thing that gives life," Abouhalima said, drawing out the analogy, "the life in this pen . . . the soul." He finished his point by saying, "the soul, the religion, you know, that's the thing that's revived the whole life. Secularism," he said, looking directly at me, "has none, they have none, you have none."

And as for secular people, I asked, who do not know the life of religion? "They're just moving like dead bodies," Abouhalima said.

Abdul Aziz Rantisi and Hamas Suicide Missions

Although their targets were not as spectacular as the World Trade Center buildings, the series of suicide terrorist attacks in Jerusalem and Tel Aviv conducted in recent years by Muslim activists associated with the radical Palestinian movement Hamas were equally terrifying—just as vicious in their killing of what are traditionally viewed as noncombatants, and just as desperate in their attempts to gain the world's attention for what was perceived by the perpetrators to be a religious as well as a political cause. Like the World Trade Center event, the intended audience included not just those in the immediate vicinity, but all who observed the media reportage and were horrified by it.

To many who witnessed them even at a distance, the horror of the bombings in Jerusalem and Tel Aviv was compounded by the knowledge that the bombers purposefully killed themselves in conducting the acts. Who would do such a thing, and why?

The answers to such questions are best given by those directly involved in them. But because anyone who successfully carries out a suicide bombing is by definition unavailable for interviewing afterward, I found that the next best way of hearing their voices is to watch the videotapes that many of them made the night before the missions. Often crudely photographed, these testimonies were filmed by their Hamas colleagues partly to memorialize the young men and partly to show to other potential volunteers as a kind of recruiting device. These tapes are clandestinely circulated within the Palestinian community in Gaza and the towns on the West Bank. I was privileged to see several that are part of a collection gathered by two American scholars, Anne Marie Oliver and Paul Steinberg, who once lived in Gaza and have written a book on the phenomenon of suicide bombings and the valorization of the young men who committed them.[21]

One of the most moving videotapes in their collection shows a handsome young man, no more than eighteen years old and perhaps less, looking oddly happy as he talked about the sacrifice that he was about to make. Dubbed "the smiling boy" by Oliver and Steinberg, he was videotaped in an outdoor setting beside a rock and a bush, wearing what appears to be a stylish bluejean jacket, his bushy dark hair and grinning face bathed in sunlight. The mission he and his friend would carry out involved plastic explosives, either strapped around his waist or carried in a knapsack, but he was portrayed holding a gun—most likely included in the video to give him a martial demeanor.

"Tomorrow is the day of encounter," the smiling boy said. It was to be "the day of meeting the lord of the Worlds." He went on to say that he and his colleagues would "make our blood cheap for the sake of God, out of love for this homeland and for the sake of the freedom and honor of this people, in order that Palestine remain Islamic, and in order that Hamas remains a torch lighting the roads of all the perplexed and all the tormented and oppressed [and] that Palestine might be liberated."[22]

Another of the volunteers, on a different tape, explained that all people have to die at some time, so one is indeed fortunate to be able to choose one's destiny. He explained that there were those "who fall off their donkeys and die," those "whose donkeys trample them and they die," those who are hit by cars and suffer heart attacks, and "those who fall off the roofs of their houses and die." But, he added, "what a difference there is between one death and another,"implying that the choice of martyrdom was a rare opportunity and that he was fortunate to have it."Truly there is only one death," he said, repeating the words of a famous Muslim martyr, "so let it be on the path of God."[23]

The young men on these tapes look so innocent, so full of life, that the viewer is moved to try somehow to reverse time and stop them from carrying out their deadly missions. Whatever sympathy they engender is superseded, however, by the sense of loss and remorse for the deaths of their victims, who were even more innocent than their attackers. Unlike the smiling boy and his colleagues, they were never given the choice of whether or not to give up their lives for the sake of these violent missions.

On the morning of August 21, 1995, for example, a packed bus carrying students to classes and police officers to their daily assignments was inching its way from stop to stop in a crowded neighborhood of limestone apartment buildings in the northern section of the city of Jerusalem, near the Mt. Scopus campus of Hebrew University. At 7:55 A.M. a lone Arab passenger sitting in the back of the bus— someone very much like the smiling boy—suddenly reached into the handbag he was carrying and detonated a ferociously explosive bomb. It contained what police later estimated to be about ten pounds of the chemical explosive 3-acetone.[24] It was an extraordinary blast, instantly incinerating the Arab, a visiting American sitting near him, and three Israelis seated nearby. The force of the explosion ripped open the side of the bus and continued outside, destroying another bus that happened to be traveling alongside. In addition to the five killed, 107 others in the two buses and passing along the street were wounded in the attack.

As I mentioned at the beginning of this book, I happened to be in Israel during those days, presenting a paper on religious violence, and I had visited the Hebrew University campus on Mt. Scopus earlier in the week on a bus that followed the same route as the one marked for disaster. The day before the blast I had been talking with members of the Hamas movement in Gaza, attempting to find answers to my questions about the suicide bombings that had occurred earlier in the year in crowded street corners in Tel Aviv. A little over two years later—after several more suicide bombings had occurred, including the savage attacks in Jerusalem's vegetable market and the Ben Yehuda shopping mall in September 1997—I received an articulate explanation for these

missions in a lengthy interview with one of the founders of the Hamas
movement, Dr. Abdul Aziz Rantisi.

I met Dr. Rantisi on March 1, 1998, in a village in the southern part
of the Gaza Strip that can best be described as only moderately less de-
pressed than the rest of Gaza.[25] Some of Gaza's Mediterranean beaches
are quite lovely, but the streets are dusty and pockmarked, crowded
with old buses and donkey carts. Dr. Rantisi's attractive new house was
on a small hillside in a suburban area. The driveway was filled with
cars, and posters related to Palestinian political issues were plastered on
the pillars of the entryway.

I was ushered into a comfortable living room containing a row of
couches and overstuffed chairs on one side and several formal-looking
chairs on the other, and was offered strong Middle Eastern coffee. It
seemed clear to me that the room was meant for meetings. At one end
of the room were bookcases and pictures of Rantisi when he was the
spokesman for a group of Hamas supporters who had been caught in
a no-man's land between Israel and Lebanon in 1992. Next to the
bookcases was a sort of shrine with several drawings and pictures of
Sheik Ahmed Yassin, the spiritual leader of the Hamas movement,
whom I had met years earlier. Sheik Yassin was freed from captivity by
the Israeli government in 1997 (and again arrested a few months
later). But on the day that I met Rantisi the sheik was in Egypt for
medical reasons.

When Dr. Rantisi came into the room, he greeted me cordially. A be-
spectacled, middle-aged man who spoke excellent English, Rantisi
seemed very much the professor and medical doctor he was trained to
be, and despite the heat he was nattily dressed in a business suit with a
vest. When I asked him how he wanted to be described, he said, "as a
founder of Hamas." Although I was interested in his views on the connection between religion and politics, I told him I wanted to understand
their relation to the current situation. It was not long until the conversation had turned to the matter of suicide bombings.

Dr. Rantisi corrected me. I should not call them "suicide bombings,"
he said. What he preferred was another term, a familiar Arabic word
that he wrote out in my notebook in both Arabic and Roman translit-
eration: *istishhadi*. "It means 'self-chosen martyrdom,'" Rantisi explained, adding that "all Muslims seek to be martyrs." The term one
used to describe this act was important, Rantisi went on to say, because
it conveyed its significance. "Suicide bomber" implied an impulsive act
by a deranged individual. The missions undertaken by the young men

in the Hamas cadres, he said, were ones that they deliberately and care-fully chose as part of their religious obligation. "We do not order them to do it," Rantisi emphasized, "we simply give permission for them to do it at certain times."[26]

But why, I wanted to know, would Hamas give such permission? Quite aside from the issue of the permissibility of self-martyrdom, there is the matter of targeting noncombatants. Why would Hamas allow a mission in which innocent civilians, including women and children, were the victims in such horrible attacks?

Rantisi answered in military terms, echoing the words that one of his colleagues used in discussing these matters with me in an earlier interview: "We're at war."[27] He added that it was a war not only with the Israeli government but with the whole of Israeli society. This did not mean that Hamas intended to wipe Israel from the face of the earth, he said, although some members of the movement said as much. Rantisi made it clear that he had no animosity toward Jewish culture or religion. "We're not against Jews just because they're Jews," he said.[28] From Rantisi's point of view, Hamas was presently in a state of war with Israel simply because of Israel's stance toward Palestine—especially toward the Hamas concept of an Islamic Palestine. It was Islamic nationalism that Israel wanted to destroy, Rantisi said, claiming that this political position was buttressed by the attitudes of Israeli society.

For this reason the war between Israel and Hamas was one with no innocent victims. In the beginning, Rantisi said, the military opera-tions of Hamas targeted only soldiers. The movement took "every measure" to stop massacres and to discourage suicide bombings. But two events changed things. One was the attack by Israeli police on Palestinians demonstrating in front of the al-Aqsa mosque near the Dome of the Rock in 1990, and the other was the massacre in Hebron by Dr. Baruch Goldstein in 1994 during the month of Ramadan. Rantisi pointed out that both of these incidents were aimed at mosques, and he thought that Goldstein's attack during Ramadan was not a coincidence. He concluded that these were attacks on Islam as a religion as well as on Palestinians as a people. He was also convinced that despite the Israeli government's denial that it supported the ex-tremist Jews who precipitated the al-Aqsa incident or caused the Hebron massacre, Rantisi was certain that the Israeli military had a hand in them. He pointed out that in Goldstein's attack, Israeli soldiers were standing nearby. Goldstein had befriended them, and he was able to change his rifle magazine clip four times during the incident without being stopped by soldiers.

Rantisi explained that the young Hamas supporters' acts of self-martyrdom—the suicide bombings—were allowed only in response to these and other specific acts of violence from the Israeli side, acts that frequently affected innocent civilians. In that sense they were defensive: "If we did not respond this way," Rantisi explained, "Israelis would keep doing the same thing."

Moreover, he said, the bombings were a moral lesson. They were a way of making innocent Israelis feel the pain that innocent Palestinians had felt. "We want to do the same to Israel as they have done to us," he explained, indicating that just as innocent Muslims had been killed in the Hebron incident and in many other skirmishes during the Israeli-Palestinian tensions, it was necessary for the Israeli people to actually experience the violence before they could understand what the Palestinians had gone through.

Dr. Rantisi then spoke to me in a manner indicating that his comments were meant not only for me but for the American people he regarded me as representing. "It is important for you to understand," he said, "that we are the victims in this struggle, not the cause of it." He repeated this at the end of my interview, when I asked Rantisi in what way he thought Hamas was misunderstood and what misrepresentations he would like to correct. "You think we are the aggressors," Rantisi said. "That is the number one misunderstanding. We are not: we are the victims."

Rantisi's passionate commitment to the Hamas cause came in large part from his own experience of victimization. "Like most Palestinians," he explained to me, "our family has horrible stories to tell." In his case, one of the stories involved the destruction of his prosperous family's home in a village that was located somewhere between the modern Israeli cities of Tel Aviv and Ashdod. The village, like the family home, was destroyed in the creation of modern Israel. When members of his family struggled against what they regarded as the Israeli occupation of their land, several were killed: Rantisi's uncle, three of his cousins, and his grandfather. In recent years Rantisi witnessed the continued encroachment of Israel into the limited land that Palestinians were allocated. According to Rantisi, one-third of the Gaza Strip is allotted to 1500 Jewish settlers, and the remaining two-thirds to the approximately one million Palestinians crowded there, many as refugees. Such developments have led to frustration. If the Israeli government continues to allow settlements to be built, Rantisi said, "we should use all means to stop it."[29]

In such a context, Rantisi said, the actions of self-martyrs are understandable; they are responses. Another Hamas activist, Imad Faluji, had earlier described them as "letters to Israel." They were ways of notifying Israelis that they were engaged in a great confrontation, whether they had been previously aware of it or not, and that their security as a people was "zero."[30] Moreover, Faluji said, these bombings showed that Israel's security "does not lie with Egypt, nor with Libya, nor with Arafat," but "with us."[31]

The notion that Hamas is engaged in a great war with Israel, one with both spiritual and political consequences, was articulated in a similar way by Sheik Ahmad Yassin, the movement's spiritual leader, when I spoke with him at his home in Gaza a number of years ago. Even then the competition between the secular Palestinian Liberation Organization and Hamas was so severe that my taxi driver, a Palestinian from Gaza who was apparently acting on orders from the PLO, took me to the secular movement's unmarked headquarters in Gaza before taking me to Sheik Yassin. I was told that the sheik and his religious nationalism should not be regarded as truly representative of the Palestinian struggle, and it was suggested that I visit an area of Gaza where the PLO was firmly in control—the Jabaliya refugee camp—before visiting the leaders of Hamas. I happily followed this suggestion—although with my PLO-supporting driver at the wheel I had little choice—and only afterward did we proceed to our original destination, Sheik Yassin's modest quarters on a hillside outside Gaza City.

At that time, shortly before he was placed under detention by the Israelis in 1989, Sheik Yassin was living in a motel-like row of rooms that comprised his residence, office, mosque, and meeting rooms. The rooms and the area outside were crowded with a variety of supporters, most of them men in their thirties and forties, who busily talked with one another until the sheik appeared, and then lapsed into respectful silence and crowded into the meeting room. On the wall of the room was the obligatory picture of the Dome of the Rock in Jerusalem and a drawing portraying the Qur'an superimposed on a map: it was drawn with hands extending out of either side of the Holy Book, stretching from Algeria to Indonesia, encompassing the whole of the Muslim world. The drawings indicated two different, though compatible, views of the political significance of Islam—one focusing on a distinctively Palestinian contribution to Muslim culture, the Dome of the Rock, and the other suggesting a transnational Islamic culture that reached from Africa to Southeast Asia.

The sheik's attendants eased an old-fashioned wooden wheelchair out of the private rooms at the end of the building and wheeled the sheik down the veranda to the public meeting room. Suffering from a degenerative nerve condition for most of his life, the sheik had to be lifted from place to place. He sat with difficulty on the carpet in the meeting room, propped up on cushions, and managed the ritual bowing that accompanies Muslim prayers with the greatest of difficulty, tottering back and forth as he uttered the sacred words. After the prayers were completed he gave a short homily to the assembled group, and then, as the group began to disperse, the sheik responded to my questions—translated by one of his aides—about why Islamic militancy was necessary at this moment in history.

"There is a war going on," the sheik explained. Just as Rantisi described it in my interview with him years later, Sheik Yassin implied that the struggle against the Israeli authorities was the expression of a larger, hidden struggle.[32] When I raised the question of why the secular Palestinian movement was not a sufficient agency to carry out this cause, the sheik was careful in his response. Without directly opposing Arafat, he said that the idea of a secular liberation movement for Palestine was profoundly misguided, because there "is no such thing as a secular state in Islam."[33]

This was the position of the Palestinian Muslim Brotherhood, with which the sheik had been associated for many years and which had close ties to the Egyptian movement of the same name. Hamas as a movement began in the late 1980s when the urban, organized strategy of the PLO had floundered and a new struggle emerged from the poorer, rural segments of Palestinian society: the *intifada*, backed by Hamas. The word *hamas* means "zeal" or "enthusiasm," but it is also an acronym for the Arabic phrase that is the formal name of the movement: Harakat al-Muqawama al-Islamiya, or "Islamic Resistance Movement." The term *Hamas* first appeared publicly in a communique circulated in mid-February 1988.[34]

Sheik Yassin and Dr. Rantisi were involved in the movement from the beginning. Both of them—and therefore the movement—had roots in the Muslim Brotherhood, with which Rantisi was associated when he was a medical student in Alexandria in northern Egypt. One of the first communiques issued by the movement described it as "the powerful arm of the Association of Muslim Brothers."[35] Perhaps for this reason,

Rantisi chafed at the notion that the Hamas movement was similar to Egypt's radical al Gamaa-i Islamiya, headed by Sheik Omar Abdul Rahman, who was convicted of conspiracy in relation to the World Trade Center bombing. "We are not like al Gamaa-i Islamiya," Rantisi told me, "but like the Muslim Brotherhood. We are legitimate."[36]

This comment indicated that Rantisi was conscious of the criticism that Hamas reflected only a fraction of Palestinian Muslim sentiment, and the most marginal and radical fraction at that. He pointed out that prominent religious figures had been associated with Hamas from the earliest days of the movement. These included Sheik 'Abd al-Aziz 'Odeh and Sheik As'ad Bayud al-Tamimi, a resident of Hebron who was a preacher at the al-Aqsa mosque in Jerusalem, as well as Sheik Ahmed Yassin from Gaza.[37] Yassin, who is described as "a charismatic and influential leader," commanded the Islamic Assembly, which had ties to virtually all the mosques in Gaza. Dr. Rantisi pointed out that the religious legitimacy for the acts of self-martyrdom came from a re-ligious decree—a *fatwa*—issued by a mufti in the Gulf emirates.

In the 1990s Hamas vastly expanded as an organization, and al-though the heart of the movement still lay in decentralized, local cadres, Hamas developed a fairly sophisticated organizational structure, di-vided between policy and military wings. Within the latter was a sepa-rate organizational structure for the secret cells that recruited and trained the young men who were to become operatives in the missions of self-martyrdom, as Rantisi called them. The men in these cells were seldom known within the wider Palestinian community, and even mem-bers of their own families were shocked to discover their involvement, which was often revealed only after the fatal completion of their mis-sions. In a videotape in the collection of Oliver and Steinberg that por-trays funeral ceremonies for these young self-martyrs, a group of young men is seen entering the crowd, masked and carrying rifles. The crowd roars in frenzied approval. These were "living martyrs," those who had already committed themselves to self-martyrdom and were awaiting their call to action.

In some cases, young people were recruited for a suicide bombing mission days before the act was to be carried out; they had no previous affiliation with Hamas and virtually no military training. The explosion at a busy street corner in downtown Tel Aviv in 1995, for example, was carried out by a nineteen-year-old student with a backpack full of ex-plosives. The shy, affable young man had been recruited three days ear-lier by a Hamas supporter who was asked to find an appropriate

volunteer. According to the Hamas organizer and recruiter who was interviewed for a segment on the CBS television program *60 Minutes,* he
found someone close at hand: his own cousin, who lived next door.[38]

A study of suicide bombings conducted by Ariel Merari and other
scholars related to the Center for the Study of Terrorism and Political
Violence at Tel Aviv University indicated that most of the members of
the suicide cell of Hamas received from three weeks to several months
of training. Based on interviews with friends and family members of
thirty three of the thirty four successful perpetrators of Hamas suicide
missions in Israel in recent years, the study showed that they were recruited through friendship networks in school, sports, and extended
families. They were held to their decision by having to commit to one
another in friendship pacts and having to write letters that would be
sent to their families after their deaths. Their parents and other immediate family members were kept in the dark about the young men's intentions, but the youths died with the knowledge that all would be rewarded: the dying young man would receive seventy virgins and
seventy wives in heaven, and his family would receive a cash payment
worth twelve to fifteen thousand U.S. dollars.[39]

Although most Israelis and other non-Palestinians have been aware
of the militant side of Hamas through their actions, in Gaza and West
Bank towns the peaceful face of Hamas has been more visible. The
movement has given support for medical clinics and primary education.
Hamas has also provided support for orphans and free food programs
and offered cash support to those in need—not only the families of self-
martyrs but also those affected by Israeli military assaults on Hamas
operatives. When the Israeli government destroyed Palestinian houses
as a way of punishing those who supported Hamas's actions, for example, the movement provided the Palestinian families with cash settlements often worth more than the values of the houses.

Some Palestinians have supported Hamas not because they agree completely with its radical platform and actions, but because they believe that
Hamas has kept Arafat and the Palestinian Authority on its toes and
made the organization stronger than it otherwise would be. "We need
Hamas," one student supporter of the movement told me at a seaside
cafe in Gaza, adding that the secular Palestinian Authority "compromises
too easily." For that reason, he concluded, Hamas is needed as a correc-
tive.[40] He thought that the strength of the movement is in its religious
base. Unlike secular organizations, he said, "Hamas won't change over
time," because it was "founded on religious principles."

Modern Islamic Justifications for Violence

The religious principles on which Hamas was founded have given the movement credibility and legitimacy, and they have also given it the most important base of power possible: the ability to justify the use of force. But Islam is ambiguous about violence. Like all religions, Islam occasionally allows for force while stressing that the main spiritual goal is one of nonviolence and peace. The Qur'an contains a proscription very much like the biblical injunction "Thou shalt not kill." The Qur'an commands the faithful to "slay not the life that God has made sacred."[41] The very name Islam is cognate to *salam*, the word for peace, and like the Hebrew word *shalom*, to which it is related, it implies a vision of social harmony and spirtual repose.

For this reason, Muslim activists have often reasserted their belief in Islamic nonviolence before defending their use of force. According to Sheik Omar Abdul Rahman in an interview shortly after the bombing of the World Trade Center, a Muslim can "never call for violence," only for "love, forgiveness and tolerance." But he added that "if we are aggressed against, if our land is usurped, we must call for hitting the attacker and the aggressor to put an end to the aggression."[42] In other cases a violent act has been justified as an exception to the rule, as when Muslim supporters of the al-Salam mosque defended the killing of Rabbi Kahane, claiming that this deed did not violate the Qur'an since Kahane was an enemy of Islam.[43] In yet other instances, the use of force has been shown to be consistent with Islamic principles. Iran's Ayatollah Khomeini said he knew of no command "more binding to the Muslim than the command to sacrifice life and property to defend and bolster Islam."[44]

The ayatollah was correct that there are some Islamic tenets that condone struggle and the use of force. In addition to the Qur'an's prohibition against killing, there are Muslim principles that justify it. Violence is required for purposes of punishment, for example, and it is sometimes deemed necessary for defending the faith. In the "world of conflict" (*dar al harb*) outside the Muslim world, force is a means of cultural survival. In such a context, maintaining the purity of religious existence is thought to be a matter of *jihad*, a word that literally means "striving" and is often translated as "holy war."[45] This concept has been used by Muslim warriors to rationalize the expansion of political control into non-Muslim regions. But Islamic law does not allow *jihad* to be used arbitrarily, for personal gain, or to justify forcible conversion to the faith: the only conversions regarded as valid are those that come about nonviolently, through rational suasion and a change of heart.

Even so, Islam has a history of military engagement almost from its beginning. Scarcely a dozen years after the prophet Muhammad received the revelation of the Qur'an in 610, he left his home in Mecca and developed a military stronghold in the nearby town of Medina. Forces loyal to Muhammad instigated a series of raids on Meccan camel caravans, and when the Meccans retaliated, they were roundly defeated by the prophet's soldiers in the Battle of Badr, the first Muslim military victory. Several years of sporadic warfare between the two camps ended in a decisive Muslim victory in the Battle of the Trench. By 630 Muhammad and his Muslims had conquered Mecca and much of western Arabia and had turned the ancient pilgrimage site of the Kaaba into a center for Muslim worship. The caliphs who succeeded the prophet as temporal leaders of the Muslim community after Muhammad's death in 632 expanded both the military control and spiritual influence of Islam, and over the years the extraordinary proliferation of the Islamic community throughout the world has been attributed in no small measure to the success of its military leaders in battle.

The Islamic sanctioning of military force is not indiscriminate, however. Most historical examples have involved the use of force by an established military or governmental power for the purpose of defending the faith. This is a far cry from justifying acts of terrorism, though there were rogue groups of Muslims in the twelfth century—the Nizari branch of Ismaili Islam—who used what might be called terrorism in establishing a small empire based in the north of Persia near the Caspian Sea. Hardly the models of virtuous society, the members of the order were said to have used drugs and were dubbed *hashshashin*—or, in medieval Latin, *assassini*, "drug users." They expanded their political power by infiltrating their opponent's camps and killing their leaders, often by slitting their throats with a knife. Although their empire was short-lived, they left their legacy on the terminology of political terrorism—the word *assassin*—even though most Muslims would regard them as quite peripheral to the mainstream of Islamic tradition.[46]

Present-day religious activists look for more traditional Islamic justifications for the use of violence. Dr. Rantisi and Sheik Yassin, for example, justified the Hamas use of violence based on the Islamic sanction for self-defense. Both Yassin and Rantisi expanded the notion to include the defense of one's dignity and pride as well as one's physical well-being.[47]

One of Yassin's colleagues, Sheik 'Abd al-Aziz 'Odeh, explained that the Islamic *intifada* differed from the *intifada* waged by secular supporters of the PLO in that the Islamic struggle was a moral struggle as well as a political one, stemming from religious commitment. It was also part of a tradition of Islamic protest against injustice.[48]

This is an interesting idea—that the approval of force for the defense of Islam can be expanded to include struggles against political and social injustice—and it is a relatively new one. Perhaps no writer has had greater influence in extending this concept and reinterpreting the traditional Muslim idea of struggle—*jihad*—than the contemporary Egyptian writer Abd al-Salam Faraj. The author of a remarkably cogent argument for waging war against the political enemies of Islam in the pamphlet *Al-Faridah al-Gha'ibah* ("The Neglected Duty"), Faraj stated more clearly than any other contemporary writer the religious justifications for radical Muslim acts. His booklet was published and first circulated in Cairo in the early 1980s.[49] What is significant about this document is that it grounded the activities of modern Islamic terrorists firmly in Islamic tradition, specifically in the sacred text of the Qur'an and the biographical accounts of the prophet in the Hadith.

Faraj argued that the Qur'an and the Hadith were fundamentally about warfare. The concept of *jihad*, struggle, was meant to be taken literally, not allegorically. According to Faraj, the "duty" that has been profoundly "neglected" is precisely that of *jihad*, and it calls for "fighting, which meant confrontation and blood."[50] Moreover, Faraj regarded anyone who deviates from the moral and social requirements of Islamic law to be targets for *jihad*; these targets include apostates within the Muslim community as well as the expected enemies from without.

Perhaps the most chilling aspect of Faraj's thought is his conclusion that peaceful and legal means for fighting apostasy are inadequate. The true soldier of Islam is allowed to use virtually any means available to achieve a just goal.[51] Deceit, trickery, and violence are specifically mentioned as options available to the desperate soldier.[52] Faraj set some moral limits to the tactics that could be used—for example, innocent bystanders and women are to be avoided, whenever possible, in assassination attempts—but emphasized that the duty to engage in such actions when necessary is incumbent on all true Muslims. The reward for doing so is nothing less than a place in paradise. Such a place was presumably earned by Faraj himself in 1982, after he was tried and executed for his part in the assassination of Anwar Sadat.

This way of thinking, though extreme, was not idiosyncratic to Faraj. He stood in a tradition of radical Islamic political writers reaching back to the beginning of this century and before. Among Sunni Muslims worldwide, the most important radical thinker was Maulana Abu al-Ala Mawdudi, the founder and ideological spokesman for Pakistan's Jamaat-i-Islami religious party.[53] His ideas were echoed by Egypt's most influential writer in the radical Muslim political tradition, Sayyid Qutb. Qutb was born in 1906 and, like Faraj, was executed for his political activities.[54] Although he was not as explicit as Faraj in indicating the techniques of terror that were acceptable to the Islamic warrior, Qutb laid the groundwork for Faraj's understanding of *jihad* as an appropriate response to the advocates of those elements of modernity that seemed to be hostile to Islam.

Specifically, Qutb railed against those who encouraged the cultural, political, and economic domination of the Egyptian government by the West. Qutb spent several years in the United States studying educational administration. This experience only confirmed his impression that American society was essentially racist and that American policy in the Middle East was dictated by Israel and what he regarded as the Jewish lobby in Washington, DC.[55] Alarmed at the degree to which the new government in Egypt was modeled after Western political institutions and influenced by Western values, Qutb, in the early 1950s, advocated a radical return to Islamic values and Muslim law. In *This Religion of Islam*, Qutb argued that the most basic divisions within humanity were religious rather than racial or nationalist, and that religious war was the only form of killing that was morally sanctioned.[56] To Qutb's thinking, the ultimate war was between truth and falsehood, and satanic agents of the latter were to be found well entrenched in the Egyptian government. It is no wonder that the government found such ideas dangerous. Qutb was put in prison for most of the rest of the 1950s, and a state execution silenced him forever in 1966.

These ideas of Mawdudi, Qutb, and Faraj have been circulated widely throughout the Muslim world through two significant networks: universities and the Muslim clergy. The two networks intersect in the Muslim educational system, especially in the schools and colleges directly supervised by the clergy. It is not surprising, then, that many who have been attracted to paramilitary movements such as the al Gamaa-i Islamiya or Hamas were former students or, like Dr. Rantisi, highly trained professionals.

When I asked Dr. Rantisi which writers he most respected, the first name the Hamas leader mentioned was the founder of modern-day Muslim political activism, Mawdudi.[57] When I posed the same question to Mahmud Abouhalima in the federal penitentiary in Lompoc, at first he gave no specific reply. When I suggested Faraj's name, Abouhalima seemed surprised that I had heard of him, though he corrected my pronunciation. Abouhalima confessed to owning both Arabic and English versions of Faraj's infamous booklet, "The Neglected Duty."

Abouhalima wanted to make certain that I would not use his knowledge of Faraj against him. In Abouhalima's first criminal case, he said, the evidence that he possessed copies of Faraj's book was used to show that he harbored hostile and violent attitudes against the secular government. For that reason, Abouhalima asked me to be careful how I described his attitude toward Faraj. "Do not say 'I was influenced by him,'" Abouhalima instructed me, but rather "'I respect him.'" Then Abouhalima leaned over, put his head close to mine, and whispered, "but he was right, you know."[58]

CHAPTER 5

The Sword of Sikhism

At five o'clock in the afternoon of August 31, 1995, when residents of India's Punjab state thought that the terrorism associated with the Sikh separatist movement for fifteen years had finally come to an end, a massive explosion rocked the parking lot in front of the modernistic secretariate building in the state capital, Chandigarh. In the blast that shuddered through the impressive complex of government buildings designed by the French architect Le Corbusier, the chief minister of the state, Beant Singh, was literally blown to pieces. Fifteen of his aides and security guards were also killed, and several cars were demolished in the conflagration that followed. In the smoldering heap that minutes before was his official vehicle, only Beant Singh's Sikh bracelet (*kara*) remained to identify the chief minister.[1]

Among the mangled and limbless bodies was one believed to belong to the bomber himself. The car that brought him to the site stood empty nearby; the accomplice who was supposed to drive it away had apparently panicked and fled. By tracing the license plate, the police were able to identify and apprehend several of the alleged conspirators. All were members of one of the Sikh movement's deadliest guerrilla cells, the Babbar Khalsa. They and members of several other groups, including the Bhindranwale Tigers and the Khalistan Commando Force, had been both victims and perpetrators in the reign of terror in Punjab since the early 1980s.

The suicide bomber behind the explosion that killed the chief minister was identified as Dilawar Singh, a tall young man in his early twenties. The details of his last days were revealed by his accomplices in response to what the police described as "rigorous interrogation"— a term that many Sikhs understand to be a code name for torture.[2] According to their testimony, Dilawar had practiced for the event for several weeks preceding the explosion in the middle-class suburb of Mohalli. As he left the comfortable, modern house to commit the crime that he knew would lead to his death, Dilawar scribbled a sentence in Punjabi on a piece of paper stating that his act was "in memory of the martyrs"—presumably the martyrs of early Sikh history. Quite likely, though, he was also referring to his own colleagues, the many members of the Babbar Khalsa, the Khalistan Commando Force, and other groups who had fallen in their futile struggle against the Indian police.

Thousands were killed between 1981 and 1994 on both the police and rebel sides, with many innocent citizens caught in between. Perhaps none of the killings was more spectacular or influential, however, than the assassination of India's prime minister Indira Gandhi on October 31, 1984, which the murder of Chief Minister Beant Singh replicated. By grim coincidence, one of Mrs. Gandhi's assassins was also named Beant Singh, although he was unrelated to the man who later became Punjab's chief minister. The killer Beant Singh—like the alleged accomplices in Chief Minister Beant Singh's death—was a member of the security forces of his victim. He and another guard, Satwant Singh, turned on Indira Gandhi with automatic rifles as they accompanied her on a lovely floral path from her home to her office to meet with the British actor Peter Ustinov, who was waiting in the garden for an interview to be aired on British television.

The assassin, Beant Singh, was killed on the spot, and his partner, Satwant Singh, and one other accomplice were brought to trial. They were convicted and hanged for the murder of Mrs. Gandhi. Although they were the only ones convicted, rumors of a wider conspiracy continued for some years. One scenario was forced out of the co-assassin, Satwant Singh, in a "rigorous interrogation" conducted by the police immediately after Mrs. Gandhi was killed. In his confession he implicated several Sikh leaders, including Kehar Singh, an elderly activist, and a former police official, Simranjit Singh Mann.

Satwant Singh identified Mann as the ringleader. Mann had resigned from the Indian Police Service in protest against Operation Bluestar, joined with militant Sikhs in criticizing the government, and gone into hiding. Within several weeks of Mrs. Gandhi's murder, he was caught by the Indian police attempting to flee the country by truck over the Nepal border, disguised as a construction worker. According to some accounts, Mann had colluded with a leading militant, Atinder Pal Singh, in an intricate plot to kill the prime minister.[3] The only evidence, however, was Satwant Singh's forced confession. Although Mann was held for some time in harsh confinement, he was never tried or convicted of the assassination. His relations with the most militant Sikhs have been ambivalent: sometimes they have supported each other, and at other times a clear line has been drawn between them. When Punjab's chief minister was killed in 1995, Mann was living comfortably but still under police surveillance in a pleasant two-story house blocks from the government secretariate where the bombing took place.

Simranjit Singh Mann and India's Assassinations

When I talked with Simranjit Singh Mann at his home in Chandigarh less than a year after the explosion that killed Beant Singh, he denied involvement in the assassination of either the chief minister or Indira Gandhi. But, he said, "no tears were spilled" when either of these political leaders was killed.[4] Mann compared their executions to the attempts to kill Hitler. "It was an act of punishment," he said, referring to the killing of Chief Minister Beant Singh. He added that "people rejoiced" throughout the Punjab on hearing the news.

The killing of the chief minister also showed the desperation of the militant Sikhs in their attempt to assert power, Mann told me. He said he did not expect the assassination to change things. What he called the "repression" of the Indian government toward the Sikhs would likely continue, he said. But this act did achieve a symbolic victory: it demonstrated to the world that the struggle would continue. "This is a war situation," Mann told me. "If we open our mouths we're in jail." Although the most militant wings of the movement had been crushed and there had been very few signs of overt hostility since Beant Singh's assassination, Mann still regarded the movement as potent. He saw himself as a kind of soldier. "It's a war situation still," he said.

What made Mann's statement remarkable was not only the apparent serenity of Punjab's post-1995 political landscape, but also the comfortable circumstances of Mann's own home. Despite his sometimes militant words, he has become an established political leader in the Punjab. When I interviewed him in 1996, he was living not in a bunker or a guerrilla hideout but in a two-story suburban house that can only be described as upper middle class. The living room boasted a large Kashmiri carpet and carefully chosen furniture. On the wall were etchings of Punjab life taken from nineteenth-century British travel books. He was surrounded by the trappings of middle-class success, including a graceful, articulate wife who served tea, a son who studied business in the United States, and a friendly cocker spaniel named May.

Mann looked exactly like the career civil servant he had intended to become after he finished college in Chandigarh and joined the police service, serving as the head of posts in Faridkot and elsewhere in Punjab as well as in Bombay. As his family name indicated, Mann was a member of one of the Punjab's most prestigious subgroups within the leading Jat caste, and when he resigned from government service in protest against the Indian army's invasion of the Golden Temple during Operation Bluestar in 1984, it was major news. In his resignation letter to the president of India, Zail Singh, Mann compared the government's heavy-handed action to the British atrocities against Indian protesters at Amritsar's Jallianwala Bagh square in 1919. In even stronger terms, he accused the Indian government of being "bent upon committing the genocide of the Sikhs."[5] The Indian government regarded it as an insult that someone with his qualifications and rank in the government's elite civil service would turn against them, and it was no surprise that he would be accused of complicity in Prime Minister Gandhi's assassination a few months later.

Since then Mann had been on the run, under investigation, or in jail—including five years of what he described as solitary confinement. He accused his captors of torture and showed me what he claimed to be evidence of their brutality. Mann pulled back his beard and showed scars where he said his beard hair had been pulled out. Other scars were evident on his legs. Toenails and teeth were missing; these he said had been broken or yanked out by his captors. He also claimed that his genitals had been injured from having electric wires attached to them. One testicle, he said, had shrunk and was now loose in his scrotum. Mann's imprisonment was officially an act of detention as he awaited trial. Although he was arrested thirty-two times, Mann was not convicted of a single offense. Mann said that this torture and harassment were characteristic of the Indian government's heavy-handed response to Sikh militancy and had helped to swell the ranks of the movement.

In addition to conspiracy to commit violence, charges leveled against Mann and then dismissed included treason and sedition. Mann told me, however, that he was not waging war against India as such. It was not the Indian nation that he disdained, but its government. He described the government sometimes as "secular," and sometimes as "pro-Hindu," offering the rise of the Hindu nationalist Bharatiya Janata Party (BJP) as evidence of the government's religious preferences. When militant Sikhs attacked supporters of the BJP being bused through Punjab on a Unity March en route to Kashmir in January 1992, killing five and wounding sixteen others, they asserted that this notion of India's religious unity was precisely what they were against. The Unity March "absolutely had to be stopped," Mann said, even "by force."

Yet the Sikh movement began long before the rise of the BJP, and the Sikh's Akali Party—though not Mann's faction of it—eventually joined the BJP in forming electoral coalitions. So the Hinduization of India's politics could not have been the sole cause of the Sikh rebellion of the 1980s and early 1990s. Mann said that the purpose of the movement as not simply to rebel against Hindu power but to "protect the Sikh community" from secular influences. The movement was also aimed at enlarging the Sikhs' ability to assert what they felt to be their rights and their warranted demands. Sikhs were a "national ethnic minority," Mann said, that had to look out for themselves.

The Sikh movement contained a diversity of points of view, however, and one of the most strident of its advocates—someone whom Mann admired—saw the struggle almost solely in religious terms. This leader was Sant Jarnail Singh Bhindranwale, a rural preacher from central Punjab who became the spokesman for Sikh militancy from its first stirrings in 1978 until his movement's nadir—and Bhindranwale's martyrdom—in the tragic events of 1984. Bhindranwale was a homespun village preacher who called for repentance and action in defense of the faith. Mann regarded him as one of Sikh history's most impressive leaders because of his ability to summarize great themes in simple phrases and clearcut images. According to Mann, he "articulated the hegemony of Hindu power and the injustice suffered by Sikhs, and he did it all with a consciousness of Sikh history and tradition."

I was particularly interested in Mann's comments about Bhindranwale, since it was Bhindranwale's sermons that triggered my interest in the relationship between religion and violence and led to my first article on this topic.[6] In that study I examined a collection of audio- and videotapes of the radical Sikh leader and rough transcriptions of the sermons that had been made by Prof. R. S. Sandhu, who kindly shared these materials with me.[7] I found that what Bhindranwale disdained—indeed loathed—above all else was what he described as "the enemies of religion."[8] These included "that lady born in a house of Brahmans"—the phrase he used to describe Indira Gandhi. But it also included his fellow Sikhs, especially those who had fallen from the disciplined fold and sought the comforts of modern life. Even his dislike of Indira Gandhi was grounded in a hatred of secularism as much in an opposition to Hinduism; in fact, he often regarded the two as twin enemies. He reflected an attitude held by many Sikhs—that what passes for secular politics in India is a form of Hindu cultural domination. So conscious are many Sikhs of what they regard as the oppressiveness of Hindu culture that they react strongly when scholars locate the origins of their tradition in a medieval Hindu milieu.

So it is understandable that the image of Bhindranwale cast a shadow over the Sikh community long after his death. Bhindranwale's role as exemplar was brought home to me several years ago, during the height of the militant movement, when I met with young Sikh activists in a room adjoining a *gurdwara* (a Sikh house of worship) in Delhi. The subject had turned from their own potential encounters with the Indian police and their probable deaths to the martyrdom of their hero, Bhindranwale. They would like to die as he died, the young men told me: they wanted to take life to the limit. Unlike the stance of easy compromise taken by most politicians, they said that Bhindranwale "went to his death for what he believed."[9]

During its heyday, from 1981 to 1994, thousands of young men and perhaps a few hundred women joined the movement. They were initiated into the secret fraternities of various rival radical organizations. These included the Babbar Khalsa, the Khalistan Commando Force, the Khalistan Liberation Force, the Bhindranwale Tiger Force of Khalistan, and extremist factions of the All-India Sikh Students Federation. Their enemies were secular political leaders, heads of police units, some Hindu journalists, and other community leaders. Over time the distinctions between valid and inappropriate targets became blurred, and virtually anyone could become a victim of the militants' wrath. By January 1988, more than a hundred people a month were killed; 1991 was the bloodiest year, with over three thousand people killed in the Punjab's triangular battle among the police, the radicals, and the populace. One of the more spectacular incidents in 1991 was the attack by Sikh extremists on the Indian ambassador to Romania in Bucharest. The Romanian government helped to capture the Sikhs. They were killed, and later that year militant Sikhs kidnaped a Romanian diplomat in Delhi in retaliation.

Accompanying the increase in violence was a general collapse of law and order, especially in rural areas of the state near the Pakistan border. The young activists had intimidated the older Sikh leaders, who became virtual pawns of the militants. The only authority in some areas came from those who ruled by gun at night. This was due in part to the erosion of idealism in the Sikh movement and in part to the movement's exploitation by what amounted to street gangs and roving bands of thugs. In addition, the Sikh movement had failed to achieve its political goals, leaving a cynical and demoralized public in its wake. In the absence of a legitimate government in the Punjab, the rural area became a no-man's-land in the battle between militants and armed police.

In the 1990s older and more responsible leaders in the Jat Sikh community found themselves in a quandary. They could not capitulate to the urban Hindu leadership of the central government because that would mean abandoning their religion and caste. They needed the young Sikh militants' support, but at the same time they wanted to regain some semblance of political control over them. One might think that it would be in the best interests of the central government to help them do that, but the Congress Party leaders were hesitant. For one thing, they resented the fact that moderate Sikh leaders identified with the Sikh's Akali Party rather than the Congress Party or one of the national coalition parties. More important, they feared that any concessions they made to Sikh leaders would have repercussions throughout India. Muslims would immediately demand similar rights, as would leaders of separatist movements in northeastern India and Kashmir.

In Kashmir, where Muslims were the majority community, the rise of Hindu nationalism throughout India had spurred a separatist movement. Protests erupted in 1986–87, led by the Muslim United Front. In 1988 some elements of the opposition took a more strident course, forming a paramilitary operation: the Kashmir Liberation Front. Allegedly supported by Pakistan, the Front called for secession from India. It organized demonstrations and responded to police attempts to suppress it by throwing bombs and firing automatic weapons, leading to bloodshed on both sides. In May 1989, the separatists began calling themselves *mujahedeen* ("holy warriors") and characterized their conflict with the government as a holy war—a war that continued through the 1990s.[10]

Although the Sikh and Kashmir separatist movements were not related, any concessions made to the Sikhs would certainly have been demanded by the Kashmiris, and vice versa. At the same time, the Indian government could not be too harsh on one group without intimidating the other. In the same week that Punjab's chief minister Beant Singh was assassinated in 1995, for example, the Indian government was involved in delicate negotiations for the release of foreign hostages in Kashmir and could not have afforded to renew hostilities with the Sikhs.

The rise of Hindu nationalism in India coincided with the decline of the Sikh movement. As we noted earlier, the attitude of Sikhs toward Hindu politics has been mixed. After the BJP gained strength in several northern Indian states, culminating in the formation of a national coalition government in 1998, some moderate factions of the Sikh's Akali Party did indeed join forces with the BJP. But these Akali-BJP coalitions achieved greater electoral success among the urban consitutencies, which were both Hindu and Sikh, than in the rural Sikh stronghold. The suspicion of Sikhs toward Hindu politics, like the hatred between many activist Sikhs and the secular Congress Party, was never completely overcome.

In 1990, in a poignant attempt to break the vicious cycle of hatred and reprisal, the Congress prime minister, Rajiv Gandhi, in what was virtually his last act of office, released Simranjit Singh Mann from prison. This was an extraordinary act, since Mann was awaiting trial for his alleged participation in the plot that led to the murder of Rajiv's mother, Indira Gandhi. Mann had won a parliamentary seat after campaigning from prison, but Rajiv claimed that his pardon was due not to Mann's electoral success but to his own desire to "heal wounds."[11]

Following Mann's release from prison the major factions of the Akali Party united under his leadership. The unity was brief, however, and in the years that followed there was considerable erosion of Mann's support. The party broke apart, and Mann's faction became one of the smallest of several groups at the Akali periphery. Mann's political power had come largely from his ability to broker alliances between moderate wings of the Sikh leadership and the militants. The militants had respected Mann not only for his radical rhetoric but also because of the persecution he had experienced from his alleged role in Indira Gandhi's murder. When the armed police were unleashed in 1990 and the reign of the militants came to an end, Mann's influence declined as well.

According to Mann, the tide began to turn against the militants in 1992. They were, in his opinion, destroyed from within as much as from without. It was a problem of leadership, Mann said. When many of the leaders were captured, they were enjoying the fruits of their

spoils, using air conditioners and driving expensive cars. "They advocated puritanical ways to the masses," Mann told me, "but they lived
in luxury themselves." The standards within the movement degener-
ated. "Guns controlled the party," he said, adding that "it should have
been the other way around." Internal disputes were rife, and many of
the militants were killed by members of rival factions rather than by the
police.

In the late 1990s Mann was among the few activists who had not
been killed, jailed, or sent into hiding abroad—mostly in Pakistan,
England, and the United States. Like the former militants with whom I
talked in India and the United States, Mann expressed bitterness at
both the Indian government, which he felt had persecuted the movement, and the extremist members of the militant cadres, who he believed had destroyed the movement from within.

I asked Mann if he thought the militancy of the movement was a
mistake. He said that given the geography of the Punjab, surrounded by
the rest of India with its vastly superior military resources, the movement could not have launched a productive military venture—with the
exception of those instances where "punishment" and "retribution"
called for violence, as in the assassinations of Prime Minister Indira
Gandhi and Chief Minister Beant Singh. But in most other cases, he
said, the violence was counterproductive in that it provided the government with a reason for exterminating the movement. Mann would
have much preferred a peaceful solution, such as the one proposed for
the separation of Quebec from Canada. But, Mann said, he was not opposed in principle to the use of force for a righteous cause. His disagreement with the use of violence in this instance was not "a moral decision," he said, "but a strategic one."

Sikh and Hindu Justifications for Violence

In considering the terrible toll of fifteen years of terror, one wonders
what could possibly have justified all the bloodshed and destruction.
The costs of the violence were palpable, especially in rural Punjab,
where the social and psychological scars were slow to heal.

In 1998 I spent a day in Sultanwind village near Amritsar with Prof.
Harish Puri and graduate students from the political science department of Guru Nanak Dev University. Sultanwind had been the headquarters of one faction of the Khalistan Commando Force during the
stormy days of the movement, and the tragedy of the militant move-

ment was still very much a part of the village's life. We talked with one of the student's relatives, a leading member of the village, Harjap Singh. The village leader seemed to have every reason to be satisfied: he had just been elected to the council of the Amritsar Municipal Corporation; he was a member of the leading subcaste in that area, the Chauhans; and he was the head of a large family farming complex, which he directed in person and through his cell phone. His family had a long history of leadership in the Sikh community, and pictures on the wall indicated an association with Punjab's great post-independence leader, Pratap Singh Kairon, and with the more recent Akali leader, Simranjit Singh Mann.[12]

Despite Harjap Singh's success, an aura of sadness surrounded his household, symbolized by the living room wall that had been devoted to a shrine for his younger brother, Kanwarjit Singh, whom the family regarded as a martyr for the Sikh community. Born in 1966, Kanwarjit grew up with two passions: Sikhism and sports, especially field hockey. In 1982, when he was only sixteen years old, he went to hear Jarnail Singh Bhindranwale and was seduced by the romance and excitement of the militant Sikh movement. In 1985, even though several families had extended offers of marriage to the handsome young athlete, Kanwarjit joined the Khalistan Commando Force. Two years later, at age twenty-one, he became commander-in-chief of the whole organization.

Those were busy times, the family recalls, as their humble village became the center of a very active and important organization. They were proud of Kanwarjit's leadership role. The other young men in the village were either under his command or intimidated into silence. There were rumors of "actions" undertaken by Kanwarjit's forces that led to the deaths of government and police officials and political leaders in surrounding areas, but members of Sultanwind village, even the police, were protected from the violence as long as Kanwarjit Singh was alive.

As with most militant Sikh leaders, however, his leadership and his life did not last long. In 1989 Kanwarjit and two of his colleagues were cornered by police in a house near the city of Jalandhar. The police apparently did not realize the importance of their catch and began to take the group by car to the police station for questioning. One of Kanwarjit's comrades jumped out of the vehicle and ran away, but Kanwarjit had a metal plate in his leg as the result of an earlier injury from a police attack and was unable to run. Instead, he swallowed one of the cyanide capsules he always carried with him for such a situation. Like many militant leaders, he preferred to kill himself rather than to

be tortured to death or forced to reveal information about the movement. Kanwarjit Singh was twenty-three at the time. A few months
later most of the other young men in the village were dead as well. An
entire generation of boys had been taken from the community.

Yet they were remembered. In addition to the shrine in the family
home, Kanwarjit's elderly mother had created another, more intimate
shrine in her bedroom, where Kanwarjit was born. Harjap and his sons
knew all the stories about the great days of the movement. Harjap and
the village elders erected a memorial in the center of the village to "all
of the lost sons" who died in police encounters during the years of terror. They wanted to name a new school in memory of the "lost sons,"
but there was a dispute with the government over the appropriateness
of locating a government facility in a building dedicated to those who
were, after all, enemies of the state. A library adjacent to the school
served as the memorial building instead.

Harjap did not want to talk with me about Kanwarjit's opposition
to the government, but he waxed eloquent about his brother's virtues
as a political leader. "Kanwarjit never used his power to get money,"
Harjap told me proudly, adding that he was only "fighting for principles." Other militant groups, such as the Bhindranwale Tigers, Harjap
said, attracted thugs who would use their weapons to get money, drugs,
and women. Kanwarjit's group, the Khalistan Commando Force,
would sometimes "eliminate" these bad elements in order to keep the
whole movement respectable. They would also eliminate members of
their own group, Harjap said, if they found them abusing their power.[13]

But what was the power for? What was the purpose of the movement?

At first he seemed somewhat perplexed about how to answer the
question. "To support the Sikh community," he finally responded.

Was it worth it? Were the deaths of his brother and all of the others
in vain?

Harjap Singh answered indirectly. "In Sikh history," he said, "young
men go away in battle and do not return. They are our martyrs."

This simple justification for young men's fighting in battle—killing
or being killed in sacred struggle—runs deep in India's religious traditions. Long before Sikhism developed as a separate religious tradition
in the sixteenth century, in India's ancient Vedic times, warriors called
on the gods to participate in their struggles and to provide a divine
leverage for victory. The potency of the gods was graphically depicted
in mythic stories filled with violent encounters and bloody acts of
vengeance.[14]

As India's religious traditions developed, images of warfare persisted. The great epics—the *Mahabharata* and the *Ramayana*—contained grand accounts of wars and battles, and the enduring sermon of Lord Krishna, the *Bhagavad Gita,* was recorded in the *Mahabharata* as being delivered on a battlefield. The *Gita* gave several reasons why killing in warfare is permissible, among them the argument that the soul can never really be killed: "he who slays, slays not; he who is slain, is not slain." Another reason is based on *dharma* (moral obligation): the duties of a member of the *ksatriya* (warrior) caste by definition involve killing, so violence is justified in the very maintenance of social order.[15] Mohandas Gandhi, like many other modern Hindus who revere the *Gita,* regarded its warfare as allegorical, representing the conflict between good and evil.[16] Gandhi, who ordinarily subscribed to nonviolence, allowed for an exception to this general rule when a small, strategic act of violence would defuse a greater violence.[17]

Most exponents of Hindu nationalism have differed with Gandhi on the religious necessity for nonviolence, however. The Hindu Rashtriya Swayamsevak Sangh (National Patriotism Organization) began training paramilitary cadres for the defense of Hindu culture in the 1920s. A former member of the RSS was Gandhi's assassin, and followers of the RSS stormed an ancient mosque in Ayodhya in 1992, setting off riots between Muslims and Hindus throughout India in which thousands were killed. Many of the leaders of the Hindu nationalist party, the BJP, have come from the RSS; and when the new BJP national government came to power in 1998, one of its first acts was to detonate a nuclear explosion as a test of its military power. Clearly, Hinduism, like most religious traditions, has been able to embrace positions of violence as well as nonviolence.

The history of Sikhism is also one of violent encounters, usually in the defense of the tradition against its foes.[18] Sikhism's bloody history, however, is something of a paradox. Guru Nanak, the sixteenth-century spiritual master regarded as the Sikhs' founder, is portrayed in literature as a gentle soul, one of India's great medieval saints.[19] Yet his successors came to be engaged in military confrontation with invading Mughal forces. Members of a tribal group, the Jats, began joining the Sikh community at the end of the sixteenth century. They were great warriors and imposed their martial values and symbols onto the whole of the Sikh community.[20] Some observers of Sikhism have contended that the most militant and aggressive aspects of the tradition—including the uprising in the last decades of the twentieth century—are legacies of the Jat influence.

At the end of the seventeenth century the tenth and final teacher in
the lineage of Sikh masters, Guru Gobind Singh, presided over an army
of considerable size. Martyrdom was the supreme honor bestowed on
those who gave their lives to the cause. The symbols Guru Gobind
Singh is said to have brought to his followers in 1699, and which are
still observed by the faithful, include such emblems of militancy as a
sword and a bracelet-like shield worn on the wrist. The most frequently
displayed symbol of Sikhism today is a double-edged blade surrounded
by a circle—or perhaps a cooking vessel—and a pair of curved swords.
Warfare, therefore, is not only a part of Sikhism's history but a central
feature of its iconography.[21]

In the eighteenth century the army of Sikhs in fact consisted of several armies, each with its own sphere of influence. Early in the nineteenth century the lands and armies of the Sikhs were consolidated by
Maharaja Ranjit Singh, whose kingdom spanned most of the Punjab. It
was the last independent region in India to fall to the British, conquered
only after a hard-fought war later in the century. The British colonial
period saw a decline of the Sikh community until a reform movement
in 1873 began to revive the tradition and imposed standards of faith
and practice. This movement, the Singh Sabha, was disturbed over the
display of what it regarded as Hindu artifacts in the Golden Temple and
other Sikh shrines and gurdwaras (houses of worship—literally, "the
threshold to the Guru").

In 1920 groups of Sikhs began agitating for reforms in gurdwara
management, calling for an ouster of those who had been in control of
the shrines, including the Udasis (a sect that traced its origins to the son
of Guru Nanak, revered Hindu gods and texts, and venerated Guru
Nanak to the exclusion of the other nine founding gurus of Sikhism).
The British government capitulated to these demands in 1925 and established a board of control, the Shiromani Gurdwara Prabandhak
Committee (Central Gurdwara Management Committee), consisting
largely of elected representatives. The SGPC became an arena for Sikh
politics. One group of partisans in the gurdwara reform movement, the
Akali Dal ("the band of the Immortal One"), later became a political
party, and after independence it successfully contested elections for legislative seats, sharing with the Congress Party the ability to form ruling
governments in the state. Sikh politicians supported India's fight for
freedom from the British, though some were suspicious of what they regarded as Hindu control of the independence movement.[22] The success
of Mohammad Ali Jinnah in creating a Muslim state in Pakistan raised

in the minds of many Sikhs the conviction that there should be a Sikh state as well.

India's independence in 1948 brought a certain amount of disillusionment to many Sikhs who had supported the struggle against the British. They felt peripheral to the mainstream of national politics. They did not even have control of their area of India, since the Sikhs constituted less than half of the electorate in the state of Punjab. In the 1950s a political movement emerged demanding that the Indian government fulfill its promise to have Punjab's boundaries drawn on linguistic lines, as in other Indian states. They wanted the Punjab to include only speakers of the Punjabi language, a demand that was tantamount to calling for a Sikh majority state. The charismatic leader of the time, Sant Fateh Singh, went on a well-publicized fast and threatened to immolate himself in the precincts of the Golden Temple. The Indian government, captained by Prime Minister Indira Gandhi, conceded, and in 1966 the old Punjab was carved along linguistic lines, and a new, smaller Punjab was created, which happened to have a narrow Sikh majority.

These early campaigns for Sikh autonomy and political power anticipated the movement that erupted in the 1980s. But in many ways the new movement was more intense, more religious.[23] The movement began during a clash in 1978 between a group of Sikhs and the Sant Nirankaris, a branch of the Nirankari movement that had splintered from the Sikh tradition. The Sant Nirankaris followed its own lineage of gurus. The leader of the Sikhs attacking the Nirankaris was Jarnail Singh, a young rural preacher who at an early age had joined the Damdami Taksal, a religious school and retreat center associated with the great Sikh martyr Baba Deep Singh. Jarnail Singh eventually became its head and assumed the name of the previous leader, who had come from a village named Bhindran and was therefore called "Bhindranwale" (a person from Bhindran). Jarnail Singh Bhindranwale began to monitor religious standards in the surrounding Sikh society and found the Sant Nirankaris' worship of a living guru to be presumptuous and offensive. In the escalating violence between the two groups, lives were lost on both sides. In 1980 the Nirankari guru was assassinated. Some suspected Bhindranwale of being implicated in the crime, but he was not charged or convicted.

Soon Bhindranwale became busy with a new organization, the Dal Khalsa ("the group of the pure"), which was supported by the prime minister's younger son, Sanjay Gandhi, and other Congress Party leaders,

including the president of India, Zail Singh.[24] The group intended to
replace the Akali Dal as the leading party in the SGPC, but it never
succeeded. The next year, the publisher of a chain of Hindu newspapers in Punjab who had been a critic of Bhindranwale was shot dead;
again, Bhindranwale was implicated but never tried or convicted. In
response to his arrest and the destruction of his personal papers,
Bhindranwale turned against the government. Bands of young Sikhs
began indiscriminately killing Hindus, and later in 1981 a group of
Sikhs hijacked an Indian Airlines plane in Pakistan. The serious violence had begun.

The situation came to a head on June 5, 1984, when Mrs. Gandhi
sent troops into the Golden Temple in what was code-named Operation
Bluestar. In a messy military operation that took two days to complete,
two thousand or more people were killed, including a number of innocent worshippers. Bhindranwale's forces put up a spirited defense, but
eventually they were all killed, including Bhindranwale. What shocked
the Sikh community was not only the leader's death but also the dese-
cration of their most sacred shrine. Even moderate Sikhs throughout
the world were horrified at the specter of the Indian army stomping
through their holiest precincts with boots on, shooting holes in the
buildings' elaborate marblework facades. The assassination of Mrs.
Gandhi on October 31, 1984, was widely regarded as revenge for this
act of profanity. On the following day more than two thousand Sikhs
were massacred in Delhi and elsewhere by angry mobs—a reprisal orchestrated, some say, by the police themselves.[25]

The sermons of Bhindranwale offer clues to his religious sensibilities
and their political implications. In a rambling, folksy manner, he called
on his followers to maintain their faith in a time of trial, and he echoed
the common fear that Sikhs would lose their identity in a flood of
resurgent Hinduism, or worse, in a sea of secularism. One of his more
familiar themes was the survival of the Sikh community; for "community" he used the term *qaum*, which carries overtones of nationhood.[26]
As for the idea of Khalistan, a separate Sikh nation, Bhindranwale said
he "neither favored it nor opposed it."[27] What Bhindranwale did support was the Sikh concept of *miri-piri*, the notion that spiritual and
temporal power are linked.[28] He projected the image of a great war between good and evil waged in the present day—"a struggle . . . for our
faith, for the Sikh nation, for the oppressed."[29] He implored his young
followers to rise up and marshal the forces of righteousness. "The Guru
will give you strength," he assured them.[30]

Violence was not the explicit theme of Bhindranwale's messages, but he did not shirk from what he felt the implications of *miri-piri* might be in an unjust world.[31] He affirmed that the Sikh tradition, like most religious traditions, ordinarily applauds nonviolence and proscribes the taking of human life.[32] He acknowledged that "for a Sikh it is a great sin to keep weapons and kill anyone." But Bhindranwale went on to justify the occasional violent act in extraordinary circumstances and said that "it is an even greater sin to have weapons and not to seek justice."[33] In an extreme moment, he praised his young lieutenants for hijacking an airplane and called for either full concessions to his demands from India's political leaders, "or their heads."[34]

One of the surviving leaders of the movement concurred that violence was sanctioned in Sikhism, but ordinarily as a defensive act. The leader, Sohan Singh, whose name is associated with one of the main coordinating bodies of the militant Sikh movement—the Sohan Singh Panthic Committee—was in his eighties when I interviewed him in the suburb of Mohalli near Chandigarh.[35] Sohan Singh spoke eloquently about the the role of love in Sikhism, saying that the tradition emphasizes love and allows for conversion only through moral suasion. But, Sohan Singh said, if others try to kill you, you are warranted in trying to kill them. He argued that the violence of the Sikhs in recent years was primarily a response to the violence of the state. Sohan Singh claimed that the killings undertaken by militants were always done for a purpose; they were "not killing for killing's sake."[36] Moreover, Sohan Singh said that warnings were given and punishment was meted out only if the offenders persisted in the conduct that the militants regarded as offensive.

One might wonder why the militants felt they had the moral authority to make judgments about others and to carry out corporal punishment on their own. In a remarkable series of interviews with Sikh militants transcribed and analyzed by Cynthia Keppley Mahmood in her book *Fighting for Faith and Nation*, the militants seem unconcerned about the issue of their moral authority.[37] According to Sikh tradition, a council of five leaders is sufficient to give the community guidance; there is no hierarchy of priests or codified authority within Sikhism. In 1986, shortly after Bhindranwale was killed, the militants created their own Panthic Committee (an authoritative committee led by five elders). One of the members of this first committee, Bhai Dhanna Singh, told Mahmood that the task of the group was to speak for Sikhs. He said the term *Sikh* meant anyone "who listens to the

Guru's command." The Guru's command, Dhanna Singh said, was "to speak against injustice." He added that "anyone who complies with an oppressive regime is never a Sikh."[38]

Thus the militants assumed a divinely ordained authority to right injustice and secure public order. Sohan Singh assumed that he and his colleagues had the moral jurisdiction to make life-and-death decisions about their constituency, especially when they thought that the government was morally bankrupt. What needed to be shown, he said, was that he and his colleagues were able to conduct their public role as upholders of political righteousness in a responsible manner. As an indication of what Sohan Singh considered to be the militants' good manners, he cited the apology they had extended to the families of those who were inadvertently killed in the explosion that took the life of Punjab's chief minister, Beant Singh, whom Sohan Singh described as "a killer" who was killed in the "heat of battle." This apology showed the "moral courage" of the militants, Sohan Singh said.[39]

Though Sohan Singh showed little reservation about the way that the militants used their force, Simranjit Singh Mann was more reflective. Although he had no moral qualms about Sikhs destroying those considered to be enemies of the faith, he felt that there were strategic choices to be made. Mann made a distinction between "random killing" and "targeted killing." The former, he said, simply scared the general population and made it vulnerable to the potential for even more terror from the state in reprisal. Targeted killing, on the other hand, could broaden the base of support for the movement by inviting sympathy and eliminating ruthless persons. The assassination of Chief Minister Beant Singh was an effective example of targeted killing, Simranjit Singh Mann said, since he was a symbol of the state's tyranny. Punjab's former police chief, K. P. S. Gill, was a similar symbol. If he were to be killed, it would also be a symbolic act. It would indicate the collective judgment of the Sikhs and the continuing power of the movement.

Another former leader of the militant movement, Major General Narinder Singh, agreed that Chief Minister Beant Singh "had to be killed," and that K. P. S. Gill would be targeted soon—"tomorrow," as he put it.[40] Narinder Singh could justify such an act, for he accepted violence for purposes of defense and punishment. He thought that the militant movement provided stability in a time of anarchy and official corruption. Yet he also felt that the militant movement had gone far beyond these purposes in the quixotic quest for power through armed struggle.

In explaining the years of terror visited on the Punjab, Narinder Singh concluded that sometimes "the boys"—as the Sikh militants were commonly described in the Punjab—"were hot-headed."[41] It was this passion that was their eventual undoing. "Eventually the people became sick of all the killings," he explained in accounting for why the movement came to an end. Someday, he added, the movement will rise again. But not now, he said. "All the boys are dead."

CHAPTER 6

Armageddon in a Tokyo Subway

Perhaps the religious tradition in which one least expects to find violence is Buddhism, and the location for which a violent act of religious terrorism is least anticipated is modern urban Japan. Yet it was an offshoot of Japanese Buddhism, Aum Shinrikyo, that was catapulted into the world's attention on March 20, 1995, when its members released vials of poisonous sarin gas in the Tokyo subway, killing a number of commuters and injuring thousands more.

It was 7:45 A.M., during the Monday morning rush hour, when five male members of the movement, scientists in Aum's elite Ministry of Science and Technology, boarded trains at different ends of Tokyo's sprawling subway system. Their trains were expected to converge almost exactly a half hour later at a single central stop: the Kasumigaseki station in the heart of the city's governmental district, blocks from the parliament building, government agencies, and the Imperial Palace.

Taking his place in a train on the Hibiya line was a young graduate student in physics at Tokyo University. At the other end of the same line was another physics graduate. Joining a Chiyoda line train was a former cardiovascular surgeon who had studied in the United States and graduated from Keio University in Japan. On one end of the Marunouchi line was a former physics student from Waseda University, and at the other end of the same line was an electronics engineer.[1] What all of these intense and dedicated young men had in common, aside from their skilled scientific training, was a deep devotion to Master Shoko Asahara. On this occasion they also shared more peculiar assets: each carried an umbrella with a sharpened tip and held in his arms a loosely wrapped newspaper. Inside the papers were plastic sacks of liquid chemicals.

As the trains began to converge on the Kasumigaseki station in central Tokyo, each of the men put his newspaper on the floor of the train and punched the plastic sack with the sharpened end of the rolled-up umbrella. The men quickly exited the trains at intermediate stops, and the trains rolled on without them. But they left behind the leaking plastic bags and an evil odor that began to permeate the subway cars. Sarin gas in its pure form is odorless, but the batch that was mixed by Aum's scientists had impurities that made it smell. According to some witnesses the odor was like mustard; others compared it with the smell of burning rubber.[2]

Within minutes, commuters on the trains were coughing, choking, and clutching themselves in fits of nausea. As the trains stopped, passengers stumbled out, vomiting and writhing on the train platform in spasms. Still, the car doors closed and the trains moved on to Kasumigaseki. Passengers inside collapsed on the floors, twisting in agony, convulsing, foaming at the mouth, unable to breathe. Even those who managed to clamber outside and escape death were sick and blinded for days. Doctors and nurses who treated the contaminated commuters themselves developed sore throats and eye irritations. Eventually twelve died, lying in subway stations or perishing in hospitals soon after, and over 5,500 people were affected, many with permanent injuries.

The public response to the event was one of shock and disbelief that innocent people could be assaulted in such a calculated and vicious manner in what most Japanese regard as the most mundane and reliable aspect of public life: the subway transportation system. The public attitude turned to anger when police investigations made clear that the perpetrators of the act were leaders of one of Japan's ubiquitous new religious movements. The unfolding investigation was followed closely by the Japanese public in a barrage of news reports. A year after the incident the leader of the movement, Shoko Asahara, and his inner circle were arrested for planning and conducting the assault. They were held in prison as their trial extended for many years.

The Tokyo nerve gas attack was one of Japan's most discussed events of the late twentieth century. Many Japanese saw in it the dark side of a modern urban society, the result of desperate searching for social identity and spiritual fulfillment. Scholars of social violence have found the case intriguing because it signaled a new kind of terrorism: one that created a colossal event for the sake of a catastrophic vision of world history and employed for the first time weapons of mass destruction. For my efforts to understand the cultures of violence that give rise to religious terrorism, it raised the question that anyone might ask on hearing about such a horrific action: why would religion, much less Buddhism, lead to such a thing?

When I went to Tokyo to find answers, I was interested in exploring the cultural context of the event as well as understanding the mindset of members of the Aum Shinrikyo movement. Despite the extraordinary public interest in the case and the nearly unanimous condemnation of the movement within Japanese society, Aum officials agreed to meet with me in their Tokyo headquarters days before it was closed down by the Japanese government. The headquarters were housed in a small office building on the corner of a major intersection in the Aoyama section of the city. When I entered I had to pass through a phalanx of television cameras, reporters, and police barricades.

During this time, less than a year after the nerve gas incident, the spiritual leader of the movement, Shoko Asahara, and the movement's spokesman, Fumihiro Joyu, were under arrest. The officers with whom I met, the general secretary and the head of public affairs of the Tokyo office, were primarily concerned with keeping the movement alive.[3] The Japanese government's attempts to outlaw Aum Shinrikyo, disband it entirely, and revise the government's liberal Religious Corporation Law worried not only these Aum Shinrikyo leaders but also many other concerned Japanese. They feared a government crackdown on religious freedom and the persecution of Japan's many new religious movements.[4]

The Aum Shinrikyo leaders were also concerned over the treatment of their jailed spiritual master. The public affairs officer, Yasuo Hiramatsu, told me that Master Asahara denied his alleged role in the attack, and he assured me that "all our members still trust our Master." Yet, Hiramatsu confessed, he had his doubts. When I asked him directly if he thought that Asahara was guilty of having planned the gas attack, Hiramatsu said, "I don't know." What if he were found to be guilty beyond a reasonable doubt, I asked. "That," Hiramatsu responded in what was something of an understatement, "would be very difficult to explain." Yet "even if he did do it," the public affairs officer professed, this would not shake his faith or cause him to abandon his belief in Master Asahara and the Aum Shinrikyo movement. If the master was involved, Hiramatsu told me, he must have had "a religious reason."[5] This view was shared by other members with whom I spoke, including volunteer clerks in the Aum Shinrikyo bookstore, which was located up several flights of stairs in a high-rise office building in the Shibuya area of Tokyo. When I spoke with the Aum volunteers, their bookstore, the last in what had been a flourishing chain throughout Japan, was due to close in a matter of days.[6]

It was a convulsive moment in the history of the movement, not only because it had come under public attack, but also because the world view that the members had so obediently and comfortably accepted was shattered. The best account I received of how the members viewed the world before and after the nerve gas event came from a young man who had been a member of the staff in the Tokyo office. This former Aum Shinrikyo member, whom I will call "Takeshi Nakamura," left the movement in the turbulent days after the attack. When I talked with him at Tokyo's International House in January 1996, less than a year later, he still had a great deal of respect for the movement's teachings and an appreciation of its role in giving him a sense of hope and confidence about life.

Takeshi Nakamura and the Aum Shinrikyo Assault

Takeshi Nakamura was a thin, nervous young man who had joined Aum Shinrikyo in January 1995, just two months before the incident that tore the movement apart.[7] The time immediately before his joining the movement, he told me, had been a difficult one in his career and his personal life. What impressed him when he joined was the movement's critique of traditional Japanese religion. Most forms of Buddhism, he said, were for scholars or existed solely to facilitate funerary rites. The form of religion that Aum offered was what Nakamura was searching for: something personally transformative and socially prophetic.

Nakamura had previously been interested in religion—especially Zen Buddhism—and in social reform. He regarded the Japanese social system as hierarchical and powerful, one that did not adequately exemplify the principles of justice, fairness, and freedom. It was also, Nakamura felt, a society that could not easily change. What the Aum Shinrikyo movement offered was not only a mystical personal experience but also an egalitarian community and a vision of a transformed social order that greatly appealed to Nakamura's social concerns.

Despite these attractions it took some profound signs to indicate to Nakamura that Aum was the proper path for him to follow. Soon after his encounter with Aum teachings, Nakamura had a dramatic experience: he felt that his soul was traveling outside of his body. Then all of Japan vicariously experienced the earthquake that leveled the city of Kobe in January 1995. Nakamura took both of these events as spiritual signs that the world was awry and that great changes were under way. On January 23, he mailed the postcard expressing his interest in Aum Shinrikyo and soon thereafter became a member of the movement.

Joining the movement was relatively inexpensive. He was charged ten thousand yen (approximately one hundred dollars) at the outset and was required to pay dues of a thousand yen (ten dollars) per month. All of the publications, videotapes, and other accouterments of the faith were available on a cash basis. During the initial stages of his membership, Nakamura was required to study books on Aum Shinrikyo, including the teachings of Shoko Asahara. He was also told to listen to audiotapes and watch videos of his teachings, and to practice meditation techniques while sitting in the lotus position. He was to live an austere existence, eschewing sporting events, avoiding movies and television, and refraining from sex. He and other members were to avoid reading or listening to reports from the news media because of "the impurity of the data that one receives about the world." To his delight, Nakamura soon began having mystical experiences while practicing meditation and reciting the five principles of Aum. He saw bright lights coming toward him, heard a bell in the darkness, and felt his consciousness rising. The latter Nakamura described as the awakening of his *kundalini*, the term for one's personal energy center that is employed in Hindu meditation practices.[8]

Nakamura was ready to be initiated into the movement. The four-day initiation began on March 5. Nakamura and three other candidates were brought into a small room, where they removed all of their clothing. They then put on diapers as if they were infants and donned pullover robes. They could eat, sleep, and go to the bathroom only when permitted. They were required to sign a note saying they would not reveal the secrets of the initiation and would not complain. They were left in silence for what seemed a very long time and then asked to complete the following sentence: "I am . . . ." After answering this question, they were asked to speculate on what happens after death.

They were assured, however, that whatever their fates, Master Asahara would be with them on that final journey.

The high point of the initiation was the appearance of Master Asahara himself. It was Asahara's charisma that had attracted Nakamura to the movement, so he regarded this as an especially dramatic moment. It was as if Christ himself had appeared. Asahara seemed so profound in his knowledge of religion, so certain in his predictions, so clear in explaining the forces that caused the world to be fractious and confused.

Part of Asahara's mystique came from his blindness. He was afflicted with infantile glaucoma shortly after he was born in 1955 in a small village in Japan's southern island of Kyushu. The disease left him completely blind in one eye; in the other he had only limited sight. When it came time for him to go to school, he was sent with his brother, who was totally blind, to a special institution. There he is said to have gained a great deal of power over the other students, all of whom were sightless, by his limited vision.[9] They gave him money and status to use his abilities to describe the world around them or guide them through the local town. One of the housemothers in the school described him as "bossy and violent."[10]

Asahara came to Tokyo for his higher education. After failing two college entrance examinations, including one that would have allowed him to attend the prestigious Tokyo University, he undertook spiritual lessons on his own. He joined a new religious movement, Agonshu, which was led by a strong, charismatic figure able to prophecy future events. The movement's teachings borrowed liberally from a variety of Buddhist traditions, and even reached out to Taoist ideas from China and yoga practices from India. It was from Agonshu that Asahara learned about the Hindu idea of the *kundalini,* a kind of inner consciousness that had to be elevated within the self through yogic practices. By 1984 Asahara had become disenchanted with Agonshu and left, taking the ideas of the movement and a dozen of its members with him to establish his own group. After a trip to the Himalayas in 1986, where he claimed to have received mystic visions from Hindu masters, he returned to Japan. He changed his name to Shoko Asahara from the one given him at birth—Chizuo Matsumoto—and in 1987 he named his new group Aum Shinrikyo. *Aum* is a variant spelling of the Hindu mantra, *om,* followed by *shinri,* the Japanese term for "supreme truth," and *kyo,* for "religious teaching." His followers regarded this supreme truth as virtually anything that Asahara uttered.

The appearance of the master during the initiation ceremony, therefore, was more than the high point of the event; it *was* the event, as far
as Nakamura was concerned. His master entered the room accompanied by a retinue of twenty assistants and was seated on a cushion.
Nakamura said that Asahara appeared to be practically blind, though
he thought he might have been able to see slightly through one eye. His
attitude was serious, even angry, and Nakamura felt he was judging
each of them personally. He took a sip from a glass and ritually passed
it around the circle of initiates. Nakamura drank from it as instructed.
Then Asahara gave a little homily. He told them that he was devoted to
both Shiva and the Buddha, and that he expected total devotion from
his initiates.

After Master Asahara spoke, the initiates were led away from him
to another room, where they were seated on a vibrating mat. They felt
the vibration move up their spines as they chanted a mantra and recited the five principles Asahara had taught them. Whatever had been
in his drink began to take effect; Nakamura later speculated that it
might have been laced with LSD. He began to hallucinate, and
Nakamura and the other candidates had mystical experiences. The initiates were asked to report what they saw and felt; they were cautioned that if they saw a dreadful god, all they had to do was to think
of Master Asahara and it would vanish. Then actors came into the
room, disguised as what Nakamura described as "terrible" and
"peaceful" gods. They told the initiates that they were in hell and challenged them to think about what they might have done to warrant
such a predicament. Nakamura confessed to being frightened by the
experience, but a woman who was a seasoned member of the movement was at his side, assuring him that if he continued to trust in
Asahara he would survive. After tearful confessions and proclamations
of forgiveness were given and the effects of drink had diminished, the
initiation was completed. They watched videos of the master's teachings, undertook meditation practices, and were administered intra-
venous fluids to end their fast.

After initiation, Nakamura was not allowed to return to his home.
He was sent instead to an Aum monastery, where he devoted himself to
meditation. He was then sent back to the Tokyo office, where he
worked with the staff. Only a few days after he had taken his position
at the office in Tokyo's Aoyama district, he discovered the movement
and his office to be at the center of public attention. It was March 20,
1995, and the city had suffered a spectacular nerve gas attack.

When Nakamura first heard the news of the incident, he knew exactly what it meant. He thought that "the weird time had come." [11] When I asked what that meant, Nakamura whispered, "Armageddon."

At the core of Asahara's prophecies was a great cloud casting its shadow over the future: the specter of a world catastrophe unparalleled in human history. Although World War II had been disastrous to Japanese society, this destructive conflagration—including the nuclear holocausts at Hiroshima and Nagasaki—was nothing compared with the coming World War III. The term that Asahara chose for this cataclysmic event, Armageddon, is an interesting one. It comes from the New Testament book of Revelation in the Christian Bible and refers to the place where the final conflict between good and evil will occur.[12] In the biblical account of this conflict, an earthquake splits a great city into parts, and in the calamity that follows all nations perish.

Asahara took the prophecies of Revelation and mixed them with visions from the Old Testament and sayings of the sixteenth-century French astrologer Nostradamus (Michel de Nostredame). It was from Nostradamus that Asahara acquired the notion that Freemasons have been secretly plotting to control the world. To these fears Asahara added the same sort of obsession that Christian Identity thinkers possess regarding Jews as a source of international conspiracy. The CIA was also thought to be involved. Asahara also incorporated Hindu and Buddhist notions of the fragility of life into his prognosis for the world, and claimed that his dire prophecies would be fulfilled in part because humans needed to be taught a lesson about mortality. "Armageddon," Asahara said, must occur because "the inhabitants of the present human realm do not recognize that they are fated to die."[13]

When Armageddon came, Asahara said, the evil forces would attack with the most vicious weapons: "Radioactivity and other bad circumstances—poison gas, epidemics, food shortages—will occur," the Master predicted.[14] The only people who would survive were those "with great karma" and those who had the defensive protection of the Aum Shinrikyo organization. "They will survive," Asahara said, "and create a new and transcendent human world."[15]

Asahara's prophecies gave Nakamura a sense of clarity about the world around him and hope for the future. He longed to be one of those survivors who would help to build a better world. Like many Japanese of his generation, he felt that the world had been moving too fast and was becoming too intense for comfort. Before he joined the movement, his own life had seemed empty and unsuccessful. It was reasonable to assume that someone must be profiting from his discomfort. When Asahara talked about an international cadre that was conspiring to enslave the world, the specter frightened him. But, he told me, intuitively Asahara's views made sense.

These prophetic statements of Master Asahara came ringing back to Nakamura when he heard the news of the incident on March 20. Nakamura told me that it felt like the moment in a play when one is suddenly called from the quiet of the wings onto the boisterous stage. Since Asahara had told them that Armageddon was expected in 1997, Nakamura and his colleagues thought that the subway incident was the harbinger of that awful cataclysm, and he fully expected a sequence of horrific events to follow within days or months. The drama, Nakamura said, had begun.

One of the things that immediately convinced Nakamura that the nerve gas attack was the forerunner of the dreaded Armageddon was the location in which it occurred: not just the subway system, but on trains converging at the Kasumigaseki station in downtown Tokyo. Since the deep underground station was located in the heart of Tokyo's government area, many journalists at the time jumped to the conclusion that the site had been chosen as an attack on the Japanese government. But inside the Aum Shinrikyo movement's headquarters in Tokyo, the members—those who were not informed that their own leaders had been implicated in the plot—offered somewhat different scenarios. Takeshi Nakamura and his colleagues thought that the assault might indeed have been an attack on the Japanese government, albeit a deceptive one. They suggested that the government officials had attacked themselves to deflect the public's attention from what the Aum members thought had really occurred: World War III had begun, and the Japanese government had been secretly captured by America. The use of nerve gas seemed to confirm this theory, since the Aum members had been told by their leaders that only the American army in Japan possessed such a weapon.[16]

A book of Asahara's prophecies published by the movement a few months before the subway attack indicated another reason the Kasumigaseki station was significant. Among the predictions of the great conflagration at the end of the twentieth century was one that nerve gas—sarin was mentioned by name—would be used against the populace. Asahara urged the public to join movements such as Aum that were preparing themselves against such an attack, since the Japanese government could not sufficiently protect them; it had prepared "a poor defense for the coming war," Asahara said.[17] He went on to say that the government had constructed only one subway station of sufficient depth and security to be used as a haven in time of nuclear or poisonous gas attack. "Only the Kasumigaseki subway station, which is near the Diet Building, can be used as a shelter," and even it was vulnerable.[18]

Nakamura felt secure since the Aum organization had developed means of protecting its members against weapons of mass destruction. He thought it significant that no members of Aum Shinrikyo had been injured in the subway gas incident. Nakamura concurred with another member of the movement when he said that this event proved that Asahara was watching over the safety of his followers. "Master predicted the gas attack," the grateful member said, adding that through this warning, "he saved us."[19] Initially Nakamura and other members of the movement did not hear the news reports about their own leaders' involvement in the incident because the movement denied them access to outside media. Later, when they began to hear rumors about the reports, Nakamura said, they did not believe them. They assumed that they were efforts to discredit the movement.

A little over a month later, Nakamura was transferred to an office some distance from Tokyo, where he became embroiled in a dispute with the local director. Nakamura wanted to help beautify the place but was told that he was not yet religious enough to help with such matters. Nakamura felt that he was not respected by the director, and the next day he decided to leave. His decision to depart Aum Shinrikyo, therefore, had nothing to do with the nerve gas incident; it was a matter of pride. He had joined the movement because he lacked a sense of worth, and it had given him a feeling of self-confidence. He was not going to sacrifice that to play what he regarded as a humiliating role, he said. So he left.

In the six months between his departure from Aum and my interview with him in Tokyo's International House—only a few subway stops away from the Kasumigaseki station—he had helped to counsel some of the estimated one thousand members who left the movement because of its negative publicity. Fearing reprisals, however, he kept his address secret. Still feeling the need for spiritual succor and personal support, he turned to Christianity. A pastor comforted him, and he began to attend church in Tokyo.

When I asked Nakamura what he now thought about Aum's teachings, he said that he never believed all aspects of the elaborate global conspiracy theory—especially the involvement of Freemasons, which he had found to be far-fetched. He still suspected, however, that Armageddon was possible. But if it did come, Nakamura told me, there was nothing we could do about it. For that reason it was best to concentrate on the present. "Why speculate on world history?" he asked me.[20]

Nakamura now believed that Asahara was indeed responsible for the Tokyo nerve gas attack. In response to my questions about Asahara's motives, Nakamura gave three reasons for his former master's role. In the first place, he said, Asahara wanted to control Japan and "be like a king." Engineering the nerve gas attack gave him a sense of power. Since Asahara had already allegedly masterminded the murders of several of the movement's former members and critics, and nothing had happened to him, he believed he could literally get away with murder. "He felt he could do anything," Nakamura said. Second, Asahara and his colleagues felt trapped by police investigations and wanted to go out "with a bang." Finally, Nakamura said, Asahara "wanted to be seen as a savior" by creating an act that appeared to fulfill his own prophecies. He "wanted to be like Christ."[21]

Can Buddhist Violence Be Justified?

Neither Christ, Buddha, nor any of Asahara's other spiritual heroes were murderers. What needed to be explained was how a community of intense spiritual devotion could be involved in such a savage act of violence. The personal megalomania of Shoko Asahara could help us understand his own actions, but it did not explain why so many intelligent and sensitive followers, including Takeshi Nakamura, assented to them. Nor did it reveal what Asahara's "religious reason" for the attack, as Hiramatsu put it, might have been.[22]

One might expect that the doctrine of *ahimsa*—nonviolence— would make any Buddhist organization, even one as eclectic in its teachings as Aum Shinrikyo, immune from religious justification for acts of terror. Yet the history and teachings of Buddhism are not spotless. The great military conquests of the Sinhalese kingdoms in Sri Lanka, for instance, have been conducted in the name of the Buddhist tradition and often with the blessings of Buddhist monks. In Thailand the tradition called for those who rule by the sword as kings to first experience the discipline of Buddhist monastic training. They had to be "world renouncers" before they could be "world conquerors," as Stanley Tambiah put it.[23]

Some traditional Buddhist teachings have tried to identify exactly when the rule of nonviolence can be broken, accepting the notion that circumstances may allow some people to be absolved from the accusation that they killed or attempted to do so. The teachings require that five conditions be satisfied in order to certify that an act of violence indeed took place: something living must have been killed; the killer must have known that it was alive; the killer must have intended to kill it; an actual act of killing must have taken place; and the person or animal attacked must, in fact, have died.[24] It is the absence of the third condition—the intention to kill—that typically allows for some mitigation of the rule of nonviolence. Many Buddhists will eat meat, for instance, as long as they have not themselves intended that the animal be killed or been involved in the act of slaughtering it. Using violence nondefensively for the purpose of political expansion is prohibited under Buddhist rules. But armed defense—even warfare—has been justified on the grounds that such violence has been in the nature of response, not intent. Like Islam, the great expansion of Buddhism in various parts of the world has been credited in part to the support given it by victorious kings and military forces who have claimed to be fighting only to defend the faith against infidels and to establish a peaceful moral order.

In Sri Lanka, where great battles in the name of Buddhism are part of Sinhalese history, acts of violence perpetrated by Sinhalese activists in the latter decades of the twentieth century have been supported by Buddhist monks. I was told by a monk who had participated in violent antigovernment protests that there was no way to avoid violence "in a time of dukkha"—the age of suffering that Buddhists regard as characteristic of recorded human history.[25] In such a time, he said, violence naturally begets violence. Politicians who were ruthless and were seen as enemies of religion could reasonably expect bloodshed as a sort of karmic revenge for their actions. During such times in Sinhalese history, he claimed, evil rulers were overthrown. "We believe in the law of karma," he added, "and those who live by the sword die by the sword."[26] The killing of Sri Lanka's prime minister, S.W.R.D. Bandaranaike, by a Buddhist monk in 1959 is evidence that Buddhists, like their counterparts in other religious traditions, have been able to justify violence on moral—or, rather, supramoral—grounds.

Precedent has thus been established for the justification of acts of killing within the Buddhist tradition, though rarely in the forms of Buddhism found in Japan. Perhaps for that reason Shoko Asahara reached out to other Buddhism traditions for interpretations of the law of karma, the rule of moral retribution, that would allow acts of destruction to be undertaken in religion's name.

In Tibetan Buddhism, Asahara claimed to have found such an exemption. Rather than concentrating on the adverse effect that killing has on the killer's moral purity, this teaching focuses on the one who is killed and the merit that comes after death. The concept of *phoa*—that consciousness can be transferred from the living to the dead to elevate their spiritual merit—was extended by Asahara to imply that in some cases people are better off dead than alive.[27] According to Asahara's interpretation of this Tibetan principle, if the persons killed are scoundrels, or are enmeshed in social systems so evil that further existence in this life will result in even greater negative karmic debt, then those who kill are doing their victims a favor by enabling them to die early. Their early deaths would be a kind of mercy killing, allowing their souls to move to a higher plane than they would otherwise have been able to achieve.

Aum members told some scholars investigating the movement that they saw Asahara's teachings on this Tibetan principle in a textbook that was made available only to advanced members.[28] Ian Reader, a Scottish scholar of Japan's new religions, has seen the text, which he described as a 360-page photocopied manuscript written in Japanese. Reader said that it contained numerous references to the moral acceptance of mercy killing and that it supported the "right of the guru and of spiritually advanced practitioners to kill those who otherwise would fall into the hells."[29] Scholars of Tibetan Buddhism with whom I have consulted doubt, however, that such a teaching is written in any authentic Tibetan text. It appears to be Asahara's own concoction. To his followers, however, it had the ring of truth.

They also accepted another notion that Asahara planted in their minds: the Hindu concept of planes of consciousness. Nakamura told me that the master had the ability to travel from one plane to the other in a fraction of human time. This ability explained in part why Asahara did things that might seem unusual from a human point of view. According to Hiromi Shimada, who at one time publicly defended Asahara and lost his position as a professor of religion at a women's college as a result, Asahara taught his followers that he lived in a non-material world.[30] He had appropriated Hindu concepts of planes of existence. At the lowest level is the worldly plane, in which ordinary historical activity occurs. Beyond that is the causal plane, which is the source of all meaning in the material world; and even further beyond is the astral plane, which has no shred of the material world whatsoever. Asahara was thought by his followers to be capable of existing in the astral plane, but for the sake of his worldly admirers he hovered in the causal and material planes, allowing those who believed in him to elevate their own souls.

Because he lived on a higher plane, however, he could see things that ordinary people could not see, and his actions were consistent with causal plane reality, not our own. For this reason anything Master Asahara might do that seemed to ordinary mortals as odd—even involvement in conspiracies to kill other people—could be explained as having its impetus and hence its justification in a higher plane of reality. The killers and their victims were simply actors in a divine scenario. When Asahara was put in jail, Nakamura told me, the members of the movement regarded this incident like a scene in a play: Asahara was playing the role of prisoner, following a script of which they were unaware, for a purpose that only he knew.

The most dramatic scenario described by Asahara was Armageddon, and that concept also justified the taking of life. Once one is caught up in cosmic war, Asahara explained, the ordinary rules of conduct do not apply. "The world economy will have come to a dead stop," he said, somewhere around August 1, 1999.[31] "The ground will tremble violently, and immense walls of water will wash away everything on earth. . . . In addition to natural disasters," Asahara prophesied, "there will be the horror of nuclear weapons."[32] Nerve gas would also be used in that horrific war—sarin gas, specifically.[33]

In a perceptive analysis of the Aum Shinrikyo movement, Ian Reader has linked Aum's concept of cosmic war to a feeling of humiliation. According to Reader, the development of Asahara's concept of Armageddon went hand in hand with a history of rejection experienced both by Asahara and by members of his movement. This sense of rejection led to conflict with the society around them, and these encounters in turn led to greater rejection. This downward spiral of humiliation and confrontation led ultimately to a paranoid attitude of "Aum against the world."[34]

In a peculiar way, the paranoia of its leaders might have been a part of Aum's appeal. Like many of Japan's other new religious movements, its attraction was due in part to its opposition to mainstream Japanese society. Where Japanese society has been hierarchical, the new religious movements have provided a spirit of family fellowship—albeit under the powerful control of paternal and maternal figures. Where society's values have been material, the new movements have given the impression of being transcendently spiritual.

According to Susumu Shimazono, Tokyo University's most respected scholar of contemporary religion, the new religious movements in his country have recently gone through two waves of activity: one in the 1970s and early 1980s, and the other in the late 1980s and 1990s. Shimazono said that the most recent wave was characterized by movements such as the Institute for Religion and Human Happiness, Worldmate, and Aum Shinrikyo. These were movements with political agendas, including a resurgent nationalism and millenarian prophecies. Shimazono said that these traits reflect an uneasiness that Japanese people feet about the future, a nervousness about Japanese identity in a global society, and a lack of trust in their political leaders to provide moral vision and social solidarity in times of economic and social disarray.[35]

Perhaps because they reflect some of the deepest concerns that Japanese have about their society, these movements experienced enormous popularity. Not even the infamy of Aum Shinrikyo dampened the public's interest in such movements, apparently including even Aum Shinrikyo itself. In 1998 there was said to have been a resurgence in Aum membership, not only in Japan but also in Russia and other parts of the world where it had previously enjoyed a sizable following.[36] Although the Japanese government had debated over whether to use its authority to limit the freedom of religious movements and outlaw the Aum movement entirely, it backed off from such harsh measures. New religious movements in Japan, including Aum, have continued to enjoy a great deal of latitude and considerable government leniency regarding their freedom of action and range of public expression.

Perhaps for this reason Takeshi Nakamura was correct in his assessment at the close of my interview that the Aum Shinrikyo movement was far from demolished. Destroying its center, he said, would likely strengthen it, since it would allow splinter groups and renegade cadres within the movement to establish their own bases of power. The reason for its persistence, Nakamura said, was that it spoke to the needs of people to find certainty and a framework for understanding the unseen forces in the world around them. It was this quest, Nakamura said, that first brought him to Aum. Though he was now regarded "as a traitor" to the movement, Nakamura said that he missed much of what Aum offers to its believers. For him personally the quest that brought him to Shoko Asahara was not over.[37]

The Logic of
Religious Violence

CHAPTER 7

Theater of Terror

Do these stories of piety and mayhem have anything in common? This is a critical question, and considering the frequency of acts of religious terrorism around the globe, either answer is significant. If the answer is no, these cases may suggest a worldwide loosening of social control that makes inexplicable acts of violence possible. If it is yes, and if we can find convincing explanations for these patterns, we may shed some light on why violence and religion have reemerged so dramatically at this moment in history, and why they have so frequently been found in combination. The question, then, is whether there are common themes in the stories of Rev. Michael Bray, Timothy McVeigh, Rev. Ian Paisley, Yoel Lerner, Dr. Baruch Goldstein, Mahmud Abouhalima, Dr. Abdul Aziz Rantisi, Simranjit Singh Mann, Takeshi Nakamura, and many other religious activists around the world.

As we begin to look for answers, the very nature of the violence may provide our first clue. After all, these have been acts not only of destruction but also of bloodshed executed in a deliberately intense and vivid way. It is as if these acts were designed to maximize the savage nature of their violence and meant purposely to elicit anger.

The catastrophic bombings of the American embassies, the World Trade Center, the Oklahoma City federal building, and the American military residence in Saudi Arabia; the burning of abortion clinics and the shooting of a clinic doctor in the face; the assassination of Israeli and Indian political leaders; the massacre of innocent worshipers at a mosque; the slaying of a busload of Hindu pilgrims in the Himalayan foothills by a band of radical Sikh youths; the agonizing effects of the nerve gas attack in a Tokyo subway; and the bloody confusion of suicide bombings on the otherwise peaceful streets of Jerusalem and Tel Aviv—all of these are not just incidents of violence. They are acts of deliberately exaggerated violence.

Perhaps nothing in recent years has demonstrated this more than the gruesome sight that greeted Kashmiri villagers on a pathway near the mountain town of Pahalgam on August 13, 1995. There they encountered the mutilated body of Hans-Christian Ostro, a twenty-seven-year-old Norwegian man who had come to India to study dance and relied on the advice of a government tourist agent in Delhi that a trek in Kashmir would be completely safe. The Kashmiri separatists who captured Ostro and several other American, British, and German tourists threatened to murder the hostages if their demands were not met. Receiving no affirmative response, they slaughtered Ostro and displayed his carcass in a vividly provocative manner: they decapitated the young man and balanced the severed head between his thighs.

The purpose of such acts was to terrorize using "the most macabre means," a Protestant activist in Belfast explained.[1] In an interview with a British journalist, Unionist activist Kenny McClinton admitted that in his struggle against Irish Republicans he advocated beheading Catholics and impaling their heads on the railing of a park in the Protestant Shankhill area of Belfast.[2] His group, the Shankhill Butchers, were accused of more than thirty gory murders, all committed for the purpose of political intimidation: to show the power of the Protestant community and to scare Catholics into withdrawing their support for the IRA. They attacked an innocent Catholic working man, for instance, chosen at random as he walked to his post as a security guard in a border area between Catholic and Protestant communities, and slowly, viciously killed him. The Catholic was stripped naked, tied, and ritually carved as a sculptor would carve a block of wood.[3] Still alive after having received 147 wounds over his body, the hapless victim was suspended from a beam by a slowly tightening noose, where he eventually died of strangulation. His mutilated corpse was then put on display for Catholics and Protestants alike to see.

Even when terrorist actions have involved less direct methods of killing—such as car bombs and suicide attacks—many were carried out in such a manner as to be both vivid and horrifying. Targets were often chosen because they were familiar and secure—shopping malls, mar-

ketplaces, and centers of mass transit. The timing of the events often en-
sured that the maximum number of people would be gathered at the
target sites—the U.S. embassies and the Oklahoma federal building, the
World Trade Center, the Tokyo subway system, and a Tel Aviv shopping center, for example. The explosive devices used were often aimed
at wounding people rather than damaging buildings. Nails were embedded in the bombs of Hamas suicide bombers, for instance, to increase their maiming capability. The Aum Shinrikyo scientists considered adding a floral scent to the deadly sarin gas they were to unleash
to encourage more people to inhale it.[4]

In the August 1998 bombing at the town of Omagh in Northern
Ireland, authorities were warned of the bombing in advance, but they
were told that the attack was to take place in a different area from
where the bombs were in fact planted. As a result, unsuspecting citizens
were herded into an area directly adjacent to the bomb site, and a larger
number were killed and wounded than would have been if they had remained where they were. Although spokespersons for the "Real IRA,"
which took responsibility for the bombing, claimed that they had not
intended so many civilians to be killed, authorities were not so sure.
Many agreed with the assessment of the secretary of Northern Ireland,
that the Real IRA's statement was a "pathetic attempt to apologize for
and excuse mass murder."[5] They remained convinced that the object of
the false information was to kill as many of the townspeople as possible, and to do so in a deliberately horrific manner.

Many terrorist incidents have been aimed at killing massive numbers
of victims. If the sarin gas unleashed in the Tokyo subways on March
20, 1995, had been 70 to 80 percent pure, rather than diluted to only
30 percent of its full strength—solely to protect the safety of the Aum
members transporting it—thousands would have perished. An incident
a few weeks later at the Shibuya station in Tokyo would have killed
twenty thousand if the device had not malfunctioned and been discovered by alert station attendants.[6] If the explosives in the World Trade
Center had been as strong as the perpetrators expected, as I noted earlier, the entire pair of buildings would have collapsed, taking at least
two hundred thousand lives. As of July 1999, the largest number of casualties in a single terrorist incident were the 329 passengers killed in
the explosion of an Air India jumbo jet off the coast of Ireland on June
23, 1985. It is only by sheer good fortune that more people have not
lost their lives in events designed to be spectacular in their viciousness
and awesome in their destructive power.

Such instances of exaggerated violence are constructed events: they are mind-numbing, mesmerizing theater. At center stage are the acts themselves—stunning, abnormal, and outrageous murders carried out in a way that graphically displays the awful power of violence—set within grand scenarios of conflict and proclamation. Killing or maiming of any sort is violent, of course, but these acts surpass the wounds inflicted during warfare or death delivered through capital punishment, in large part because they have a secondary impact. By their demonstrative nature, they elicit feelings of revulsion and anger in those who witness them.

Performance Violence

How do we make sense of such theatrical forms of violence? One way of answering this is to view dramatic violence as part of a strategic plan. This viewpoint assumes that terrorism is always part of a political strategy—and, in fact, some social scientists have defined terrorism in just this way: "the use of covert violence by a group for political ends."[7] In some cases this definition is indeed appropriate, for an act of violence can fulfill political ends and have a direct impact on public policy.

The Israeli elections in 1996 provided a case in point. Shortly after the assassination of Yitzhak Rabin, his successor, Shimon Peres, held a 20 percent lead in the polls over his rival, Benjamin Netanyahu, but this lead vanished following a series of Hamas suicide attacks on Jerusalem buses. Netanyahu narrowly edged out Peres in the May elections. Many observers concluded that Netanyahu—no friend of Islamic radicals— had the terrorists of Hamas to thank for his victory.

When the Hamas operative who planned the 1996 attacks was later caught and imprisoned, he was asked whether he had intended to affect the outcome of the elections. "No," he responded, explaining that the internal affairs of Israelis did not matter much to him. This operative was a fairly low-level figure, however, and one might conjecture that his superiors had a more specific goal in mind. But when I put the same question to the political leader of Hamas, Dr. Abdul Aziz Rantisi, his answer was almost precisely the same: these attacks were not aimed at Israeli internal politics, since Hamas did not differentiate between Peres and Netanyahu. In the Hamas view, the two Israeli leaders were equally opposed to Islam.[8] "Maybe God wanted it," the Hamas operative said of Netanyahu's election victory. Even if the Hamas leaders were being disingenuous, the fact remains that most of their suicide bombings have served no direct political purpose.

Other examples of religious terrorism have also shown little strategic value. The release of nerve gas in the Tokyo subways and the bombing of the World Trade Center did not provide any immediate political benefits to those who caused them. Although Mahmud Abouhalima, convicted for his part in the World Trade Center bombing, told me that assaults on public buildings did have a long-range strategic value in that they helped to "identify the government as enemy," in general the "political ends" for which these acts were committed seemed distant indeed.[9]

A political scientist, Martha Crenshaw, has shown that the notion of "strategic" thinking can be construed in a broad sense to cover not just immediate political achievements but also the internal logic that propels a group into perpetrating terrorist acts. As Abouhalima said, many of those who committed them felt they were justified by the broad, long-range benefits to be gained.[10] My investigations indicate that Crenshaw is right—acts of terrorism are usually the products of an internal logic and not of random or crazy thinking—but I hesitate to use the term *strategy* for all rationales for terrorist actions. *Strategy* implies a degree of calculation and an expectation of accomplishing a clear objective that does not jibe with such dramatic displays of power as the World Trade Center bombing. These creations of terror are done not to achieve a strategic goal but to make a symbolic statement.

By calling acts of religious terrorism "symbolic," I mean that they are intended to illustrate or refer to something beyond their immediate target: a grander conquest, for instance, or a struggle more awesome than meets the eye. As Abouhalima said, the bombing of a public building may dramatically indicate to the populace that the government or the economic forces behind the building were seen as enemies, to show the world that they were targeted as satanic foes. The point of the attack, then, was to produce a graphic and easily understandable object lesson. Such explosive scenarios are not *tactics* directed toward an immediate, earthly, or strategic goal, but *dramatic events* intended to impress for their symbolic significance. As such, they can be analyzed as one would any other symbol, ritual, or sacred drama.

I can imagine a line with "strategic" on the one side and "symbolic" on the other, with various acts of terrorism located in between. The hostage taking in the Japanese embassy by the Tupac Amaru in Peru in 1997—clearly an attempt to leverage power in order to win the release of members of the movement held prisoner by the Peruvian government— might be placed closer to the political, strategic side. The Aum Shinrikyo nerve gas attack in 1995 might be closer to the symbolic, religious side.

Each was the product of logical thought, and each had an internal ratio-nale. In cases such as the Tokyo nerve gas attack that were more symbolic than strategic, however, the logic was focused not on an immediate po-litical acquisition, but at a larger, less tangible goal.

The very adjectives used to describe acts of religious terrorism—symbolic, dramatic, theatrical—suggest that we look at them not as tac-tics but as *performance violence*. In speaking of terrorism as "perfor-mance," I am not suggesting that such acts are undertaken lightly or capriciously. Rather, like religious ritual or street theater, they are dra-mas designed to have an impact on the several audiences that they af-fect. Those who witness the violence—even at a distance, via the news media—are therefore a part of what occurs. Moreover, like other forms of public ritual, the symbolic significance of such events is multifaceted; they mean different things to different observers.

This suggests that it is possible to analyze comparatively the perfor-mance of acts of religious terrorism. There is already a growing literature of studies based on the notion that civic acts and cultural performances are closely related.[11] The controversial parades undertaken each year by the Protestant Orangemen in Catholic neighborhoods of Northern Ireland, for instance, have been studied not only as cultural events but also as political statements.[12] So it is not unreasonable to view public vi-olence as performances as well.

In addition to referring to drama, the term *performance* also implies the notion of "performative"—as in the concept of "performative acts." This is an idea developed by language philosophers regarding certain kinds of speech that are able to perform social functions: their very utterance has a transformative impact.[13] Like vows recited during marriage rites, certain words not only represent reality but also shape it: they contain a certain power of their own. The same is true of some nonverbal symbolic actions, such as the gunshot that begins a race, the raising of a white flag to show defeat, or acts of terrorism.

Terrorist acts, then, can be both *performance events,* in that they make a symbolic statement, and *performative acts,* insofar as they try to change things. When Yigal Amir aimed his pistol at Israel's prime minister, Yitzhak Rabin, and when Sikh activists targeted Punjab's chief minister with a car bomb in front of the state's office buildings, the ac-tivists were aware that they were creating enormous spectacles. They probably also hoped that their actions would make a difference—if not in a direct, strategic sense, then in an indirect way as a dramatic show so powerful as to change people's perceptions of the world.

But the fact that the assassins of Prime Minister Rabin and Chief Minister Beant Singh hoped that their acts would make such a statement does not mean that they in fact did. As I noted, public symbols mean different things to different people, and a symbolic performance may not have the intended effect. The way the act is perceived—by both the perpetrators and those who are affected by it—makes all the difference. In fact, the same is true of performative speech. One of the leading language philosophers, J. L. Austin, has qualified the notion that some speech acts are performative by observing that the power of the act is related to the perception of it. Children, for example, playing at marriage are not wedded by merely reciting the vows and going through the motions, nor is a ship christened by just anyone who gives it a name.[14]

The French sociologist Pierre Bourdieu, carrying further the idea that statements are given credibility by their social context, has insisted that the power of performative speech—vows and christenings—is rooted in social reality and is given currency by the laws and social customs that stand behind it.[15] Similarly, an act of terrorism usually implies an underlying power and legitimizing ideology. But whether the power and legitimacy implicit in acts of terrorism are like play-acted marriage vows or are the real thing depends in part on how the acts are perceived. It depends, in part, on whether their significance is believed.

This brings us back to the realm of faith. Public ritual has traditionally been the province of religion, and this is one of the reasons that performance violence comes so naturally to activists from a religious background. In a collection of essays on the connection between religion and terrorism published some years ago, one of the editors, David C. Rapoport, observed—accurately, I think—that the two topics fit together not only because there is a violent streak in the history of religion, but also because terrorist acts have a symbolic side and in that sense mimic religious rites. The victims of terrorism are targeted not because they are threatening to the perpetrators, he said, but because they are "symbols, tools, animals or corrupt beings" that tie into "a special picture of the world, a specific consciousness" that the activist possesses.[16]

The street theater of performance violence forces those who witness it directly or indirectly into that "consciousness"—that alternative view of the world. This gives the perpetrators of terrorism a kind of celebrity status and their actions an illusion of importance. The novelist Don DeLillo goes so far as to say that "only the lethal believer, the person who kills and dies for faith," is taken seriously in modern society.[17]

When we who observe these acts take them seriously—are disgusted
and repelled by them, and begin to distrust the peacefulness of the
world around us—the purposes of this theater are achieved.

Setting the Stage

In looking at religious terrorism as theater, the appropriate place to
begin is the stage—the location where the acts are committed, or rather,
performed. When followers of an expatriate Muslim sheik living in
New Jersey chose to make a statement about their unhappiness with
American and Jewish support for Middle East leaders whom they perceived to be enemies of Islam, they found the most dramatic stage in
sight: the World Trade Center. It turned out to be an apt location for a
variety of symbolic reasons.

Designed to be the tallest buildings in New York City, and at one
time the highest in the world, the 110-story twin towers of the World
Trade Center house the headquarters of international businesses and financial corporations. Among its many offices are quarters for the federal Secret Service and the governor of the state of New York. More
than fifty thousand employees daily enter the huge edifice, which also
includes a hotel, shops, and several restaurants. From the windows of
the penthouse restaurant, Windows on the World, the executives who
come to lunch can scarcely identify Jersey City and the other industrial
areas stretched out across the Hudson River in a distant haze.

From across the river in Jersey City, the twin towers of the building
are so tall that when no other part of the skyline in New York City is
visible, the tower tops are seen ethereally suspended above the eastern
horizon. When Muhammad A. Salameh came to the Ryder Truck
Rental lot on Jersey City's busy Kennedy Boulevard on Wednesday,
February 24, 1993, to rent a ten-foot Ford Econoline van, therefore, he
could catch glimpses of the World Trade Center in the distance.

Two days later, at noon, shortly after the van was driven to level B2
of the parking basement of the World Trade Center, an enormous blast
shuddered through the basement levels, collapsing several floors, killing
several workers instantly, and ripping a 180-foot hole in the wall of the
underground Port Authority Trans-Hudson train station. On the 110th
floor, in the Windows on the World restaurant, young executives who
were attending a career-launching lunch felt a thump and heard what
seemed to be a mild earthquake or a clap of thunder. When the elec-
tricity went off and they were told to evacuate the building, they

headed downstairs jauntily singing "One Hundred Bottles of Beer on the Wall." Their joviality turned to nervous apprehension when they were greeted with clouds of soot and smoke as they groped their way down 110 flights of stairs into a scene of confusion and suffering on the ground floor.[18]

Throughout the world the news media projected images of American power and civic order undermined. Based on the belief by government officials that the World Trade Center was targeted primarily as a public symbol, security was rushed to federal monuments and memorials in Washington, DC, later that afternoon. Although six people were killed in the blast, it was the assault on the building itself that received the most prominent reportage. Within an hour of the World Trade Center bombing, a coffeehouse in Cairo was attacked—allegedly by the same group implicated in the World Trade Center incident. This bombing killed more people but garnered very little attention outside of Cairo. Regardless of the number killed, a coffeehouse is not the World Trade Center. The towers are in their own way as American as the Statue of Liberty or the Washington Monument, and by assaulting them activists put their mark on a visibly American symbol.

The same can be said about the bombing of the Alfred P. Murrah Federal Building in Oklahoma City on April 19, 1995, by Timothy McVeigh and Terry Nichols. In this case the number killed was much greater than at the World Trade Center, and an enormous outpouring of public sympathy for the victims overshadowed any concern about damage done to the building. Yet there were several similarities between the two events: McVeigh and Nichols used a mixture of ammonium nitrate fertilizer and diesel fuel not unlike that used in the World Trade Center blast, and they mimicked the World Trade Center bombers by employing a Ryder rental truck. Like Mahmud Abouhalima and his colleages, these self-designated soldiers were fighting a quasi-religious war against the American government, and they chose a building that symbolized what they regarded as an oppressive government force.

In the downtown area of Oklahoma City, the Murrah building was an imposing edifice. It served as the regional headquarters for a variety of agencies linked with the federal government. The overwhelming majority of these offices were related to the beneficent side of governmental affairs, such as welfare and social security. But the building also housed the regional offices of the federal Bureau of Alcohol, Tobacco, and Firearms (ATF), from which agents were sent to Waco, Texas, to

enforce firearm laws in a confrontation that led to the standoff at the
Branch Davidian headquarters. For this reason the Oklahoma City offices of the ATF, along with the regional offices of the FBI (whose headquarters were also in Oklahoma City, but some fifty blocks away from
the Murrah building), had been the frequent target of verbal abuse by
protesting members of right-wing militias. The sidewalk in front of the
Murrah building had been the site of antigovernment demonstrations
from both ends of the political spectrum: antiwar protestors from the
left and firearms supporters from the right.

If one had to choose a single building that symbolized the presence
of centralized federal governmental power in this region of mid-
America, the Murrah building in Oklahoma City would be it. When the
dust settled after the devastating roar of the enormous explosion on
Wednesday morning, April 19, 1995, the entire front of the building
had been sheared off, killing 168 and injuring more than five hundred.
Among the dead and injured were scores of children in the building's
day care center, but only four ATF officials were injured, and none were
killed. Clearly, the target of the attack was not so much the government
agents, or even an agency such as the ATF, as it was the building itself
and its everyday staff of government workers.

What was targeted was a symbol of normal government operations.
In this scenario of terrorism, the lives of the workers were, like the
building, a part of the scenery: they and the edifice constituted the stage
on which the dramatic act was to be performed. If the building were attacked at night without the workers present, the explosion would not
have been a serious blow to government operations, nor would the pain
of the event be felt as acutely by society at large. If the building's employees had been machine-gunned as they left their offices, with the
building itself left unscathed, the symbolism of an attack on normal
government operations would have been incomplete. Such targets as
the World Trade Center and the Oklahoma City federal building have
provided striking images of a stable, seemingly invulnerable economic
and political power. Yet all buildings are ultimately vulnerable, a fact
that performers of terror such as Abouhalima and McVeigh have been
eager to demonstrate.

Some groups that have targeted the lifeblood of modern society have
chosen a different symbol of centrality: its major transportation systems. In today's cities, the most vibrant structures are often the airports.
Their importance is demonstrated by the sheer size of their landing
fields and the frequency of their air traffic as much as by the grandeur

of their architecture. Therefore, some terrorist attacks have focused on airport buildings and landing fields.

But because air traffic itself is indicative of a society's economic vitality, often airplanes rather than airports have provided terrorism's stage. The most dramatic example is Ramzi Yousef's Bojinka plot, aimed at eleven U.S. trans-Pacific passenger airplanes and alleged to have been funded by Saudi millionaire Osama bin Laden, which would have created a catastrophic event on one fateful day in 1995. The term *Bojinka* was one that Yousef himself had chosen and was the label for the file in the hard disk of his white Toshiba laptop computer that listed the details of the plot—where flights would depart, what routes they would take, and where the participants in the plot should deplane in order to escape the explosions caused by the bombs that they were to leave behind. In the trial that convicted him of conspiring to commit these acts of terrorism, Yousef, acting as his own lawyer, offered as his main defense the notion that anyone with computer expertise could have planted such information on his hard disk. Yet he was not able to refute the testimony of witnesses who heard him talk about the plot and the Philippines airline stewardess who saw him sitting in the very seat under which a bomb exploded on a later leg of the flight, after Yousef had departed. In December 1994, Yousef is said to have boarded the plane and, once it was aloft, entered one of the bathrooms and mixed a highly inflammable cocktail involving a liquid form of nitroglycerin. He sealed it in a container and attached a blasting cap and a timer. Returning to his seat, he strapped the device underneath the cushion and departed the plane at its next stop, leaving the bomb beneath the seat to explode in midair as the plane journeyed on to its next destination. It is a scenario eerily similar to one account of how TWA Flight 800 may have exploded shortly after takeoff at Kennedy Airport in New York on July 17, 1996, two months after Yousef's trial began, which is one reason some journalists jumped to the conclusion that the plane must have been downed by Muslim activists allied with Yousef.[19]

According to a chronology of terrorist acts maintained by Bruce Hoffman at the RAND Corporation and St. Andrews University, twenty-two airliners were bombed worldwide from 1969 to 1996, and many others were hijacked. A nation can feel dishonored by the bombing of one of its airlines even when the plane, such as the downed Pan Am 103, is far from home. In that case the bomb—plastic explosives hidden in a portable radio–tape player, allegedly placed by Libyan intelligence agencies operating out of Malta—blew up the aircraft as it flew above Scotland in 1988, the shredded pieces of the plane landing near the small town of Lockerbie.

When an Air India jumbo jet exploded in midair over the Irish coast in 1985, in what was assumed to be a terrorist act, the plane was also far from home. It was also far from the struggle for a Sikh homeland in the northern Indian state of Punjab, which many people believe was connected to the bombing. Although Sikh activists deny that any of their groups were involved—"It simply did not serve our purposes," one Sikh leader told me—the act was most likely committed by someone with a grievance against the Indian government, perhaps a renegade Sikh unit unknown even to the movement's leaders.[20] Although the airplane was downed thousands of miles from India's soil, the attack on the Air India airliner was regarded by the Indian press and by the country's leaders as an attack on India itself.

Especially when the struggle that serves as the context for terrorist acts is a local feud—between two factions or between a separatist movement and the state—the transportation system targeted is often not an international carrier but a local one. In the conflict between the militant Muslim Hamas movement and the secular Israeli state, buses were the targets of suicide bombers in Jerusalem and Tel Aviv. Buses were also a favored target of Sikh activists in the Punjab, as were trains, during the heyday of the separatist movement in the late 1980s.[21]

In the United States, saboteurs derailed an Amtrak train in October 1995 near Phoenix, Arizona, killing one person on the train and injuring seventy-eight. A note at the scene signed by "Sons of the Gestapo"—a little-known local right-wing group—specified retaliation for the federal government's brutality at Waco and Ruby Ridge as the reason for the attack. Although Amtrak is a nongovernmental corporation, presumably the fact that the trains lumbering through the empty Arizona desert were part of a national transportation system was sufficient reason to identify the train as a symbol of an oppressive governmental presence in the American hinterlands.

In Paris, subway trains and stations have been the objects of a series of terrorist attacks in the 1990s allegedly undertaken by Algerian supporters of the Islamic Front Party (FIS) unhappy over the French government's support for the Algerian military regime. The regime canceled elections in the former French colony that would have brought the Islamic party into power. One of the most publicized of the Parisian attacks was a bomb placed in the St. Michel station, one of the busiest in Paris, located near the Notre Dame Cathedral.

The placement of this bomb was strikingly similar to a terrorist action undertaken by a quite different group in another part of the world:
the subway nerve gas attack committed by members of the Aum
Shinrikyo movement in Tokyo. As I noted in the previous chapter, the
multiple bags of deadly sarin that were unsealed on several subway
lines were designed to achieve their maximum destructive power when
the trains converged at the central Kasumigaseki subway station. The
choice of this location was telling because it was calculated to simultaneously humiliate the government, whose main buildings were within
walking distance of the Kasumigaseki stop, and cast questions on the
ability of the government to protect the public and itself. Like acts of
terrorism by groups in other parts of the world, the movement was assaulting the very concept of national security.

In virtually every other recent example of religious terrorism, the building, vehicle, structure, or locale where the assault took place has had symbolic significance. In some cases the symbolism of the locale was specific:
the abortion clinics in the United States that were bombed by religious
pro-life activists or the tourist boats and hotels in Egypt that were attacked
by Islamic activists who regarded them as impositions from a foreign culture. Sheik Abdul Rahman had proclaimed such tourist sites as "sinful"
and insisted that "the lands of Muslims will not become bordellos for sin-
ners of every race and color."[22] The shrine of the Tomb of the Patriarchs
in Hebron, where Dr. Goldstein killed scores of praying Muslims, also had
specific symbolic significance, for Goldstein and his group regarded the
shrine as emblematic of the Muslim occupation of Jewish territory.

The symbolism of other locations has been more general: the locations represented the power and stability of the society itself. As we
have seen, buildings such as the World Trade Center and the Oklahoma
City federal building, along with transportation systems, are examples
of such general symbols. One group—the Islamic al Fuqra ("the im-
poverished") movement based in upstate New York—attacked the
power of the government in a literal as well as a figurative sense: it was
accused of hatching a plot to disable Colorado's electrical system.[23]
Computer networks and Internet channels are also symbols of a society's centrality—its central communication system. As the Melissa virus
in 1999 demonstrated, acts of sabotage can cripple large corporations
and government agencies. In response to NATO's bombing in Serbia
and Kosovo in May 1999, hackers electronically entered the computer
systems of several United States government agencies, leaving antiwar
messages in their wake.

By revealing the vulnerability of a nation's most stable and powerful entities, movements that undertake these acts of sabotage have touched virtually everyone in the nation's society. Any person in the United States could have been riding the elevator in the World Trade Center, visiting the Oklahoma City federal building, traveling on Pan Am 103, or using a computer when a virus invaded it, and everyone in the United States will look differently at the stability of public buildings, transportation networks, and communication systems as a result of these violent incidents.

Why is the location of terrorist events—of performance violence—so important? David Rapoport has observed that the control of territory defines public authority, and ethnic-religious groups have historically gained their identity through association with control over particular places.[24] Roger Friedland and Richard Hecht have taken this point further in an article comparing the struggle between Hindus and Muslims over a sacred site in the town of Ayodhya in India, and the conflict between Muslims and Jews over Temple Mount in Jerusalem. The authors point out that religious conflicts are often not only about space, but about the centrality of space.[25]

Such central places—even if they exist only in cyberspace—are symbols of power, and acts of terrorism claim them in a symbolic way. That is, they express for a moment the power of terrorist groups to control central locations—by damaging, terrorizing, and assaulting them— even when in fact most of the time they do not control them at all. Even before the smoke had cleared at the World Trade Center, life inside was returning to normal. Although the Murrah Federal Building was destroyed, the governmental functions that had been conducted there continued unabated. Yet during that brief dramatic moment when a terrorist act levels a building or damages some entity that a society regards as central to its existence, the perpetrators of the act assert that they—and not the secular government—have ultimate control over that entity and its centrality.

The very act, however, is sometimes more than symbolic: by demonstrating the vulnerability of governmental power, to some degree it weakens that power. Because power is largely a matter of perception, symbolic statements can lead to real results. On the whole, however, the small degree to which a government's authority is discredited by a terrorist act does not warrant the massive destructiveness of the act itself. More significant is the impression—in most cases it is simply an illusion—that the movements perpetrating the acts have enormous power and that the ideologies behind them have cosmic importance. In the war between religious and secular authority, the loss of a secular government's ability to control and secure public spaces, even for a terrible moment, is ground gained for religion's side.

A Time to Kill

Much the same can be said about the dramatic time—the date or season or hour of day that a terrorist act takes place. There are, after all, centralities in time as well as in space. Anniversaries and birthdays mark such special days for individuals; public holidays demarcate hallowed dates for societies as a whole. To capture the public's attention through an act of performance violence on a date deemed important to the group perpetrating the act, therefore, is to force the group's sense of what is temporally important on everyone else.

When Timothy McVeigh and his colleagues chose the date of their explosion at the Oklahoma City federal building, they were essentially imposing a public holiday—a dramatic public recognition—as a memorial to several events. April 19, 1995, was a special day for McVeigh and other Christian Identity activists for a number of reasons. It was Patriot's Day in New England, the day the American Revolution had begun in 1775; it was the day in 1943 that the Nazis moved on the Warsaw ghetto to destroy the Jewish population on what in that year was the Day of Passover; and it was the day in 1993 when the Branch Davidian compound in Waco, Texas, burned to the ground. It was also the day in 1995 when a Christian Identity activist, Richard Wayne Snell, was due to be executed in prison for murder charges. According to Kerry Noble, one of Snell's colleagues in the Arkansas compound called the Covenant, the Sword, and the Arm of the Lord (CSA), Snell himself had planned to bomb the Oklahoma City federal building in 1983 in opposition to what he regarded as the demonic and oppressive actions of the U.S. government.[26] For various reasons that project was aborted. Was it only coincidence that the building was finally destroyed on the day of Snell's death? Noble suggested that McVeigh knew Snell through his contacts with Elohim City, also a Christian Identity compound, which McVeigh is known to have visited from time to time. The leader of Elohim City, Robert Millar, was Snell's primary adviser and defender.

The date, April 19, clearly had significance to McVeigh. Soon after Snell's execution date had been set, McVeigh created a fake driver's identification card that listed his birth date as April 19; his real birth-day was April 23. Eleven days before the bombing, McVeigh is said to have gone to a bar with one of the leaders of Elohim City and bragged to another customer, "You're going to remember me on April 19."[27] Hours after the Oklahoma City bombing, as he was being prepared for his own execution later that evening, Snell caught glimpses on television of the devasted building that he had once planned to destroy. "Hail his victory," Snell is said to have proclaimed shortly before he was put to death.[28] His body was taken to Elohim City for burial.

In some cases the days that are held sacred by an activist group are known only to that group; according to Noble, "The entire right wing was aware of Snell's pending execution date." In other instances public religious holidays create times of heightened sensitivities and hold the potential for violent reprisals. Noble warned government agencies that they should not provoke radical groups associated with the Christian Identity movement during three times of the year. One is mid-April, with its association with Easter and the resurrection of Jesus; some groups believe that anyone who is killed at that time of the year will be resurrected three days later. A second period is mid-August, historically a time of persecution for Jews and by implication the "real Jews" of the Christian Identity tradition. The third period to avoid is September and October during the Feast of Tabernacles, thought to be a time of miracles.[29]

One of the most notorious incidents in recent Jewish history—Dr. Goldstein's massacre at the shrine of the Tomb of the Patriarchs at Hebron—also occurred during a religious holiday. Goldstein chose Purim as the time for his assault, a day that is revered by Jews as the celebration of vengeance against Amalek. The scroll of Esther notes that Haman was a direct descendant of the Amalekite king Agag, and according to one Israeli author, "Goldstein wasn't killing innocent men at prayer, but Haman and Hitler and Arafat, sanctifying God's name by avenging Amalek."[30] In that sense, Goldstein was calling on Jews everywhere to reclaim their tradition, redress the humiliation of Jews, and give an immediate political meaning to the ideas they professed to honor on their sacred days.

Goldstein's attack occurred on a date that is sacred not only to Jews, however. As luck would have it, his attack occurred during Muslims' most sacred month, Ramadan. This fact was not lost on many Muslim activists in the Hamas movement, who saw Goldstein's timing not only as a way of honoring Jewish tradition but as an attempt to discredit

Islam. They became convinced of this interpretation when they heard rumors—never confirmed—that Goldstein had acted not alone, but on the behest of the Israeli government and army. Regardless of whether or not Goldstein had acted under official Israeli sanction, from the Hamas point of view the facts spoke for themselves: the attack was done in a mosque, during worship, and during Ramadan. When "the Israelis killed our women and children during the holy month of Ramadan," one Hamas leader told me, "we wanted to do the same to Israel, to show them that even their women and children are vulnerable: none are innocent."[31] Timing, it turned out, was as important to Hamas leaders as it was to Goldstein, and many of their suicide missions coincided with the anniversaries of the deaths of Hamas heroes killed by Israelis. With the choice of those dates, the attacks created a macabre sort of memorial to these martyrs.

Ramadan has also been a time for heightened violence in Algeria. The country has been devastated by violence ever since the military halted the elections of 1991–92, denying the leading religious party, the Islamic Salvation Front, an opportunity for victory. Perhaps the most horrific events have been the wholesale slaughter of villagers at night-time. The villages appeared to have been chosen at random for an act undertaken in an almost sacrificial manner: the throats of the villagers were slit in a style not unlike that of the ritual killing of animals for religious sacrifices. Moreover, the most frequent occurrence of these massacres was in the weeks immediately preceding the holy month of Ramadan. In December 1998, for instance, seven villagers were attacked in this manner in the town of Merad, sixty miles west of Algiers, two weeks before Ramadan began.[32] Another thirty were killed in neighboring villages at the end of the month.[33]

Independence Day 1999 was the date chosen by Benjamin Nathaniel Smith to go on a shooting spree across central Illinois and Indiana. The shootings, though random, were all aimed at racial minorities: Smith, a member of a white supremacist church, killed an African American basketball coach and a Korean graduate student, and he seriously wounded six Orthodox Jews, a Taiwanese student, and two other African Americans. According to Smith's former girlfriend, the Independence Day timing was not a coincidence. Smith wanted to proclaim the freedom of white Americans, she said, from the increasing pluralism of American society.

"There is a time to kill," Rev. Michael Bray wrote, paraphrasing a passage from the book of Ecclesiastes in the Bible.[34] In his case, however,

Bray was talking not about particular dates but about a period of history, a moment justifying what he called "defensive actions on behalf of the unborn" and what others have called terrorist acts against abortion clinics and their staffs. From Bray's perspective an appropriate time could also have been a sequence of events—one that led to what he regarded as virtually an inevitable occurrence of violence. Bray offered this sense of timing as one explanation for why his friend, Rev. Paul Hill, killed a doctor and his escort at a Florida clinic. Bray said that the timing was right—indeed, it required it—and if Hill had not done the deed at that time, Bray would have felt called upon to do it himself.[35]

Bray set the context. He and his colleagues had long held the conviction that killing abortion clinic staff members was justified. Their moral calculations were supported by one of the tenets of the just-war theory in Christian theology: a small act of violence may be justified in order to stop a much greater violent assault. In Bray's view, the hundreds of "unborn babies," as he termed them, who were daily killed in what Bray called "abortuaries" warranted an act of violence in an attempt to stop the slaughter. The issue, then, was not whether violent attacks on abortion clinic staff were justified, but when they should be implemented.

The issue was one of timing. There had been two botched attempts at killing abortion clinic staff in the years immediately prior to Paul Hill's act, and Bray and Hill felt that this momentum of failure had to be reversed. It was essential to members of Bray's circle that this "defensive action" be done right. In Pensacola, Florida, on March 10, 1993, prior to Hill's attack, Michael Griffin shot Dr. David Gunn three times in the back, killing him instantly. At first Hill was jubilant over the incident and appeared on television's *Donahue* show, praising Griffin's action. But as the case moved to trial, Griffin tried to defend himself by blaming his rash actions on the pro-life movement. In the view of Bray and Hill, Griffin had lost his nerve.[36] According to Bray, Hill was deeply disappointed over this turn of events. Hill had hoped that the killing of Dr. Gunn would be a watershed in the pro-life movement and that an IRA sort of paramilitary uprising would occur. But this did not happen, and Hill blamed Griffin for robbing his act of the significance Hill thought it deserved.

Hill was equally disappointed by another attempt at killing an abortion doctor that went awry. In this instance Shelly Shannon, who was part of Hill and Bray's circle of activists, attempted to kill Dr. George Tiller at a Wichita, Kansas, abortion clinic in August 1993. After firing at the doctor she was immediately caught. As she was being led away by the police, she was heard to yell out, "Did I kill him?" The answer was no. The doctor was wounded but still quite alive. Shannon did not try to wriggle out of her charges, and she received a lengthy prison sentence for the act, but because the abortion clinic doctor lived to work another day—in fact, was back at work the very next day—in the eyes of Hill and Bray her attempt was flawed. "Shelly had great character but fell short," Bray said, adding that "Griffin did the job but not with good character."

According to Bray, these attempts set up a need—a "destiny" in his way of thinking—that this act be done, and that it be done correctly. It should be an effective military operation carried out by a soldier of righteous and unwavering motives. This soldier could have been Rev. Michael Bray, but the lot fell to his friend, Rev. Paul Hill. Bray told me that Hill had the Christian "calling" to do the action.[37] "The Lord had called me and He showed me the way," Hill confirmed in a letter that he wrote to Bray and other supporters after the killing.[38]

On Friday, July 29, 1994, as Dr. John Britton and his volunteer escort, James Barrett, drove up to the clinic where abortions were to be performed, Hill shot through the windows of the truck, hitting them both in the head, killing them instantly and wounding Barrett's wife, June, who was accompanying her husband. As Hill was being taken away, he shouted, "No innocent babies are going to be killed in that clinic today."[39] After the attack Bray and others in his circle were kept under surveillance by police, who feared that more violence was forthcoming. But according to Bray they need not have worried. After Hill's action was completed, he said, it was no longer necessary for a similar one to be attempted. The deed had finally been done correctly, the symbolic statement had been made, and Hill, in Bray's eyes, had made the ultimate sacrifice. The moment had been fulfilled, and time had moved on.

This sense of a great momentum in history leading to a cataclysmic moment punctuated with violence has characterized other movements as well. Perhaps the most spectacular example in recent history was the Tokyo nerve gas incident. Immediately preceding the event the leaders of Aum Shinrikyo had felt that the government and police were closing in on them for crimes of murder and kidnaping that had been committed earlier, and for which the nerve gas incident provided a denouement and a deflection of the police's attention. But although this may have precipitated the attack, there was another, grander purpose that was related to the movement's notion of cataclysmic history. For years the

movement's leader, Shoko Asahara, had predicted that history wa.·
gathering momentum toward an awesome conflagration, a battle even
greater than World War II: Armageddon.

Asahara's worst predictions were supposed to materialize sometime
around the year 2000. As the months and years moved toward the end
of the millennium, the anticipation had become so great that the followers felt that something had to happen. When the nerve gas was released in the Tokyo subways, many of Asahara's followers received the
news with a sense of excitement and relief. They saw this attack as a
vindication of Asahara's prophecies and thought that Armageddon was
indeed upon them. This is what Takeshi Nakamura meant when he told
me he thought that the "weird time" had come.[40]

The year 2000 is momentous for other movements as well. Early in
1999, fourteen members of an American group called the Concerned
Christians were suddenly deported from Israel, where they had come to
prepare for the coming of the millennium. Based in Denver, Colorado,
they had abandoned their worldly possessions and come to Jerusalem
with the expectation that the end of the millennium would be the occasion for the apocalyptic confrontation predicted in the book of
Revelation—Armageddon—after which Christ would return to earth.
The group was charged with planning to instigate a series of terrorist
acts in order to precipitate Armageddon, and perhaps to kill themselves
in an act of mass suicide in the process. Other religious groups shared
their anticipation of a cataclysmic end to the millennium. By mid-1999,
more than a hundred Christians from Europe and the United States had
moved to Jerusalem to await the coming of the Messiah. Israeli authorities feared that some of them shared the designs of the Concerned
Christians to precipitate Armageddon through an act of terrorism—
"the most serious of crimes that harm state security," as the Israeli mag-
istrate who deported the Concerned Christians had called it.[41]

In all of these cases a certain time, or timing, was critical to the terrorist act. It provided a proscenium for the event. An aura of specialness
was imparted by the day or moment in history in which the act occurred.
By locating themselves within a transcendent temporal dimension, the
perpetrators declared their missions to be of transcendent importance as
well. Ultimately they were attempting to capture and reshape what society regarded as central in time as well as in space.

What was significant about such symbolically central times and
places—and for that matter, central things, including subways and airplanes—is that they represented power. They were centers, in Clifford

Geertz's use of the term: "concentrated loci of serious acts."[42] Such places and times constituted the "arenas" of society "where its leading ideas come together with its leading institutions" and where "momentous events" were thought to occur.[43] When activists attacked such a place, be it the World Trade Center or the Kasumigaseki subway station in central Tokyo, during one of those momentous times, they challenged the power and legitimacy of society itself.

Reaching the Audience

As the novelist Don DeLillo once said, terrorism is "the language of being noticed."[44] Without being noticed, in fact, terrorism would not exist. The sheer act of killing does not create a terrorist act: murders and willful assaults occur with such frequency in most societies that they are scarcely reported in the news media. What makes an act terrorism is that it terrifies. The acts to which we assign that label are deliberate events, bombings and attacks performed at such places and times that they are calculated to be observed. Terrorism without its horrified witnesses would be as pointless as a play without an audience.

Rev. Michael Bray said as much when he explained the secondary effect of bombing abortion clinics. He admitted that bombing one or two clinics did not make much of a dent in the volume of abortions committed on a particular day in American society. Yet, he said, the actions had "symbolic value" in that they deterred abortionists and their clients who heard about the attacks and were intimidated by them.[45] Bray implied that the primary purpose of such attacks was to have the image of burned and damaged abortion clinics portrayed across the nation. Indeed, Bray regularly published such images in his own newsletter. The images of such terrorist acts were more important than whatever direct effect the acts themselves had.

Perhaps the most enduring image from the tragic bombing of the Oklahoma City federal building on April 19, 1995, was the photograph of the bloody, mangled body of an infant carried in the arms of a rescue worker who attempted—futilely, as it turned out—to save the small child's life. Perhaps no other picture could have portrayed as poignantly the pathos of innocence defiled or evoked so strongly the righteous anger of many over what appeared to be a hideous and senseless act. The perpetrators of the bombing were not the photographers of this picture, of course, nor were they the ones who distributed it on the front pages of newspapers around the world. Yet this picture, its wide circulation, and the public revulsion it produced were an intrinsic part of the terrorist event, magnifying its horror far beyond the number of people immediately affected by the blast.

For many who have been involved in plotting terrorist attacks, the ability to seize the attention of the public through the news media is precisely the point. When I asked Mahmud Abouhalima what he felt to be the greatest threat to Islam, he gave a surprising answer: media misrepresentation.[46] He told me that secularism held a virtual lock on media control and that Islam did not have news sources to present its side of contemporary history. By implication, acts of terrorism such as the one for which he was convicted—the bombing of the World Trade Center—laid claim to the images and headlines of the world's media, at least for a moment. Abouhalima himself was very media conscious. He carefully read news accounts about him and his group, indicating which ones he felt were fair (*Time* magazine, for example), and which ones he thought were scurrilous (*New York Times* and *Newsday*, for instance). Abouhalima was particularly incensed over a book written by *Newsday* reporters, *Two Seconds under the World,* in which he was characterized as the master conspirator behind the World Trade Center bombing.[47] On the other hand, he proudly kept in his cell a copy of *Time* magazine in which his picture appeared on the cover and the account of his life was the lead story. In this case, he felt that the facts about him were portrayed fairly and nonjudgmentally.

In my own attempts to interview activists supporting or involved in terrorist acts, I found individuals fairly receptive to meeting with me and telling their stories. My initial contacts with them were through academic colleagues or journalists. Many of them were more open to the possibility of my interviewing them if the contacts came through news media connections. The more international the media network, the better. In Japan, for instance, I was told by officials in Aum Shinrikyo that they would speak with me as long as I was not accompanied by Japanese journalists or scholars. I had the impression that they were concerned not only with objectivity—suggesting that non-Japanese could judge their situation more honestly—but also with the breadth of their audience. In talking with an American scholar they hoped to get their message to the wider world.

Moreover, there was not much more the Japanese media could have discovered about the Aum Shinrikyo movement: the media coverage of the group in Japan was already at a saturation level. The March 20, 1995, nerve gas incident marked the beginning of an extraordinary media frenzy that lasted most of that year and much of the next, encompassing hundreds of hours of television time and thousands of articles and books. One of the journalists reporting the story herself became a celebrity as a result of her reportage, and other journalists clamored to interview her.[48] One American journalist working in Japan told me that this story was "bigger than the Kobe earthquake—bigger than the O. J. Simpson trial," and he added that "the Japanese public can't get enough of it."[49] Just as the American public was drawn into the events following the bombing of the U.S. embassies in Africa, the World Trade Center, and the Oklahoma federal building, and as the news media of the Middle East have been dominated by the terrorist acts of Muslim and Jewish activists, the Japanese came to look on terrorism as a kind of national drama.

The *New York Times,* in considering whether to publish the Unabomber's 35,000-word manifesto in 1995, agonized over the role that the news media was being coerced into playing, and questioned whether the newspaper's coverage—especially its willingness to publish the bomber's writings—would alleviate terrorism by helping to solve the mystery of the bomber's identity or add to terrorism's suffering by inadvertently encouraging other activists to seek the exposure that the newspaper seemed willing to offer. The publisher of the *Times,* Arthur Sulzberger, Jr., lamented the idea of "turning our pages over to a man who has murdered people." But he added that he was "convinced" that they were "making the right choice between bad options."[50]

The fact that the publication of the manifesto eventually led to the identification of Theodore Kaczynski as the bomber by his brother David would seem to vindicate the decision of the *Times* publishers. It brought to an end a seventeen-year string of violence involving sixteen letter bombings that wounded twenty-three and left three others dead. Still, it is unclear whether other activists might have been spurred on by the newspaper's capitulation to a terrorist's media demands. In the case of the visual medium of television, however, there is little that terrorists need to demand, since the highly sensational nature of their activities captures television's attention immediately and completely.

In a collection of essays on contemporary culture, Jean Baudrillard described the terrorism of the late twentieth century as "a peculiarly modern form" because of the impact that it has on public consciousness through electronic media. According to Baudrillard, terrorist acts have emerged "less from passion than from the screen: a violence in the nature of the image."[51] Baudrillard went so far as to advise his readers "not to be in a public place where television is operating, considering the high probability that its very presence will precipitate a violent event."[52] His advice was hyperbolic, of course, but it does point to the reality that terrorist events are aimed at attracting news media exposure and perhaps would not happen as frequently, or in the same way, if the enormous resources of the news media were not readily at hand to promote them.

The worldwide media coverage of the bombings of the U.S. embassies in Africa, the World Trade Center, and the Oklahoma City federal building illustrates a new development in terrorism: the extraordinary widening of terror's audience. Throughout most of history the audiences for acts of terrorism have been limited largely to government officials and their supporters, or members of rival groups. What makes the terrorism of recent years significant is the breadth of its audience, a scope that is in many cases virtually global.

When television does not adequately report the ideas and motivations behind their actions, many activist groups have found the Internet and the World Wide Web to be effective alternatives. Movements such as Hamas and Aryan Nations have well-established web sites. An anti-abortion site, "The Nuremberg Files," which advocated the killing of abortion clinic doctors and maintained a list of potential targets, was removed by its Internet service provider in February 1999, after a red line was drawn through the name of Dr. Barnett Slepian on the day after he was killed by an assassin. The creator of the site, Neal Horsley, said that the move was "a temporary setback" and vowed to return to the World Wide Web.[53] Other groups, including Christian Identity and militia activists, have protected their sites with passwords that allow only their members to gain access. Thus, even when the audience is selective, the message has been projected through a public medium.

In some cases an act of violence sends two messages at the same time: a broad message aimed at the general public and a specific communication targeted at a narrower audience. In cases of Islamic violence in Palestine and Sikh terrorism in India, for instance, one of the purposes of the assaults was to prove to movement members that the leadership was still strong enough to engender the life-and-death dedication of their commandos. In other cases, the point was to intimidate followers of the movement and to force them to follow a hard-line position rather than a conciliatory one.

Motives such as these help to explain one of the most puzzling forms of contemporary violence: silent terror. These intriguing acts of terrorism are ones in which the audience is not immediately apparent. The public is often mystified by an explosion accompanied only by an eerie silence, with no group claiming responsibility or explaining the purpose of its act. As days passed after bombs ripped through the American embassies in Kenya and Tanzania on August 7, 1998, and no person or group took credit for the actions, questions arose as to why no group had owned up to the attacks in order to publicize its cause.

This question has also been posed after other, similarly unexplained terrorist events. The 1985 bombing of the Air India jetliner, the 1994 truck bomb that destroyed a Jewish center in Buenos Aires, and the 1996 explosion of a U.S. military housing complex in Dhahran, Saudi Arabia, were all followed with silence. In cases where the anonymous perpetrators have been identified, such as the Pan Am 103 bombing over Lockerbie, Scotland, in which Libyan government officials were accused, acknowledgment of the crime by the perpetrators still has not been forthcoming.

Even in the cases where the accused were brought to trial and convicted—such as the World Trade Center and Oklahoma City bombings and the Tokyo subway attack—the guilty have still denied their complicity. Mahmud Abouhalima, even after being convicted of participation in the World Trade Center bombing, told me that he was "nowhere near" the building at the time of the blast and that he had no relationship with Sheik Omar Abdul Rahman, the spiritual leader of the group convicted of the bombing.[54] Assuming for the moment that the government case against him was strong and that he was in fact involved in the crime for which he was convicted, why would he or any other activist involved in a violent incident deny it?

When he discussed the Oklahoma City bombing, Abouhalima said that it made no difference who the perpetrators of that event were, as long as the event made the point that the American government was an enemy. This was significant, Abouhalima said, since one of the things that frustrated him was the American public's complacency, its inability to recognize that great struggles were going on in the world, and its denial that the U.S. government was deeply involved in them. Bombing a public building demonstrated the reality of that hidden war. Since terrorism is theater, the catastrophes at the World Trade Center, the Oklahoma City federal building, and the U.S. embassies in Africa broadcast that message to the world. From the point of view of the perpetrators, this was enough; the message was successfully sent, and they did not need to brag about their ability to convey it.

In a world in which information is a form of power, public demonstrations of violence have conveyed potent messages indeed. When groups are able to demonstrate their capacity for destruction simultaneously in different parts of the world, as in the case of the U.S. embassy bombings in 1998, this is an even more impressive display than single-target events. It is no less so if the only audiences who know who did it, who can appreciate the perpetrators' accomplishment, and who can admire their command over life and death are within the group itself. The act demonstrates their ability to perform a powerful event with virtually global impact.

The forms of religious terrorism that have emerged in the last decade of the twentieth century have been global in two senses. The choices of targets have often been transnational. Egyptians and Palestinians bombed the World Trade Center in New York City to protest against secular governments in the Middle East, and U.S. embassies in Kenya and Tanzania were attacked by a group with ties to Afghanistan, Egypt, and Sudan. These incidents have also been global in their impact, in large part because of the worldwide, instantaneous coverage by transnational news media. This has been terrorism meant not just for television but for CNN.

Increasingly, terrorism has been performed for a television audience around the world. In that sense it has been as real a global event as the transnational events of the global economy. Ironically, terrorism has become a more potent global political force than the organized political efforts to control and contain it. The United Nations lacks the military capability and intelligence-gathering capacity to deal with worldwide terrorism. Instead, consortia of nations have been forced to come together to handle the information sharing and joint operations required to deal with forces of violence on an international scale.

This global dimension of terrorism's organization and audience, and the transnational responses to it, gives special significance to the understanding of terrorism as a public performance of violence—as a social event with both real and symbolic aspects. As Bourdieu has observed, our public life is shaped as much by symbols as by institutions. For this reason, symbolic acts—the "rites of institution"—help to demarcate public space and indicate what is meaningful in the social world.[55] In a striking imitation of such rites, terrorism has provided its own dramatic events. These rites of violence have brought an alternative view of public reality—not just a single society in transition, but a world challenged by strident religious visions of transforming change.

Figure 1.   Rev. Paul Hill (*left*) and Rev. Michael Bray (*center*) holding a sign saying "Is it wrong to use force to stop the murder of innocent babies?" (Property of Michael Bray, 1993)

Figure 2.   Timothy McVeigh, convicted bomber of the Oklahoma City federal building. (AP/Wide World Photos)

Figure 3. The Oklahoma City federal building after the bombing. (AP/Wide World Photos)

Figure 4.   Sinn Féin headquarters in Belfast. The large stones placed in front
are meant to deter the exploding of car bombs in front of the building. (Mark
Juergensmeyer)

Figure 5.   Aftermath of the bombing in Omagh, Northern Ireland, on
August 16, 1998. The worst single attack in three decades of violence killed
twenty-eight people and injured more than two hundred. (AP Photo/Alastair
Grant)

Figure 6.   The western wall of the ancient Jewish temple adjacent to the
Muslim shrine the Dome of the Rock, in old Jerusalem. (Mark Juergensmeyer)

Figure 7.   Yoel Lerner, an activist
for right-wing Jewish causes, in his
study in old Jerusalem. (Mark
Juergensmeyer)

Figure 8. Guard at gravesite of Baruch Goldstein near Hebron (*left*) with the author. (Mark Juergensmeyer)

Figure 9. Mahmud Abouhalima (*bottom center*) hoisting defense lawyer William Kuntsler onto his shoulders after the 1991 acquittal of El Sayyid Nosair on charges of murdering Rabbi Meir Kahane the previous year. Abouhalima was accused but never convicted of being the cab driver for the bungled getaway attempt following the assassination. (Newsday, Inc. ©1991)

Figure 10. Victims from the World Trade Center bombing following the blast, on February 26, 1993. (AP/Wide World Photos)

Figure 11.   Dr. Abdul Aziz Rantisi,
political leader of Hamas, in Khan
Yunis, Gaza, with a drawing of
Sheik Ahmed Yassin in the background. (Mark Juergensmeyer)

Figure 12.   Sheik Ahmed Yassin, founder and spiritual leader of Hamas, in
Gaza with the author. (Mark Juergensmeyer)

Figure 13. Osama bin Laden, the elusive Muslim activist alleged to have bankrolled terrorist acts, including the bombing of U.S. embassies in Africa in 1998. (AP/Wide World Photos)

Figure 14. Simranjit Singh Mann, Sikh political leader, imprisoned under suspicion of masterminding the assassination of Indira Gandhi, showing where his beard hair had allegedly been pulled out in acts of torture during his imprisonment. (Mark Juergensmeyer)

Figure 15. Aum Shinrikyo nerve gas laboratories located near Mt. Fuji, Japan, guarded by police after the subway attack. (Mark Juergensmeyer)

Figure 16. Shoko Asahara, leader of the Aum Shinrikyo sect, after being taken into custody by Japanese police, August 16, 1996. (AP Photo)

CHAPTER 8

Cosmic War

The world is at war, Osama bin Laden proclaimed in a fatwa delivered in February 1998, months before the bombing of the American embassies in Kenya and Tanzania—bombings he was accused of masterminding and financing. Bin Laden wanted to make clear that it was not he who started the war, however, but Americans, through their actions in the Middle East. These had constituted, in bin Laden's words, "a clear declaration of war on God, His messenger and Muslims."[1] His own acts of violence, by implication, were merely responses to a great ongoing struggle.

Bin Laden's was not the only war recognized by religious activists around the world, nor was it the only one targeting America. When Bo Greitz, the leader of the American Patriot movement, led a posse into the woods of South Carolina in August 1998 to hunt for the alleged abortion clinic bomber, Eric Robert Rudolph, he explained that Rudolph considered himself "a soldier at war"—one whose enemy was the American government. Greitz could be confident of that assessment, since many of his militia colleagues viewed themselves in exactly the same way. The acronym RAHOWA, which stands for "racial holy war," is in fact a greeting and a rallying cry in the World Church of the Creator, the group associated with Benjamin Nathaniel Smith's racially targeted killings in Illinois and Indiana in July 1999.

"The Lord God is a man of War," Christian Identity leader Kerry Noble reminded his followers in the Arkansas compound of the

Covenant, the Sword, and the Arm of the Lord.[2] In 1998, after he had
served prison time and left the movement, Noble regretted his radical
stance but explained that he then felt it necessary, since his group
"needed to know that it was time to cross the line into violence," and
that these actions would be "acceptable to the Lord."[3] When one of
Noble's former colleagues, Bob Matthews, took seriously this mandate
for violence and killed a Jewish radio talk show host, he secluded himself in a hideout on Whidbey Island, north of Seattle, where he issued
a statement declaring that he and his comrades were in "a full and un-
relenting state of war" against the U.S. government.[4] The Bible is "a
book of war, a book of hate," another Christian Identity activist remarked.[5]

These images of divine warfare are persistent features of religious activism. They provide the content and the themes that are played out in
the grand scenarios that lie behind contemporary acts of performance
violence. In many cases these images are not new but are a part of the
heritage of religious traditions that stretch back to antiquity, and abundant examples of warfare may be found in sacred texts. In a booklet en-
titled *Prepare War!,* for instance, Kerry Noble provided a scriptural ra-
tionale for his martial stance and for his involvement in the Christian
Army of God. Because God was "a man of war" (Ex 15:3) and took
vengeance on his enemies, Noble argued, it behooved his followers to
do the same. Like many activists who have turned to terror, he has been
driven by an image of cosmic war.

I call such images "cosmic" because they are larger than life. They
evoke great battles of the legendary past, and they relate to metaphysical conflicts between good and evil. Notions of cosmic war are intimately personal but can also be translated to the social plane.
Ultimately, though, they transcend human experience. What makes religious violence particularly savage and relentless is that its perpetrators
have placed such religious images of divine struggle—cosmic war—in
the service of worldly political battles. For this reason, acts of religious
terror serve not only as tactics in a political strategy but also as evoca-
tions of a much larger spiritual confrontation.

The script of cosmic war is central to virtually all of the incidents of
performance violence described in the first part of this book. In
Christian movements, the literature of the militia and the Christian patriots—including Timothy McVeigh's favorite book, *The Turner
Diaries*—is rife with images of warfare.[6] A brochure published by the

Christian Identity–affiliated group Aryan Nations included this statement in their creed of faith: "We BELIEVE there is a battle being fought
this day between the children of darkness (today known as Jews) and
the children of Light (God), the Aryan race, the true Israel of the
Bible."[7]

The Christian Reconstruction preacher Rev. Michael Bray described
his violent abortion clinic protests as part of a "culture war" being
waged in the United States that includes, among other issues, conflicts
between "big and little government, high and low taxation, gun control
and no gun control, abortion rights and no abortion rights, rights to
sodomy and no sodomy rights."[8] In Northern Ireland Rev. Ian Paisley,
who has frequently spoken in military terms about faith and politics,
launched a magazine in October 1997 named *The Battle Standard*.[9] A
follower of Paisley who was convicted of terrorist acts assented to the
notion that his assaults on Irish Catholics were part of a "religious
war."[10]

Jewish activists following Rabbi Meir Kahane have also been convinced that their violent acts have been authorized as weapons in a divine warfare sanctioned by God. Dr. Baruch Goldstein's massacre at the
shrine of the Tomb of the Patriarchs in Hebron in 1994 was described
as a military act. "All Jews," one of his supporters told me—implying
that it was common knowledge—are "at war with the Arabs."[11]

In an odd echo of this Jewish activist's statement, Hamas supporters
claim that they too are "at war"—a war with Israel.[12] It is this great
conflict that has created the need for Hamas, Sheik Ahmed Yassin told
me.[13] Mahmud Abouhalima warned me that Americans are unaware
that there is "a war going on."[14] Shortly before the bombing of the
World Trade Center, when Abouhalima was driving a taxicab in New
York City, an ABC journalist recalls riding with the Muslim activist and
being lectured that America would lose the war against Islam without
even knowing that it was in it, or when the moment of defeat had arrived.[15]

The Muslim concept of struggle—jihad—has been employed for centuries in Islamic theories of both personal salvation and political redemption. "Life is faith and struggle," said Iran's Ayatollah Khomeini,
indicating that the notion of fighting is basic to human existence and on
a par with religious commitment.[16] As noted earlier, Abd al-Salam
Faraj and others have exploited the idea of jihad to call for physical
force, if necessary, in the struggle against all ideas, ideologies, and

political institutions that they regard as alien to Islam. But the concept
of jihad is not a carte blanche for violence. The use of the idea to justify nondefensive attacks—such as acts of terrorism—has been highly
controversial within Muslim theological circles. An American scholar
of Islam, Bruce Lawrence, has argued that the term changes in meaning
depending on its historical context and has always had social and economic, as well as military and political, dimensions.[17]

Regardless of the nuances of its usage, however, jihad is fundamentally
a concept of struggle, an image that abounds in the rhetoric of violent religious activists in both Abrahamic and non-Abrahamic faiths. When the
militant Sikh leader Jarnail Singh Bhindranwale exhorted his followers to
action, he called for "a struggle . . . for our faith, for the Sikh nation, for
the oppressed."[18] On the personal level it is a conflict between faith and
the lack of faith; on the social level it is a battle between truth and evil.
Supporters of the Bharatiya Janata Party in India evoked images of the
great wars of the Hindu epics, the *Mahabharata* and the *Ramayana*. The
leader of the Buddhist syncretist movement Aum Shinrikyo imagined
warfare in the grandest of terms: a global war that would surpass World
Wars I and II in its savage intensity and powers of destruction.[19]

These nearly ubiquitous images of warfare evoked by militant religious groups in the 1990s are significant for the understanding of violence and religion that will be explored in the remainder of this book.
In this chapter and the next, we will see how the notion of cosmic war
provides the script being played out in the violent performances of militant religious activists and is linked to notions of conquest and failure,
martyrdom and sacrifice. In Chapter 10, we will see how violence can
be part of a broader justificatory scheme that is empowering on both
the personal and social levels. In the final chapter we will explore ways
that images of struggle have helped to make religion an agent of honor
and legitimization, thereby raising the importance of religion as an ideology of order that sustains public life.

Grand Scenarios

Looking closely at the notion of war, one is confronted with the idea of
dichotomous opposition on an absolute scale. It is not just a matter of
differing opinions or an even contest with an opponent. After all, the
articulation and adjudication of differences are not advanced by warfare. War suggests an all-or-nothing struggle against an enemy whom
one assumes to be determined to destroy. No compromise is deemed

possible. The very existence of the opponent is a threat, and until the enemy is either crushed or contained, one's own existence cannot be secure. What is striking about a martial attitude is the certainty of one's position and the willingness to defend it, or impose it on others, to the end.

Such certitude on the part of one side may be regarded as noble by those whose sympathies lie with it and dangerous by those who do not. But either way it is not rational. One of the first rules of conflict resolution is willingness to accept the notion that there are flaws on one's own side as well as on the opponent's side. This is the sensible stand if one's goal is to get along with others and avoid violence.[20]

But what if that is not one's goal? A bellicose stance fundamentally contradicts the purpose of compromise and understanding, and adopting an inflexible position of militancy early in a dispute calls into question the motive for doing so. A warring attitude implies that its holder no longer thinks compromise is possible or—just as likely—did not want an accommodating solution to the conflict in the first place. In fact, if one's goal is not harmony but the empowerment that comes with using violence, it is in one's interest to be in a state of war. In such cases, war is not only the context for violence but also the excuse for it. War provides a reason to be violent. This is true even if the worldly issues at heart in the dispute do not seem to warrant such a ferocious position.

This may explain why acts of terrorism seem so puzzling to people outside the movements that perpetrate them and entirely understandable to those within them. The response to abortion clinic bombings and the killing of abortion doctors is a case in point. To many people in the United States the issue of abortion is a serious moral concern, a matter of public policy worth discussing, debating, protesting, and fighting over. But as heated as the subject may be, few on either side would regard this issue as one for which they are prepared to die or to kill.

Rev. Michael Bray takes a different position. He has defended the need to kill and, if necessary, to die over the issue of abortion, but not because he sees it as a matter of public policy. Rather, he sees the imposition of laws accepting abortion—and homosexuality, for that matter—as symptoms of a much greater conflict and a more devious form of social control. From his perspective American society has been in the grip of a demonic force for some time, and the great struggle to liberate it has only begun. There has been a great war going on, he alleges, one that goes unseen largely because the enemy has imposed its control gradually and subtly. As a result, the masses are unaware of the enemy's power and unconcerned over its effects.

From Bray's point of view the world is already at war, one that he regards as similar to World War II. "The issues are comparable," Bray told me, adding that "the issues that would justify violence now are the same."[21] Bray is impressed by the enormous sense of guilt that has saddled many Christians as they recall the gradual imposition of Nazi power and their indifference and inactivity during those awful years. The Nuremberg trials brought to public awareness much of what had transpired and implicated otherwise sensitive Christians in a silent complicity with the Nazis. Now, Bray reflected, Christians say to themselves, "would that we had moved earlier" to stop the killing. This situation Bray compares with the killing involved in abortions.

What disturbs Bray is not just the slaughter of what he describes as the "unborn," but also what he feels is a Nazi-like attitude—a disregard for human life and a penchant for indiscriminate killing—that characterizes the ruling powers of contemporary American society. He despairs that overt rebellion or revolution against this power will occur only with an economic collapse or social chaos sufficiently catastrophic to make people aware of the situation, "to give people the strength or the zeal to take up arms."[22] In the meantime, what he calls "defensive acts," and what most Americans call terrorism, can provide public reminders of the silent war that is going on and perhaps serve as a wake-up call for Americans to join the rebellion.

Michael Bray's vision of a world caught in an imminent and almost eschatological confrontation between the forces of good and evil arrayed on the battlefield of politics is not idiosyncratic: it is remarkably similar to the view promoted by militant Sikhs in India, the Aum Shinrikyo in Japan, Rabbi Kahane's Kach party in Israel, Sheik Omar Abdul Rahman's following in Egypt and New Jersey, and other groups associated with recent acts of terrorism. Theirs have been acts of desperation in response to what they perceive as a desperate situation: a world gone terribly awry. What is strikingly similar about the cultures of which they are a part is their view of the contemporary world at war.

In Japan, for instance, the members of Aum Shinrikyo have posited that the world is on the brink of a conflagration similar to World War II. What the Japanese remember about that war is not so much the genocide of Hitler as the annihilation of Japanese cities under the rain of American bombs, including the largest weapons of mass destruction ever used against an opponent: the atomic bombs that destroyed

Hiroshima and Nagasaki. It is this reign of terror that is returning, the spiritual master of Aum Shinrikyo prophesied, in a war that will be even more catastrophic than World War II. "The weapons used in World War III," Asahara told his followers, "will make the atomic and hydrogen bombs look like toys."[23] Although the full force of the great war would not be apparent until 1999, the first stages of Armageddon, as he called it, had arrived years earlier at Japanese shores.

Master Asahara waxed eloquent about the nature of this great conflagration, this Armageddon. Its goal, he said, would be "to completely annihilate the cities, produce a state of anarchy, and then establish a worldwide, unified political power."[24] The shadowy forces behind this plot included Jewish capitalists, Freemasons, the American army, and the Japanese government. The takeover was so subtle, however, that most people were not aware of it. This is where the prophetic teachings of Aum Shinrikyo were so important: they allowed the enlightened few to be cognizant of the coming disaster and to prepare for it. As far as its followers knew, the creation of nerve gas in Aum chemical laboratories was solely for the purpose of developing preventive medicines and devices to protect those in the movement against poisonous gases once Armaggedon arrived and the evil forces began to use chemical weapons against the populace. Only the most loyal were willing to believe these prophecies without any evidence that World War III was in fact beginning. The release of nerve gas in the Tokyo subways provided dramatic proof of the prophecies—at least to Asahara's followers, and to them only until it became clear that Asahara himself was implicated in the attack.

The Christian Identity scenario of cosmic war is also something of a self-fulfilling prophecy. According to Identity teaching, contemporary social struggles can be traced back to a conflict as old as the creation of the universe, when Lucifer, the satanic anti-God of the underworld, became jealous of God's order, conspired to seize the world, and yearned to establish his own kingdom of evil.[25] Christianity was a major effort by God to counteract Lucifer, but it was plagued from the start by Lucifer's forces. Some of Lucifer's agents came in the guise of people who claimed to be Jews but in fact were not; the true Jews were Aryans, according to Identity doctrine. Those who called themselves Jews were in fact Lucifer's henchmen out to confound Christians. Even the apostle Paul was suspect. The emergence of Roman Catholicism as the dominant form of European Christianity was a "fraud." Freemasons were also implicated in this conspiracy. In recent years the "Jewish-Catholic-

Freemason agents of Satan" were thought to have received powerful allies in the form of communists and liberal democrats.

Followers of Christian Identity offer a book as proof that all of these forces are allied against the relatively small band of pure white Protestant Christians. This spurious manual, *The Protocols of the Learned Elders of Zion*, is alleged to be the handiwork of a Zionist congress held at Basel, Switzerland, in 1897 under the leadership of Theodor Herzl. According to James Aho, a sociologist who was shown a copy of the document, it contains twenty-four specific steps necessary for the Jewish-communist conspiracy to take over the world. They itemize trends in global society that presumably were occurring when the fictional document was written but are presented as prophetic, as if they had been written at the time alleged, at the end of the nineteenth century. These trends include the establishment of corporate monopolies, arms races, the promotion of civil rights for minorities, the advocacy of free speech, the encouragement of pornography, progressive income taxes, and the establishment of a national bank (such as the Federal Reserve Corporation, widely thought by Christian Identity followers to be an instrument of sinister economic control).[26] Credit cards that could be electronically traced and the use of social security numbers for identification purposes were cited as further indications of governmental control. The fact that all of these items are part of modern society and are promoted or protected by the government constitutes simple proof to Identity activists that such a conspiracy exists and is succeeding.

Christian militias, therefore, are defensive responses to an ancient and ongoing war that Identity activists believe is threatening their lives and their way of living. The Michigan Militia, for example, the twelve thousand–member paramilitary survivalist organization to which Timothy McVeigh has been linked, has promoted the idea that the U.S. government has already initiated a program to completely control the life of every American. Accordingly, through training in guerrilla warfare and survivalist techniques, the militia has prepared itself to resist what it maintains are plans by the Clinton administration to deploy United Nations forces utilizing cast-off Soviet military equipment or hordes of communist Chinese troops, backed by Latino and black inner-city American street gangs, to crush any opposition.

The Christian Identity–influenced novel *The Turner Diaries* imagines a scenario that begins with a liberal-dominated Congress enacting a law abolishing private ownership of firearms. To enforce the act, legions of "jackbooted" federal agents stalk the countryside, seizing weapons wherever they find them. Seeing this as a move toward federal dictatorship, a group of white Christian patriots form an underground cell to resist. They adopt guerrilla tactics, creating a homemade bomb from ammonium nitrate and fuel oil, which they load on a delivery truck parked outside FBI headquarters in Washington, DC. According to the novel, the subsequent explosion kills seven hundred people. The *Washington Post* supposedly receives a telephone call with the message "White America shall live." It is a scenario that was played out in chilling detail in real life by Timothy McVeigh and his colleagues in demolishing the Oklahoma City federal building.

Religious struggles in other parts of the world—even those that seem more rational, in that they relate to contentions over the control of land to which both sides have legitimate claims—nonetheless have employed images of warfare on a grand scale. Yochay Ron, the young Jewish activist with whom I talked at the graveside of Dr. Goldstein near Hebron, told me that the war with the Arabs did not begin with the intifada in the 1980s, or even with the establishment of the state of Israel. It goes back "to biblical times," Ron explained, indicating that the present-day Arabs are simply the modern descendants of the enemies of Israel described in the Bible for whom God has unleashed wars of revenge.[27] Ultimately, he thought that the warfare could end, but only when Arabs leave the land and Israel is, in his view, complete. Sarah Nachshon, who like Ron lived in the embattled Beit Hadassah settlement in Hebron, also understood the violence of the present day to be explained as warfare: "It's written in the Bible," she said, "that until the Messiah comes there will be a big war, and the war will be in Jerusalem."[28]

The Palestinian conflict is conceived as something larger than a contest between Arabs and Jews: it is a cosmic struggle of Manichaean proportions. This view is shared by religious activists on both sides. Sheik Yassin, for example, described the conflict in virtually eschatological terms as "the combat between good and evil." A communiqué issued by Hamas when Americans sent troops to the Saudia Arabian desert following Saddam Hussein's invasion of Kuwait in 1990 declared it to be "another episode in the fight between good and evil" and "a hateful Christian plot against our religion, our civilization and our land."[29]

Insofar as the Islamic use of this grand polarity suggests a metaphysical duality between the spiritual and material order, it is theologically out of line with a strict monotheism that encompasses everything ultimately within the sphere of God. Khomeini's one-time associate

Banisadr wrote at some length about the notion of struggle, explaining how, although the monotheism of Islam does not allow for a division between the world and the spirit—for it does not recognize that duality—it does allow for a struggle against duality itself.[30] Thus it is possible, Banisadr argued, for grand conflict to occur even within the theological borders of Islam.

The absolutism of cosmic war makes compromise unlikely, and those who suggest a negotiated settlement are as excoriated as the enemy. In the Palestinian situation, the extreme religious positions on both sides condemn the carefully negotiated compromise created by Israel's Yitzhak Rabin and Palestine's Yasir Arafat. "There is no such thing as coexistence," Yoel Lerner told me, explaining that there is a biblical requirement for Jews to possess and live on biblical land. This is why he despises the peace accords, and regards Israeli leaders as treasonous for signing them.[31] Later on the same day in which I had this conversation with Lerner, I met with Hamas leaders in Gaza and heard Dr. Abdul Aziz Rantisi say essentially the same thing about the necessity for Arab Muslims to occupy what he regarded as their homeland. Like Lerner, Rantisi expressed anger toward the secular leadership—in his case, Arafat—for having entered into a dangerous and futile path toward an accommodation deemed to be impossible.[32] The extremists on both sides—Lerner and Rantisi—preferred war over peace.

One of the reasons a state of war is preferable to peace is that it gives moral justification to acts of violence. Violence, in turn, offers the illusion of power. Christian Reconstruction theologians argue that public executions are appropriate in a time of warfare, implying that they, rather than the state, can mete out punitive judgments. In a similar vein, followers of Christian Identity claim that in a time of war the ends justify the means, thereby rationalizing their attempts to confound the everyday workings of secular society. When asked if he would consider the use of poison to contaminate the water supply of a major American city, a member of the Phineas Priesthood said, "When one is at war, one has to consider such things, unfortunately."[33] Rev. Michael Bray made an ethical distinction between what is legal in a peaceful society and what is morally justified in a situation of warfare: the latter includes transgressing property rights and laws against murder. In an interesting way, Bray's argument is similar to that of the assassin of Mohandas Gandhi, Nathuram

Godse, who in his court trial eloquently justified what he called his "moral" though "illegal" act of killing the mahatma.[34]

The idea of warfare implies more than an attitude; ultimately it is a world view and an assertion of power. To live in a state of war is to live in a world in which individuals know who they are, why they have suffered, by whose hand they have been humiliated, and at what expense they have persevered. The concept of war provides cosmology, history, and eschatology and offers the reins of political control. Perhaps most important, it holds out the hope of victory and the means to achieve it. In the images of cosmic war this victorious triumph is a grand moment of social and personal transformation, transcending all worldly limitations. One does not easily abandon such expectations. To be without such images of war is almost to be without hope itself.

Symbolic War

"That was the most marvellous experience of my life," explained Richard Butler, describing his first reaction to the Christian Identity theory of cosmic war. "The lights started turning on, bang-bang-bang," Butler, the dean of the Identity movement, told a reporter for the *Los Angeles Times* in 1999.[35] Butler went on to say that the knowledge that "war had been going on for over six thousand years between the sons of Cain and the sons of God" was a cathartic experience for him, "opening up who we were, where we came from, and why we were there." He added that this epiphany was "the greatest thrill" he ever had, and from this moment on he knew "what my mission was."

"Wow, this is it," Denver Parmenter exclaimed in similar terms as he related how he discovered Christian Identity teachings. He claimed that this view of ancient and continuing warfare led to a sudden stroke of awareness that provided him "the reason things are going wrong."[36] This grand scenario gave him a view of the world that he could participate in, thus helping him not only to understand his destiny but to control it.

Like the rituals provided by religious traditions, warfare is a participatory drama that exemplifies—and thus explains—the most profound aspects of life. It has great appeal, then, for people such as Butler and Parmenter who feel not only confused about what is going on in their lives but also buffeted by unseen forces. Parmenter was able to directly participate in this struggle by taking part in the plot to kill a Jewish radio talk show host whom Parmenter and his Identity colleagues thought was an agent of Satan.

The idea of warfare has long had an eerie and intimate relationship with religion. History is studded with overtly religious conflicts such as the Crusades, the Muslim conquests, and the Wars of Religion that dominated the politics of France in the sixteenth century. Although these have usually been characterized as wars in the name of religion rather than wars conducted in a religious way, historian Natalie Zemon Davis has uncovered what she calls "rites of violence" in her study of religious riots in sixteenth-century France. These constituted "a repertory of actions, derived from the Bible, from the liturgy, from the action of political authority, or from the traditions of popular folk practices, intended to purify the religious community and humiliate the enemy and thus make him less harmful." Davis observed that the violence was "aimed at defined targets and selected from a repertory of traditional punishments and forms of destruction."[37] According to Davis, "even the extreme ways of defiling corpses—dragging bodies through the streets and throwing them to the dogs, dismembering genitalia and selling them in mock commerce—and desecrating religious objects" had what she called "perverse connections" with religious concepts of pollution and purification, heresy, and blasphemy.[38]

Anthropologist Stanley Tambiah showed how the same "rites of violence" were present in the religious riots of South Asia.[39] In some instances innocent bystanders would be snatched up by a crowd and burned alive. According to Tambiah, these horrifying murders of defenseless and terrified victims were done in a ritual manner, in "mock imitation of both the self-immolation of conscientious objectors and the terminal rite of cremation."[40]

In a macabre way, the riotous battles described by Davis and Tambiah were religious events. But given the prominence of the rhetoric of warfare in religious vocabulary, both traditional and modern, one can turn this point around and say that religious events often require the participants to invoke images of battle. One can argue that the task of creating a vicarious experience of warfare—albeit one usually imagined as residing on a spiritual plane—is one of the main businesses of religion.

Virtually all cultural traditions have contained martial metaphors. The ideas of a Salvation Army in Christianity and a Dal Khalsa ("army of the faithful") in Sikhism characterize disciplined religious organizations. Images of spiritual warfare are even more common. The Muslim

notion of *jihad* is the most notable example, but even in Buddhist leg-
ends great wars are to be found. In Sri Lankan culture, for instance, virtually canonical status is accorded to the legendary history recorded in
the Pali Chronicles, the *Dipavamsa* and the *Mahavamsa*, that relate the
triumphs of battles waged by Buddhist kings. In India, warfare has con-
tributed to the grandeur of the great epics, the *Ramayana* and the
Mahabharata, which are tales of seemingly unending conflict and military intrigue. More than the Vedic rituals, these martial epics defined
subsequent Hindu culture. Whole books of the Hebrew Bible are devoted to the military exploits of great kings, their contests related in
gory detail. Though the New Testament did not take up the battle cry,
the later history of the Church did, supplying Christianity with a
bloody record of crusades and religious wars.

Warfare has not just been relegated to religion's legendary histories,
however; it is also intricately related to its contemporary symbols.[41]
Protestant Christianity is an example. Though the reformed tradition is
strongly pacifist, martial images abound in the rhetoric and symbolism
of the faith. Protestant preachers everywhere have encouraged their
flocks to wage war against the forces of evil, and their homilies are followed with hymns about "Christian soldiers," fighting "the good
fight," and struggling "manfully onward."[42] One scholar of popular
Protestantism, Harriet Crabtree, surveyed the images that are prominent in what she called the "popular theologies" projected in the
hymns, tracts, and sermons of modern Protestant Christianity, and
found the "model of warfare" to be one of the most enduring.[43]

What is significant about the popular Protestant talk about war,
Crabtree stated, is that the image was meant to be taken more than
metaphorically. When the writers of hymns urged "soldiers of the
Cross" to "stand up, stand up for Jesus," this was interpreted as a requirement for real, albeit spiritual, combat. Protestant writers such as
Arthur Wallis have claimed that "Christian living *is* war." Wallis explained that the warfare is not "a metaphor or a figure of speech" but
a "literal fact"; the character of the war, however—"the sphere, the
weapons, and the foe"—are spiritual rather than material.[44] Crabtree
asserted that the image of warfare is attractive because it "situates the
listener or reader in the religious cosmos."[45]

The images of warfare in Protestant Christianity situated the faithful
in a religious cosmos that inevitably had a moral valence, but this has
not been the case in all traditions. The battles of the *Mahavamsa*, the
Hebrew Bible, and the Hindu epics, for example, testify to a different

sort of ultimate encounter. The motif that runs through these mythic scenes of warfare is the theme of us versus them, the known versus the unknown. In the battles described in the Hebrew Bible and in such epics as the *Ramayana,* the enemies were often foreigners from the shady edges of known civilization—places such as Canaan, Philistine, and Lanka. These foes often embodied the conceptual murkiness of their origins; that is, they represented what was chaotic and uncertain about the world, including those things that defied categorization altogether. In cases where the enemy possessed a familiar face—as in the *Mahabharata,* where war was waged between sets of cousins—chaos is embodied by the battle itself. It is the wickedness of warfare itself that the battle depicts, as the mythic figure Arjuna observed at the outset of his encounter with Lord Krishna on the battlefield.[46] To fight in such a circumstance was to assent to the disorder of this world, although the contestants knew that in a grander sense this disorder is corrected by a cosmic order that is beyond killing and being killed. Such was the message of Lord Krishna in his address to Arjuna in the *Bhagavad Gita.*[47]

Ultimately, such struggles are battles against the most chaotic aspect of reality: death. Among scholars, there is a persistent recognition that much of the religious imagination has been built around notions of the afterlife and the overcoming of human frailty and corruption—often symbolized by rituals involving the avoidance of pollution. The Jewish notion of raising the dead, the Christian and Muslim notions of heaven and hell, the Roman Catholic concept of purgatory, the Buddhist idea of levels of consciousness (and, in the Mahayana tradition, heavenly mansions), and the Hindu theory of karmic cycles of reincarnation—all of these offer ways of avoiding what humans know to be a fact: eventually they will die. Even bodily decay and corruption can supposedly be postponed by Jewish, Hindu, and other rituals of pollution avoidance. All of this adds up to what Ernest Becker has called religion's "denial of death."[48]

I agree with Becker, but what strikes me is the way religion has employed symbols of violence not only to deny death but to control all that is intimately related to death: disorder, destruction, and decay. By evoking and then bridling images of warfare, religion has symbolically controlled not only violence but all of the messiness of life. It is interesting in this regard that the etymology of the modern English term *war* is the Old English word *werra* (or *guerra* in Old French), which means "confusion," "discord," or "strife" and in verb form implies the bring-

ing into a state of confusion or discord. In this sense war is the ultimate
state of confusion, as many soldiers who have been in battle can confirm.

When religious cultures portray warfare as something that is acknowledged and ultimately controlled, therefore, they are presenting an
almost cosmological reenactment of the primacy of order over chaos.
In the stained glass windows of the great European cathedrals portraying Christ as king, emerging from his grave like a general victorious in
battle, the designers were stating something fundamental about
Christianity and every other religious tradition: religion reaffirms the
primacy of order, which requires that violence and other forms of disorder be conquered.

The irony of these bloody images is that the object of faith has always been peace. But in order to portray a state of harmony convinc-
ingly, religion has had to emphasize disharmony and its ability to contain it. Religion has dealt with violence, therefore, not only because
violence is unruly and has to be tamed, but because religion, as the ultimate statement of meaningfulness, must always assert the primacy of
meaning in the face of chaos. For that reason, religion has been order
restoring and life affirming even though it has justified the taking of life
in particular instances. Jesus' heroic and sacrificial act in allowing himself to be painfully put to death, for instance, has been seen by the faithful as a monumental act of redemption for humankind, tipping the balance of power and allowing a struggle for order to succeed.

Religious images have been mechanisms through which peace and
order can conquer violence and chaos, so it is understandable that the violence portrayed in religion has been in some way controlled—in the air
of normalcy with which the "body of Christ" is eaten in the Christian ritual of Eucharist, for instance, and the lack of self-consciousness with
which Christians sing hymns filled with talk of blood and battle. In ritual, violence is symbolically transformed. The blood of the Eucharistic
wine is ingested by the supplicant and becomes part of living tissue; it
brings new life. In song a similarly calming transformation occurs as the
images are absorbed aurally. As Christian theology explains, in Christ violence has been bridled. Christ died in order for death to be defeated, and
his blood was sacrificed so that his faithful followers could be rescued
from a punishment as gruesome as that which he suffered.

Other religious traditions have dealt with violence in much the same
way. In the Sikh tradition, for instance, the two-edged sword provides
an image of the domestication of violence. This familiar symbol has

been worn on lockets and proudly emblazoned on shops and garden gates, and it stands in front of Sikh *gurdwaras*, where it is treated as reverently as Christians treat their own emblem of destruction and triumph, the cross. Other images of violence in Sikhism also have functioned like their counterparts in Christianity: the gory wounds of Sikh martyrs, like those of Christian saints, bleed on in calendar art as a reminder that because their blood was shed, the faithful need fear no harm. Sikh theologians and writers, like those in the Christian faith, have been eager to explain the meaning of such symbols and stories allegorically. They point toward the war between belief and unbelief that rages in each person's soul. In a similar way, interpreters of Jewish and Islamic culture have transformed the martial images in their traditions. The chroniclers of the Hebrew Bible have seen acts of war as God's vengeance. So too have Muslim historians; some Islamic mystics have even spoken of the true jihad as the one within each person's soul.

Thus violent images have been given religious meaning and domesticized. These acts, although terribly real, have been sanitized by becoming symbols; they have been stripped of their horror by being invested with religious meaning. They have been justified and thereby exonerated as part of a religious template that is even larger than myth and history. They are elements of a ritual scenario that makes it possible for the people involved to experience safely the drama of cosmic war.

When Symbols Become Deadly

But if religious images are meant to conquer violence, one must ask the obvious but difficult question: why and how are these symbolic presentations of violence occasionally linked to real acts of violence? They should prevent violent acts by allowing the human urges to conquer and control to be channeled into the harmless dramas of ritual. Yet we know that the opposite is often the case. The riotous rites of violence described by Natalie Davis and Stanley Tambiah in the texts cited earlier in this chapter and the abundant examples of religious terrorism referred to throughout this book have demonstrated that the violence of religion has, at times, been savagely real.

The question of why images of cosmic struggle are translated into real acts of violence is complicated, since the line between symbolic and actual violence is thin. Symbols are sometimes more than just fictional representations of the real thing. Rites of sacrifice, for instance, often involve killing, and feats of martyrdom lead to death. This symbiosis between symbolic and real violence is profound and goes to the very heart of the religious imagination. It is a relationship that we will explore more fully in the next chapter.

For now, however, we can speculate on the conditions that make it likely for cosmic war to be located on a worldly stage. One way of doing this is to identify the aspects of religious thinking that link spiritual struggle with worldly conflict. It was this approach that I attempted several years ago when I was studying the rhetoric of religious violence in Sikhism. I came up with a list of several conditions, including the following, indicating when Sikhism—or any religious tradition—is susceptible to becoming associated with actual acts of violence:

The cosmic struggle is understood to be occurring in this world rather than in a mythical setting.

Believers identify personally with the struggle.

The struggle is at a point of crisis in which individual action can make all the difference.[49]

Although I still regard this as a useful list of conditions, my comparative study of terrorism has encouraged me to think about the problem in another way, one that complements this perspective. In many of the cases discussed in this book, not only have religion's characteristics led spiritual persons into violence, but also the other way around: violent situations have reached out for religious justification. The two approaches are not contradictory: extremism in religion has led to violence at the same time that violent conflicts have cried out for religious validation. But because I emphasized the former approach in my earlier studies, I wish to focus on the latter here.

Rather than beginning with religious images, then, this approach starts with real-life situations; rather than why religion leads to violence, the question is why real-world struggles involve religion. The following characteristics, based on the case studies in this book, indicate when a confrontation in the world is likely to take on the trappings of cosmic war:

WHEN CONFRONTATION IS LIKELY TO BE CHARACTERIZED
AS COSMIC WAR

1. *The struggle is perceived as a defense of basic identity and dignity.* If the struggle is thought to be of ultimate significance—a defense not only of lives but of entire cultures, such as Sikhism or Islam—the pos-

sibility is greater that it will be seen as a cultural war with spiritual implications. The Irish confrontation, for instance, became spiritualized
when Rev. Ian Paisley interpreted it as an attack on Protestantism, and
the Palestinian struggle took on a religious aura after a significant number of sheiks and mullahs interpreted it as a defense of Islam. In other
cases, the very nature of the issues—such as abortion or the sanctity of
life—can attract religious activists, such as the followers of Christian
Identity and Christian Reconstruction, whose involvement has spiritualized the anti-abortion struggle. A sense of personal humiliation, such as
Dr. Goldstein's belief that Jews were being humiliated by the Israeli
government's protection of Arab Muslims, can lead to desperate attempts to recover both personal dignity and cultural pride.

2. *Losing the struggle would be unthinkable.* If a negative outcome
to the struggle is perceived as beyond human conception, the struggle
may be viewed as taking place on a transhistorical plane. Some
Palestinian Muslims, for instance, have refused to even consider the
idea of a Jewish state in what they regard as Arab territory. Similarly,
some radical Jews have regarded the Israeli government's return of biblical lands to Arabs as unthinkable. The more that goals are reified and
made inflexible, the greater the possibility that they will be deified and
seen as the fulfillment of holy writ.

3. *The struggle is blocked and cannot be won in real time or in real
terms.* Perhaps most important, if the struggle is seen as hopeless in
human terms, it is likely that it may be reconceived on a sacred plane,
where the possibilities of victory are in God's hands. When Shoko
Asahara felt trapped by the Japanese police, he created an act that he
thought would elevate the struggle to the level of cosmic war, just as
Rev. Jim Jones did in Guyana when he chose a suicidal act of violence
to escape what he feared would be capture and defeat. According to
Weston LaBarre, these moments of desperation precipitate religion. He
described a poignant historical moment in 1870 when a group of Plains
Indians from the Paiute tribe were trapped by the U.S. Cavalry and responded by spontaneously creating a ritual of dancing and hypnotic
trances known as the Ghost Dance religion.[50] LaBarre's study indicates
when religion and its grand scenarios of cosmic war are needed most:
in hopeless moments, when mythical strength provides the only resources at hand.

The presence of any of these three characteristics increases the likelihood that a real-world struggle may be conceived in cosmic terms as

a sacred war. The occurrence of all three simultaneously strongly suggests it. A struggle that begins on worldly terms may gradually take on the characteristics of cosmic war as solutions become unlikely and awareness grows of how devastating it would be to lose. The Arab-Israeli conflict, for example, was not widely regarded as a sacred battle from the perspective of either side until the late 1980s. Then the process of sacralization overtook the conflict and transformed it, in the eyes of religious activists on both sides, into cosmic war.

When a struggle becomes sacralized, incidents that might previously have been considered minor skirmishes or slight differences of understanding are elevated to monumental proportions. The use of violence becomes legitimized, and the slightest provocation or insult can lead to terrorist assaults. What had been simple opponents become cosmic foes. As the next chapter shows, the process of satanization can transform a worldly struggle into a contest between martyrs and demons. Alas, this inescapable scenario of hostility does not end until the mythology is redirected, or until one side or the other has been destroyed.

CHAPTER 9

Martyrs and Demons

When Timothy McVeigh was sentenced to death on August 14, 1997, he was allowed to say a few words to the court. The convicted bomber of the Oklahoma City federal building chose this special occasion to do something that many in the courtroom thought odd, especially considering the highly antisocial nature of his crime: he quoted from Supreme Court Justice Louis Brandeis. The passage came from a statement in which the justice had cautioned the government against acting improperly in the case of illegal wiretaps during Prohibition. "Our government is the potent, the omnipresent teacher," Justice Brandeis wrote, adding that "for good or ill, it teaches the whole people by its example."[1]

Most interpreted McVeigh's use of this quotation as an assertion that the government was setting a bad example by sentencing him to death. In this sense it was a classic case of the murderer blaming his victim. It was the government, McVeigh seemed to say, that was doing the killing rather than him. In another sense, however, this is what McVeigh had been saying all along—that the government was the enemy. In his dramatic moment in the courtroom, Timothy McVeigh was vaunting his actions as part of an enormously important and historical struggle and articulating what he felt this larger scenario was about: a conflict between liberty and slavery, a cosmic war in which both he and the government had critical, though opposing, roles to play.

The fact that McVeigh was sentenced to death might appear to indicate that the war was nearly over and he had lost. Yet by putting his actions into the larger frame of history, McVeigh was stating that the war was far from over, and the resolution was still uncertain. Dr. Abdul Aziz Rantisi, the political leader of Hamas, told me virtually the same thing about his movement's struggle against Israel. Although he admitted that things did not look promising now, he assured me that the fight would be waged for years, perhaps generations, to come. "Look at history," he said. "Palestine has been occupied before, for two hundred years, and then liberated. This time," he added, "we have been occupied for only fifty years. We have to wait."[2] Rantisi said that the apotheosis might not come in his lifetime, but perhaps in his children's lifetime. Eventually it would come.

As Dr. Rantisi implied, the point of every story is its ending. Insofar as the scenario of cosmic war is a story, it carries a momentum toward its completion and contains the seeds of hope for its outcome. I use the term *hope* rather than *fear*, for no one wants to believe in a story that cannot produce a happy ending. Those who accept that their life struggles are part of a great struggle, a cosmic war, know that they are part of a grand tale that will ultimately end triumphantly, though not necessarily easily or quickly. The epic character of the story implies that the happy ending may indeed be long delayed—perhaps until after one's lifetime or after the lifetimes of one's descendants. In the meantime, the story will involve sadness and travail. Christians recall that Jesus, for example, triumphed over death only after being subjected to the gruesome and humiliating spectacle of public execution.

Overcoming defeat and humiliation is the point of war. The story of warfare explains why one feels for a time beaten and disgraced—that is part of the warrior's experience. In cases of cosmic war, however, the final battle has not been fought. Only when it has can one expect triumph and pride. Until that time, the warrior struggles on, often armed only with hope. Our personal tales of woe gain meaning, then, when linked to these powerful stories. Their sagas of oppression and liberation lift the spirits of individuals and make their suffering explicable and noble. In some cases suffering imparts the nobility of martyrdom. In such instances the images of cosmic war forge failure—even death—into victory.

Sacrificial Victims

This notion of a heroic, transforming death is the message projected by the architecture of the shrine that for a time accompanied Dr. Baruch Goldstein's grave near Hebron—an elegant plaza surrounded by plaques set inside boxes accompanied by votive candles that looked not unlike the stations of the cross in a Catholic sanctuary. It was clearly a shrine, a shrine for someone the young man guarding it described as both a martyr and a "hero in war."[3] A similar attitude attended the funeral celebrations for the young Muslim men who gave up their lives in acts of "self-martyrdom," as the Hamas leaders like to call them. These celebrations were remarkable events recorded on the videotapes of the men giving their ardent last statements the night before their deaths. The tapes were then clandestinely circulated throughout Gaza and the West Bank as a sort of recruitment device for likeminded young men. These events were not really funerals, a fact symbolized by the drinking of sweetened rather than bitter coffee, the distribution of sweets, and the singing of wedding songs. A cross between a marriage and a religious festival, these affairs were a modern example of an ancient religious ritual: the sanctification of martyrs.

Similar events have attended the memorials for martyrs in other religious movements. Activist Sikhs have proudly displayed pictures of the fallen leader Sant Jarnail Singh Bhindranwale, who died as a result of the military operation ordered by India's prime minister Indira Gandhi in 1984. His image has been displayed as prominently as those of the founding gurus of the tradition, and he has been remembered on both his birthday and his martyrdom day. Followers revere Bhindranwale for what they regard as his exemplary model of commitment. As one of his young followers told me, "He went to his death for what he believed."[4] The brother of one of the Khalistani leaders killed in a government encounter told me virtually the same thing: Bhindranwale "didn't just say words, he backed them up with deeds."[5]

It was a sentiment echoed by Rev. Michael Bray with regard to his friend, Rev. Paul Hill. In 1997, as the date of Hill's execution drew near, Bray began to produce publications announcing Hill's impending martyrdom, not only to rally support that might keep that event from happening, but also to give it religious significance in the likelihood that it would. "We must plead with the powers that are," Bray wrote, to spare the life of a man "who was called by God to the sacrificial, public witness he made" and was sentenced to die only "for doing justice and showing mercy." Bray regarded Hill as a martyr, and he lashed out at the brutality of a government that would take such a noble person's life.[6]

Absent from Bray's sense of outrage was any respect for the lives of Dr. John Britton and his volunteer escort, James Barrett, which Hill terminated—or "aborted," as Bray put it—in a brutal act of double murder. In a curious twist of logic, Bray had made out Hill to be the victim rather than the murderer that the state and most of the American public regarded him to be. In this way Bray was like those who mourned the deaths of Dr. Baruch Goldstein, Sant Jarnail Singh Bhindranwale, and the Hamas suicide bombers—each of whom sent scores of innocent people to early graves. Billy Wright, who had been convicted for his role in the terrorist acts conducted by the Protestant Ulster Volunteer Force paramilitary group, said that "there's no doubt" that within "every terrorist" there is the conviction that "he is the victim." According to Wright, this allows the terrorist to justify his action "morally within his own mind."[7]

A similar point was made by Dr. Rantisi when he stressed in his interview that Arab Muslims were the true victims in the confrontation rather than the savage perpetrators of suicide attacks the Western media portrayed them to be. He recounted the injustices done against himself, his family, and other Arabs over the years to demonstrate that the experience of victimage had preceded these violent attacks. It was an argument similar to the one made by Osama bin Laden in his February 1998 fatwa against America, in which he claimed that his acts were defensive, since it was America who declared war on Muslims by its "crimes and sins" committed in the Middle East.[8] The incidents of terrorism undertaken by activists such as Rantisi, bin Laden, and their operatives were thus justified by their followers as defensive acts of noble fighters. If they succeeded in their mission unscathed, they were heroes; if they died in the process, they were martyrs.

The idea of martyrdom is an interesting one. It has a long history within various religious traditions, including early Christianity. Christ himself was a martyr, as was the founder of the Shi'i Muslim tradition, Husain. The word *martyr* comes from a Greek term for "witness," such as a witness to one's faith. In most cases martyrdom is regarded not only as a testimony to the degree of one's commitment, but also as a performance of a religious act, specifically an act of self-sacrifice.

This dimension of martyrdom links it to the activity that some scholars see as the most fundamental form of religiosity: sacrifice. It is a rite of destruction that is found, remarkably, in virtually every religious tradition in the world. The term suggests that the very process of destroying is spiritual since the word comes from the Latin, *sacrificium,* "to make holy." What makes sacrifice so riveting is not just that it involves killing, but also that it is, in an ironic way, ennobling. The destruction is performed within a religious context that transforms the killing into

something positive. Thus, like all religious images of sacrifice, martyrdom provides symbols of a violence conquered—or at least put in its
place—by the larger framework of order that religious language provides.

There is some evidence that ancient religious rites of sacrifice, like
the destruction involved in modern-day terrorism, were performances
involving the murder of living beings. The later domestication of sacrifice in evolved forms of religious practice, such as the Christian ritual
of the Eucharist, masked the fact that in most early forms of sacrifice a
real animal—in some cases a human—offered its life on a sacred chopping block, an altar. In the Hebrew Bible, which is sacred to Jews,
Christians, and Muslims, the book of Leviticus gives a detailed guide
for preparing animals for sacrificial slaughter. The very architecture of
ancient Israeli temples reflected the centrality of the sacrificial event.
The Vedic Agnicayana ritual, some three thousand years old and probably the most ancient ritual still performed today, involves the construction of an elaborate altar for sacrificial ritual, which some claim
was originally a human sacrifice.[9] This was certainly so at the other side
of the world at the time of the ancient Aztec empire, when conquered
soldiers were treated royally in preparation for their role in the sacrificial rite. Then they were set upon with knives. Their still-beating hearts
were ripped from their chests and offered to Huitzilopochtli and other
gods, eventually to be eaten by the faithful, and their faces were
skinned to make ritual masks.

Why are such gory acts of sacrifice central to religion? The attempt
to find answers to that question has been a preoccupation of scholars
for over a century. The insights of such pioneering thinkers as Émile
Durkheim and Sigmund Freud have been revived by recent scholars, including Maurice Bloch, René Girard, Walter Burkhert, and Eli Sagan,
who give social and psychological reasons for the virtual universality of
violence in religious images and ideas.[10] Most of them see the symbols
of violence as playing an ultimately nonviolent and socially useful role.

According to Freud, for instance, violent religious symbols and sacrificial rituals evoke, and thereby vent, violent impulses in general.
Accepting Freud's main thesis, Girard amended it by suggesting that the
motivation for violence is "mimetic desire"—the desire to imitate a
rival—rather than the psychological instincts of sexuality and aggression.
Like Freud, Girard claimed that ritualized violence performs a positive
role for society. By allowing individuals to release their feelings of hostility toward members of their own communities, symbols of violence en-

able affinity groups to achieve greater social cohesion. "The function of ritual," claimed Girard, "is to 'purify' violence; that is, to 'trick' violence into spending itself on victims whose death will provoke no reprisals."[11] Those who participate in ritual are not consciously aware of the social and psychological significance of their acts, of course, for Girard claimed that "religion tries to account for its own operation metaphorically."[12]

Much of what Freud and Girard said about the function of symbolic violence in religion has been persuasive. Even if one questions, as I do, Girard's idea that mimetic desire is the sole driving force behind symbols of religious violence, one can still agree that mimesis is a significant factor. One can also agree with the theme that Girard borrows from Freud, that the ritualized acting out of violent acts plays a role in displacing feelings of aggression, thereby allowing the world to be a more peaceful place in which to live. But the critical issue remains as to whether sacrifice should be regarded as the context for viewing all other forms of religious violence, as Girard and Freud have contended.

My own conclusion is that war is the context for sacrifice rather than the other way around. Of course, one can think of religious warfare as a blend of sacrifice and martyrdom: sacrificing members of the enemy's side and offering up martyrs on one's own. But behind the gruesome litany is something that encompasses both sacrifice and martyrdom and much more: cosmic war. As Durkheim pointed out, religious language contains ideas of an intimate and ultimate tension, one that he described as the distinction between the sacred and the profane. This fundamental dichotomy gives rise to images of a great encounter between cosmic forces—order versus chaos, good versus evil, truth versus falsehood—which worldly struggles mimic. It is the image of war that captures this antinomy, rather than sacrifice.

At a seminar on the comparative study of the subject of disorder and order, Girard was challenged by a colleague who questioned Girard's assumptions about the anthropological origins of the image of sacrifice. He suggested that perhaps Girard was wrong—that the primal hunt started first, and sacrifice was meant to imitate the hunt. "If I accepted your theory," Girard replied, "I could no longer connect my theory of desire with my theory of victimage." His comment was followed by laughter.[13] My guess, however, is that it was nervous laughter, since the intervention of the scholar Eric Gans pointed to what most of his colleagues at the seminar must have known to be true, that the social activity of organized conflict, whether against an animal in a hunt or against other people in battle, is a primal form of human activity. Warfare organizes people into a "we" and a "they," and it organizes social history into a storyline of persecution, conflict, and the hope of redemption, liberation, and conquest.[14] The enduring and seemingly ubiquitous image of cosmic war from ancient times to the present continues to give the rites of sacrifice their meaning.

I think the concept of sacrifice makes sense only within the context of cosmic war. The sacrificial victim represents the destruction endemic to battle. Like the enemy—and like violence itself—the victim is often categorically out of place and is therefore a symbol of disorder. Animals used for sacrifice, for instance, are usually domesticated beasts: they lie in the ambiguous middle ground between the animal kingdom and the human.

When sacrificial victims were human, they also frequently came from an uncertain category. In India, for example, in the case of the *sati* of widows, the victims were anomalies: married women bereft of living husbands.[15] Among the Huron and Seneca Indians a sacrifice was made of a warrior out of place: during a state of war between tribes, an enemy soldier was captured, brought into the community, made a member of a household where a son had been lost in battle, and became for a time that missing son. The brave was feted and adored and then, knowing what the outcome would be and yet displaying his courage, he was ritually tortured to death. The final acts included plucking out his eyes and crushing and mutilating his genitals while the young man, still alive, writhed in pain. But he courageously accepted his fate.[16]

Sometimes it was God him- or herself who was offered up, or a divinely inspired person such as Jesus or Husain, whose very existence was extraordinary. It was not just their sacrifice that made them divine; rather, their almost unhuman holiness was what made them candidates for slaughter. Herman Melville's *Billy Budd* played on this theme: though he stuttered, in every other way Billy was as morally pure as his antagonist, Claggart, was evil. His very goodness was an indication that he did not fit into society and eventually had to be destroyed. A group of scholars who compared the issues of sainthood and morality cross-culturally came to a similar conclusion about saints, but put it the other way around: social misfits make good candidates for sainthood. They must be perceived as sublimely wacky in order for their martyrdom and self-sacrifice to be seen as pure.[17]

The sacrifices made during acts of religious terrorism in recent years have been consistent with this theme. In a study of the young men chosen by the Hizbollah and Amal sects in Lebanon to be sacrificed as martyrs in the bombing of American and Israeli targets, Martin Kramer concluded that they met the traditional criteria of purity and anomaly required of sacrificial beings. They were no longer children but were not yet married, they were members of the community but were free from family responsibilities, and they were pious but not members of the clergy.[18] In the case of the youths who volunteered for participation in Hamas suicide missions, interviews with their families and tapes of their last testimonies indicated that they were often regarded as somewhat shy but good kids. They were serious in their manners, perhaps slightly aloof from their crowd, and ultimately accepted in society in a grand way when their suicidal acts were remembered joyously as events of martyrdom.

When Dr. Rantisi objected to my use of the term "suicide bombers" to describe his young colleagues in Hamas who chose to blow themselves up in acts of violence against Israel, he was objecting to the idea that their acts were done idiosyncratically or thoughtlessly. As I mentioned, he preferred to think of them as "self-chosen martyrs," soldiers in a great war who diligently and reverently gave up their lives for the sake of their community and their religion. The videotapes taken of the young men the night before their deaths indicated that they thought of themselves in just that way. They were trying not to avoid life but to fulfill it in what they considered to be an act of both personal and social redemption.

The Invention of Enemies

Every struggle has its heroes, but even more fundamentally, the struggle must have a foe. As James Aho observed in his study of Idaho and Montana militia movements, the concept of enemy is "socially assembled."[19] Our discussion of the scenarios of war has indicated that this is indeed true of virtually every instance of religious terrorism: enemies have to be invented if they do not already exist. If the point of scenarios of cosmic war is to give those who believe in them a sense of empowerment and hope, these feelings could not be generated without the role of an evil foe, a negative reference to which one can position oneself and over which one can hope to triumph. Put simply, one cannot have a war without an enemy.

This means that some enemies have to be manufactured. As Stanley Tambiah noted in his analysis of ethnic conflict, the "rites of violence" in religious riots in South Asia led inevitably to the "demonizing of victims and their expulsion or annihilation in the idiom of exorcism."[20]

The demonization of an opponent is easy enough when people feel oppressed or have suffered injuries at the hands of a dominant, unforgiving, and savage power. But when this is not the case, the reasons for demonization are more tenuous and the attempts to make satanic beings out of relatively innocent foes more creative.

In the case of the Aum Shinrikyo movement in Japan, for instance, the melange of enemies is quite remarkable. Its numbers include the Japanese government, which the leader of the movement claimed is interested only in materialism and therefore is out to crush any form of spirituality, and the United States. The appearance of American military installations in Japan was basis enough for Asahara's conjecture that the U.S. is hell-bent on global domination. These enemies are reasonably understandable, since they are relatively close at hand.

More peculiar is the inclusion of Freemasons and Jews in the Aum Shinrikyo's unholy pantheon, foes that one would not ordinarily suspect of causing Japanese society much harm. Master Asahara's inclusion of Freemasons seems to stem from the writings of European mystics who saw treachery in Freemasons' secret societies and mysterious sayings. Asahara explained that Freemasons are trying to create Armageddon because "they think the reign of Christ will not come unless the final war is fought."[21] Jews were included because of similar conspiratorial theories alleging them to have designs on global economic and political control. For some reason, books on the so-called Jewish threat have been popular in Japan.[22] Added to these foes in Asahara's diatribes was a vague, generic enemy, a sort of inchoate force of evil, represented by the Japanese police, the news media, and virtually anyone he thought might be opposed to him.

The enemies of Sikhism, as described by the activist leader of the movement, Sant Jarnail Singh Bhindranwale, are similarly varied. They include both politicians and shadowy figures with no names. What Bhindranwale disdained—indeed loathed—was what he described as "the enemies of religion." These include heretics who have fallen from the disciplined Sikh fold and sought the easy comforts of modern life, and "that lady born in a house of Brahmans"—the phrase he used to describe Indira Gandhi. Bhindranwale's epithet for Indira Gandhi seems to have indicted both secular and Hindu politicians—the former because of party, the latter because of caste—and, in fact, he often regarded the two as twin evils. He was reflecting an attitude held by many Sikhs—that what passed for secular politics in India was in fact a form of Hindu cultural domination.

A similar political twist characterizes the satanization of Catholics by the Irish Protestant leader Rev. Ian Paisley. In calling the pope a "black-coated bachelor," he was insulting the religion of the community that he and other Protestants feared could eventually overwhelm them by their numbers in Ulster and by their strength in the adjacent Republic of Ireland. But Paisley was also attempting to turn an ordinary opponent—a leader of a rival religious group—into a caricature and thus dehumanize both him and the Catholics for whom he is an honored figure. On other occasions he not only denied that Catholics were Christian but also implied that they were subhuman. In these ways Paisley was doing what is commonly done to enemies: deny them personhood.

In some cases, the enemy has been literally caricatured. Rev. Michael Bray is fond of publishing cartoons in his newsletter portraying abortion clinic doctors and political leaders in the Clinton administration as bulbous buffoons. He has also distributed a joke book of the Polish-joke variety, but with the butt of the humor aimed at abortionists. It contains lines such as "How do you tell if an abortionist has class?" The answer: "All the words on his tatoo [sic] are spelled correctly." Inadvertently compounding the humor is the fact that the word *tattoo* is misspelled, presumably by mistake. In the summer, 1995, issue of his newsletter, Bray explained that jokes that "mock evildoers' reinforce a "right posture" of "loathing, not a happy tolerance."

Bray admits that behind his humor is a serious attempt at depersonalization, a quality that is found in virtually every group's attitude toward its enemy—the more so if it is a grand enemy, a satanic foe in the scenario of cosmic war. Shortly after Benjamin Nathaniel Smith went on a shooting spree in 1999 on the Fourth of July, killing or wounding eleven members of racial minorities before destroying himself, the leader of the World Church of the Creator, with which the killer was affiliated, mourned the "loss of one white man": Smith. The eleven other killed or wounded did not count, since they were "subhuman" or "mudpeople," as Matthew Hale, the leader of the movement, called them, using the same pejorative epithets used by Christian Identity writers.[23]

Robert Matthews, the leader of an Aryan Nations splinter group, The Order, who was later killed in a government shootout, used the Christian Identity term *mudpeople* to describe blacks and Hispanics. He advocated that they, along with what he called the "so-called white race traitors" who supported them, be exterminated in what he characterized as "a racial and religious Armageddon."[24] The grandfather of Christian Identity activists, Richard Butler, once invited his followers to his compound in Hayden Lake, Idaho, for what he described as "a summer conference and nigger shoot." He said that any blacks who attended would be treated as "live targets," and any who "refused to run or can't for any reason will be fed to the dogs."[25]

The principal recipients of Christian Identity's wrath, however, are not blacks but Jews. According to the movement's ideology, they have subverted the Bible's teachings from the very beginning by claiming they were the real Jews of the Bible, the inheritors of God's kingdom, and not the children of Satan that Christian Identity claims them to be. Denver Parmeter explained that he was mandated by Christian Identity teachings to participate in a plot to kill Alan Berg, a Denver talk-show host, because the radio personality was Jewish. Jews "had to be killed," he said, explaining that "Blacks diluted the white race" and are to be despised, but Jews are even worse because, according to Identity teachings, they are the "origins of evil."[26]

In light of these wretched characterizations of Jews, and considering how frequently Jews have been depersonalized as enemies over the centuries, it is troubling to see some Jewish activists adopting the same attitudes toward their own enemies, the Arabs. Nowhere was this depersonalizing stance more apparent than during the funeral of Dr. Baruch Goldstein after he was killed in the melee created by his massacre of innocent Arab Muslims at prayer in the Tomb of the Patriarchs in Hebron. At the funeral, Rabbi Yitzhak Ginsburgh, head of the yeshivah located in Joseph's Tomb in Nablus, comforted the assembled followers of Goldstein by explaining that Gentile blood was worth less than Jewish blood.[27] Followers of Kahane's Kach group, on the bus en route to Goldstein's funeral, passed around newspaper pictures showing Arabs who were killed in Goldstein's slaughter. One picture showed an Arab man with his head opened and the gray matter exposed. "This proves that Arabs have brains!" said a teenager. His friends laughed and passed around plastic cups filled with sweet Kiddush wine to toast the memory of Dr. Goldstein.[28]

These blanket characterizations of a people make the process of dehumanizing an enemy easier. It is difficult to belittle and kill a person whom one knows and for whom one has no personal antipathy. As most Jews are aware from centuries of experience at the receiving end of anti-Semitism, it is much easier to stereotype and categorize a whole

people as collective enemies than to hate individuals. The Christian
Identity activists still regard Jews this way, and as we have seen, some
Jewish extremists collectively brand Arabs in such a manner. To many
Muslim activists, America and Americans are collective enemies, with
the particulars of how and why they threaten Muslim people and their
culture left unspecified.

This phenomenon of the faceless collective enemy explains in large
part why so many terrorist acts have targeted ordinary people—individuals whom most observers would regard as innocent victims. In the
eyes of those who planned the Hamas bombings in the buses of
Jerusalem and Tel Aviv, the schoolchildren on their way to class and the
housewives on their way to the shopping mall were not innocent: they
were representatives of a collectivity—Israeli society—that was corpo-
rately the foe. An Israeli on the other side of the struggle confirmed that
he regarded innocent Arabs as enemies as well, since there were no such
things as civilians in "a cultural war."[29] Echoing this sentiment, a leader
in the Hamas movement told me, "No one is innocent in the war between Arabs and Jews."[30] He indicated that he regarded all Israelis as
soldiers or as potential soldiers, including women and children.

Since it is relatively easy to kill someone who is unknown, the perpetrators of terrorist acts have sometimes been apologetic after the fact,
as were the members of the "Real IRA" after the August 1998 attack
in the village of Omagh, Northern Ireland. More often, however, even
when the extent of the victims' suffering has become known, the perpetrators have remained defensive about what they have done. Timothy
McVeigh, for instance, in his words of sympathy to the families of the
victims of the Oklahoma City bombing essentially repeated a scene
from *The Turner Diaries*. In that novel, after the fictional bombers had
destroyed a federal building, they picked their way through the rubble
and helped one of the women who had been injured, whose "pretty
face was smudged and scraped . . . and blood was spurting from a deep
gash in her thigh." The bombers regretted that so many "thousands of
innocent victims" had to die but remained convinced that there was
"no way" that they could "destroy the System without hurting many
thousands of innocent people—no way."[31]

Since these victims did not possess individual personality, they
could represent a collective enemy such as the American "system," or
they could be a stand-in for a more diffuse notion of evil, a sort of
"enemy-in-general." In the sermons of Sant Jarnail Singh Bhindranwale, for instance, he seemed deliberately vague about who the

enemy really was. "To destroy religion," Bhindranwale informed his congregation, "mean tactics have been initiated," and they came from "all sides and in many forms."[32] But rather than explain what these forces were, who was behind them, and why they would want to destroy religion, Bhindranwale dwelled on what the response should be: a willingness to fight and defend the faith—if necessary, to the end. "Young men: with folded hands, I beseech you," Bhindranwale implored, reminding them that the ultimate decision between truth and evil was up to them.[33]

Moreover, there is a poetic appropriateness to the image of the enemy as a shadowy, almost subhuman figure—"mudpeople," in Christian Identity's way of thinking. Since the point of a religious vision of cosmic war is to assert the triumph of order over disorder, it is understandable that the foes would be considered amorphous. They are, in fact, symbols for amorphousness itself. Even when the symbols have been particular peoples and governments, such as Jews, Arabs, and America, the concepts have been so broad and generic as to be virtually metaphoric in character.

The idea of the enemy is sufficiently flexible that it can include more than one group. In fact, as political scientist Ehud Sprinzak has argued, the efforts to "delegitimize" an opponent by considering it to be an enemy has often been "split." The hatred inspired by what Sprinzak has called "the radicalization of a group of extremists" has been directed toward "two separate entities."[34] In such instances the enemy includes not only the primary target, but also a secondary target. It could be any person or entity that is seen as supporting or defending the primary target.

The primary enemy is the religious rival or local political authority that directly threatens the activist group and against which there is usually a commonsense basis for conflict and animosity. The secondary enemy is a less obvious threat: a moderate leader on one's own side, for example, or a governmental authority who is trying to be fair-minded. Both can infuriate an activist who has bifurcated the world into heroes and enemies in a cosmic war. Secondary enemies, such as government authorities, are seen as not only defending the primary enemy but also belittling the very notion of cosmic war. One of these secondary enemies' greatest failures, from a radical's point of view, is their inability to take seriously the notion of an absolute, sacred struggle. Instead they treat disputes as if they were rational differences over which reasonable people can come to some sort of accommodation or even agreement. This view is anathema to those who see the world at war.

Some of Rev. Ian Paisley's harshest rhetoric has been reserved for "apostates," as he calls them—moderates from his own, Protestant side. These include preachers of tolerance such as Billy Graham and ecumenical entities such as the World Council of Churches. Once, when a delegation of Protestants called on him and acknowledged their respect for his position but encouraged him to be more modest in the way he proclaimed it, Paisley threatened to kick them out the door. Later he explained who he thought they were: "emissaries from hell, that is who they were, sent by Beelzebub, commissioned by Satan to tell the man of God to compromise."[35]

Jarnail Singh Bhindranwale lambasted modern-minded Sikh men in his congregation. His wrath was aimed especially at those who, in opposition to Sikh custom, did not let their beards and hair grow long and those who "hankered after government administrative positions."[36] Christian Identity activists hate white liberal defenders of civil rights almost more than they hate the blacks. "O.J. Simpson was a national hero," Aryan Nations leader Richard Butler remarked, referring to Simpson's alleged murders of his white wife and her Jewish friend, since he "got a Jew and a race traitor at the same time."[37]

Government authorities make easy secondary targets. They protect the primary enemy and belittle the notion that ordinary mortal conflict can be elevated to the level of cosmic war. Moreover, as upholders of order within society, they are the natural enemies of those who feel that a certain amount of revolutionary disorder is necessary to transform the system. Rabbi Meir Kahane told me that he despised the secular government of Israel more than the Palestinian Arabs—whom he pitied, he said, rather than hated.[38] Mahmud Abouhalima said he loathed secular Muslims such as Egypt's president, Hosni Mubarak, who he claimed are not really Muslims at all. He regarded Mubarak as a wolf in sheep's clothing, who wore the label of Islam but "watered down" Islamic law.[39] In Rev. Ian Paisley's case, he was able to despise the government of Great Britain even while demanding that it support his Unionist cause. It was the moderate, accommodating stance of London toward the Catholics that so incensed him and led him to describe Prime Minister Margaret Thatcher as a "wicked, treacherous, lying woman."[40]

This hatred of government as a primary or secondary enemy in a cosmic war has made political leaders targets of assassination. Irish nationalists in the Provisional IRA killed Britain's Lord Mountbatten in 1979. In Egypt President Anwar Sadat was assassinated in 1981 by Muslim extremists associated with the al Jihad movement. In India

Prime Minister Indira Gandhi was killed by her own Sikh bodyguards in 1984 as a reprisal against her orders to the Indian army to invade the Golden Temple. In 1990 the speaker of the Egyptian Assembly, Rifaat al-Mahgoub, was killed by members of the same radical Muslim group that killed Sadat. In Algeria in 1992, the civilian head of the military-supported Council of State was assassinated, allegedly by followers of the outlawed Islamic Salvation Front. In 1995 Israel's prime minister Yitzhak Rabin, flushed with the victory of a peace accord with the Palestinians, was struck down by a Jewish extremist who could not bear the idea of compromise with the Arabs.

The assassination of Rabin followed months of increasing satanization of Israeli political figures. In the year before Rabin's killing, for example, the deep disdain for Israel's secular leaders was evident at the funeral of the perpetrator of the Hebron massacre, Dr. Baruch Goldstein. Just as members of Hamas had accused the Israeli government of secretly supporting Goldstein and causing the deaths of innocent Muslims, Goldstein's supporters accused the government of conniving with the Arabs and thus causing Goldstein's death. Though Goldstein was beaten to death at the shrine of the Tomb of the Patriarchs by Arabs attempting to stop the massacre, Goldstein's supporters at his funeral blamed the Israeli government for his demise. The mere mention of Rabin or other government officials was greeted with hissing and catcalls. On the bus that brought Kach supporters to the funeral, one woman told friends proudly that her son had propped up pictures of Rabin and other government leaders in the toilet and drawn concentric rings around their faces to provide targets while he urinated.[41]

America as Enemy

More than any other government, America has been assigned the role of primary or secondary foe. The wrath has been directed largely toward political leaders and governmental symbols, but the wider circle has included American businessmen, American culture, and the American "system"—a generic term that has included all responsible persons and every entity that has kept the country functioning as a political, economic, and social unit. According to the RAND Chronicle of International Terrorism, since 1968 the United States each year has headed the list of countries whose citizens and property were most frequently attacked.[42] The U.S. State Department's counterterrorism unit reported that during the 1990s, 40 percent of all acts of terrorism worldwide have been against American citizens and facilities.[43]

Mahmud Abouhalima has said that he regards America as a world-wide enemy. The reason, he says, is not only because the United States supports the secular Egyptian government that he and his colleagues find directly oppressive, but also because of its history of terrorist acts. The bombing of Hiroshima, for instance, Abouhalima compared with the bombing of the Oklahoma City federal building.[44] Abouhalima's spiritual leader, Sheik Omar Abdul Rahman, during a lengthy court-room speech at the end of the trial convicting him of conspiring to bomb the World Trade Center, predicted that a "revengeful" God would "scratch" America from the face of the earth.[45]

Osama bin Ladin, implicated in the bombing of the American embassies in Kenya and Tanzania in 1998, explained in an interview a year before the bombing that America deserved to be targeted because it was "the biggest terrorist in the world."[46] It may be only co-incidence that after the embassy bombings U.S. National Security Advisor Samuel Berger called Osama "the most dangerous nonstate terrorist in the world."[47] The reason bin Laden gave for targeting America was its list of "crimes," which included "occupying the lands of Islam in the holiest of places, the Arabian Peninsula, plun-dering its riches, dictating to its rulers, humiliating its people, ter-rorizing its neighbors and turning its bases in the peninsula into a spearhead through which to fight the neighboring Muslim peo-ples."[48] In response to what bin Laden regarded as a declaration of war on Muslims by America, he issued a fatwa calling on "every Muslim" as "an individual duty" to join him in a righteous war "to kill the Americans and their allies." Their obligation was not only "to kill the Americans" but also to "plunder their money wherever and whenever they find it." He sealed his fatwa with the reassurance that "this is in accordance with the words of Almighty God" and that "every Muslim who believes in God and wishes to be rewarded" should "comply with God's order."[49]

Why is America the enemy? This question is hard for observers of in-ternational politics to answer, and harder still for ordinary Americans to fathom. Many have watched with horror as their compatriots and sym-bols of their country have been destroyed by people whom they do not know, from cultures they can scarcely identify on a global atlas, and for reasons that do not seem readily apparent. From the frames of reference of those who regard America as enemy, however, several motives appear.

One reason we have already mentioned: America is often a secondary enemy. In its role as trading partner and political ally, America
has a vested interest in shoring up the stability of regimes around the
world. This has often put the United States in the unhappy position of
being a defender and promoter of secular governments regarded by
their religious opponents as primary foes. Long before the bombing of
the World Trade Center, Sheik Omar Abdul Rahman expressed his disdain for the United States because of its role in propping up the
Mubarak regime in Egypt. "America is behind all these un-Islamic governments," the Sheik explained, arguing that the purpose of American
political and economic support was "to keep them strong" and to try
to "defeat the Islamic movements."[50] In the case of Iran prior to the
Islamic revolution, Ayatollah Khomeini saw the shah and the American
government linked as evil twins: America was tarred by its association
with the shah, and the shah, in turn, was corrupted by being a "com-
panion of satanic forces"—that is, of America.[51] When Khomeini
prayed to his "noble God for protection from the evil of every wicked
traitor" and asked Him to "destroy the enemies," the primary traitor
he had in mind was the shah and the chief enemy America.[52]

A second reason America is regarded as enemy is that both directly and
indirectly it has supported modern culture. In a world where villagers in
remote corners of the world increasingly have access to MTV, Hollywood
movies, and the Internet, the images and values that have been projected
globally have been American. It was this cultural threat that brought an
orthodox rabbi, Manachem Fruman, who lived in a Jewish settlement on
the West Bank of Israel near Hebron, to regular meetings with Hamas-
related mullahs in nearby villages. What they had in common, Rabbi
Fruman told me, was their common dislike of the "American-style" traits
of individualism, the abuse of alcohol, and sexy movies that were widespread in modern cities such as Tel Aviv. Rabbi Fruman told me that
"when the mullahs asked, who brought all this corruption here, they answered, 'the Jews.' But," Fruman continued, "rabbis like me don't like this
corruption either." Hence the rabbi and the mullahs agreed about the
degradation of modern urban values, and they concurred over which
country was ultimately responsible. When the mullahs asserted that the
United States was the "capital of the devil," Rabbi Fruman told me, he
could agree.[53] In a similar vein, Mahmud Abouhalima told me he was bitter that Islam did not have influence over the global media the way that
secular America did. America, he believed, was using its power of information to promote the immoral values of secular society.[54]

The third reason for the disdain of America is economic. Although most corporations that trade internationally are multinational, with personnel and legal ties to more than one country, many are based in the United States or have American associations. Even those that were identifiably European or Japanese are thought to be American-like and implicitly American in attitude and style. When Ayatollah Khomeini identified the "satanic" forces that were out to destroy Islam, he included not only Jews but also the even "more satanic" Westerners—especially corporate leaders with "no religious belief" who saw Islam as "the major obstacle in the path of their materialistic ambitions and the chief threat to their political power."[55] The ayatollah went on to claim that "all the problems of Iran" were due to the treachery of "foreign colonialists."[56] On another occasion, the ayatollah blended political, personal, and spiritual issues in generalizing about the cosmic foe—Western colonialism—and about "the black and dreadful future" that "the agents of colonialism, may God Almighty abandon them all," have in mind for Islam and the Muslim people.[57]

What the ayatollah was thinking of when he prophesied a "black and dreadful future" for Islam was the global domination of American economy and culture. This fear of globalization is the fourth reason America is often targeted as an enemy. The apprehensions of Ayatollah Khomeini were shared by many not only in the Muslim world but elsewhere, including the United States. There right-wing militias were convinced that the "new world order" proclaimed by President George Bush was more than a mood of global cooperation: it was a conspiratorial plot to control the world. Accepting this paranoid vision of American leaders' global designs, the Aum Shinrikyo master Shoko Asahara linked the U.S. army with the Japanese government, Freemasons, and Jews in the image of a global conspiratorial band.

Like all stereotypes, each of these characterizations holds a certain amount of truth. America's culture and economy have dominated societies around the world in ways that have caused concern to protectors of local societies. The vast financial and media networks of American-backed corporations and information systems have affected the whole of the globe. There has indeed been a great conflict between secular and religious life throughout the world, and America does ordinarily support the secular side of the fight. Financial aid provided to leaders such as Israel's Benjamin Netanyahu and Egypt's Hosni Mubarak has shored up the political power of politicians opposed to religious nationalism. Moreover, after the fall of the the Soviet Union, the United States has been virtually the only coherent military power in the world. Hence it has been an easy target for blame when people have felt that their lives were going askew or were being controlled by forces they could not readily see. Yet to dislike America is one thing; to regard it as a cosmic enemy is quite another.

When the United States has been branded as an enemy in a cosmic war, it has been endowed with superhuman—or perhaps subhuman— qualities, ones that have had little to do with the people who actually live in America. It is the image of the country that has been despised— a reified notion of Americanism, not its people. Individual Americans have often been warmly accepted by those who hate the collective image that they hold as cosmic enemy. This was brought home to me in Gaza when I talked with Dr. Abdul Aziz Rantisi about the Hamas movement's attitude toward America and its pro-Israeli stance. As Dr. Rantisi offered me coffee in the comfortable living room of his home, he acknowledged that the United States was a secondary enemy be- cause of its complicity in Israel's existence and its oppression of Palestinian Arabs. From his point of view, it deserved to be treated as an enemy. What about individual Americans, I cautiously asked him, raising the example of American professors. Would such people be targeted?

"You?" Rantisi responded, somewhat surprised. "You don't count. You're our guest."[58]

Satanization and the Stages of Empowerment

Everyone has enemies in the sense of opponents, but to become objects of religious terrorism such enemies must become extraordinary: cosmic foes. When Osama bin Laden spoke of America as embodying the "forces of evil," he was not just identifying a problem to which he needed to respond, but a mythic monster with which he had to battle— one that ultimately only divine power could subdue. The question is how this happened—how a view of an opponent could cross the line into a deep and enduring hatred for a satanic entity.

I call this process satanization. The process of creating satanic ene- mies is part of the construction of an image of cosmic war, and some of the same criteria listed at the end of the previous chapter that make sa- cred warfare possible also make possible a satanic opponent. When the opponent rejects one's moral or spiritual position; when the enemy ap- pears to hold the power to completely annihilate one's community, one's culture, and oneself; when the opponent's victory would be unthinkable; and when there seems no way to defeat the enemy in human terms—all of these conditions increase the likelihood that one will envision one's opponent as a superhuman foe, a cosmic enemy. The process of satanization is aimed at reducing the power of one's opponents and discrediting them. By belittling and humiliating them—by making them subhuman—one is asserting one's own superior moral power.

Satanization is to some extent a process of "delegitimization," as Sprinzak has described it. He has identified a three-stage series of progressive steps aimed at discrediting one's opponents, humbling them, and reducing their power.[59] The first stage involves a *crisis of confidence* over the authority of a regime or its policies. The second stage is a *conflict of legitimacy,* in which a challenge group is "ready to question the very legitimacy of the whole system."[60] The third stage is a full *crisis of legitimacy.* At this stage the challenge group extends its hostility to everyone in society associated with a regime it regards as illegitimate, and both the regime and ordinary citizens are satanized—or as Sprinzak puts it, they are "derogated into the ranks of the worst enemies or subhuman species."[61] It is this dehumanization that allows a group to "commit atrocities without a second thought."[62] It is in this stage, according to Sprinzak, that acts of terrorism can be justified.

In general, I agree with Sprinzak that the effect of satanization is to delegitimize an opponent. When Rev. Ian Paisley called the pope a black-coated bachelor from hell, his aim was to reduce the credibility of Catholic leadership and to undermine its authority. Sometimes the process has worked. Not just name calling, but acts of terrorism over which an opponent seems to have no control can be a powerful way of undermining the opponent's legitimacy, as Prime Minister Shimon Peres discovered in the 1996 Israeli elections. Terrorism in this case was an agent of delegitimization.

But that has not always been the case. Sometimes governmental authority has been strengthened in the eyes of its supporters by the way it has responded to terrorism. British and French responses to terrorism are cases in point. In other cases, terrorism—especially religious terrorism—has not been undertaken with the intention to delegitimize, even in cases where that has been the outcome. It is a question of motive: did the people who perpetrated terrorist acts do so for the purpose of destroying their opponents' credibility? When this question was put directly to those involved in incidents of terrorism—such as Dr. Rantisi and the operatives behind the Hamas suicide bombings and Mahmud Abouhalima and his colleagues in the World Trade Center bombing—their answers were obscure. They said that they were involved in great conflicts in which such acts were understandable and inevitable.

Based on what these activists have said, it would appear that the delegitimization of the opponent was not the primary objective in their minds. Most religious activists do not appear to think tactically. Rather than trying to deal strategically with their opponents, craft tactics, and conceive ways to discredit them, the activists see themselves as engaged in a great struggle, in which the discrediting of opponents comes naturally and perhaps even secondarily. Prior to delegitimization and satanization is the sense of being involved in a cosmic war.

As we have seen, the idea of cosmic war is compelling to religious activists because it ennobles and exalts those who consider themselves a part of it—especially those who have been desperate about their situations and defiant in resisting them. In that sense the concept is not just an effort at delegitimization but at dehumiliation: it provides escape from humiliating and impossible predicaments for those who otherwise would feel immobilized by them. They become involved in terrorism not only to belittle their enemies but also to provide themselves with a sense of power.

Rabbi Meir Kahane saw the cosmic struggle as a series of humiliations. The Jews throughout history have been humbled by their opponents, whom God, in turn, has humbled. Kahane spoke of God's vengeance against the Gentiles. It began with the humiliation of the pharaoh in the exodus from Egypt over three thousand years ago and continued in the modern era with the humiliation of the Gentiles in the creation of Israel.[63] "When the Jews are at war," Kahane added, "God's name is great." Yoel Lerner echoed Kahane's words, telling me that "God always fights against His enemies." He added that activists such as himself "are the instruments of this fight."[64]

One can view the process of satanization and the construction of ideas of cosmic war as part of an effort at ennoblement, empowerment, and dehumiliation. It is an incremental process in which acts of terrorism appear only in the later stages of a pattern that begins with a feeling of helplessness. The stages are as follows.

STAGES OF SYMBOLIC EMPOWERMENT

1. *A world gone awry.* The process begins with real problems: the Israeli occupation of Palestine, the corruption of secular governments

in Egypt and India, the discrediting of traditional values, and the dehumanization of modern societies in Japan and the United States. Most people are able to cope with such situations. Others rebel against them politically and culturally. A few take these situations with ultimate gravity and perceive them as symptoms of a world gone badly awry. These few are part of emerging cultures of violence.

2. *The foreclosure of ordinary options.* Most people who feel so strongly about such desperate conditions to want to change them join in political or social campaigns that sometimes are successful, sometimes not. But they persist with the expectation that eventually changes can be made through ordinary means: electing new leaders, advocating changes in public policy, and rallying public support. The few who are part of cultures of violence, however, see no possibility of improvement through normal channels. Their sense of frustration about the world around them is experienced as the potential for personal failure and a meaningless existence.

3. *Satanization and cosmic war.* For those in cultures of violence who experience both despair and defiance over what they perceive to be hopeless situations, religion provides a solution: cosmic war. As opponents become satanized and regarded as "forces of evil" or "black-coated bachelors from hell," the world begins to make sense. Those who felt oppressed now understand why they have been humiliated and who is behind their dismal situation. Perhaps most important, they feel the exhilaration of hope, that in a struggle with divine dimensions God will be with them and, despite all evidence to the contrary, somehow they can win.

4. *Symbolic acts of power.* The final stage is the performance of acts that display symbolically the depth of the struggle and the power that those in cultures of violence feel they possess. These performances include holding private rallies and public demonstrations, publishing newsletters and books and staging media events that humiliate the cosmic foe, flaunting weapons in an effort to show military might, developing communications systems and organizations, and creating alternative governments with courts and cabinet ministers and social services. In moments of dramatic intensity those within cultures of violence who want to express power symbolically may also choose an explosive act—terrorism—either as an isolated incident or as a part of a protracted state of guerrilla war.

Satanization is thus part of a larger pattern of behavior in which people desperately try to make sense of the world and maintain some control over it. Perpetrating acts of terrorism is one of several ways to symbolically express power over oppressive forces and regain some nobility in the perpetrator's personal life. Those who have been part of cultures of violence and who have participated in acts of empowerment—even vicariously—have experienced the exuberance of the hope that the tide of history will eventually turn their way. Such performances of power have provided the anticipation that victory is at hand. Alas, the experience has often been fleeting. Sadder still, it has been purchased at an awful cost.

CHAPTER 10

Warriors' Power

To outsiders, the struggles in which most members of terrorist groups see themselves engaged appear to be of such cosmic proportions that they cannot conceivably be won. This point was amply demonstrated by the explosions at the American embassies in Africa in 1998 and the tragic suicide bombings in Israel in recent years. The very means by which these and similar battles have been waged—violent blasts set off by small minorities against opponents who are infinitely better armed— seem destined to failure. It is hard to take seriously the notion that these are rational efforts to achieve power, at least by ordinary calculations. Yet, to those undertaking them, there may be something exhilarating, perhaps even rewarding, about the struggle itself. This sense of empowerment may make the effort seem worthwhile.

"To die in this way"—through suicide bombings—the political head of the Hamas movement told me, "is better than to die daily in frustration and humiliation."[1] He went on to say that, in his view, the very nature of Islam is about the defense of "dignity, land, and honor." He then told a story that the prophet had told about a woman who fasted daily, and yet because she humiliated her neighbors, she was doomed to hell.[2] The point of the story, he said, is that dishonoring someone is the worst act that one can do, and the only thing that can counter it is dignity: the honor provided by religion and the courage of being a defender of the faith. In a curious way, then, both religion and violence are seen as antidotes to humiliation.

The countering of dishonor with piety and struggle is a theme that runs through many incidents of religious violence in recent years. Dr. Baruch Goldstein is said to have been driven to kill innocent Muslims in the shrine of the Tomb of the Patriarchs in Hebron because he felt Jews had been dishonored. A similar sense of pride is exhibited in the nervous bravado of the Hamas suicide bombers in the videotapes taken the night before their actions, and in the swagger of the convicted conspirator of the World Trade Center bombing, Ramzi Yousef, appearing in a New York City courtroom, as described by *Los Angeles Times* correspondent Robin Wright.[3] When a black Muslim whom Iranians employed to kill their enemy Ali Tabatabayi in Washington, DC, in 1980 was asked why he agreed to do it, he explained that he was lured by the "opportunity" to be "involved in something that's bigger than that"—the experience of being in an African American minority in the United States.[4] Sikh militants were so angered that the government ignored them that they felt the need to force the government to take them seriously.[5] Japan's Shoko Asahara wanted to be not only "like a king," as one of his former followers told me, but "like Christ."[6]

In all these cases, the act of being involved in violence provided a sense of empowerment disproportionately greater than what the violence actually achieved. For this reason, I describe this feeling of strength as "symbolic empowerment." By using the term *symbolic,* I do not mean to imply that the empowerment is not real. After all, a sense of power is largely a matter of perception, and in many cases the power that the activists obtained had a very real impact on their community, their relationships, and themselves, as well as on the political authorities who feared them and granted them the respect of notoriety. But symbolic expressions of violence—performance violence, as I earlier described it—are empowering in a special way, for they do not lead to conquests of territory or personnel in the traditional definition of military success. For most of these quixotic fighters, their great success was simply in waging the struggle—the heady confidence they received by being soldiers for a great cause, even if the battles were not won, or were even winnable, in ordinary military terms.

Empowering Marginal Men

A society provides an accepted—even heroic—social role for its citizens who participate in great struggles and have been given the moral license to kill. They are soldiers. Understandably, many members of radical reli-

gious movements see themselves that way. Sheik Abdul Rahman, for instance, described himself as "a soldier and servant in the cause of
Allah."[7] Rev. Michael Bray, who had once attended the naval academy
at Annapolis but never completed his military training, called himself "a
soldier for Christ."[8] A former staff member of the Aryan Nations said
that he had been drawn to the movement by the flags, the military uni-
forms, and the parades.[9] For many activists, though, the militant posture
is not just an affectation. They were indeed soldiers at one time in real
wars, and continue their identities as war heroes—or perhaps fulfill their
frustrated careers—in the imagined wars of politico-religious struggles.

Timothy McVeigh and Terry Nichols, for example, were veterans of
the Gulf War. In Operation Desert Storm, McVeigh is said to have enjoyed the act of killing and once boasted of decapitating an Iraqi with his
cannon at a distance of 1100 meters. During the last battle—a no-contest
encounter that amounted to virtual slaughter of all remaining Iraqi
forces—McVeigh is reported to have been furious when ordered to stop
shooting. He then took out his camera and wandered over the battlefield,
taking pictures of the Iraqi dead.[10] When McVeigh returned to the United
States after the war, he continued to wear his army fatigues and tote
weapons as if preparing for battle.

In this respect McVeigh was not unlike thousands of uniformed militia
activists throughout the United States. Gordon Sellner, a militia member
who subscribed to a Christian Identity ideology similar to McVeigh's and
shot a deputy sheriff in Montana, barricaded himself inside his cabin and
sent out directives that he signed, "a soldier for Christ and country."[11]

Muslim activists have also had military connections. Mahmud
Abouhalima and other followers of Sheik Omar Abdul Rahman had
served as mujahadeen in the battlefields of Afghanistan. On several
tours of duty in Afghanistan in 1988–89, Abouhalima is said to have
volunteered to undertake the most treacherous of missions.[12] When I
interviewed him, Abouhalima said he submitted himself to dangerous
situations in the Afghan war because "as a Muslim," it was his "job."[13]
A leader in Abouhalima's mosque said most Muslims like Abouhalima
who went to the war in Afghanistan from America left "as ordinary
men and came back so devout and so proud." He went on to explain
that the Afghan war "reminded them of the glorious old days, many
hundreds of years ago, when the Muslims were fighting the infidel."[14]

During the height of the Sikh separatist movement some of India's
most highly ranked soldiers crossed over and joined the Khalistani revolt.
Sant Jarnail Singh Bhindranwale's military adviser, Shabeg Singh, had

been a general in the Indian army. Shabeg Singh's former superior officer, Major General Narinder Singh, also joined the movement after his retirement. When I interviewed the former major general in the Punjab capital city, Chandigarh, in 1996, he told me that his involvement in the movement initially was a matter of personal pride. He felt lost after leaving the military and was flattered when a group of retired Sikh military officers were brought to Amritsar and asked to support the struggles of their people. Narinder Singh said that for several years thereafter he traveled around the state, serving as adviser to five or six major paramilitary organizations.[15]

Other Sikh activists have had police connections. Dilawar Singh, the suicide bomber who killed Punjab's chief minister Beant Singh in 1995, was a dismissed special police officer from Patiala. An accomplice, Balwant Singh, was a police constable. The alleged mastermind of Indira Gandhi's assassination, Simranjit Singh Mann, had served as a superintendent of police in the Punjab.[16]

In the radical religious movements on both sides of the Palestine-Israeli confrontation, military images have abounded. Hamas cadres have had military as well as religious training, and some of the volunteers are former armed police of the Palestinian authority. On the Jewish side, both the assassin of Prime Minister Yitzhak Rabin and the perpetrator of the massacre in Hebron's Tomb of the Patriarchs had been soldiers in the Israeli army. The latter, Dr. Baruch Goldstein, maintained good relations with the Israeli military, and though long retired from the army he dressed up in his old military uniform the morning he entered the mosque at the sacred site on February 25, 1994, and with an army weapon killed scores of Arabs kneeling at prayer.[17]

Such soldiers have found new battles: the grand spiritual and political struggles in which their movements envision themselves to be engaged. These cosmic wars impart a sense of importance and destiny to men who find the modern world to be stifling, chaotic, and dangerously out of control. The imagined wars identify the enemy, the imputed source of their personal and political failures; they exonerate these would-be soldiers from any responsibility for failures by casting them as victims; they give them a sense of their own potential for power; and they arm them with the moral justification, the social support, and the military equipment to engage in battle both figuratively and literally. It is an incendiary combination, one that has led to horrendous acts.

Like soldiers in real armies, the imagined soldiers of cosmic wars tend to be young and male. They also tend to be members of financially and socially marginal groups for which there is a great need for empowerment. Like all generalizations, however, there have been significant exceptions: the leaders of the groups, for instance, have often been middle-aged and affluent.

The very youthfulness of most members of the movements makes them socially marginal. A tabulation of the ages of Sikh extremists killed by police indicated that most of the men were in their early twenties.[18] According to Emmanuel Sivan, one of the leading scholars of modern Islamic history, Hamas has consisted largely of "urban males in their teens."[19] In most societies, young people between the ages of sixteen and twenty-two are in a liminal state between life stages. They are no longer children in their parents' families, and they have not yet created familes of their own. Their marginality is especially acute in traditional societies built around family units, in which one does not find the highly developed youth cultures of modern urban and industrialized societies. These activist youths are family members without a family, for whom religious movements provide a home and an extended kinship.

In the cultures of violence that have led to religious terrorism, the anxieties of all young men—concerns over careers, social location, and sexual relationships—have been exacerbated. Experiences of humiliation in these matters have made them vulnerable to the voices of powerful leaders and images of glory in a cosmic war. In Palestine, for example, where the unemployment rate among young men in their late teens and early twenties has hovered around 50 percent, economic frustration has led to sexual frustration. Without jobs, which is usually a prerequisite to searching for a wife in traditional societies, they cannot marry. Without marriage, in strict religious cultures such as that of Palestinian Arabs, they cannot have sex. The Hamas movement has provided a way of venting the resulting frustrations in a community that supplies a family and an ideology that explains the source of their problems and gives them hope.

The same can be said about many other movements of religious activism, including the Islamic Resistance in Algeria. There religious opposition to the secular National Front Party was fueled by a 20 percent inflation rate, a 25 percent unemployment rate, and a youthful population—70 percent of citizens are under twenty-five years of age—who could not hope for marriage, an apartment, or a job under Algeria's dire economic conditions.[20] A U.S. State Department official told me that an improvement in Algeria's economic climate would quickly quell the agitation of religious revolutionaries. The implication of his comments was that Algeria's religious revolution was an economic rebellion in disguise. Although I suspect that religious ideology permeated the Algerian resistance more deeply than he suggested, there is no question in my mind that much of what he said was right: economic despair led to a sense of desperation and anger that was aimed—appropriately or not—at the secular junta that seized power when the election appeared to be moving toward victory for the Islamic party.

In some movements, however, the economic situation is not one of extreme poverty, but of relative deprivation. This was the case in the Aum Shinrikyo movement in Japan, where most of the followers were middle class and many of them professionals. Yet they were often frustrated in their careers. Chemists and nuclear scientists who reached a plateau in their professions and could not move higher up the corporate ladder, or who had been laid off in their companies' downsizing, were recruited into the Aum Shinrikyo science program to make devices to protect against the effects of chemical and nuclear weapons. Their experimentation also involved the creation of some of those weapons; the scientists were assured that this was for the purpose of making certain that their protective devices would work.

The members of the Christian militia in the United States also do not wholly fit the stereotype of young and poor: most of them are employed and no longer youthful—though many of the most violent members are in their twenties. Some, like Timothy McVeigh, are unemployed and drifting in their careers, but others, like Paul Hill, are more established. What they all have in common is a fear of social marginality in the future. Although they are white Protestant males and currently members of a privileged class, they perceive American society to be moving in a direction that would make this class increasingly peripheral. They are terrified at statistical projections, based on the rise of Asian and Hispanic immigrants in the 1980s and 1990s, that put Caucasians in the minority in California and other West Coast states some time in the twenty-first century.

These fears of impending marginality have undoubtedly helped to fuel the racism of many radical religious movements. Kerry Noble, one of the leaders of the Christian Identity compound the Covenant, the Sword, and the Arm of the Lord, said that he used to preach sermons describing blacks as the "beasts of the field" mentioned in the Bible. Jews, he once alleged, were products of sexual intercourse between Eve and Satan. Even though Noble and his colleagues "had never personally known a Jew," that did not hinder them from blaming Jews for most of the problems in the modern world: "for the pornography, for the lack of morality, for the economic situation in America, for minority rights over white rights, and for kicking God out of the schools."[21] By implying that Jews were responsible for these problems, Noble was expressing his own frustration over the inability of white Christian men like himself to control the world around them.

In India, the movement of Sikh empowerment was also composed largely of young men from a privileged class, the agrarian Jats, who saw their world similarly endangered. They feared that the social and economic status they regarded as their birthright was slipping away. Some of the most fanatical members of the movement, including Beant Singh, the assassin of Indira Gandhi, were Sikhs who came from the lowest stratum of society—the so-called untouchable castes.[22] The bulk of the militant Sikh movement, however, was composed of young Jats, rural youths with little education. In earlier generations they would automatically have assumed positions of leadership and economic power within Punjab society. In the last decades of the twentieth century, however, as northern India became increasingly urban and industrial, money and social status within the Sikh community moved away from rural Sikhs and toward members of merchant and administrative castes—both Hindus and Sikhs—who live in cities. Urban groups such as Khatris and Aroras had begun to challenge the Jats for power in the Punjab, and young Jats were desperate to reassert the primacy of their caste—and themselves. In some cases, this desperation led to participation in movements of religious violence, such as the one that took the life of the chief minister of Punjab in 1995. On the morning that the young Jat, Dilawar Singh, ignited the bomb that killed the chief minister and fourteen others, he said, "Today I will make the Jats feel proud."[23]

Not all Sikhs who supported the militant movement lived in India, however. Sikhs abroad are examples of another kind of marginalized people who have become involved in paramilitary activity: expatriates. A considerable amount of money and moral support for Punjabi militants came from such faraway places as London, Houston, and Los Angeles. Sikhs in these places heard in the video- and audiotaped messages of Sant Jarnail Singh Bhindranwale a message of belonging. Although they were on the periphery of society in England, Canada, the United States, and the many other parts of the world to which Sikhs migrated in the twentieth century, militant movements provided them with the opportunity to display their commitment and prove their importance to the community in a powerful way.

This phenomenon might be called "e-mail ethnicities": transnational networks of people tied culturally despite the diversity of their places of residence and the limitations of national borders.[24] These ethnicities, united by Web sites and the Internet, are extensions of traditional societies whose adherents and cultures are dispersed throughout the world.[25] Among these expatriate groups have been some notoriously politically active ones—Sikhs, Sri Lankans, and Arabs—including the followers of Sheik Omar Abdul Rahman, who lived variously in Egypt, the Sudan, and New Jersey. Among his adherents was Muhammad Salameh, whose story is paradigmatic of the religious radical expatriate experience.

In New Jersey, Salameh lived virtually from hand to mouth, sharing addresses with several other people. One, at 34 Kensington Street, Jersey City, was a modest apartment on the fourth floor of an overcrowded building without elevators; another, on Weldom Street a few blocks away, was in a smelly, decrepit tenement building; and another, at 40 Pamrapo Avenue, was found to contain what FBI agents called "bomb-making paraphernalia." All were situated in a busy working-class neighborhood that, like other industrial neighborhoods of Jersey City, teemed with new immigrants from Haiti and the Middle East. The setting was in some ways not unlike the social and economic conditions in the crowded Palestinian refugee camps on the West Bank and in Jordan, where Salameh was born and raised and from which he departed in 1987 for America to improve his educational and financial situation. In the United States, where his limited English was a continuing social barrier, Salameh associated primarily with other Arabs. His life became focused around a local mosque located above a Chinese restaurant, led by the charismatic Egyptian cleric Sheik Omar Abdul Rahman. The trajectory of his life led ultimately to his participation in the bombing of the World Trade Center, where the world came to know him as the terrorist who foolishly returned to the Ryder rental agency to retrieve his deposit for the van he had rented and subsequently blown up, and was immediately caught by waiting agents of the FBI.[26]

Muhammad Salameh exemplifed several aspects of marginality. He was a refugee first in the Middle East and then in America. He came from abject poverty and was a man with little skills and few hopes of developing a career. He was a bachelor without good prospects for marriage. Yet one could say the same of thousands of others who immigrate to the United States in any given year, many of whom settle into respectable if not lucrative positions, and few of whom end up trying to destroy major urban buildings. At the same time, many of

Salameh's comrades in the World Trade Center conspiracy were not so-cially or economically marginal at all: some, like Mahmud Abouhalima and Nidal Ayyad, a chemical engineer, were well-educated profession-als with suburban homes and families.

Thus the case of Muhammad Salameh, while exemplifying a famil-iar pattern of marginality, also raises questions. What kind of causal connections should be made between marginality and the propensity for violent action? I hesitate to move too quickly. I do not think that economic or social despair leads automatically to violence, since virtu-ally everyone on the planet has experienced some sort of economic and social hardship in his or her life. In the cases that we have examined, however, it appears that the combination of factors has made a differ-ence, as has the intensity with which these factors are experienced and the availability of a religious and political vocabulary with which the frustrations can be articulated. Most important is the intimacy with which the humiliation is experienced and the degree to which it is re-garded as a threat to one's personal honor and respectability. These can create the conditions for a desperate need for empowerment, which, when no other options appear to be open, are symbolically and vio-lently expressed.

Why Guys Throw Bombs

Nothing is more intimate than sexuality, and no greater humiliation can be experienced than failure over what one perceives to be one's sexual role. Such failures are often the bases of domestic violence; and when these failures are linked with the social roles of masculinity and femi-ninity, they can lead to public violence. Terrorist acts, then, can be forms of symbolic empowerment for men whose traditional sexual roles—their very manhood—is perceived to be at stake.

Before we rush into an analysis of terrorism as a man's occupation, however, we have to acknowledge the fact that some women have played active roles in terrorist movements. The assassin who in 1991 killed Rajiv Gandhi, the son and successor of India's prime minister Indira Gandhi, was a female suicide bomber who hid her lethal cargo in her sari. She had been a member of a Sri Lankan Tamil separatist group that was angry at Rajiv Gandhi's support of the neighboring Sri Lankan government's attempts to quell their separatist uprising. When the Tupac Amaru movement invaded the Japanese embassy in Lima, Peru, in 1996, several young rural women were prominent among the cadres, who held the diplomats hostage. A Kurdish rebel suicide bomber in Turkey who killed nine people, including herself, on June 31, 1996, in the town of Tunceli was dressed as a pregnant woman in order to hide the bomb that she was carrying beneath her skirt.

In all of these incidents, however, the groups of which the young terrorist women were a part were motivated by secular political ideologies or ethnic separatism; they were not religious. I cannot think of a single religious activist movement in which women have played a prominent role, although some groups—especially those that are less conservative in their religious ideology—have provided an ancillary role for women.

In the Irish nationalist movement, for example, women formed their own paramilitary group, Cumann Na Mbann. Their main role, however, was to carry guns and explosives for the men to use in the military cadres of the Provisional Irish Republican Army.[27] The movement for Sikh separatism in India adopted much the same position. Cynthia Keppley Mahmood reported that when a young woman pleaded with the leader of the Khalistan Commando Force to allow her to become a member, he finally assented but restricted her to support roles—carrying munitions and messages—rather than being involved in "combat actions."[28] Mahmood said that the woman waited for the day when she would have the opportunity to be more active. That time came when she broke into the house of a Hindu shopkeeper whom she suspected as having reported her to the police. She held a gun at his head, berating him for turning her in. The shopkeeper denied that he had done so, and was "begging for pardon" and "crying that I was like his daughter," the young woman said. But she was not dissuaded. "I shot him down with my revolver," she went on to say, "with my own hands."[29]

In reporting this grisly story, the young Sikh woman said that one of her purposes in murdering the Hindu shopkeeper was to spur Sikh men into what she regarded as even greater acts of courage. If they saw that "girls could be so brave," she reasoned, then Sikh boys "could be even more brave."[30] The implication was that the task of killing was ordinarily the work of men—or "boys," as the young Sikh activists were called—and the role of women was to provide support, to challenge them, and to spur them on.

Her position was essentially that of the great martyr in the Sikh movement, Jarnail Singh Bhindranwale, who addressed his congregations as if the men (especially the young men) were the only ones listening, encouraging them to let their beards grow in the long Sikh fashion and describing their cowardice in the face of government opposition as "emasculation." In general, Bhindranwale's attitude was in line with the prevailing values of virtually all cultures of violence based on strong traditional religious ideologies. These have been postures of "radical patriarchalism," as Martin Riesebrodt has called it.[31] The role of men is in public life; the role of women is in the home.

Religious activists often have shown a certain paternalistic respect for women, as long as they have remained in their place. During the 1991–92 Muslim uprising in Algeria, Ali Belhaj, one of the Islamic Front leaders, said that a woman's primary duty was to "bear good Muslims"; and Sheik Abdelkhader Moghni, another Islamic Front leader, complained about women working and taking jobs from men. Women, he said, just "spend their salaries on makeup and dresses, they should return to their homes."[32] A businesswoman in Algiers responded by saying she feared that if the Islamic Front succeeded, it would usher in a reign of "pig power." "They're all male chauvinist pigs," she explained, adding, "believe me, we are worried."[33] The worst of these fears came true in Afghanistan, where the Taliban party promoted a male-dominant culture that did not tolerate women in public life, even as teachers, doctors, or nurses. Although they claimed that eventually Afghan society would become somewhat more liberal, they stated that society would not be regularized until the fighting was over. Such cases exemplify an assertion of masculinity and a recovery of public virility that is at once sexual, social, and political.

Does this explain why terrorism is primarily a male occupation, and why bombs are most often thrown by guys? I use the term *guys* in this case because it evokes the camaraderie of young males slightly on the edge of social acceptance. Moreover, it is etymologically rooted in religious activism. The term *guy* came into use in England in the seventeenth century after Guy Fawkes was tried and executed in 1606 for his role in the Gunpowder Plot. This extraordinary conspiracy planned by radical English Catholics involved thirty-six barrels of gunpowder hidden in a cellar under the House of Lords, set to be ignited on the opening day of Parliament. Intended as a protest against laws they thought would restrict their religious freedom, the explosion would have blown up both British legislative houses and King James I. Thus the religious terrorist, Fawkes, was the original "Guy," and his name came to be applied to all roguish men who skirted danger.

The religious terrorists of recent years are today's guys: bands of rogue males at the margins of respectability. The gender specificity of their involvement suggests that some aspect of male sexuality—sexual roles, identity, competence, or control—is a factor in the attitude of these "urban males in their teens."[34] Perhaps the easiest aspect to understand is the matter of sexual competence—by which I mean the capacity to have sex, an ability that is limited in traditional societies by moral restrictions and lack of opportunities. There is a certain amount of folklore about men and guns that cannot easily be dismissed—the notion, for instance, that sexual frustration leads to a fascination with phallic-shaped weaponry that explodes in a way that some men are unable to do sexually. As I mentioned earlier, the young bachelor self-martyrs in the Hamas movement enter into their suicide pacts almost as if it were a marriage covenant. They expect that the blasts that kill them will propel them to a bed in heaven where the most delicious acts of sexual consummation will be theirs for the taking. One young man who had committed himself to becoming a suicide bomber said that "when I exploded" and became "God's holy martyr," he was promised a place for himself and his family in paradise, seventy-two virgins, and a cash settlement for his family equivalent to six thousand dollars.[35] It was the virgins that seemed to interest the young man the most.

Sexual power for many men involves not only sexual competence—the ability to have sex—but also sexual control. This means knowing when not to have sex, and putting sex in its place. Their aversion to what appear to be sexual aberrations—including misplaced gender roles, such as women assuming dominant positions in the public arena—are examples of sex out of control. To many men these phenomena also exemplify a wider form of social disorder: they are illustrations of the encroaching power of evil, demonstrations of the pervasiveness of the lack of moral values, and examples of how social definitions have become skewed. In *The Turner Diaries,* for instance, William Pierce spoke of what he called "Women's lib" as being "a form of mass psychosis . . . promoted and encouraged by the System as a means of dividing our race against itself."[36]

This concern with sexual roles elevates the issue beyond one of simple sexual competence or control on a personal level. For Pierce, sex is a social problem: roles and conduct out of place in what he regards as a society in moral decline. Moreover, it is a public problem that leads in some cases to hostility. It is anger against sex out of place that is often evident in the targets of violence, such as abortion clinics and gay bars. At other times the violence itself has had sexual overtones, as in India and Algeria, where the rape of women has been employed as part of a terrorist act, or in Ireland, where torture of enemies has involved mutilation of the men's genitals—literally, in some cases, emasculating them.

What is the connection between these forms of violence, this macho religiosity, and these yearnings for political power? The antipathy toward modern women—the notion of female sexual roles out of place—is one clue. The hatred of homosexuality is another. It is true that the disdain of homosexuality has been a theme of conservative religion for centuries and was one of the criticisms that the religious opponents of the Enlightenment leveled against the values of secular morality in eighteenth-century France.[37] But it has returned with a peculiar stridency in contemporary religious cultures of violence, where the fear of homosexuality—homophobia—has been a prominent theme.

Virtually all radical religious movements of the final decades of the twentieth century have had a homophobic twist. In 1999 a gay couple was killed in northern California and gay bars were attacked allegedly by Christian Identity activists. Gays were included among the "mudpeople" that Benjamin Smith hoped to destroy in his 1999 Illinois rampage, and *The Turner Diaries* described homosexuality as a kind of aberration that "healthy males" would not consider.[38] Some have gone so far as to misquote the Bible in prescribing "the penaltys [sic] for race-mixing, homo-sexuality [sic], and usury" as "death."[39] The gay subculture of Tehran was one of the facets of modern Iranian life that angered Ayatollah Khomeini, and hundreds associated with it perished following the Islamic revolution in Iran. The acceptance of homosexuality in secular Israeli society has dismayed right-wing Jewish activists, who offered the rumors of Yasir Arafat's alleged penchant for boys as evidence of the moral corruption of Palestine's leadership.[40]

In Belfast, one of Ian Paisley's main criticisms of liberal Protestantism is its acceptance of gays. "Lesbianism, homosexuality held up as taught in the Bible and to be practiced by Christian people," he thundered in one of his sermons, "think of it!"[41] Along the same lines, one of Paisley's complaints about Catholic clergy is that they never marry, a matter of some suspicion to the arch-heterosexual Paisley. Regarding salvation, for instance, he assured his parishioners that the Protestant method was much more efficacious than the Catholic, in large part because of the morally suspect nature of the clergy. "You do not need to kneel at a confessional box," Paisley told them, "before a bachelor priest who has more sins than you have and yet pretends to forgive you."[42]

Kerry Noble said that his group, the Covenant, the Sword, and the Arm of the Lord, regards American cities to be like Sodom and Gomorrah largely because they harbor homosexuals.[43] Noble said that one of the turning points in his disaffection with the Christian Identity movement was when he entered a gay church in Kansas City with the intention of igniting a bomb he was carrying in his briefcase, and decided not to do it. After looking around and seeing men embrace other men, watching women kiss other women, and hearing the preacher speak about his male lover, Noble hesitated. He had second thoughts about the loss of life that would have resulted—at least fifty would have been killed—and he also questioned the effectiveness of the bombing. It would not, he reasoned, precipitate the revolution that he had hoped for. It was only later, after he had rejected the ideology and the personal ties to Christian Identity, that he also abandoned his homophobia and saw gays as scapegoats for what he and his group had regarded as society's immoralities.

Rev. Michael Bray told me that the secular government's tolerance for abortion and homosexuality were the two marks of its moral degeneracy. Considering Bray's prejudices, it is interesting to note that when Bray was sent to prison for bombing abortion clinics, he was placed in the same cell with a pedophile convicted of preying on boys. Bray and his cellmate became fast friends, Bray told me, but only after the pedophile repented of his sins. Still, the man acknowledged to Bray that his sexual inclination toward young men persisted. When Bray refused to take part in a prison prayer meeting with an out-of-the-closet gay prisoner who was unrepentant about his sexuality, this led to tensions within the cell. His cellmate became angry and accused Bray of being antigay. Bray tried to assure his cellmate that same-sex attractions were understandable as long as one did not act on those impulses, and as long as one felt remorseful if indeed such acts were committed.[44]

Why have such aversions to homosexuality been held so strongly by contemporary religious activists? One answer is a loss of identity: the kind of heterosexual male who is attracted to such movements is precisely the sort who loses power in a society in which women and gays have access to straight males' traditional positions of authority. They see women and gays as competition.

But there is another answer to the question of why radical religious groups are so homophobic: a loss of control. As Kerry Noble said, homosexuals have been scapegoats for a perceived systemic problem in society. When men have perceived their roles as diminished in a socioeconomic system that denies a sense of agency to individuals, either by being incompetent or overly competent—a faceless mechanical bureaucracy—this challenge has led to a defense of traditional roles. Because men have so frequently held the reins of public order as their gendered responsibility in society in the past, they have felt particularly vulnerable when the public world has fallen apart or has seemed beyond control. In this case, they have seen active women and gays not just as competition, but as symptoms of a world gone awry.

This is a deeper fear, and there is not much that men can do about it. If the problem were just one of competition, they could hope to better themselves, and at least some would be able to succeed on an individual basis. If the problem is more systemic, then it is a matter of social disorder or worse: a sinister hand controlling and disrupting the world. This perception has led naturally to the satanization of enemies and to theories of cosmic war. It has also led naturally to a kind of tribal instinct that encourages members of such cultures of violence to band together and fight.

In such a context, then, though same-sex erotic acts are suspect, male bonding makes sense. Like the camaradie of a football team facing a dangerous enemy in an uncertain struggle, the close community of men creates a primal form of social order. Unlike heterosexual bonding, which leads to private communities—families—the bonding of groups made up of the same sex, such as nuns and monks and football players, represents a primitive attempt to create a personalized form of public society. Individuals have a direct relationship with authority and a shared sense of responsibility in clearly delineated social roles. All-male radical religious groups, therefore, attempt to create and defend a righteous order in the face of massive social disorder.

These forms of marginal, male-bonding, anti-institutional, semipolitical movements are not idiosyncratic to the contemporary era. There have been occasions in past centuries when noninstitutional men's associations have spun off from mainstream religious traditions, often with violence on their agenda. The *assassini* of medieval Islam are one example. The murderous, goddess-worshiping *thugs* of India—from which we get the English word *thug*—are another. In Christianity we have had the "guys" of Guy Fawkes's seventeenth-century Catholic terrorists and before them the Crusaders—blessed by Church officials, at least at the outset of their ventures. The Freemasons of the eighteenth century are a Protestant example of men springing from the domesticity of Church religion and founding their own secret order. Though not known for its violence, the organization has skirted the edges of institutional Christianity. So the precedent of somewhat marginal male movements has been set within religious history. But the proliferation of noninstitutional male paramilitary orders, such as the Christian militia, is a relatively recent phenomenon. What is interesting is how intense the internal cohesion of the groups has been.

The Turner Diaries describes an initiation into just such an intimate male circle: the elite of the Order, as it is described in the novel. As he entered the initiation rites, the lead character observed a torchlight flickering over "the coarse, gray robes of the motionless throng" and thought to himself that these men were "the best my race has produced in this generation." They were truly men with whom he wished to bond. "These were no soft-bellied, conservative businessmen assembled for some Masonic mumbo-jumbo," the character affirmed to himself, and they were "no pious, frightened churchgoers whining for the guidance or protection of an anthropomorphic deity." They were *"real men, White* men, men who were now *one* with me in spirit and consciousness as well as in blood."[45]

As this romantic rhetoric from Pierce's novel suggests, such close male bonding could have a homoerotic element—perhaps paradoxically so, considering the aversion that most men in right-wing religious groups have to sex out of place, including publicly identified homosexual roles. Yet same-sex intimacy has been a strong feature of many right-wing movements. The residents of Richard Butler's Aryan Nations compound in Idaho, for instance, have virtually all been young unmarried men.[46] Even married male adherents of Christian Identity have found in their religious and political groupings a certain male bond. The friendship between Timothy McVeigh and Terry Nichols, for example, was so tight and time-consuming that Nichols's wife became jealous.

Young men who volunteered for suicide bombing missions sponsored by the Hamas movement usually worked in pairs and were sent out on missions accompanied by ritual elements often associated with marriage. On one of the videotapes depicting Hamas volunteers for suicide bombings, a young man no more than eighteen years old, wearing stylish dark glasses and a camouflage military cap, tells about his friend, who was sent on a suicide mission from which he never returned: "My brother Hatim, we were friends for the sake of God." The night before he left, the young man said emotionally, "he bequeathed me this gift." It was a dagger. The purpose was "to cut off the head of a collaborator or a Jew." He added, "and God living I will remain alive, and I will be able to fulfill the vow."[47]

The pattern of male bonding in radical religious groups was also found in the movement of Sikh activism that uprooted India's Punjab in the 1980s. Being part of the Sikh movement was to join in a "bond of love," one young militant told Cynthia Keppley Mahmood.[48] The portraits of Sukha and Jinda, the Sikh assassins of General Vaidya, that many militants kept on their walls portrayed what Mahmood called "comradely love." With their arms around each other's shoulders, they exemplified the "tight bond of solidarity among comrades-in-arms" that she said accounted for much of the courageous behavior of Sikh militants in the field and the cycles of revenge killing that quickly escalated in the Punjab. In confronting death, Sukha and Jinda were said to have stated in their farewell address that they imagined the hangman's rope "as the embrace of a lover," and they "longed for death as for the marital bed." Their own "dripping blood" would be the "outcome of this union," and they hoped it would "fertilize the fields of Khalistan."[49] Friendships such as that of Sukha and Jinda are common in societies where extramarital male-female relationships are not allowed, and relationships within one's own sex can develop to considerable intensities. The Hindi and Punjabi languages have terms for such buddies who are more than just friends: they are *yar,* "intimate friends," or *yaro-ki yar,* "the best of friends."

Friendship may also have played a role in the dramatic events in 1984 that led to the death of the leader of the Sikh movement, Sant Jarnail Singh Bhindranwale. Bhindranwale had befriended his young lieutenant, Surinder Singh Sodhi, whom the Sikh leader described as "my brother."[50] Journalists considered him Bhindranwale's "right hand man," "personal bodyguard," and "key hit-man."[51] It was the murder of Sodhi on April 17, 1984, that exacerbated the internal struggles between Bhindranwale's followers and the Akali Party forces linked with Gurcharan Singh and Sant Harchand Singh Longowal, both sequestered in the Sikhs' main shrine, the Golden Temple in Amritsar. Bhindranwale accused Gurcharan Singh of having plotted Sodhi's murder, and claimed that the death of his young comrade was like "chopping my right hand."[52] Bhindranwale spent the week following the youth's murder confined to his quarters. Within days Sodhi's killer and several members of the Akali camp were killed in reprisal. As tensions mounted between the two factions, the Indian army invaded the Golden Temple on June 5 in what became known as Operation

Bluestar. In the exchange of fire, Bhindranwale's forces killed the Akali leader, Gurcharan Singh, and Bhindranwale himself was killed. After Prime Minister Indira Gandhi was assassinated later that year, her son and successor, Rajiv, signed a peace accord with Longowal, who was himself soon thereafter assassinated, thus completing the spiral of violence that began with the killing of Bhindranwale's friend, Sodhi, in 1984.

The theme of male bonding was also found in the Hindu nationalist movement, the RSS, composed of celibate men who boasted of their manhood and took inordinate interest in providing political and religious training to boys and young men in Boy Scout–type outings. Yet when an American scholar published a study of one of the RSS's spiritual heroes, Ramakrishna, revealing the homosexual aspects of his mysticism, the clamor of protest in India was enormous, especially among right-wing supporters of the RSS and the political party they have spawned, the Bhartiya Janata Party (BJP).[53]

In the hostile Indian response to Jeffrey Kripal's book about Ramakrishna, it was not so much the suggestion of homosexual attraction that was seen as offensive but the modern Western role of the homosexual. The Indian critics found it inconceivable that a spiritual hero such as Ramakrishna could be capable of such a thing. In an e-mail rejoinder to Kripal on an Internet listserv that circulated among American scholars of South Asian religion, Narasingha Sil, a professor of Indian origin, assailed Kripal for making it appear as if Ramakrishna's homosexual tendencies—his "diseased and disturbed mental proclivities"—were "normal or natural." Sil was clearly upset that the guru was put in the same category as those Indian lads "cavorting up and down the streets of the elite quarters of Calcutta or Mumbai, sporting nose rings or earrings." Although the professor acknowledged in India a certain "fondness for young boys on the part of some adult men," it was primarily "a pathetic option for aged impotent males."[54]

Another scholar, Sarah Lee Caldwell, writing in the same listserv, ruminated over what she described as "deep connections between male sexual prowess, virility, and Hindu nationalist violence."[55] In her thinking, the uproar in India over Kripal's suggestion of Ramakrishna's homosexuality was a defensive "hypermasculine" response that had "roots in the colonial period." It was not just that Ramakrishna had a fondness for boys: the idea that he rejected playing the heterosexual male role and that his disciple, Vivekananda, may have played a pas-

sive role in satisfying his guru's sexual desires was, to many Hindu nationalists, "deeply threatening."[56] According to Caldwell, the notion
that a man would willingly play the woman's role of receiver in a sexual act raised specters of the "feminine" male of India. As several other
writers on India have observed, the British view of Indian males as effeminate was part of what has been described as "colonial discourse."[57]

India's nationalist leaders from Gandhi to current members of the BJP
have felt obligated to reassert the manliness and potency of India's leadership. As scholars such as Ashis Nandy have demonstrated, the rhetoric
of the British colonial period that referred to Indians in effeminite terms
had a deep and enduring impact on India's nationalist movement, an impact that continues to the present day.[58] When the BJP came to power
and shocked the world by conducting a series of nuclear tests on May 11,
1998, this demonstration of power was overwhelmingly approved within
India. As one Indian scholar observed, the BJP's display of power showed
the "hyper-masculinity" inherent in the Hindu nationalism movement
represented by such Hindu chauvinists as Balasaheb K. Thackeray, leader
of the Shiv Sena party, who responded to the nuclear tests with the comment that they proved that Indians were "not eunuchs."[59] In testing the
bomb, India's BJP leaders were not only asserting their national power
but also rejecting the colonial dominance of the West and its accompanying sense of emasculation.

Although supporters of the Christian militia in the United States
have not had the Indians' experience of being a colonized people, their
attitudes toward modern liberal government is similar to those of neo-
conservative Hindu nationalists. Both would agree with the characteri-
zation offered by William Pierce that liberal government expects an
obedience that is "feminine" and "infantile."[60] These are fears not only
of sexual impotence but of government's role in the process of emasculation. Men who harbor such fears protect themselves, therefore, not
only by setting up veiled defenses against the threats of powerful
women and unmanly men, but also by attempting to reassert control in
a world that they feel has gone morally and politically askew.

In Israel, the Jewish activist Avigdor Eskin, who accused Yasir Arafat
of having a sexual penchant for boys, meant this as not so much a character assault as a political criticism. Eskin offered the example of
Arafat's alleged bisexuality to show that the Palestinian leader could not
even control his own passions, much less the destiny of a geographical
region that Eskin regarded as sacred.[61] Eskin, a somewhat effete musi-
cian and philosopher, might have gained encouragement in his attitudes

from the American religious right, for whom antihomosexuality is something of a virtue, and with whom Eskin had frequent contact. Raised in
Russia, Eskin for a time traveled through the United States appearing on
the television programs of evangelists such as Pat Robertson and Jerry
Falwell as a spokesperson against the Soviet oppression of the Russian
Jewish community. Eventually emigrating to Israel, he became politically
active among the Russian Israeli community and was selected in 1998
by Russian immigrants as the fourth most well-known person in the
country. When I visited him in March 1998, he was deeply involved in
anti-Arab political activism and was under detention for charges of
planning to toss a pig's head into the quarters of the Muslim shrine the
Dome of the Rock, charges he denied. Whether or not the charges where
true, however, his comments confirmed that Eskin's main social concern
was not homosexuality but politics and the restoration of what he regarded as righteous biblical order.

The point I have been making is that the homophobic male-dominant
language of right-wing religious movements indicates not only a crisis of
sexuality but a clash of world views, not just a moral or psychological
problem but a political and religious one. It is political in that it relates
to the crisis of confidence in public institutions that is characteristic of
postmodern societies in the post–Cold War world. It is religious in that
it is linked with the loss of spiritual bearings that a more certain public
order provided.

When the lead character in *The Turner Diaries* saw on television the
horrific scenes of mangled bodies being carried from the federal building he had just demolished with a truckload of explosive fertilizer and
fuel oil, he could still confirm that he was "completely convinced" that
what he had done was necessary to save America from its leaders—
these "feminine," "infantile" men "who did not have the moral tough-
ness, the spiritual strength" to lead America and give it and its citizens
a moral and spiritual purpose. From his point of view, his wretched act
was redemptive.

Trivializing the effect of their violence, this character and his real-life
counterparts Timothy McVeigh, Mahmud Abouhalima, and many
other calculating but desperate men have tried to restore what they perceive to be the necessary social conditions for their sexual and spiritual
wholeness. Their rhetoric of manhood has been a cry to reclaim their
lost selves and their fragile world.

What they have in common, these movements of cowboy monks, is
that they consist of anti-institutional, religio-nationalist, racist, sexist,

male-bonding, bomb-throwing young guys. Their marginality in the modern world is experienced as a kind of sexual despair that leads to violent acts of symbolic empowerment. It could almost be seen as poignant, if it were not so terribly dangerous.

Fighting for the Rule of God

This conceptual shift from a feeling of loss of personal integrity and sexual potency to an anger directed at public authorities may be a distinctively male trait. Men, after all, gain much of their sense of self-identity from the public roles they play. Men are more likely than women to feel diminished when public order does not perform properly. In the 1998 crisis of the U.S. presidency, polls indicated that it was American men more than women who felt betrayed by the actions of President Clinton.

It is understandable, then, that such men could focus their anger on the state. After Paul Hill killed an abortion clinic doctor and his escort, he said he had "cast off the State's tyranny." Hill said that in the weeks prior to the shooting he had felt burdened with "the oppressive feeling" that he was "not free." His act, which gave him "inner joy and peace," was therefore aimed not just at the abortion clinic staff but at the government that he thought was responsible for the staff's actions and for his own sense of humiliation.[62]

It is also understandable that in a time when public authority is discredited, one looks for alternative sources of leadership. In a situation where it is believed that public morality is amiss, leaders are degenerate, and even laws are based on shaky ethical footing, one may retreat to the only authority that one can easily grasp: the direct confidence of a respected person. Similarly, one may look for a familiar basis of public legitimacy in religion.

This is a reversion to what Erik Erikson has described as "basic trust": the sense of self-assurance that comes from a solid personal relationship. In Erikson's understanding of an individual's psychological development, a bedrock of trust is established in a child's relationship with his or her parents; it is "the first component of a healthy personality."[63] When early bonds of trust are lost or outgrown later in life, they must be supplanted by something else that is trustworthy. "Religion, through the centuries," Erikson observed, has provided this bedrock of confidence. In times of crisis it has served to "restore a sense of trust."[64]

This need to create a climate of public trust based on personal relationships explains in part why so much of the efforts of groups within
cultures of violence have been spent on building and maintaining their
own communities. In some cases groups have established separate com-
munes, such as the Christian Identity communities of Elohim City; the
Covenant, the Sword, and the Arm of the Lord; and the Freeman
Compound. In Japan, Aum Shinrikyo formed its own towns administered by its own governments. Jewish groups took over settlements in
Arab territories, and Meir Kahane spoke of creating an independent
state of Judaea on the West Bank. Muslim and Sikh movements have
also had communal headquarters, such as Osama bin Laden's encampment in Afghanistan, which was bombed by American missiles in 1998,
and Sant Jarnail Singh Bhindranwale's command center in India, which
was based first in the Damdani Taksal ashram and then in the Sikhs'
Golden Temple in Amritsar.

Even groups that did not physically live together, such as Sheik
Omar Abdul Rahman's followers in New Jersey, developed such an intense relationship and such tight bonds of association that it was difficult for outsiders—including government informants—to penetrate.
The bonds that held such groups together were often fragile, and only
strong leadership and ideological commitment enabled them to cohere.
At times even these ties were frayed. At such times acts of violence—
though targeted at the cosmic enemy—were often directed at an internal audience, especially wayward or schismatic factions, that needed
demonstrations of power to be held in line. As I noted earlier in this
book, this was why many terrorist acts were not proclaimed to the
world: the intended audience had already received the message.

The internal dynamics of a movement can affect its stance toward
the surrounding society. In fact, one can look at terrorist movements
organizationally, as Martha Crenshaw has, and argue that the internal
tensions in the movement are greater predictors of the group's actions
than its interactions with its sworn enemies.[65] As we have seen, the
leaders of the radical Sikh group the Khalistan Commando Force regularly ordered killings of members of its own or a rival group whom they
felt had gotten out of line. If individuals in the groups were using their
military power "to get money, drugs, or women," one of the former
members told me, the KCF "would sometimes eliminate them to keep
the whole movement more respectable."[66]

In other movements also, as we have seen, recalcitrant members
were disdained as much or more than their enemies. It was Ian Paisley

who said that "we have no respect at all for the system of Romanism [Catholics], and we have less respect for the system of apostate Protestantism."[67] Rabbi Meir Kahane was said to have welcomed the idea of a Jewish civil war and predicted the political assassination of secular Jewish leaders. We earlier noted the rumors that Mahmud Abouhalima was involved in the murder of a moderate Muslim leader who rivaled Sheik Omar Abdul Rahman. Thus many acts of terrorism undertaken by a group have been aimed not at a wider audience but at its own members.

Michel Wieviorka has taken this idea of organizational causes for terrorism a step further and argued that terrorism is the result not only of a movement's internal dissension but also of its collapse. He has claimed that violence comes only when a splinter group is alienated from a larger movement and it—or the larger movement itself—has abandoned its ideology.[68] Wieviorka argued that what he calls "the organized practice of indiscriminate and irredeemable violence" is a "substitute for a movement which has either become imaginary or has fallen out of sync with the hopes pinned on it."[69] If Wieviorka's argument has merit, then one could see terrorism as the mark of a breakup of political movement, rather than a sign of its strength.

There is some evidence in Wieviorka's favor. Members of Aum Shinrikyo, for instance, released nerve gas into the Tokyo subways only when the police were closing in on them. Some of the most violent actions of Hamas came after the signing of the peace accord between Israel's Yitzhak Rabin and Palestine's Yasir Arafat, signaling to the leaders of Hamas that they were peripheral to the Palestinian leadership. The Sikh explosion that killed Chief Minister Beant Singh came two years after the movement had been virtually eradicated from the Punjab. And the incident that killed the greatest number of civilians in the years of troubles between Catholics and Protestants in Northern Ireland occurred after the peace settlement in 1998.

These cases indicate that terrorism has been a response to humiliation—a point that I have made throughout this book. While they also show that Wieviorka has been right in some cases and violence may have come with the dissolution of a movement's purpose, other examples show that this is not necessarily the case. The actions of Hamas and Jewish activists such as Dr. Goldstein have been justified in terms of the primary ideologies of the groups. When Mike Bray attacked an abortion clinic, he explained to me, he was showing his disappointment not only with the moderate policies of the pro-life movement but with those of the American government. He said that the attacks on clinics were also attacks on the government that stood behind them and on the secular values that supported such institutions.[70] Religious violence may indeed come as a result of internal tensions, schisms, and a sense of failed momentum, but it is usually justified in terms of cosmic war and the primary struggle with an external foe—the satanic enemy.

In fact, activist groups have often gone to some effort to make themselves respectable and credible in the eyes of their opposition and rival groups. Some acts of violence, such as the U.S. embassy bombings in Africa, were perpetrated to fulfill threats made against enemies. The Kashmiri rebels who killed their American and European hostages were said to have found themselves in a dilemma: they did not necessarily want to murder the young men, they said, but felt they had an obligation to be true to their word after they had threatened to kill them if their demands were not met. Mike Bray told me that Paul Hill was goaded into shooting abortion clinic staff by people such as Flip Benan, the head of Operation Rescue, who allegedly told him that if he believed in the moral necessity of such acts, he should carry them out.[71] Sikhs in the Punjab did not want to lose face with the Indian government; hence, according to Cynthia Keppley Mahmood, they felt obliged to kill Hindus and government officials once they had threatened to do so.

Although it may appear as if these acts were meant to win the respect of opponents, they also signified something else: the movements were attempting to establish themselves as their opponents' equals. In a display of what René Girard has described as mimesis, they were not only imitating their rivals but also showing their superiority in terms that they believed their rivals would understand. Many activists have used their courtroom trials as arenas to convey the message that through their acts they were sparring with the government and taunting it by accusing it of abandoning the very values it professed. As we have seen, Timothy McVeigh cited Justice Brandeis in implying that the U.S. government had set a bad example, and the World Trade Center defendants called the U.S. Department of Justice the department of "injustice." Paul Hill, during his trial in Miami on October 4, 1994, also accused the government that was convicting him of murder as "unjust."[72]

In the same vein, the suicide bombings perpetrated by the Hamas movement in residential neighborhoods of Tel Aviv and Jerusalem were, as one leader described them, "letters to Israel." They were invasions of the most domestic of their rival's quarters, with messages intended to show that "Hamas cannot be ignored" and "the security for Israel's people is zero."[73] In that sense the message was the medium in which it was sent: the bombing provided a moment of chaos, warfare, and victimage that the Hamas movement wanted Israeli society to experience. It made the point that war was at hand by providing a bloody scene of battle in Israel's own quiet neighborhoods.

What was buttressed in these acts of symbolic empowerment was not just the credibility of the Hamas leadership and their equality with government officials, but also the legitimacy of their ideology of religious social order. Through the currency of violence they were drawing attention to what they thought was significant about the social arena around them. In the language of Bourdieu they were creating a perverse "habitus," a dark world of social reality, and forcing everyone—Israelis and Palestinians alike—to take stock of their perception of the world.[74]

To some extent the empowerment worked, in that these symbolic events did affect the wider social and political arena. Mike Bray, in responding to my suggestion that bombing abortion clinics did not have any practical effect, gave the example of the IRA's Gerry Adams, who was visiting the White House at the time. "Look at Adams," Bray said, "wining and dining with Bill Clinton." Bray said that the public accepted this "as long as there was some distance between that moment and the time the last bomb went off." Bray concluded that whatever else the IRA's bombings achieved, they enabled Adams "to get the ear of people."[75]

Adams, like most activists, was aware that such displays of power not only elevated his movement's credibility but also advertised its sociopolitical agenda. Adams and other activists were also aware that the very act of performing violence in public is a political act: it announces that the power of the group is equal or superior to that of the state. In most cases this is exactly the message that the group wants to convey.

In Israel, for instance, the Jewish right has long accused the secular government of using its devotion to democracy as an excuse for not fully embracing the idea that Israel is a Jewish religious entity. Years before his attack on innocent Muslims at the Tomb of the Patriarchs in Hebron, Dr. Baruch Goldstein, in a letter to the editor of the *New York Times*, wrote that "Israelis will soon have to choose between a Jewish state and a democratic one."[76] Goldstein's massacre, I was told by one of his followers, displayed how serious he was about that choice. The supporter went on to tell me that now "Jews will have to learn to worship in a national way."[77] Yoel Lerner agreed with this position, telling me that in his opinion Israel should not be a democracy but a "Torahcracy"—a society based on the principle of Jewish law.[78]

This idea of a nation based on religious law is on the minds of Christian religious activists as well. Activists associated with Christian Identity advocate the creation of a Christian Republic.[79] White supremacists from throughout the United States and Canada met in Idaho allegedly to plot the forcible overthrow of the federal government and to create a separate Aryan nation within the United States. A government indictment based on information gleaned from this meeting stated that they planned to "carry out assassinations of federal officials, politicians and Jews, as well as bombings and polluting of municipal water supplies."[80]

Mike Bray, reflecting a Christian Reconstruction perspective, advocates the need for a return to "Christian law and order."[81] The models he has in mind are not only European Christian monarchies and Roman Catholic canon law, for which he has a certain respect, but also the Protestant governments of the early American colonies. Bray believes that the way that they grounded their constitutions in biblical law could set a precedent for a new kind of Christian government in the United States, though he recognizes that not everyone in the country would be enthusiastic about such a development.

For that reason, Bray advocates state's rights, a radical federalism that would allow for different forms of political rule in each state. Bray suggested a "translocation" of power that would allow "Christian civilization" to flourish in some states and "other civilizations" in others.[82] States would need to be bound together only for their common military defense. It is a proposal not unlike the "10 percent solution" offered by the Aryan Nations leader, Richard Butler, who advocates that 10 percent of American territory—such as the states of Idaho and Montana—be dedicated to white Christians.

Bray is encouraged in his dream of radical federalism by a statement by the governor of Florida, who declared Florida to be part of a Christian nation, and by the governor of Pennsylvania, who refused to use welfare money from Medicaid for the purpose of abortion. Bray pointed to countries such as South Africa, which once had what he described as a "Christian constitution," and he admires the attempts of Muslims in Iran, Sudan, and Afghanistan to create regimes grounded in Islamic law. To Bray, freedom of religion means freedom to live under religious law. Since America's secular government has denied Bray this freedom, he regards it as hypocritical.

The establishment of a rule based on religious law is the primary aim of many Muslim groups. Members of Hamas regard this as the main difference between their organization and secular groups such as Fateh associated with Yasir Arafat's Palestinian Authority. A similar argument has been made by activists in Egyptian movements. Mahmud Abouhalima told me that President Hosni Mubarak could not be a true Muslim because he does not make *shari'a*—Islamic law—the law of the land.[83] A cleric in Cairo's conservative Al-Azhar theological school told me he resented his government's preference for Western law. "Why should we obey Western laws when Muslim laws are better?" he asked me.[84] It is this position that is assumed by many Muslim activists: Western political institutions and the ideology on which they are based should be banished from their territories. They want to rebuild their societies on Islamic foundations.

In some cases activist groups have carried this critique to an extreme. They have not only rejected secular political authority but also created alternatives to it. Aum Shinrikyo, for instance, designated the leaders in its organization with government administrative titles such as minister of defense, minister of intelligence, minister of internal affairs, and minister of science and technology. The idea was not only to show that their organization could do the government's job but also to prepare the movement for actually doing that job after the arrival of the global catastrophe predicted by Shoko Asahara. When that dark day came, the government of Aum Shinrikyo would be the only one remaining to administer civil order.

In India, during the height of the Sikh rebellion in the 1980s, militants were treated as if they possessed an authority rivaling that of police and other government officials. Villagers in terrorist zones around the Punjab cities of Batala and Tarn Taran were unwilling to report violent incidents to officials, and radical youths set up their own courts and governmental offices. "Politics can be beautiful," I was told by a former head priest of Sikhism's central shrine.[85] "But it must be the right kind of politics." By this he meant a politics fused with religion, where "religion dominated politics" rather than the other way around.[86] When the country of Khalistan was created and Sikh rule established, one of the leaders of the movement told me, it would be a rule of law that would bring justice to all, not just Sikhs, in a regime that lauded the tenets of the Sikh scriptures and the guru Granth Sahib as supreme.[87] Exactly how this differed from the current form of political organization in India, however, remained obscure.

This goal of righteous rule is sometimes touted by members of activist groups as the singular purpose of their terrorist acts. Yet in fact, with the possible exception of the Palestinian Authority and the independent commissions of Northern Ireland, no governmental apparatus has ever been created through the means of terrorism. When religious regimes have been established (in Afghanistan, Sudan, and Iran; briefly in Turkey and Tajikistan; and nearly in Algeria), they rode into power through the vehicle of peaceful democratic elections or through well-organized military takeovers. It was not through the sporadic and extreme performances of power that characterize guerrilla terrorist acts.

In fact, despite their bravado, groups associated with terrorism have largely shied from politics. They have eschewed elections. When given the opportunity to run for office, they have usually rejected it, as Hamas did in Palestine in 1996 and radical Sikhs did in Punjab in 1992. If they did attempt to win at the polls, as Aum Shinrikyo did in 1990, they failed miserably. Nor have they attempted to develop effective fighting forces other than those needed for a hit-and-run style of terrorist bombing.

The images of political order that they yearn to create have been deliberately fuzzy. Sometimes they have appeared to be democratic, sometimes socialist, sometimes a sort of religious oligarchy. Sometimes they have been nationalist, at other times international in scope. Islamic movements especially have projected the illusion of waging a global struggle. The Hamas leader Abdul Aziz Rantisi told me that what distinguishes his organization from Yasir Arafat's is that the Palestinian Authority is waging a "national struggle" whereas Hamas is "transnational."[88] Similarly, the assemblage of activists coordinated by Sheik Omar Abdul Rahman and Osama bin Laden have been proudly multinational in membership. But what has that meant politically? Although it is clear who they hate, nowhere in their program have they given a design for a global political entity—Islamic or otherwise—that could actually administrate the results of a victory over American and secular rule and the emergence of a religious revolution, should they ever achieve it.

My conclusion is that although some movements for religious nationalism are indeed serious alternatives to secular rule, proponents of religious terrorism often have a less tangible goal. These acts are often devices for symbolic empowerment in wars that cannot be won and for goals that cannot be achieved. The very absence of thought about what the activists would do if they were victorious is sufficient indication that they do not expect to be, and perhaps do not even want to be. They represent a peculiar corollary to the advice of the French theorist Frantz Fanon during Algeria's war of independence some years ago, when he advocated terrorism as the Algerians' mobilizing weapon. Fanon reasoned that even a small display of violence could have immense symbolic power by jolting the masses into an awareness of their own potency.[89] What Fanon did not realize is that for some activist groups the awareness of their potency is all that they desire.

Yet these acts of symbolic empowerment have had an effect beyond whatever personal satisfaction and feelings of potency they have imparted to those who supported and conducted them. The very act of killing on behalf of a moral code is a political statement. Such acts break the state's monopoly on morally sanctioned killing. By putting the right to take life in their own hands, the perpetrators of religious violence have made a daring claim of power on behalf of the powerless, a basis of legitimacy for public order other than that on which the secular state relies. In doing so, they have demonstrated to everyone how fragile public order actually is, and how fickle the populace's assent to the moral authority of power can be.

CHAPTER 11

The Mind of God

When the shy young man grinned into the videocamera the day before he was to become a martyr in a Hamas suicide operation, proclaiming that he was "doing this for Allah," he was demonstrating one of the remarkable facts about those who have committed acts of terrorism in the contemporary world: they would do virtually anything if they thought it had been sanctioned by divine mandate or conceived in the mind of God.[1] The power of this idea has been enormous. It has surpassed all ordinary claims of political authority and elevated religious ideologies to supernatural heights.

In this book we have observed the potency of religion in certain pockets of public life. We have seen how religious ideas and the sense of religious community have been endemic to the cultures of violence from which terrorism has sprung; how the drama of religion has been especially appropriate to the theater of terror; how images of martyrdom, satanization, and cosmic war have been central to religious ideologies; and how these images and ideas have been agents of social empowerment, personal pride, and political legitimization. The conclusion is inescapable: even at the dawn of a new millennium, religion continues to make a claim on public life. As the cases in this book show, the claim has sometimes been violent.

Religion has given an extraordinary twist to the practice of public terrorism, though some of the hallmarks of religious terrorism described in this book are similar to those associated with terrorist acts motivated solely by prospects of political gain. All terrorism is violent, and its violence may be performed for symbolic as well as strategic reasons. Much of what I have said about religious terrorism in this book may be applied to other forms of political violence—especially those that are ideological and ethnic in nature. To some degree all of them—acts of leftists, separatists, and religious nationalists—are expressions of what I have called performance violence.

What is striking about religious terrorism is that it is almost exclusively symbolic, performed in remarkably dramatic ways. Moreover, these disturbing displays of violence have been accompanied by strong claims of moral justification and an enduring absolutism, characterized by the intensity of the religious activists' commitment and the transhistorical scope of their goals.

The absolutism of religion has been revealed especially in the notion of cosmic war. Although left-wing movements subscribe to what may seem a similar idea—the concept of class conflict—ordinarily this contest is thought to take place only on a social plane and within the temporal limitations of history. In fact, in the more humane versions of Marxist conflict theory, persons can be separated from their class roles: capitalists, for instance, can be reeducated, as the leaders in Mao Zedong's Chinese communist regime attempted to do with former landlords and businessmen. Religious concepts of cosmic war, however, are ultimately beyond historical control, even though they are identified with this-worldly struggles. A satanic enemy cannot be transformed; it can only be destroyed.

The vast time lines of religious struggles also set them apart from secular conflicts. Most social and political struggles have sought conclusion within the lifetimes of their participants. But religious struggles have taken generations to succeed. As we have seen, the leaders of Hamas have claimed that they can persevere even in the face of Israel's overwhelming military superiority. "Palestine was occupied before," Dr. Rantisi reminded me, "for two hundred years." He assured me that he and his Palestinian comrades "can wait again—at least that long."[2] In some cases religious activists have been prepared to wait for eons—and some struggles have not been expected to be completed within human history; they must await their fulfillment in some transtemporal realm. There is no need, therefore, to compromise one's goals in a struggle that has been waged in divine time and with the promise of heaven's rewards. There is no need, also, to contend with society's laws and limitations when one is obeying a higher authority. In spiritualizing violence, therefore, religion has given terrorism a remarkable power.

Ironically, the reverse is also true: terrorism has given religion power as well. Although, as I have noted, sporadic acts of terrorism do not lead to the establishment of new religious states, they make the political potency of religious ideology impossible to ignore. Along with empowering individuals and movements, therefore, violence has empowered religion: it has given religious organizations and ideas a public importance that they have not enjoyed for many years. When Mike Bray told me he hoped that the bombing of abortion clinics would make people reflect "not on what they think, but what God thinks," he was asserting a claim for the primacy of religion in public life.[3]

Empowering Religion

But what does God think? Regardless of what Mike Bray thinks God thinks, not everyone—not all Christians, not all Lutherans, not even all members of Bray's church or the culture of violence with which he has been associated—would agree. Interpretations of scripture vary widely, and much of the controversy within religious traditions has been precisely over the issue of God's will. The discipline of theology emerged as a human attempt to try to construe *theo-logos,* literally, the knowledge, or thinking, related to God. Only rarely does this thinking justify acts of violence, and yet these rare occasions have appeared in virtually every religious tradition. The Christian, Jewish, Muslim, Hindu, Sikh, and Buddhist cultures of violence described earlier in this book rely on these precedents and justifications for their own acts of religious violence.

With these justifications for violence in mind, the religious activists cited in this book have been able to go about their business of killing with the certainty that they were following the logic of God. In each case, however, other members of their traditions have strongly disagreed. In fact, all of the groups that have sanctioned violence in the form of terrorism have been marginal—in varying degrees—to their own religious societies. Their violence has been in part a counterbalance to their marginality, a way of empowering them within their own religious communities. This marginality often preceded their acts of violence, and became more extreme afterward. In some cases the movements were proudly peripheral, and the disdain that the wider religious community displayed toward them was reciprocated.

The Aum Shinrikyo movement, for instance, regarded itself as a perfect synthesis of all forms of Buddhism, and indeed all religions. But in the public outcry after the nerve gas incident, many religious leaders denied that Aum was even a religion, much less a form of Buddhism. Even the movement to which it was most closely related—a new religion called Agonshu, in which Shoko Asahara had once participated—questioned Aum's legitimacy as a religious organization.[4] Asahara, for his part, questioned the legitimacy of Agonshu and other forms of Japanese Buddhism.

In America, members of Christian militia groups have disdained liberal Protestantism and even mocked Christian conservatives. Richard Butler left the Presbyterian ministry to form his own Church. William Pierce, writing in *The Turner Diaries,* observed that "the Jewish takeover of the Christian churches and corruption of the ministry is now virtually complete."[5] Pierce went on to say that the liberal clergy was less interested in the teachings of Christianity than in "government 'study' grants, 'brotherhood' awards, fees for speaking engagements, and a good press." He was even more vituperative about conservative Christians, whom he called "the world's greatest cowards." Adding insult to injury, Pierce claimed that the cowardice of most Christian conservatives was "excelled only by their stupidity."[6] It was the rare Christian who saw, as Pierce's characters did, that the governmental system played a key role in "undermining and perverting Christendom" and that its destruction was essential for the emergence of true Christianity.[7] Matthew Hale took this position one step further and rejected Christian churches entirely, claiming them to be a Jewish conspiracy. His World Church of the Creator was intended, therefore, to be not just a branch of Christianity but an antidote to it.

The tension between militant and mainstream religion has existed within virtually every tradition. In Judaism, for example, at the time of the assassination of Yitzhak Rabin, the orthodox Jewish leadership in Israel was dubious that rabbis could be found who would give religious sanction to such an act, and their doubt turned to astonishment when several rabbis were located who indeed gave authorization for killing another Jew under the moral precedents of traditional law. Yoel Lerner told me that he regarded the rabbinic establishment in Israel as "comfortable" and "cowardly"—"unwilling to rock the boat" over political issues that he thought their beliefs should command them to champion.[8]

Among Muslim groups, Hamas has also been marginal. Though the movement has had its clerical supporters—sheiks and mullahs who have provided religious legitimization for its ventures and been widely revered throughout Palestinian society, Hamas has not been authorized by all members of the Islamic hierarchy in Palestine, nor has it ever sought such authorization. Only in Gaza has it enjoyed much support from traditional Muslim clerics. Elsewhere in Palestine it has prided itself on its prophetic role, somewhere on the margins of social respectability.

Much the same can be said of other militant Islamic movements. The men who were members of the al Gamaa-i Islamiya (Islamic Party) led by Sheik Omar Abdul Rahman and were sentenced to life in prison for their part in the bombing of New York City's World Trade Center in 1993 were participants in a semisecret male society that had an uneasy relationship with the immigrant Muslim community to which they were connected. In fact, one of the first signs of the movement's violence in the United States was the takeover of the Abu Bakr mosque in Brooklyn. In 1992 Mahmud Abouhalima is said to have engineered a leadership coup over the protests of its more moderate members.[9]

Perhaps the most successful of the recent radical male Islamic movements, Afganistan's Taliban, also has had an uneasy relationship with the more moderate clergy of its country. Shoving aside many of the traditional leaders, these former students of Islamic schools seized power through military means, capturing the capital, Kabul, in 1995. In August 1998 the last outposts of opposition in northern Afghanistan crumbled to their control. Still the young leaders displayed the trappings and organization of their brigand past. They wore the traditional clothing of their rural homelands and treated the modern city of Kabul as if it were a village. Adopting an even stricter interpretation of Islamic law than most of the Kabul clergy, the Taliban leaders refuse to let women work, even as nurses and doctors in the hospitals or as teachers in women's schools.

In India, the radical Sikh leader Jarnail Singh Bhindranwale emerged from the pastorate of a relatively obscure religious shrine—marginal to the traditional bases of Sikh political power—and was elevated to the leadership of a large and potent movement. Although after his death many Sikhs revered Bhindranwale as a martyr, and some Sikh congregations (*gurdwaras*) were dedicated to his memory, many Sikhs have expressed uncertainty about his legitimacy in their tradition and questioned the role that history would ultimately accord him.

In many recent cases of religious terrorism, therefore, the function of violence has been not only to empower individuals and their ideological causes, but also to vault marginal religious movements into positions of power vis-à-vis their moderate, mainstream rivals. Aum Shinrikyo, for example, in a moment when its leadership seemed trapped and the movement was dying off, chose to demolish itself in a dramatic way, thus ensuring its place in history.

Yet violence alone does not allow marginal religious groups to enjoy positions of prominence, at least not for very long. The groups that have made a long-term impact, such as Hamas, the Khalistan movement, Christian Identity, and the Jewish right wing, have used violence not only to draw attention to themselves but also to articulate the concerns of those within their wider cultures. Within these circles they have not been marginal at all. Radical though they may be, they have represented widely held feelings of alienation and oppression, and for this reason their strident language and violent acts have been considered by their cohorts as perhaps intemperant but understandable.

This point was brought home to me in Gaza when a young man who worked as a waiter at a seaside cafe and attended business school told me that although he was not a member of Hamas, he was glad it existed. He supported the movement, he told me, because he thought that it kept Yasir Arafat "more Islamic and more aggressive towards Israel."[10] Even Aum Shinrikyo had a kind of tacit support within Japan. Though few Japanese outside the movement would publicly support it, the members of Aum were not unlike those of Japan's many other new religious movements. They shared the same dedication to a cause, the same disaffection toward society, and the same sense of alienation that many young Japanese felt toward the bureaucracy and competition of modern urban life.

The radical religious movements that emerged from these cultures of violence throughout the world are remarkably similar, be they Christian, Jewish, Muslim, Buddhist, or Sikh. What they have in common are three things. First, they have rejected the compromises with liberal values and secular institutions that were made by most mainstream religious leaders and organizations. Second, they refuse to observe the boundaries that secular society has imposed around religion—keeping it private rather than allowing it to intrude into public spaces. And third, they have replaced what they regard as weak modern substitutes with the more vibrant and demanding forms of religion that they imagine to be a part of their tradition's beginnings.

The fact that these movements are marginal, however, does not mean that they are intrinsically different from mainstream religion. As strident as some of them appear, I hesitate to label them "cultic" or "fundamentalist," as some observers have described these politically active religious movements that have emerged in the late twentieth century. In my view, it is not their spirituality that is unusual, but their religious ideas, cultural contexts, and world views—perspectives shaped by the sociopolitical forces of their times. These movements are not simply aberrations but religious responses to social situations and expressions of deeply held convictions. In talking with many of the supporters of these cultures of violence, I was struck with the intensity of their quests for a deeper level of spirituality than that offered by the superficial values of the modern world.

Mahmud Abouhalima told me that the critical moment in his religious life came when he realized that he could not compromise his Islamic integrity with the easy vices offered by modern society. Abouhalima claimed that he had spent the early part of his life running away from himself. Although involved in radical Egyptian Islamic movements since his college years in Alexandria, he felt there was no place where he could settle down. He told me that the low point came when he was in Germany, trying to live the way that he imagined Europeans and Americans carried on: a life in which the superficial comforts of sex and inebriants masked an internal emptiness and despair.[11] Abouhalima said his return to Islam as the center of his life carried with it a renewed sense of obligation to make Islamic society truly Islamic—to "struggle against oppression and injustice" wherever it existed.[12] What was constant, Abouhalima said, was his family and his faith. Islam was both "a rock and a pillar of mercy."[13] But it was not the Islam of liberal, modern Muslims: they, he felt, had compromised the tough and disciplined life the faith demanded.

Abouhalima wanted his religion to be hard, unlike the humiliating, mind-numbing comforts of secular modernity. His newfound religion was what he perceived to be traditional Islam. This was also the case with born-again Sikhs in the separatist movement in India: theirs, they claimed, was real Sikhism.

Followers of Aum and of movements related to Christian Identity and Christian Reconstruction, though aware that they were involved in nontraditional forms of religion, have insisted that their new religions have ancient roots. They have claimed that their groups are in fact revivals of the original forms of their traditions. The name of Richard Butler's new church, based on Christian Identity teachings, was meant to emphasize its authority: the Church of Jesus Christ, Christian. In Timothy McVeigh's favorite novel, *The Turner Diaries,* William Pierce wrote about the role that his militants played in restoring Christianity's "spiritual strength" and "spiritual health."[14] But because churches had subverted the Christian message, Pierce's Cosmotheist ideology had to invent its own version of traditional religion.

Pierce's new "old religion" was a curious amalgam: partly mystical, partly medieval, and partly a juvenile revival of Boy Scout and fraternity rites. Without the benefit of clergy, the members of the fictional Order in Pierce's novel undertook an initiation similar to the rites of joining a monastic order. The central character in the novel told of being required to wear "something like a monk's robe" and being led to a dark ceremony room where the leader's face was illuminated by candles. The leader explained that the initiates had "passed the test of the Word and the test of the Deed" and shown "a correct attitude toward the Cause." The high point of the initiation came when the members were told to take an oath—"a mighty Oath, a moving Oath," the central character in the novel recalled, saying that it "shook me to my bones and raised the hair on the back of my neck."[15] With this oath the members of the Order were spiritually armed to be "bearers of the Faith" in a godless world.[16] (The capitalizing of "Word," "Deed," "Cause," "Oath," and "Order" is in the novel.)

Activists such as McVeigh and Abouhalima—and for that matter, Abdul Rahman, Rantisi, Bhindranwale, Asahara, Kahane, Lerner, Bray, and Hill—have imagined themselves as defenders of ancient faiths. But in fact they have created new religious forms: like many present-day spiritual leaders, they have used the language of traditional religion to build bulwarks around aspects of modernity that have threatened them and to suggest ways out of the mindless humiliation of modern life. It was vital to their image of religion, however, that it be perceived as ancient.

The need for religion—a "hard" religion as Abouhalima called it, an "ancient" one as Pierce imagined it—was a response to the soft treachery they observed in the new societies around them. The modern secular world that Abouhalima, Pierce, and the others inhabited was a dangerous, chaotic, and violent sea for which religion was an anchor in a harbor of calm. At some deep and almost transcendent level of consciousness, they sensed their lives slipping out of control, and they felt both responsible for the disarray and a victim of it. To be abandoned by religion in such a world would mean a loss of their own individual identities. In fashioning a "traditional religion" of their own, they exposed their concerns not so much with their religious, ethnic, or national communities as with their own personal, imperiled selves.

These intimate concerns of Abouhalima, McVeigh, and other activists were prompted by the perceived failures of public institutions. As Pierre Bourdieu has observed, social structures never have a disembodied reality; they are always negotiated by individuals in their own strategies for maintaining personal identity and success in life. Such institutions are legitimized by the "symbolic capital" they accrue through the collective trust of many individuals.[17] When that symbolic capital is devalued, when political and religious institutions undergo what Jürgen Habermas has called a "crisis of legitimacy," this devaluation of authority is experienced not only as a political problem but as an intensely personal one, as a loss of agency.[18]

It is this sense of a personal loss of power in the face of chaotic political and religious authorities that is common, and I believe critical, to Abouhalima's al Gamaa-i Islamiya, Timothy McVeigh's circle of militia activists, and most other movements for Christian, Muslim, Jewish, Sikh, Buddhist, and Hindu nationalism around the world. The syndrome begins with the perception that the public world has gone awry, and the suspicion that behind this social confusion lies a great spiritual and moral conflict, a cosmic battle between the forces of order and chaos, good and evil. Such a conflict is understandably violent, and this violence is often felt by the victimized activist as powerlessness, either individually or in association with others of his gender, race, or ethnicity. The government—already delegitimized—is perceived to be in league with the forces of chaos and evil.

Postmodern Terror

One of the reasons government is easily labeled the enemy of religion is that to some degree it is. By its nature, the secular state is opposed to the idea that religion should have a role in public life. From the time that modern secular nationalism emerged in the eighteenth century as a product of the European Enlightenment's political values, it has assumed a distinctly antireligious, or at least anticlerical, posture. The ideas of John Locke about the origins of a civil community and the "social contract" theories of Jean Jacques Rousseau required very little commitment to religious belief. Although they allowed for a divine order that made the rights of humans possible, their ideas had the effect of taking religion—at least Church religion—out of public life. At the time, religious "enemies of the Enlightenment"—as the historian Darrin McMahon described them—protested religion's public demise.[19] But their views were submerged in a wave of approval for a new view of social order in which secular nationalism was thought to be virtually a natural law, universally applicable and morally right.

Enlightenment modernity proclaimed the death of religion. Modernity signaled not only the demise of the Church's institutional authority and clerical control, but also the loosening of religion's ideological and intellectual grip on society. Scientific reasoning and the moral claims of the secular social contract replaced theology and the Church as the bases for truth and social identity. The result of religion's devaluation has been "a general crisis of religious belief," as Bourdieu has put it.[20] This has been a problem not just for believers but for society as a whole, for it has undercut the public's ability to rely on public symbols. According to Bourdieu, "The crisis of religious language and its performative efficacy" is part of the collapse of an old world view: "the disintegration of an entire universe of social relations."[21]

In countering this disintegration, resurgent religious activists have proclaimed the death of secularism. They have dismissed the efforts of secular culture and its forms of nationalism to replace religion. They have challenged the notion that secular society and the modern nation-state can provide the moral fiber that unites national communities or the ideological strength to sustain states buffeted by ethical, economic, and military failures. Their message has been easy to believe and has been widely received because the failures of the secular state have been so apparent.

The moral leadership of the secular state has become increasingly challenged in the last decade of the twentieth century following the end of the Cold War and the rise of a global economy. The Cold War provided contesting models of moral politics—communism and democracy—that have been replaced by a global market that has weakened national sovereignty and is conspicuously devoid of political ideals. The global economy became characterized by transnational businesses accountable to no single governmental authority and with no clear ideological or moral standards of behavior. But while both Christian and Enlightenment values were left behind, transnational commerce transported aspects of Westernized popular culture to the rest of the world. American and European music, videos, and films were beamed across national boundaries, where they threatened to obliterate local and traditional forms of artistic expression. Added to this social confusion were convulsive shifts in political power that followed the breakup of the Soviet Union and the faltering of Asian economies.

The public sense of insecurity that has come in the wake of these cataclysmic global changes has been felt not only in the societies of those nations that were economically devastated by them—especially countries in the former Soviet Union—but also in economically stronger industrialized societies. The United States, for example, has seen a remarkable degree of disaffection with its political leaders and witnessed the rise of right-wing religious movements that feed on the public's perception of the inherent immorality of government.

Is the rise of religious terrorism related to these global changes? We know that some groups associated with violence in industrialized societies have an antimodernist political agenda. At the extreme end of this religious rejection of modernism in the United States are members of the American anti-abortion group Defensive Action, the Christian militia and Christian Identity movement, and isolated groups such as the Branch Davidian sect in Waco, Texas. When Michael Bray and other members of the religious right cast aspersions at "the new world order" allegedly promoted by President Bill Clinton and the United Nations, what he and his colleagues feared was the imposition of a reign of order that was not just tyrannical but atheist. They saw evidence of an antireligious governmental pogrom in what they regarded as a pandering to pluralist cultural values in a society with no single set of religious moorings.

Similar attitudes toward secular government have emerged in Israel—the religious nationalist ideology of the Kach party is an extreme example—and, as the Aum Shinrikyo movement demonstrated, in Japan. Like the United States, contentious groups within these countries became disillusioned about the ability of secular leaders to guide their countries' destinies. They identified government as the enemy. In Israel, for instance, Hamas and the Jewish right have been in opposition not so much to each other as to their own secular leaders. This fact was demonstrated by the reaction of Jewish settlers in Gaza to a Hamas suicide bombing attempt in 1998, soon after the Wye River accords, in which an activist attempted to ram a car loaded with explosives into a school bus filled with forty of the settlers' children. One of the parents immediately lashed out in hatred—not against the Arabs who tried to kill her child, but against her own secular leader, Netanyahu, whom she blamed for precipitating the action by entering into peace agreements with Arafat.[22] Her comments demonstrated that the religious war in Israel and Palestine has not been a war between religions, but a double set of religious wars—Jewish and Muslim—against secularism.

The global shifts that have given rise to antimodernist movements have also affected less-developed nations. India's Jawaharlal Nehru, Egypt's Gamal Abdel Nasser, and Iran's Riza Shah Pahlavi were once committed to creating versions of America—or a kind of cross between America and the Soviet Union—in their own countries. But new generations of leaders no longer believed in the Westernized visions of Nehru, Nasser, or the shah. Rather, they were eager to complete the process of decolonialization and build new, indigenous nationalisms.

When activists in Algeria demonstrating against the crackdown on the Islamic Salvation Front in 1991 proclaimed that they were continuing the war of liberation against French colonialism, they had the ideological rather than political reach of European influence in mind. Religious activists such as the Algerian leaders, Ayatollah Khomeini in Iran, Sheik Ahmed Yassin in Palestine, Sayyid Qutb and his disciple Sheik Omar Abdul Rahman in Egypt, L. K. Advani in India, and Sant Jarnail Singh Bhindranwale in India's Punjab have asserted the legitimacy of a postcolonial national identity based on traditional culture.[23]

The result of this disaffection with the values of the modern West has been what I have called a "loss of faith" in the ideological form of that culture, secular nationalism.[24] Although a few years ago it would have been a startling notion, the idea has now become virtually commonplace that secular nationalism—the principle that the nation is rooted in a secular compact rather than a religious or ethnic identity—is in crisis. In many parts of the world it is seen as an alien cultural construction, one closely linked with what has been called "the project of modernity."[25] In such cases, religious alternatives to secular ideologies have had extraordinary appeal.

The uncertainty about what constitutes a valid basis for national identity is a political form of postmodernism.[26] In Iran it has resulted in the rejection of a modern Western political regime and the creation of a successful religious state. Increasingly, even secular scholars in the West have recognized that religious ideologies might offer an alternative to modernity in the political sphere.[27] Yet what lies beyond modernity is not necessarily a new form of political order, religious or otherwise. In nations formerly under Soviet control, for example, the specter of the future beyond the socialist form of modernity has been one of cultural anarchism. The fear of a spiritual as well as a political collapse at modernity's center has, in many parts of the world, led to terror.

Both violence and religion have emerged at times when authority is in question, since they are both ways of challenging and replacing authority. One gains its power from force and the other from its claims to ultimate order. The combination of the two in acts of religious terrorism has been a potent assertion indeed. Whether or not the perpetrators of these acts consciously intended them to be political acts, any public act of violence has political consequences. Insofar as they have been attempts to reshape the public order, they have been examples of what José Casanova has called the increasing "deprivatization" of religion.[28] In various parts of the world where attempts have been made by defenders of religion to reclaim the center of public attention and authority, religious terrorism is often the violent face of these attempts.

The postmodern religious rebels that we have examined in this book have therefore been neither anomalies nor anachronisms. From Algeria to Idaho, these small but potent groups of violent activists have represented growing masses of supporters, and they have exemplified currents of thinking and cultures of commitment that have risen to counter the prevailing modernism—the ideology of individualism and skepticism—that has emerged in the past three centuries from the European Enlightenment and spread throughout the world. They have come to hate secular governments with an almost transcendent passion. These guerrilla nationalists have dreamed of revolutionary changes that would establish a godly social order in the rubble of what the citizens of most secular societies have regarded as modern, egalitarian democracies. Their enemies have seemed to most people to be both benign and banal: modern, secular leaders such as Yitzhak Rabin and Anwar Sadat, and such symbols of prosperity and authority as the World Trade Center and the Japanese subway system. The logic of this kind of militant religiosity has therefore been difficult for many people to comprehend. Yet its challenge has been profound, for it has contained a fundamental critique of the world's post-Enlightenment secular culture and politics.

For this reason these acts of guerrilla religious warfare have been not only attempts at "delegitimization," as Ehud Sprinzak has put it, but also relegitimization: attempts to purchase public recognition of the legitimacy of religious world views with the currency of violence.[29] Since religious authority can provide a ready-made replacement for secular leadership, it is no surprise that when secular leaders have been deemed inadequate or corrupt, the challenges to their legitimacy and the attempts to gain support for their rivals have been based on religion. When the proponents of religion have asserted their claims to be the moral force undergirding public order, they sometimes have done so with the kind of power that a confused society can graphically recognize: the force of terror.

Curing Violence

How will it end, all this mayhem and bloodshed? When the United States responded to attacks on its embassies in Africa allegedly perpetrated by Muslim extremists in August 1998, Secretary of State Madeleine Albright proclaimed that America was at war with religious terrorists. It would be "a long-term struggle," she predicted, adding that "unfortunately, this is the war of the future."[30]

Although her dismal prognosis was probably correct, it is also true that all wars eventually end. Even long-term struggles that sputter on sporadically for decades come to a conclusion, as the Cold War did in 1990, when the Soviet Union dissolved and the dream of a global conquest of communism was abandoned. Moreover, in long struggles especially, the pace of war sometimes changes: there are small victories, occasional breaks, tentative resolutions, and attempts to forge a reconciliation.

The war with religious terrorism has been from the point of view of military and diplomatic leaders a kind of global guerrilla war. It has been difficult to fight with weapons designed for conventional and technological warfare. Yet military officers have deemed it a war that can be won. Many secular political leaders have described it as a war that must be won for civilization as the modern West has known it to survive. From the point of view of many religious activists, as we have seen, religious terrorism has been an aspect of cosmic war, one that need not be won in ordinary history, and one in which they are convinced they will eventually triumph. It is, in any event, a war that they cannot conceive of losing.

In such a war, one that seems so absolute and unyielding on both sides, what can be the possible outcomes? Extrapolating from current trends and recent examples, I see the following five possibilities.

Destroying Violence

The first scenario is one of a solution forged by force. It encompasses instances in which terrorists have literally been killed off or have been forcibly controlled. If Osama bin Laden had been in residence in his camp in Afghanistan on August 20, 1998, along with a large number of leaders of other militant groups when the United States launched one hundred Tomahawk cruise missiles into his quarters, for instance, this air strike might have removed some of the persons involved in planning future terrorist acts in various parts of the world.

It would not have removed all of them, however, and the attempt may well have elevated the possibility of more terrorist acts in reprisal. The war-against-terrorism strategy can be dangerous, in that it can play into the scenario that religious terrorists themselves have fostered: the image of a world at war between secular and religious forces. A belligerent secular enemy has often been just what religious activists have hoped for. In some cases it makes recruitment to their causes easier, for it demonstrates that the secular side can be as brutal as it has been portrayed by their own religious ideologues.

The 1998 U.S. attack on Osama bin Laden's camp neither destroyed the militant Muslim's operations nor deterred his aggression. Immediately after the attack several other American embassies were targeted, and several months later, in February 1999, George Tenet, head of the U.S. Central Intelligence Agency, announced to the press that he had "no doubt" that "Osama bin Laden and his world-wide allies and sympathizers" were plotting "further attacks" against U.S. installations and symbols of American power.[31] In Algeria, attempts to eliminate Muslim militants also had violent repercussions. When the military junta in Algeria halted the elections and began running the country with an iron hand, popular support for the Islamic party and violent resistance against the junta escalated.

In order for the destructive strategy to work, a secular government must be willing to declare total war against religious terrorism and wage it over many years, as the Israeli government attempted to do against its terrorist opponents. Even under these conditions the prognosis for victory has been good only when the opponents were easily identified and—perhaps more important—contained within a specific region. Because Israel's enemies have been mobile, its attempts to squash them have had a limited degree of success. The government of India, on the other hand, was able to virtually obliterate the most militant Sikhs in 1992, in part because it embarked on a ruthless search-and-destroy mission against the activists within the confines of the state of Punjab.

Legal means of quelling a religious insurrection have also been effective, but only if the government has had direct legal authority over the group. In Japan, for instance, the government was able not only to bring the Aum Shinrikyo leaders to trial and imprison them, but also to use its legislative and police powers to restrict the movement's activities. In 1999 China outlawed the Falun Gong movement, which it considered dangerous. But as the United States discovered in the case of the Libyan terrorists who allegedly destroyed Pan Am flight 103 over Lockerbie, Scotland, controlling activists in another country—especially an unfriendly one—can be a difficult matter.

Activist groups sometimes have destroyed themselves, however. The infighting within some movements has become so severe that they literally killed themselves off, or so weakened their military defenses that their government opponents could handily subdue them. The internal squabbling of various Sikh factions, for instance, made it easier for the movement to be conquered by the Indian government. In some extreme cases, such as the nonterrorist but heavily armed Branch Davidian movement in Waco, the members of the movement have resorted to suicide when they perceived no viable options for the future. In the year before he instigated the nerve gas attack in the Tokyo subways, Shoko Asahara mentioned group suicide as a way out of what he thought was a government conspiracy against his movement.[32] Thus although it is difficult for a government's military power to obliterate a terrorist band, sometimes its own internal tensions can accomplish the task.

Terrifying Terrorists

A second scenario is one in which the threat of violent reprisals or imprisonment so frightens religious activists that they hesitate to act. This is the strategy adopted by many law enforcement agencies to "crack down" on terrorists: even if the authorities cannot eliminate the terrorists completely, they can at least frighten them by raising the stakes associated with involvement in terrorist activity.

Though some fringe members of activist groups may have been sobered by such threats, it is doubtful that the "get tough with terrorists" strategy has had much of an effect on the more dedicated members. In the view of most of them, the world is already at war, and they have always expected the enemy to act harshly. In fact, they would be puzzled if it did not. So the threat of an additional increment of penalty to be meted out for their actions has had little if any deterrent effect.

The case that is sometimes offered as a successful instance of terrorist intimidation is the one involving Libya. In the mid-1980s Libya was thought to harbor Muslim activists responsible for a series of acts of international terrorism against the United States. In 1986 the United

States undertook an air strike against the leader of the country, Muammar el-Qaddafi, in reprisal. The missiles were aimed at one of his residences, and in fact a member of his family was killed in the attack, but el-Qaddafi himself survived. Over ten years later there were very few terrorist acts aimed at the United States attributed to Libya. Were the air strikes effective?

It is doubtful. Although it is possible that Libya was eventually intimidated by the strikes, the immediate response was quite different. According to the RAND–St. Andrews Chronology of International Terrorism, the number of terrorist incidents linked to Libya and directed against the United States rose in the two years following the U.S. air strikes: fifteen in 1987 and eight in 1988.[33] The most devastating terrorist attack against the United States in which Libya has been implicated—the tragic explosion of Pan Am flight 103 over Lockerbie, Scotland, killing all 259 on board—occurred in December 1988.

It is not clear why the number of terrorist attacks from Libya has decreased in the years since then. Comments made by el-Qaddafi in 1998 indicated that the economic sanctions leveled against Libya were much on his mind. He broke off relations with Arab states in a pique of anger after they failed to support the abandonment of the boycott.[34] Perhaps he was eager to normalize relations with other governments for trade reasons as much as any other. In any event, there is no clear evidence that he or any other supporter of international terrorism has been intimidated by America's show of military might.

There is a possibility that in some cases, however, terrorists have frightened themselves. In some instances the magnitude of their destructive acts has been so enormous that they were shaken into a realistic understanding of what their symbolic violence can in fact produce. After Timothy McVeigh fulfilled a horrific vision from the novel *The Turner Diaries* by destroying the Oklahoma City federal building in 1995, the number of violent incidents from Christian militia members diminished. After Paul Hill killed abortion clinic staff in Florida in 1994, according to Rev. Michael Bray, there was no need for further action from his circle of activists; the killing of abortion clinic doctors since then has been done by other groups. In other cases, activists have had an epiphany on their way to committing their deeds of destruction. Kerry Noble reported that when he was sent to destroy a gay church and its parishioners in Kansas City, the moments in which he sat in the pew before he was to trigger his bomb and depart was an occasion for him to seriously reflect on what his intended act would achieve: "All I could envision was torn bodies, limbs ripped from torsos," Noble recalled. Sobered and shaken, he left the sanctuary with the briefcase containing the bomb still in his hand.[35]

Violence Wins

The third scenario is the reverse of those cases in which terrorism is defeated or diffused: it is when terrorism, in some way, wins. This is the outcome for which every religious activist, understandably, has yearned. When I asked the Hamas leader Dr. Abdul Aziz Rantisi whether Jews and Muslims could live in harmony in the area he described as Palestine, he affirmed that they could—but not under the present arrangement. He could not accept "Israel's sovereignty over Palestinian land," he said. But the two groups could live in peace if the situation were reversed and the land were controlled by Palestinian Arabs.[36] "Jews would be welcomed in our nation," Rantisi explained, adding that he did not hate Jews as such. He pledged not to mistreat them "when we become strong."[37] He hoped for a South Africa–type solution, where the whole of the area would be united—Israel, Gaza, and the West Bank—and the Palestinians who had left the region would be allowed to return. With Arabs then a majority, Rantisi would accept democratic rule over the united region, which would be called something other than Israel.

It is a solution that would delight Palestinians both inside and outside the Hamas movement. Needless to say, it has not been a solution enthusiastically embraced by Israel. Given that fact, and considering that Israel holds a preponderance of military power in the region, could any part of the radical Islamic Palestinian objective be achieved? As I suggested earlier, acts of terrorism tend to be strategically unproductive and do not usually lead to transformations of power. If one is not willing to wait, as Dr. Rantisi claimed he was willing to do, beyond his own generation and perhaps the next, symbolic action will have to be replaced by the kind of strategic planning aimed at achieving goals either totally or incrementally. Revolutionary changes can occur through a well-organized mass movement, as in Iran, or an effective military force, as in Afghanistan. They might also come about through political pressures, as in Sudan and Pakistan, where regimes have capitulated to religious nationalist ideologies in what have been incremental but virtually bloodless coups. But as noted earlier, none of these cases has involved terrorist acts as the primary means of achieving power.

There have been instances, however, where the power accrued through terrorist acts was converted into bargaining chips for negotiated settlements, and where formerly terrorist organizations were forged into effective political parties. An example of this process, which might be called the domesticization of violence, was the negotiated peace settlement in Northern Ireland and the emergence of Sinn Féin as an effective force in local elections. Yet, as the bombing in the village of Omagh in August 1998 revealed, such compromises are not always accepted gracefully by renegade members of activist movements, who insist on continuing their violent paramilitary campaigns. After all, the ideology of cosmic war does not easily submit to accommodation. Yet, as the Omagh incident also indicated, public support for a compromise solution may isolate perpetrators of acts of violence, and their continued terrorism may undercut their public support.

The approach taken by the opponent—the old enemy of a terrorist struggle—has sometimes made all the difference in a successful transition from violence to the politics of compromise. The attempted resolutions of the Northern Ireland and Palestine conflicts are interesting cases in point. In Northern Ireland, the British did not blame Sinn Féin for the Omagh violence, and both British and Sinn Féin leaders formed a united front against it. Hence the public perception of Omagh was that of a senseless act, one that was peripheral and counterproductive to the political purposes of the Northern Irish Catholic community. In Israel, however, when Hamas terrorist activities were renewed after the peace accords, Benjamin Netanyahu and other Israeli leaders publicly blamed the Palestinian peacemaker, Yasir Arafat, for the terrorism. Thus, perhaps inadvertently, the Hamas activists were given credibility by Netanyahu through his equating them with Arafat, and the legitimacy of the secular Palestinian leader was undercut by his being blamed for the acts of renegade activists whom he could hardly control. With Arafat weakened and Hamas emboldened by the effect of their incidents of terrorism, the spiral of violence continued.

Thus a negotiated compromise with activists involved in terrorism is fraught with difficulties. It is a solution that does not always work. A few activists may be appeased, but others may be angered by what they regard as a sellout of their principles. The case of Arafat and Hamas was complicated not only by the lack of cooperation from the Israeli side following the elections that brought Netanyahu into power, but also by the intractability of Hamas and its own fears of losing whatever leverage it had gained through its previous tactics. In 1996 some members of the movement advocated a shift of strategy and participation in Palestinian elections as a political party. It was a shift that the leadership of Hamas rejected. One of their concerns was political: they knew that although they might have won in Gaza, their level of support in the West Bank was not sufficient to rout Fateh and the other parties that supported Arafat's Palestinian Authority. Another concern of the Hamas leadership was ideological: once one has entered into the rhetoric of cosmic war, the struggle cannot easily be abandoned without forsaking the will of God.

Separating Religion from Politics

The fourth scenario for peace is one in which religion is taken out of politics and retired to the moral and metaphysical planes. As long as images of spiritual warfare remain strong in the minds of religious activists and are linked with struggles in the social world around them, the scenarios we have just discussed—achieving an easy victory over religious activists, intimidating them into submission, or forging a compromise with them—are problematic at best. In some cases where religious politics had previously been strong, however, the image of cosmic war itself has been transformed. A more moderate view of the image of religious warfare has been conceived, one that is deflected away from political and social confrontation.

The extreme form of this solution—one in which religion returns to what Casanova described as its privatization in the post-Enlightenment world—is unlikely, however.[38] Few religious activists are willing to retreat to the time when secular authorities ran the public arena and religion remained safely within the confines of churches, mosques, temples, and synagogues. Most religious activists regard the social manifestation of cosmic struggle to be at the very heart of their faith and dream of restoring religion to what they regard as its rightful position at the center of public consciousness.

Yet, in the 1990s, many Islamic countries witnessed a certain reaction against politicized religion. In 1999, Iranian students demonstrated in support of such leaders as the moderate theologian Abdol Karim Soroush, who argued that interpretations of religion are relative and change over time.[39] He made a distinction between ideology and religion, and claimed that Muslim clergy had no business being in politics.[40] Similar statements have been made by such moderate Islamic thinkers as Hassan Hanafi in Egypt, Rashid Ghannouchi in Tunisia, and Algeria's Mohammed Arkoun. For them, the image of struggle consists largely of a spiritual battle or a contest between moral positions rather than between armed enemies.

To some degree these thinkers advocated what René Girard recommended in his analysis of how religion can cure violence. He regarded the rite of sacrifice as deflected violence—a token of what I call ritualized cosmic war. According to Girard, when religion conducts its business adequately, it provides for society a symbolic way of acting out violent impulses so that they need not be expressed in the real world.[41] One of Girard's colleagues, Mark Anspach, observed that Islam lacks the developed sacrificial ritual structure of many other religious traditions, and hence it has always skirted the danger of "the confusion of ritual and history," resulting in ritualized—albeit real—violence against its sacred enemies.[42] What Soroush and his fellow Islamic thinkers proposed was not necessarily a moderate Islam but a revitalized one, a Muslim religiosity sufficiently vital and symbolically rich to do what Girard and Anspach argued all religion should be able to do: deflect violence through its ritual enactment.

Moreover, Soroush's vision of Islam allows religion to play a significant albeit a noncontrolling public role. Like the Protestant Reformation's Martin Luther, Soroush advocates an unmediated form of religion that is both personal and public. He places little stock in the clerical hierarchy and its privileges—a position that has gotten him into a fair amount of difficulty in Iran—but at the same time his reformed Islam is not privatistic. Like socially responsible Protestants, he sees a prophetic role for religion in the public arena. This is a form of social activism that eschews political power in favor of moral suasion, and it has transformed the idea of struggle into a contestation of ideas rather than opposing political sides.

Solutions such as the one Soroush formulated in Iran do not require the image of cosmic war to be removed from public life or abandoned altogether. Rather, it is redirected to the battlefield of ideas. For such a transformation to come about, however, two conditions must be met: members of the activists' religious community have to embrace this moderate form of social struggle as a legitimate representation of cosmic war, and the opponents have to accept it without being threatened by it. Secular authorities can do little about the first criterion, since it requires a transformation of thinking and leadership within the religion itself. But they can effect the second criterion by resisting the temptation to act like an enemy in a cosmic war and being open to a social role for religion on a less violently confrontational level.

When one is treated like an enemy, however, the temptation to re-spond like an enemy is considerable. This has been especially so when the provocations have been savage. After American embassies in Africa were bombed in August 1998, for instance, the U.S. government found itself in a position similar to that of the Israeli government in being mo-tivated to retaliate swiftly and strongly in order to appease their con-stituencies. Yet such retaliations have seldom been effective. As we have seen, retaliatory strikes usually have not destroyed their targets com-pletely, they have invited more terrorist acts in return, and they have played into the terrorists' scenarios of war in which there can be no easy compromise.

Understandably, governments cannot afford to let acts of terrorism go unaddressed. Governments must be vigilant in their surveillance of potential terrorist groups, diligent in their attempts to apprehend those suspected of committing terrorist acts, and swift in bringing them to courts of law. But the tit-for-tat approach to terrorism has usually failed if for no other reason than that few governments have been will-ing to sink to the savage levels and adopt the same means of gutter combat as the groups involved in terrorist acts. Moreover, government authorities are usually aware that those within cultures of violence from which acts of terrorism have emerged are watching to see how the authorities respond to the violence. Any response to the perpetra-tion of violent acts, even in the form of retaliatory strikes, will enhance the credibility of the terrorists within their own community. Supporting moderate leadership within the communities, however, would diminish support for the extremists.

Examples of attempts to respond to terrorism in a moderate way may be found in the British reactions to the violence of the Irish Republican Army, and at least one moment in the Israeli response to Palestinian ac-tivism. When Britain's prime minister Tony Blair befriended Gerry Adams, the leader of the IRA's political wing, Sinn Féin, and when Israel's prime minister Yitzhak Rabin shook the hand of Palestine's Yasir Arafat, many in these prime ministers' respective countries were con-vinced that they had sold out to terrorists. Within Adams's and Arafat's camps were those who felt that the Sinn Féin and Palestinian leaders had also abandoned their principles. As we have seen, the Omagh tragedy and the Hamas suicide bombings were violent expressions of this dis-pleasure and were aimed at both the governments' and the bombers' own moderate leaders. Yet the British and Israeli authorities persevered because they recognized the opportunity to support a peaceful solution over a violent one, and—for the most part—they continued on a path of reconciliation that rewarded those who favored a transformation from terror to cooperation.

Healing Politics with Religion

These moderate solutions have required the opponents in the conflict to summon at least a minimal level of mutual trust and respect. This respect has been enhanced and the possibilities of a compromise solution strengthened when religious activists have perceived governmental authorities as having a moral integrity in keeping with, or accommodating of, religious values. This, then, is the fifth solution: when secular authorities embrace moral values, including those associated with religion.

In some cases where religious violence has been quelled, religion has literally been subsumed under the aegis of governmental authorities. In Sri Lanka, for instance, the efforts of the government to destroy the Janatha Vimukthi Peramuna (JVP)—the People's Liberation Front—a movement supported by many radical Buddhist monks, were double-pronged. The harsh measures involved tracking down and killing the most dedicated members of the movement. The more accommodating measures included efforts to win the support of militant religious leaders. In 1990 President Ranasinghe Premadasa provided a fund for the financial support of Buddhist schools and social services, and created a Ministry of Buddhist Affairs, naming himself the first minister. Premadasa created a council of Buddhist advisers, including Buddhist monks who had been quite critical of the secular government previously. One of these told me in 1991 that after Premadasa's pro-religious measures, the government was finally beginning to "reflect Buddhist values."[43]

In other cases, such as the British response to Irish terrorism, the government's stance in following the rule of law and not overreacting to terrorist provocations demonstrated its subscription to moral values. This made it difficult for religious activists—with the exception of Rev. Ian Paisley—to portray the government as a satanic enemy. It also increased the possibility of some sort of accommodation with religious activists on both sides of the Northern Ireland dispute—leading to the signing of a peace accord in 1998.

Governments that chose the other route—abandoning their own democratic principles in response to terrorism—have embarked on perilous journeys. A case in point is the Algerian military junta that seized control and annulled the elections that appeared to be leading to a victory for the Islamic Salvation Front in 1992. The result was years of increased terrorism, in part due to the perception that the government had discredited itself and demonstrated that it could not meet the mundane moral standards of secular democracies, much less the presumably higher standards suggested by religion.

It is poignant that the governments of modern nations have so often been perceived as being morally corrupt and spiritually vacuous since the Enlightenment concepts that launched the modern nation-state were characterized by a fair amount of moralistic fervor. Jean-Jacques Rousseau coined the term civil religion to describe what he regarded as the moral and spiritual foundation essential for any modern society that wanted to sustain an enduring political order. Such a "religion," Rousseau claimed, was to be based not on the "dogmas of religion" but on what he called the "the sanctity of the social contract."[44]

Despite the noble rhetoric of these Enlightenment thinkers, their opponents at the time belittled the secularists' morality just as their modern critics have done; and just as they have done today, they accused them of hypocrisy. As McMahon has pointed out, religious critics of thinkers such as Rousseau accused them, perhaps unfairly, of cloaking self-interest in the garb of high-minded abstractions.[45] It is this apparent hypocrisy—and what they regard as the inherent vacuousness of secular life—that has continued to disturb religious activists from the time of the Enlightenment to the present day.

This point was made clear to me in a direct way in a peculiar place— the federal penitentiary in Lompoc, California— where a convicted terrorist lectured me on my lack of moral and spiritual purpose. Mahmud Abouhalima accused American people in general, and me in particular, of secularism. He challenged our dedication to the virtue of tolerance when we have been unwilling to tolerate religious enthusiasts such as himself. He insisted that he knew what people like me lacked: "the soul of religion," he said, "that's what's missing." He went on to say that people in the secular world "are just living day by day, looking for jobs, for money to live." They were living, he said, "like sheep."[46]

I accepted that there was some truth to Abouhalima's analysis, but that most people did not want to live like sheep. Like him, they longed for a life of dignity and quiet pride. I interpreted what Abouhalima advocated to be not just religious doctrine, or even a "born-again" religious conversion, but a longing for vitality and meaning in life. What he wanted was a tough, grounded existence, not one simply floating toward a pointless death. I agreed with Abouhalima that religion at its best helps to give people that sense of purpose.

I wondered, though, to what extent Abouhalima was correct in his assessment that secular politics and modern social values have prevented individuals from having this kind of satisfying life. Can social and political institutions in society be blamed for our lack of spirituality? Answers to this question have been varied. Those who have responded "no" include those who have accepted the modernist assumption that private and public lives are separate, and that individuals are solely responsible for whatever integrity and morality they possess. Among those who have answered "yes" are modernity's critics, who have pointed to the deleterious effects of a consumer culture and its numbing assault on the senses by seemingly endless media images, and the cynicism with which most people view the moral integrity of those in public life. Robert Bellah argued in 1998 that the bland multicultural climate that has overcome American society at the dawn of the twenty-first century has been fostered by what he regards as the great agents of socialization—education and television—and encouraged through public policy.[47]

But even those who have condemned modern society for its aesthetic and ethical poverty may wonder if the entrance of religion into public life would help to leaven these negative influences. Several thoughtful observers of Western society have suggested that indeed it might—if religion could enter the public arena in an undogmatic and unobtrusive way. A French theorist, Marcel Gauchet, has called for Western society to recover the spiritual roots that it abandoned when it transferred the sense of sacrality from God to the nation.[48] An American theologican, Reinhold Niebuhr, has made a similar argument, even though Niebuhr was wary of religion's intrusion into politics.

Niebuhr was suspicious of religion because it absolutizes and moralizes political calculations that realistically are made for reasons of self-interest. Yet he could see a political role for what he called the "illusions" of religion in providing the ties that bind people together "in spite of social conflict." He described these as "the peculiar gifts of religion to the human spirit." Niebuhr claimed that secular imagination is not capable of producing them, for they require "a sublime madness which disregards immediate appearance and emphasizes profound and ultimate unities."[49]

I agree with Niebuhr that what religion provides society is not just high-mindedness, but also a concern with the quality of life—a goal more ennobling than the simple accretion of power and possessions. For that reason religious rhetoric has entered into political discourse at times when the moral and spiritual roots of a community have been challenged or have been in danger of being severed. Especially within the religious cultures of violence that we have examined in this book, people have criticized the vacuousness of modern secular life. They have sought religion as a balm for their fractured existences. For some, religion—like art, education, or sports—can be an escape from political turmoil. For others, these elements of public life give the turbulence meaning. During the height of the conflict in Bosnia in the mid-1990s, for instance, mosques stayed open and the symphony orchestra of Sarejevo kept to its concert schedule, performing to audiences of mixed ethnic identities.

In Palestine it has been higher education and sports along with religion that have symbolized this unity beyond the violence of ethnic conflict. When I asked a member of Hamas where the future generation of Palestinians and Israelis might come together, he told me, "it would be in a university." He could imagine a situation in which his son and the child of one of his Israeli opponents might relate to one another someday as friends and fellow students on a neutral arena—"perhaps on your campus of the University of California," he suggested.[50]

"I miss soccer," a young Hamas supporter told a journalist who interviewed him in an Israeli prison for the documentary film *Shaheed* (*Martyr*). The young man had been designated to be a suicide bomber but was intercepted by the Israeli police before he could demolish himself and his target, a crowd of innocent Israeli bystanders. He explained to the interviewer that he hated the Jews. "I despise them," he said. "They took our land." But when asked about Israel's soccer team, he said that he greatly admired Israeli players and knew many by name. When the journalist asked him what he would do if he were asked to carry out his suicide mission in a soccer stadium—one that was filled with his enemies, Zionists and nonbelievers—the young man seemed genuinely troubled. "On a soccer field?" he asked, his sensibilities clearly offended. "No," he said, "I couldn't do that."[51]

In the mind of the erstwhile suicide bomber, soccer rose above the turmoil of terrorism, just as higher education and symphony concerts have provided neutral planes beyond ethnic, religious, and ideological tensions. Religion can also provide such a neutral space: in Israel, rabbis and mullahs have shared ideas almost as extensively as their political counterparts have. Though religion has scarcely been perceived as being neutral in the same way that art, education, and sports have been, virtually every religious tradition has projected images of tranquility that are even more profound and unifying. It is, after all, for the sake of the tranquil and universal ideal of sacred transformation that one struggles in the battles of a cosmic war. In a curious way, then, the goal of all this religious violence is peace.

As we have seen in the case studies in this book, religious ideas have given a profundity and ideological clarity to what in many cases have been real experiences of economic destitution, social oppression, political corruption, and a desperate need for the hope of rising above the limitations of modern life. The image of cosmic struggle has given these bitter experiences meaning, and the involvement in a grand conflict has been for some participants exhilarating. It has even been empowering. Persons and social movements engaged in such a conflict have gained a sense of their own destinies. In such situations, acts of violence, even what appear to those of us outside the movements as vicious acts of terrorism, have been viewed by insiders in cultures of violence as both appropriate and justified.

Why, in a few extreme instances, violence has accompanied religion's renewed political presence is something that this book has tried to explore. My conclusion is that it has much to do with the nature of the religious imagination, which always has had the propensity to absolutize and to project images of cosmic war. It also has much to do with the social tensions of this moment of history that cry out for absolute solutions, and the sense of personal humiliation experienced by men who long to restore an integrity they perceive as lost in the wake of virtually global social and political shifts.

To some extent it is also related to the role that violence has played in public life. Since public violence is a display of power, it appeals to those who want to make dramatic statements and reclaim public space. In moments of social transition and uncertainty it can simultaneously hold both political currency and religious meaning. It can be used to remind the populace of the godly power that makes a religious ideology potent, and it can be used to render divine judgments. It can create man-made incidents of fear on heaven's behalf, as if its perpetrators could discern the mind of God.

This is one of history's ironies, that although religion has been used to justify violence, violence can also empower religion. Perhaps understandably, therefore, in the wake of secularism, and after years of waiting in history's wings, religion has made its reappearance as an ideology of social order in a dramatic fashion: violently. In time the violence will end, but the point will remain. Religion gives spirit to public life and provides a beacon for moral order. At the same time it needs the temper of rationality and fair play that Enlightenment values give to civil society. Thus religious violence cannot end until some accommodation can be forged between the two—some assertion of moderation in religion's passion, and some acknowledgment of religion in elevating the spiritual and moral values of public life. In a curious way, then, the cure for religious violence may ultimately lie in a renewed appreciation for religion itself.

Notes

Chapter 1. Terror and God

1. "Global Terror," *Los Angeles Times*, August 8, 1998, A16.
2. Bruce Hoffman, *Inside Terrorism* (New York: Columbia University Press, 1998), 91.
3. Warren Christopher, "Fighting Terrorism: Challenges for Peacemakers," address to the Washington Institute for Near East Policy, May 21, 1996. Reprinted in Warren Christopher, *In the Stream of History: Shaping Foreign Policy for a New Era* (Stanford, CA: Stanford University Press, 1998), 446.
4. See, for example, the essays from a conference on the psychology of terrorism held at the Woodrow Wilson International Center for Scholars, in Walter Reich, ed., *Origins of Terrorism: Psychologies, Ideologies, Theologies, States of Mind* (New York: Cambridge University Press, 1990).
5. Baruch Goldstein, letter to the editor, *New York Times*, June 30, 1981.
6. Interview with Rev. Michael Bray, Reformation Lutheran Church, Bowie, Maryland, April 25, 1996.
7. Interview with Sohan Singh, leader of the Sohan Singh Panthic Committee, Mohalli, Punjab, August 3, 1996.
8. Interview with Mahmud Abouhalima, convicted coconspirator in the World Trade Center bombing case, federal penitentiary, Lompoc, California, September 30, 1997.
9. Interview with Abdul Aziz Rantisi, cofounder and political leader of Hamas, Khan Yunis, Gaza, March 1, 1998.
10. Lance W. Small, an assistant professor of mathematics at the University of California, Berkeley, at the time Kaczynski taught there, quoted in David Johnston and Janny Scott, "The Tortured Genius of Theodore Kaczynski," *New York Times*, May 26, 1996, A1. According to the authors, Kaczynski's brother David thought that Kaczynski was unaffected by any particular political movement at the time.

11. In using the phrase "cultures of violence," I realize that for some this will evoke the term "cultures of poverty," coined by Oscar Lewis and other anthropologists in the 1960s to describe the mindset of the barrios of Latin America and African American ghettos in the United States. Lewis was accused of presenting a static set of values, forged through desperate conditions, that on the one hand explained away many of the moral and intellectual shortcomings of the people who came from such cultures, and on the other hand seemed to imply that nothing could be done to help them. My term, "cultures of violence," does not carry these implications.

12. Michel Foucault, *The Order of Things: An Archaeology of Human Sciences* (New York: Vintage, 1973), 168.

13. Pierre Bourdieu, *Outline of a Theory of Practice* (Cambridge: Cambridge University Press, 1977), 76.

14. Clifford Geertz, "Ideology as a Cultural System," in David Apter, ed., *Ideology and Discontent* (New York: Free Press), 1964; and "Religion as a Cultural System," reprinted in William A. Lessa and Evon Z. Vogt, eds., *Reader in Comparative Religion: An Anthropological Approach*, 3rd ed. (New York: Harper & Row, 1972).

15. Bernard Lewis, *The Assassins: A Radical Sect in Islam* (London: Al Saqi Books, 1985); Walter Laqueur, *Terrorism* (Boston: Little, Brown, 1977), revised and republished as *The Age of Terrorism* (Boston: Little, Brown, 1987); Hoffman, *Inside Terrorism*.

16. Walter Reich, *Origins of Terrorism: Psychologies, Ideologies, Theologies, States of Mind* (New York: Cambridge University Press, 1990); Robert S. Robins and Jerrold Post, *Political Paranoia: The Psychopolitics of Hatred* (New Haven, CT: Yale University Press, 1997).

17. Martha Crenshaw, *Revolutionary Terrorism: The FLN in Algeria, 1954–1962* (Stanford, CA: Hoover Institution, 1978); Peter Merkl, "West German Left-Wing Terrorism," in Martha Crenshaw, ed., *Terrorism in Context* (University Park: Pennsylvania State University Press, 1995). See also Crenshaw's article on instrumental and organizational approaches to the study of terrorism, "Theories of Terrorism," in David C. Rapoport, ed., *Inside Terrorist Organizations* (New York: Columbia University Press, 1988).

18. Paul Wilkinson, *Political Terrorism* (London: Macmillan, 1974); Brian Jenkins, *International Terrorism: Trends and Potentialities* (Santa Monica, CA: RAND Corporation, 1978). See also Paul Wilkinson and A. M. Stewart, eds., *Contemporary Research on Terrorism* (Aberdeen: Aberdeen University Press, 1987); Bruce Hoffman, *An Agenda for Research on Terrorism and LIC [Low Intensity Conflict] in the 1990s* (Santa Monica, CA: RAND Corporation, 1991).

19. Jeffrey Kaplan, "The Context of American Millennarian Revolutionary Theology: The Case of the 'Identity Christian' Church of Israel," *Terrorism and Political Violence* 5:1, Spring 1993, 30–82, and "Right Wing Violence in North America," in Tore Bjørgo, ed., *Terror from the Extreme Right* (London: Frank Cass, 1995), 44–95; James Aho, *The Politics of Righteousness: Idaho Christian Patriotism* (Seattle: University of Washington Press, 1990); Martin Dillon, *God and the Gun: The Church and Irish Terrorism* (New York: Routledge, 1998); Cynthia Keppley Mahmood, *Fighting for Faith and Nation: Dialogues with*

Sikh Militants (Philadelphia: University of Pennsylvania Press, 1997); Ehud Sprinzak, *The Ascendance of Israel's Radical Right* (New York: Oxford University Press, 1991); Paul Steinberg and Annamarie Oliver, *Rehearsals for a Happy Death: The Testimonies of Hamas Suicide Bombers* (New York: Oxford University Press, forthcoming).

Chapter 2. Soldiers for Christ

1. Michael Bray, *A Time to Kill: A Study Concerning the Use of Force and Abortion* (Portland, OR: Advocates for Life Publications, 1994), 9.

2. Interview with Rev. Michael Bray, Reformation Lutheran Church, Bowie, Maryland, April 25, 1996, and March 20, 1998. The quotations from Bray in this section, unless otherwise cited, are from these interviews.

3. *Nightline*, March 9, 1998.

4. Interview with Bray, March 20, 1998. Bray clarified his position in correspondence to me on March 9, 1999, from which this quotation is taken.

5. Bray, *A Time to Kill*. The book was written before Hill's murder of Britton and Barrett. It defended Michael Griffin's slaying of Dr. David Gunn, also in Florida (p. 124). Articles written by Bray after Hill's action indicate that the argument in his book extended to Hill and may indeed have have been a justification in advance for Hill's act.

6. Paul Hill, "Why I Shot an Abortionist," December 22, 1997, open letter to Rev. Michael Bray and the attendees of the White Rose Banquet, circulated by Bray.

7. See Reinhold Niebuhr, *Moral Man and Immoral Society* (New York: Scribner's, 1932), and *Why the Christian Church Is Not Pacifist* (London: Student Christian Movement Press, 1940).

8. For a somewhat controversial statement of the position that early Christianity was perceived during its own time as a political movement, see S. F. G. Brandon, *Jesus and the Zealots: A Study of the Political Factor in Primitive Christianity* (New York: Charles Scribner's Sons, 1967).

9. See Albert Marrin, ed., *War and the Christian Conscience: From Augustine to Martin Luther King, Jr.* (Chicago: Henry Regnery, 1971); James Turner Johnson, *Ideology, Reason, and the Limitation of War: Religious and Secular Concepts, 1200–1740* (Princeton, NJ: Princeton University Press, 1975); Hal Drake, *Constantine and the Bishops: Tolerance and Coercion in the Early Church* (forthcoming). See also my article "Nonviolence," in Mircea Eliade, ed., *The Encyclopedia of Religion*, vol. 10 (New York: Macmillan, 1987), 463–67.

10. See Ralph Potter, *War and Moral Discourse* (Richmond, VA: John Knox Press, 1969); Paul Ramsey, *The Just War: Force and Political Responsibility* (New York: Charles Scribner's Sons, 1968); Thomas Merton, *Faith and Violence: Christian Teaching and Christian Practice* (Notre Dame, IN: University of Notre Dame Press, 1968).

11. See Robert McAfee Brown, *Religion and Violence*, 2nd ed., (Philadelphia: Westminster Press, 1987), esp. 56–61; Gustavo Gutierrez, *A Theology of Liberation: History, Politics, and Salvation*, rev. ed. (Maryknoll,

NY: Orbis Books, 1988); Teofilo Cabastrero, *Revolutionaries for the Gospel: Testimonies of Fifteen Christians in the Nicaraguan Government* (Maryknoll, NY: Orbis Books, 1986).

12. Niebuhr, *Why the Christian Church Is Not Pacifist.*

13. See Niebuhr, *Moral Man and Immoral Society.*

14. "Manifesto for the Christian Church," *Crosswinds.* Quoted in Chip Berlet, *John Salvi, Abortion Clinic Violence, and Catholic Right Conspiracism* (Somerville, MA: Political Research Associates, 1996), 8.

15. Gary North, *Lone Gunners for Jesus: Letters to Paul J. Hill* (Tyler, TX: Institute for Christian Economics, 1994), 2.

16. The book that established Reconstruction Theology as a movement is Rousas John Rushdoony's two-volume *Institutes of Biblical Law* (Nutley, NJ: Craig Press, 1973). Introductions to Cornelius Van Til's thought are found in R. J. Rushdoony, *By What Standard?* (Tyler, TX: Thoburn Press, 1978) and Richard Pratt, *Every Thought Captive* (Phillipsburg, NJ: Presbyterian and Reformed Publishing Company, 1982). The journal of Reconstruction thought, *Chalcedon Report*, is published in Vallecito, California.

17. Gary North, *Backward, Christian Soldiers? An Action Manual for Christian Reconstruction* (Tyler, TX: Institute for Christian Economics, 1984), 267. According to North, the four main tenets of Christian Reconstruction are biblical law, optimistic eschatology, predestination, and "presuppositional apologetics," which North defines as a "philosophical defense of the faith" (267). North has authored or edited over twenty books, including *An Introduction to Christian Economics* (Tyler, TX: Institute for Christian Economics, 1973), *Millennialism and Social Theory* (Tyler, TX: Institute for Christian Economics, 1990), and *Unconditional Surrender: God's Program for Victory* (Tyler, TX: Institute for Christian Economics, 1988).

18. North, *Lone Gunners for Jesus*, 25.

19. North, *Lone Gunners for Jesus*, 6–8.

20. Paul Hill, *Paul Hill Speaks* (pamphlet published by Reformation Press, Bowie, Maryland, June 1997), 1.

21. Hill, *Paul Hill Speaks*, 2.

22. Bray, *A Time to Kill*, 158.

23. Michael Bray, "Running with Rudolph," *Capitol Area Christian News*, 28, Winter 1998–1999, 2.

24. Bray, "Running with Rudolph," 2.

25. Morris Dees, *Gathering Storm: America's Militia Threat* (New York: HarperCollins, 1996), 165. Reports of McVeigh visiting Elohim City are made in David Hoffman, *The Oklahoma City Bombing and the Politics of Terror* (Venice, CA: Feral House, 1998), 83–84.

26. Andrew Macdonald [William Pierce], *The Turner Diaries* (New York: Barricade Books, 1996) (orig. published by National Alliance Vanguard Books, Arlington, VA, in 1978).

27. Dees, *Gathering Storm*, 154.

28. Dees, *Gathering Storm*, 158.

29. Although Pierce, the author of *The Turner Diaries*, denies knowing McVeigh or talking to him, two separate law enforcement sources claim to have

telephone records proving that McVeigh placed a lengthy call to Pierce's un-listed number in West Virginia in the weeks before the bombing. This informa-tion was first reported by CNN and is mentioned in Dees, *Gathering Storm*, 165.

30. Amy C. Solnin, *William L. Pierce: Novelist of Hate*, research report of the Anti-Defamation League (New York: Anti-Defamation League, 1995), 8.

31. Macdonald [Pierce], *Turner Diaries*, 64.

32. Michael Barkun, *Religion and the Racist Right: The Origins of the Christian Identity Movement* (Chapel Hill: University of North Carolina Press, 1994).

33. Barkun, *Religion and the Racist Right*, 7.

34. Leonard Zeskind, *The "Christian Identity" Movement: Analyzing Its Theological Rationalization for Racist and Anti-Semitic Violence* (New York: Division of Church and Society of the National Council of Churches of Christ in the U.S.A., 1986), 12.

35. Zeskind, *"Christian Identity" Movement*, 14.

36. Jeffrey Kaplan, *Radical Religion in America: Millenarian Movements from the Far Right to the Children of Noah* (Syracuse: Syracuse University Press, 1997), 175.

37. Zeskind, *"Christian Identity" Movement*, 45.

38. Gerald Baumgarten, *Paranoia as Patriotism: Far-Right Influences on the Militia Movement* (New York: Anti-Defamation League, 1995), 17.

39. Gordon "Jack" Mohr (founder of the Christian Patriot Defense League), *Know Your Enemies*, 1982 pamphlet. Quoted in James Aho, *The Politics of Righteousness: Idaho Christian Patriotism* (Seattle: University of Washington Press, 1990), 96.

40. Aho, *Politics of Righteousness*, 91.

41. Kim Murphy, "Last Stand of an Aging Aryan," *Los Angeles Times*, January 10, 1999, A1.

42. Kim Murphy, "Hate's Affluent New Godfathers," *Los Angeles Times*, January 10, 1999, A14.

43. Aho, *Politics of Righteousness*, 85.

44. See Gerry Adams, *Before the Dawn: An Autobiography* (London: Mandarin Paperbacks, 1996), 246, 274-75.

45. Interview with Tom Hartley, councillor and leader of the Sinn Féin party in the Belfast City Council, Belfast, July 31, 1998.

46. Dennis Cooke, *Persecuting Zeal: A Portrait of Ian Paisley* (Kerry, Ireland: Brandon Book Publishers, 1996), 23.

47. Ian Paisley, *The Preaching of Ian Paisley* (Belfast: Martyrs' Memorial Recordings, 17 November 1985). Cited in Cooke, *Persecuting Zeal*, 1.

48. Notice in *The Battle Standard: The Journal of the European Institute of Protestant Studies* 1:1, October 1997, 8.

49. *The Battle Standard*, 1:1, October 1997, 8.

50. Ian Paisley, quoted in Marjorie Miller, "Two Northern Ireland Leaders Share Nobel Peace Prize," *Los Angeles Times*, October 17, 1998, A1.

51. Interview with Stuart Dignan, staff member, Belfast office of the Democratic Unionist Party, Belfast, July 30, 1998.

52. Ian Paisley, sermon reprinted in *The Revivalist*, September 1983. Cited in Cooke, *Persecuting Zeal*, 42. Cooke persuasively argues that Paisley is even less tolerant of Catholics than the Protestant reformers he quotes. Unlike Paisley, he notes, Calvin accepted Catholics as Christians, and although John Wesley rejected the authority of the pope, he accepted Catholics into the wider, hidden fellowship of Christians (47–53).

53. Ian Paisley, "Swearing Allegiance to King Jesus," sermon of March 24, 1991, Belfast. Reprinted in Ian Paisley, *Sermons on Special Occasions* (Belfast: Ambassador Productions, 1996), 114.

54. Martin Dillon, *God and the Gun: The Church and Irish Terrorism* (New York: Routledge, 1998), 73.

55. Dillon, *God and the Gun*, 64–65.

56. Interview with Hartley, July 31, 1998.

57. Dillon, *God and the Gun*, 89–90.

58. Dillon, *God and the Gun*, 93.

59. Conor Cruise O'Brien, *Ancestral Voices: Religion and Nationalism in Ireland* (Dublin: Poolbeg Press, 1994), 3–4.

60. O'Brien, *Ancestral Voices*, 4.

61. Ian Paisley, editorial, *Protestant Telegraph*, August 12, 1972, 5. Cited in Cooke, *Persecuting Zeal*, 57.

62. Interview with Hartley, July 31, 1998.

63. Dillon, *God and the Gun*, 93.

Chapter 3. Zion Betrayed

1. Aharan Domb, Jewish settler on the West Bank, quoted in Norman Kempster, "Arafat, Netanyahu Sign Pact," *Los Angeles Times*, October 24, 1998, A1.

2. Margot Dudkevitch, "Settlers: Netanyahu No Longer Our Leader," *Jerusalem Post* (Internet edition), October 26, 1998.

3. Interview with Yoel Lerner, director of the Sanhedrin Institute, Jerusalem, March 2, 1998.

4. Ehud Sprinzak, *The Ascendance of Israel's Radical Right* (New York: Oxford University Press, 1991), 278. See pp. 274–79 for Sprinzak's description of Lerner and his views.

5. Interview with Lerner, January 20, 1989.

6. Interview with Lerner, August 17, 1995.

7. Sprinzak, *Ascendance of Israel's Radical Right*, 278.

8. Interview with Lerner, March 2, 1998.

9. Interview with Leah Rabin, Tel Aviv, March 2, 1998.

10. Prime Minister Yitzhak Rabin, quoted in Serge Schmemann, "Rabin Assassinated in Jerusalem," *New York Times*, November 5, 1995, 1.

11. Yigal Amir, quoted in Joel Greenberg, "Rabin's Assassin," *New York Times*, November 5, 1995, A1.

12. Serge Schmemann, *New York Times*, November 11, 1995, A1.

13. Arieh O'Sullivan, "Netanyahu Flies to Capital to Avoid Protestors," *Jerusalem Post* (International edition), October 26, 1998; Deborah Sontag,

"Israelis Get an Eerie Reminder That Words Do Kill," *New York Times*, November 1, 1998, D3.

14. Interview with Lerner, March 2, 1998.

15. Yossi Klein Halevi, "Kahane's Murderous Legacy," *Jerusalem Report*, March 24, 1994, 12.

16. Interview with Yochay Ron, Kiryat Arba settlement, Hebron, August 18, 1995.

17. Interview with Lerner, March 2, 1998. Ben Gurion had given the orders, transmitted by a young Yitzhak Rabin, to attack a boat, the *Altalena*, which contained illegal weapons brought to Israel by the right-wing Irgun militia group. Ben Gurion feared the weapons might be used to undermine his own moderate authority in the new state. The boat was set on fire near Tel Aviv, and fifteen men were killed in the skirmish.

18. Sprinzak, *Ascendance of Israel's Radical Right*, 90.

19. Rivka Zerbib, quoted in Marjorie Miller, "Hebron's Fifty Jewish Families Unsettle Mideast," *Los Angeles Times*, October 20, 1996, A1.

20. Interview with Yochay Ron, August 18, 1995.

21. Interview with Rabbi Meir Kahane, Jerusalem, January 18, 1989.

22. See Robert Friedman, *The False Prophet: Rabbi Meir Kahane — From FBI Informant to Knesset Member* (London: Faber and Faber, 1990).

23. M. K. Michael Eitan, 1984 speech to the Knesset Rules Committee, quoted in Gerald Cromer, *The Debate about Kahanism in Israeli Society, 1984–1988*, Occasional Papers of the Harry Frank Guggenheim Foundation, No. 3 (New York: H. F. Guggenheim Foundation, 1988), 37–38.

24. Yair Kotler, *Heil Kahane* (New York: Adama Books, 1986).

25. John Kifner, "A Militant Leader, Fiery Politician and Founder of Anti-Arab Crusade," *New York Times*, November 7, 1990, B12.

26. Ehud Sprinzak, "Violence and Catastrophe in the Theology of Rabbi Meir Kahane: The Ideologization of Mimetic Desire," in Mark Juergensmeyer, ed., *Violence and the Sacred in the Modern World* (London: Frank Cass, 1991), 48–70; and Sprinzak, *Ascendance of Israel's Radical Right*, 220–23. See also Kahane's writings, including *Listen World, Listen Jew* (Jerusalem: Institute of the Jewish Idea, 1978) and *They Must Go* (Jerusalem: Institute of the Jewish Idea, 1981); Ehud Sprinzak, *Brother against Brother: Violence and Extremism in Israeli Politics from Altalena to the Rabin Assassination* (New York: Free Press, 1999); Cromer, *Debate about Kahanism in Israeli Society*.

27. See Sprinzak, *Ascendance of Israel's Radical Religious Right* and *Brother against Brother*; and Ian S. Lustick, *Jewish Fundamentalism in Israel* (New York: Council on Foreign Relations, 1989).

28. Alter B. Z. Metzger, *Rabbi Kook's Philosophy of Repentance: A Translation of "Orot Ha-Teshuvah,"* Studies in Torah Judaism, vol. 11 (New York: Yeshiva University Press, 1968), 111. See also Jacob B. Agus, *Banner of Jerusalem: The Life, Times, and Thought of Abraham Isaac Kuk* (New York: Bloch Publishing Company, 1946).

29. Interview with Kahane, January 18, 1989.

30. According to Sprinzak, Kahane did not make the usual nationalist argument that the Jews deserved the land because it was their ancient birthplace;

rather, the Jews *"expropriated* it in the name of God and his sovereign will" (*Ascendance of Israel's Radical Right*, 225, italics in the original).

31. See M. Landsbaum and E. Litschblau, "Pair Suspected in Bombings Held in Israel," *Los Angeles Times*, March 25, 1991, A1. My thanks to Rimah Khouri, a student in the Global Peace and Security Program at the University of California, Santa Barbara, for providing information on the investigation related to the killing of Alex Odeh, her uncle.

32. Interview with Kahane, January 18, 1989.

33. Interview with Kahane, January 18, 1989. See also similar comments by Kahane in an interview published in Raphael Mergui and Philippe Simonnot, *Israel's Ayatollahs: Meir Kahane and the Far Right in Israel* (London: Saqi Books, 1987) (originally published as *Meir Kahane: Le rabbin qui fait peur aux juifs* by Editions Pierre-Marcel Favre, Lausanne, 1985), 43, 44, 68, 76–77, 150.

34. Interview with Lerner, Jerusalem, January 20, 1989.

35. Interview with Kahane, January 18, 1989.

36. See David Biale, *Power and Powerlessness in Jewish History* (New York: Schocken Books, 1987); and Salo Baron, George S. Wise, and Lenn Goodman, eds., *Violence and Defense in the Jewish Experience* (Philadelphia: Jewish Publication Society of America, 1977).

37. Speech given by Kahane, Jerusalem, January 18, 1989. I am indebted to Prof. Ehud Sprinzak and his students for providing me with a simultaneous English translation at the event. For a summary of the discussion in the Gush Emunim about the appropriateness of using violence, see Ian S. Lustick, *For the Land and the Lord: Jewish Fundamentalism in Israel* (New York: Council on Foreign Relations, 1988), 93–100.

38. Speech given by Kahane, Jerusalem, January 18, 1989.

39. Interview with Lerner, January 20, 1989.

40. Mergui and Simonnot, *Israel's Ayatollahs*, 52.

41. Mergui and Simonnot, *Israel's Ayatollahs*, 50.

42. Mergui and Simonnot, *Israel's Ayatollahs*. See also Kotler, *Heil Kahane*.

43. "The Legacy of Hate," New York Times, November 7, 1990, A30.

44. Jim Dwyer, David Kocieniewski, Deidre Murphy, and Peg Tyre, *Two Seconds under the World: Terror Comes to America—The Conspiracy behind the World Trade Center Bombing* (New York: Crown, 1994), 112.

45. Dwyer et al., *Two Seconds under the World*, 111. Nosair was never convicted of killing Kahane but received a prison sentence on a lesser charge of weapons possession.

Chapter 4. Islam's "Neglected Duty"

1. See, for example, Richard Behar, "The Secret Life of Mahmud the Red," *Time*, October 4, 1993, 54–64.

2. Benjamin Weiser, Susan Sachs, and David Kocieniewski, "U.S. Sees Brooklyn Connection to Embassy Bombings," *New York Times*, October 22, 1998, A1.

3. Interview with Mahmud Abouhalima, federal penitentiary, Lompoc, California, August 19, 1997, and September 30, 1997.

4. Jim Dwyer, David Kocieniewski, Deidre Murphy, and Peg Tyre, *Two Seconds under the World: Terror Comes to America—The Conspiracy behind the World Trade Center Bombing* (New York: Crown, 1994), 192.

5. Dwyer et al., *Two Seconds under the World*, 1–5.

6. Interview with Abouhalima, August 19, 1997. A similar account of what happened in the trial is described in Dwyer et al., *Two Seconds under the World*, 278–79. He repeated his claim of innocence in correspondence to me on May 20, 1999.

7. Interview with Abouhalima, September 30, 1997.

8. Interview with Abouhalima, August 19, 1997. The topic of the relationship between Islam and public order was discussed in both interviews, and clarified in his correspondence to me on May 20, 1999.

9. Interview with Abouhalima, August 19, 1997.

10. Behar, "The Secret Life of Mahmud the Red," p. 58.

11. Interview with Abouhalima, August 19, 1997.

12. Interview with Abouhalima, August 19, 1997.

13. *Newstand*, CNN television news program, December 20, 1998.

14. Dwyer et al., *Two Seconds under the World*, 148. In his correspondence to me on May 20, 1999, Abouhalima underscored the point that he was in Afghanistan solely "for civil purposes."

15. Interview with Abouhalima, August 19, 1997.

16. Dwyer et al., *Two Seconds under the World*, 148; see also Behar, "The Secret Life of Mahmud the Red," 60.

17. Sheik Omar Abdul Rahman, quoted in the British newspaper *The Independent*. Cited in Kim Murphy, "Have the Islamic Militants Turned to a New Battlefront in the U.S.?" *Los Angeles Times*, May 5, 1993, A20.

18. Interview with Abouhalima, August 19, 1997.

19. Interview with Abouhalima, August 19, 1997.

20. Judge Michael B. Mukasey, quoted in John J. Goldman, "Defendants Given 25 Years to Life in N.Y. Terror Plot," *Los Angeles Times*, January 18, 1996, A1.

21. Anne Marie Oliver and Paul Steinberg, *Rehearsals for a Happy Death* (New York: Oxford University Press, forthcoming).

22. Hamas videotape from the collection of Anne Marie Oliver and Paul Steinberg.

23. Hamas videotape from the collection of Anne Marie Oliver and Paul Steinberg. The quotation is from the words of Abdullah Azzam.

24. Lisa Beyer, "Jerusalem Bombing," *New York Times*, August 21, 1995.

25. Interview with Dr. Abdul Aziz Rantisi, Khan Yunis, Gaza, March 1, 1998.

26. Interview with Rantisi, March 1, 1998.

27. Interview with Imad Faluji, journalist and member of the policy wing of Hamas, Gaza, August 19, 1995. Faluji has since left the Hamas movement and joined Arafat's Palestinian Authority.

28. Interview with Rantisi, March 2, 1998.

29. Interview with Rantisi, March 2, 1998.

30. Interview with Faluji, August 19, 1995.

31. Interview with Faluji, August 19, 1995.

32. Interview with Sheik Yassin, January 14, 1989.

33. Interview with Sheik Yassin, January 14, 1989.

34. For an overview of the Hamas movement, see Roger Friedland and Richard Hecht, *To Rule Jerusalem* (Cambridge: Cambridge University Press, 1996), 366–84; and Mark Juergensmeyer, *The New Cold War? Religious Nationalism Confronts the Secular State* (Berkeley: University of California Press, 1993), 69–77.

35. Quoted in Jean-Francois Legrain, "The Islamic Movement and the Intifada," in Jamal R. Nassar and Roger Heacock, eds., *Intifada: Palestine at the Crossroads* (New York: Praeger, 1990), 182.

36. Interview with Rantisi, March 2, 1998.

37. See Elie Rekhess, "The Iranian Impact on the Islamic Jihad Movement in the Gaza Strip," in David Menashvi, ed., *The Iranian Revolution and the Muslim World* (Boulder, CO: Westview Press, 1990). An excerpt from this article, under the title "The Growth of Khomeinism in Gaza," was published in *Jerusalem Post Magazine*, January 26, 1991, 12.

38. Interviews with Hassan Salameh and Mohammad Abulwardi by Bob Simon in "Suicide Bomber," produced by Michael Gavson, aired on *60 Minutes*, October 5, 1997.

39. Interview with Ariel Merari, Center for the Study of Terrorism and Political Violence, Tel Aviv University, March 3, 1998.

40. Interview with Ashraf Yaghi, Gaza, August 19, 1995.

41. *Holy Qur'an,* 6:152.

42. Sheik Omar Abdul Rahman, quoted in James Mann and Robert L. Jackson, "Motive Behind Trade Center Bombing Remains a Mystery," *Los Angeles Times*, March 20, 1993, A16.

43. John Kifner, "Suspect in Kahane Case Is Muslim Born in Egypt," *New York Times*, November 7, 1990, A1.

44. Imam [Ayatollah] Sayyed Ruhollah Mousavi Khomeini, *Collection of Speeches, Position Statements*, Translations on Near East and North Africa no. 1902 (Arlington, VA: Joint Publications Research Service, 1979), 7.

45. See Rudolph Peters, *Islam and Colonialism: The Doctrine of Jihad in Modern History* (The Hague: Mouton, 1979); Richard C. Martin, "Religious Violence in Islam: Towards an Understanding of the Discourse on Jihad in Modern Egypt," in Paul Wilkinson and A. M. Stewart, eds., *Contemporary Research on Terrorism* (Aberdeen: Aberdeen University Press, 1969), 54–71; John Kelsay, *Islam and War: A Study in Comparative Ethics* (Louisville, KY: Westminster/John Knox Press, 1993).

46. See David Rapoport, *Assassination and Terrorism* (Toronto: Canadian Broadcasting Corporation, 1971), 3–4.

47. Interview with Sheik Yassin, January 14, 1989; interview with Dr. Rantisi, March 2, 1998.

48. Interview with Sheik 'Odeh, in *Islam and Palestine*, Leaflet 5 (Limasol, Cyprus, June 1988).

49. It was published in *Al-Ahrar*, an Egyptian newspaper, on December 14, 1981. An English translation, accompanied by an extensive essay about the

document, can be found in Johannes J. G. Jansen, *The Neglected Duty: The Creed of Sadat's Assassins and Islamic Resurgence in the Middle East* (New York: Macmillan, 1986). I have also found helpful the analysis of this document by David Rapoport in "Sacred Terror: A Case from Islam," unpublished paper delivered at the 1988 Annual Meeting of the American Political Science Association, Washington DC, September 1–4, 1988. The political implications of the document are discussed in Mohammed Heikal, *Autumn of Fury: The Assassination of Sadat* (London: Andre Deutsch, 1983).

50. Faraj, par. 84, in Jansen, *Neglected Duty*, 199.

51. Faraj, pars. 102 and 109, in Jansen, *Neglected Duty*, 210–11.

52. Faraj, par. 113, in Jansen, *Neglected Duty*, 212–13; see also par. 109, 211.

53. According to an Egyptian scholar who interviewed in prison members of the group responsible for Sadat's assassination, the writings of Mawdudi were "important in shaping the group's ideas." See Saad Eddin Ibrahim, "Islamic Militancy as a Social Movement: The Case of Two Groups in Egypt," in Ali E. Hillal Dessouki, ed., *Islamic Resurgence in the Arab World* (New York: Praeger, 1982), 125.

54. For a discussion of the significance of Sayyid Qutb's life and work, see Martin, "Religious Violence in Islam"; Gilles Kepel, *Muslim Extremism in Egypt: The Prophet and Pharaoh* (Berkeley: University of California Press, 1986), 36–69; Yvonne V. Haddad, "Sayyid Qutb: Ideologue of Islamic Revival," in John L. Esposito, ed., *Voices of Resurgent Islam* (New York: Oxford University Press, 1983); Ronald L. Nettler, *Past Trials and Present Tribulations: A Muslim Fundamentalist's View of the Jews* (New York: Pergamon Press, 1987).

55. Qutb studied in Washington, DC, and California from 1949 to 1951; see Haddad, "Sayyid Qutb," 69.

56. Sayyid Qutb, *This Religion of Islam (Hadha 'd-Din)* (Palo Alto, CA: Al-Manar Press, 1967), 87.

57. Interview with Rantisi, March 2, 1998.

58. Interview with Abouhalima, August 19, 1997.

Chapter 5. The Sword of Sikhism

1. Ramesh Vinayak, "Striking Terror," *India Today*, September 30, 1995, 27.

2. Vinayak, "Striking Terror," 34.

3. Ritu Sarin, *The Assassination of Indira Gandhi* (New Delhi: Penguin Books, 1990) 125–33.

4. Interview with Simranjit Singh Mann, Chandigarh, India, August 4, 1996.

5. Simranjit Singh Mann, letter to Zail Singh, June 1984. Reprinted in Ian Mulgrew, *Unholy Terror: The Sikhs and International Terrorism* (Toronto: Key Porter Books, 1988).

6. Mark Juergensmeyer, "The Logic of Religious Violence," in David Rapoport, ed. *Inside Terrorist Organizations* (London: Frank Cass, 1988), 172–93.

7. Jarnail Singh Bhindranwale, "Address to the Sikh Congregation," transcript of a sermon given in the Golden Temple in November 1983 (translated

by Ranbir Singh Sandhu, April 1985, and distributed by the Sikh Religious and Educational Trust, Dublin, Ohio); and "Two Lectures," July 19, 1983, and September 20, 1983 (translated from the videotaped originals by R. S. Sandhu and distributed by the Sikh Religious and Educational Trust, Dublin, Ohio).

   8. Bhindranwale, "Address to a Sikh Congregation." Among the other sources of Bhindranwale's words are Surjeet Jalandhary, ed., *Bhindranwale Sant* (Jalandhar, India: Punjab Pocket Books, n.d. [c. 1985]); and Joyce Pettigrew, "In Search of a New Kingdom of Lahore," *Pacific Affairs* 60:1, Spring 1987, 334–52.

   9. Interview with Jasvinder Singh, member of the Delhi branch, All-India Sikh Students Federation (Mehta-Chawla group), at Rakabganj Gurdwara, New Delhi, January 13, 1991.

   10. See Salman Khurshid, *Beyond Terrorism: New Hope for Kashmir* (New Delhi: UBS Publishers' Distributors, 1994).

   11. Sarin, *Assassination of Indira Gandhi*, 149.

   12. Interview with Harjap Singh, Sultanwind village, Amritsar district, Punjab, January 21, 1998, in English and Punjabi (with translation assistance of Prof. Harish Puri, Raminder Bir Singh, and Harbhajan Singh).

   13. Interview with Harjap Singh, January 21, 1998.

   14. See, for example, Wendy Doniger O'Flaherty, *Tales of Sex and Violence: Folklore, Sacrifice, and Danger in the Jaiminiya Brahmana* (Chicago: University of Chicago Press, 1984).

   15. For violence in later Hindu mythology, see David Kinsley, *The Sword and the Flute: Kali and Krsna, Dark Visions of the Terrible and the Sublime in Hindu Mythology* (Berkeley: University of California Press, 1975).

   16. Mohandas Gandhi, *Discourses on the Gita* (Ahmedabad: Navajivan Publishing House, 1960) (trans. from the original Gujarati by V. G. Desai).

   17. See Mark Juergensmeyer, *Fighting with Gandhi* (San Francisco: Harper & Row, 1984), reprinted as *Gandhi's Way* (Berkeley: University of California Press, forthcoming).

   18. This history of Sikh nationalism is drawn from Mark Juergensmeyer, *The New Cold War? Religious Nationalism Confronts the Secular State* (Berkeley: University of California Press, 1993), 90–99.

   19. The leading scholarly work on Guru Nanak is W. H. McLeod, *Guru Nanak and the Sikh Religion* (Oxford: Clarendon Press, 1968). See also the introduction to Nanak's writings in John Stratton Hawley and Mark Juergensmeyer, trans., *Songs of the Saints of India* (New York: Oxford University Press, 1988).

   20. This transition is described in W. H. McLeod, *Evolution of the Sikh Community* (Oxford: Clarendon Press, 1976), 1–19. See also McLeod's *Guru Nanak and the Sikh Religion* and *Who Is a Sikh? The Problem of Sikh Identity* (Oxford: Clarendon Press, 1989).

   21. The idea that the circular form in the Sikh symbol is a cooking vessel has been offered in Gurinder Singh Mann, *Your Sikh Neighbors* (Richmond Hill, NY: Sikh Cultural Society, 1999), 8.

   22. See Ainslie Embree, "A Sikh Challenge to the Indian State," in Embree's *Utopias in Conflict* (Berkeley: University of California Press, 1990), 113–32.

   23. For accounts of the Punjab crisis in the 1980s, see Mark Tully and Satish Jacob, *Amritsar: Mrs. Gandhi's Last Battle* (London: Cape, 1985);

Amarjit Kaur, *The Punjab Story* (New Delhi: Roli Books International, 1984); and Kuldip Nayar and Khushwant Singh, *Tragedy of Punjab: Operation Bluestar and After* (New Delhi: Vision Books, 1984).

24. See Tully and Jacob, *Amritsar.*

25. See *Who Are the Guilty? Report of a Joint Inquiry into the Causes and Impact of the Riots in Delhi from 31 October to 10 November* (Delhi: People's Union for Democratic Rights and People's Union for Civil Liberties, 1984). An interesting study of the Delhi event and other riots in South Asia is Stanley Tambiah, *Leveling Crowds: Ethnonationalist Conflicts and Collective Violence in South Asia* (Berkeley: University of California Press, 1996).

26. For a discussion of the political implications of the concept of *qaum* in the Punjab, see Mark Juergensmeyer, *Religion as Social Vision* (Berkeley: University of California Press, 1982), 45.

27. Bhindranwale, "Address to the Sikh Congregation," 9.

28. Joyce Pettigrew examines Bhindranwale's use of the concept of *miri-piri* in "In Search of a New Kingdom of Lahore."

29. Bhindranwale, "Two Lectures," 2.

30. Bhindranwale, "Address to the Sikh Congregation," 1.

31. For the ethic of nonviolence in Sikhism, see W. Owen Cole and Piara Singh Sambhi, *The Sikhs: Their Religious Beliefs and Practices* (London: Routledge and Kegan Paul, 1978), 138; Avtar Singh, *Ethics of the Sikhs* (Patiala, India: Punjabi University Press); and S. S. Kohli, *Sikh Ethics* (New Delhi: Munshiram Manoharlal, 1975).

32. See Mohinder Singh, "Gandhi, Sikhs and Non-Violence," *Khera: The Journal of Religious Understanding* 9:3, July–September 1990, 72–87.

33. Bhindranwale, "Two Lectures," 21.

34. Excerpt from one of Bhindranwale's speeches, quoted in Pettigrew, "In Search of a New Kingdom of Lahore."

35. Interview with Sohan Singh, Mohalli, Punjab, August 3, 1996. For the role of his coordinating body, also known as the Second Panthic Committee, see Cynthia Keppley Mahmood, *Fighting for Faith and Nation: Dialogues with Sikh Militants* (Philadelphia: University of Pennsylvania Press, 1996), 159–61.

36. Interview with Sohan Singh, August 3, 1996.

37. Cynthia Keppley Mahmood, *Fighting for Faith and Nation: Dialogues with Sikh Militants* (Philadelphia: University of Pennsylvania Press, 1997). See also the interviews with Sikh militants in Joyce Pettigrew, *The Sikhs of the Punjab: Unheard Voice of State and Guerrilla Violence* (Atlantic Highlands, NJ: Zed Books, 1995).

38. Mahmood, *Fighting for Faith and Nation*, 149.

39. Interview with Sohan Singh, August 3, 1996.

40. Interview with Narinder Singh, Chandigarh, Punjab, August 3, 1996.

41. Interview with Narinder Singh, August 3, 1996.

Chapter 6. Armageddon in a Tokyo Subway

1. David E. Kaplan and Andrew Marshall, *The Cult at the End of the World: The Terrifying Story of the Aum Doomsday Cult* (New York: Crown, 1996), 2.

2. Kaplan and Marshall, *Cult at the End of the World*, 246.

3. Interview with Tatsuko Muraoka and Yasuo Hiramatsu, Aoyama, Tokyo, January 13, 1996.

4. Teresa Watanabe and Hilary E. MacGregor, "Plan to Rein in Religious Groups Worries Japanese," *Los Angeles Times*, October 16, 1995, A1.

5. Interview with Hiramatsu, January 13, 1996.

6. Interview with Tomoko and Ayako (no last names given), Satian Bookstore, 1-15-3 Dogenzaka, Shibuya, Tokyo, January 11, 1996.

7. Interview with "Takeshi Nakamura," Tokyo, January 12, 1996 (translation assistance provided by Amy Arakane and Prof. Susumu Shimazono). At his request I changed his name and omitted any personal information that might allow current members of the movement to identify him.

8. Interview with Nakamura, January 12, 1996.

9. D. W. Brackett, *Holy Terror: Armageddon in Tokyo* (New York: Weatherhill, 1996), 60.

10. Brackett, *Holy Terror*, 60.

11. Interview with Nakamura, January 12, 1996.

12. Revelation 16:16–21.

13. Shoko Asahara, *Disaster Approaches the Land of the Rising Sun: Shoko Asahara's Apocalyptic Predictions*, Aum Translation Committee, trans., ed. (Tokyo: Aum Publishing Co., Shizuoka Japan, 1995), 190.

14. Asahara, *Disaster Approaches*, 135–36.

15. Asahara, *Disaster Approaches*, 136.

16. Interview with Nakamura, January 12, 1996.

17. Asahara, *Disaster Approaches*, 190.

18. Asahara, *Disaster Approaches*, 190.

19. Brackett, *Holy Terror*, 183.

20. Interview with Nakamura, January 12, 1996.

21. Interview with Nakamura, January 12, 1996.

22. Interview with Hiramatsu, January 13, 1996.

23. Stanley J. Tambiah, *World Conqueror and World Renouncer* (Cambridge: Cambridge University Press, 1987).

24. Hajime Nakamura, "Violence and Nonviolence in Buddhism," in Philip P. Wiener and John Fisher, eds., *Violence and Aggression in the History of Ideas* (New Brunswick, NJ: Rutgers University Press, 1974), 173–86. See also H. Saddhatissa, *Buddhist Ethics* (London: George Allen and Unwin, 1970).

25. Interview with Venerable Palipana Chandananda, Mahanayake, Asigiriya chapter, Sinhalese Buddhist Sangha (Kandy, Sri Lanka), January 4, 1991.

26. Interview with Chandananda, January 4, 1991.

27. See Ian Reader, *A Poisonous Cocktail? Aum Shinrikyo's Path to Violence* (Copenhagen: NIAS Books, 1996), 17.

28. These accounts were related to me by Susumu Shimazono, professor of religion, Tokyo University Faculty Club, January 9, 1996.

29. Ian Reader, personal correspondence, January 12, 1999.

30. Interview with Hiromi Shimada, Suginami-ku, Tokyo, January 10, 1996.

31. Asahara, *Disaster Approaches*, 274.

32. Asahara, *Disaster Approaches*, 275.

33. Asahara, *Disaster Approaches*, 169.

34. Reader, *A Poisonous Cocktail?*, 35.

35. Interview with Shimazono, January 9, 1996. See also his articles "In the Wake of Aum," *Japanese Journal of Religious Studies* 22:3–4, 1995, 381–415 (which is a condensed version of Shimazono's book *Aum Shinrikyo no kiseki*, Robert Kisala trans.); and "New 'New Religions' and This World: Religious Movements in Japan after the 1970s and Their Beliefs about Salvation," *Social Compass* 42:2, 1995, 193–202.

36. "Resurgence of Interest in Aum Shinrikyo," *New York Times*, October 28, 1998, A3.

37. Interview with Nakamura, January 12, 1996.

Chapter 7. Theater of Terror

1. Kenny McClinton, quoted in Martin Dillon, *God and the Gun: The Church and Irish Terrorism* (New York: Routledge, 1998), 27.

2. McClinton, quoted in Dillon, *God and the Gun*, 27.

3. Dillon, *God and the Gun*, 27.

4. D. W. Brackett, *Holy Terror: Armageddon in Tokyo* (New York: Weatherhill, 1996), 184.

5. Mo Mowlam, quoted in "Apology Comes as First Victims Are Buried," *San Francisco Chronicle*, August 19, 1998, A3.

6. Brackett, *Holy Terror*, 157.

7. Walter Laqueur, *The Age of Terrorism* (Boston: Little, Brown, 1987), 72. For a discussion of the problem of defining terrorism, see Bruce Hoffman, *Inside Terrorism* (New York: Columbia University Press, 1998), 13–44; Michel Wieviorka, "Terrorism in the Context of Academic Research," in Martha Crenshaw, ed., *Terrorism in Context* (University Park: Pennsylvania State University Press, 1995), 599–600; Thomas Perry Thornton, "Terrorism as a Weapon of Political Agitation," in Harry Eckstein, ed., *Internal War: Problems and Approaches* (New York: Free Press, 1964); David Rapoport, "The Politics of Atrocity," in Y. Alexander and S. Finger, eds., *Terrorism: Interdisciplinary Perspectives* (New York: John Jay, 1977).

8. Interview with Abdul Aziz Rantisi, Khas Yunis, Gaza, March 2, 1998. The quotation from Hassan Salameh, the Hamas operative who planned the 1996 suicide bombings in Jerusalem and Tel Aviv, is from a televised interview with Bob Simon, "Suicide Bomber," produced by Michael Gavson, aired on *60 Minutes*, October 5, 1997.

9. Interview with Mahmud Abouhalima, federal penitentiary, Lompoc, California, September 30, 1997.

10. Martha Crenshaw, "The Logic of Terrorism: Terrorist Behavior as a Product of Strategic Choice," in Walter Reich, ed., *Origins of Terrorism: Psychologies, Ideologies, Theologies, States of Mind* (Cambridge: Woodrow Wilson International Center for Scholars and Cambridge University Press, 1990), 7–24.

11. See Catherine Bell, *Ritual Theory, Ritual Practice* (New York: Oxford University Press, 1992); Richard Schechner, *The Future of Ritual: Writings on Culture and Performance* (London: Routledge, 1993); Felicia Hughes-Freeland, *Ritual, Performance, Media* (London: Routledge, 1998); David Parkin, Lionel Caplan, and Humphrey Fisher, *The Politics of Cultural Performance* (Providence: Berghahn Books, 1996). I am grateful to Shawn Landres for keeping me up to date on this growing field of academic study.

12. Neil Jarman, *Material Conflicts: Parades and Visual Displays in Northern Ireland* (Oxford: Berg, 1997).

13. See J. L. Austin, *How to Do Things with Words* (Oxford: Clarendon Press, 1962).

14. Austin, *How to Do Things with Words*, 4.

15. Pierre Bourdieu, *Language and Symbolic Power* (Cambridge, MA: Harvard University Press, 1991) (translated from the 1982 French original by Gino Raymond and Matthew Adamson, edited by John B. Thompson), 117.

16. David C. Rapoport, "Introduction," in David C. Rapoport and Yonah Alexander, eds., *The Morality of Terrorism: Religious and Secular Justifications* (New York: Pergamon Press, 1982), xiii.

17. Don DeLillo, *Mao II* (New York: Penguin, 1991), 157.

18. John J. Goldman and William C. Rempel, "Blast Rips World Trade Center in N.Y.," *Los Angeles Times*, February 27, 1993, A1.

19. The question of whether the bombing was undertaken by Yousef's accomplices as an act of revenge for his indictment is discussed in Robin Wright, "Suspect Search Is Wide Open and Baffling," *Los Angeles Times*, July 22, 1996, A1.

20. Interview with Simranjit Singh Mann, Chandigarh, India, August 4, 1996. Two writers who examined the Air India bombing make the astounding suggestion that, since the public would rush to the conclusion that the bombing was a Sikh terrorist act, it might have been committed by Indian government agents seeking to discredit the Sikh movement. See Zuhair Kashmeri and Brian McAndrew, *Soft Target: How the Indian Intelligence Service Penetrated Canada* (Toronto: J. Lorimer, 1989).

21. Bruce Hoffman, *"Holy Terror": The Implications of Terrorism Motivated by a Religious Imperative* (Santa Monica, CA: RAND Corporation, 1993), 10.

22. Sheik Omar Abdul Rahman, quoted in Kim Murphy, "Militant Mullah Speaks Out," *Los Angeles Times*, March 5, 1993, A1.

23. Hoffman, *Holy Terror*, 13. See also Mark Hosenball, "Another Holy War, Waged on American Soil: Al-Fuqra, a Muslim Sect with a Dangerous Agenda," *Newsweek*, February 28, 1995, 29–31.

24. David C. Rapoport, "Observations on the Importance of Space in Violent Ethno-Religious Strife," paper presented at the seminar "Religious and Ethnic Conflict," University of California, Riverside, April 28, 1995.

25. Roger Friedland and Richard Hecht, "The Bodies of Nations: A Comparative Study of Religious Violence in Jerusalem and Ayodhya, *History of Religions*, November 1998, 101–49; and "Divisions at the Center: The Organization of Political Violence at Jerusalem's Temple Mount/al-Haram al-

Sharif—1929 and 1990," in Paul Brass, ed., *Riots and Pogroms: The Nation State and Violence* (New York: Macmillan, 1996).

26. Kerry Noble, *Tabernacle of Hate: Why They Bombed Oklahoma City* (Prescott, Ontario: Voyageur, 1998), 206.

27. Noble, *Tabernacle of Hate*, 207. According to Noble, the producers of a Canadian Broadcasting Corporation program, *The Fifth Estate*, secured footage from a security camera documenting the customer's report and verifying that McVeigh mentioned the April 19 date.

28. Noble, *Tabernacle of Hate*, 9.

29. Noble, *Tabernacle of Hate*, 225.

30. Yossi Klein Halevi, "Kahane's Murderous Legacy," *Jerusalem Report*, March 24, 1994, 17.

31. Interview with Imad Faluji, August 19, 1995. The same idea was conveyed by Dr. Abdul Aziz Rantisi in my interview with him on March 1, 1998.

32. "Death Toll in Algeria Rises to 52 in Pre-Ramadan Violence," *Los Angeles Times*, December 7, 1998, A7. I am indebted also to an unpublished paper on this topic by Michelle Zimney, "Ramadan's Killing Fields: Sacrifice and National Struggle in Algeria."

33. "Groups Attack Two Algerian Villages," *Los Angeles Times*, December 29, 1998.

34. Michael Bray, *A Time to Kill: A Study Concerning the Use of Force and Abortion* (Portland, OR: Advocates for Life Publications, 1994).

35. Interview with Rev. Michael Bray, Bowie, Maryland, April 25, 1996.

36. Interview with Bray, April 25, 1996.

37. Interview with Bray, April 15, 1996.

38. Paul Hill, "Why I Shot an Abortionist," December 22, 1997, an open letter to Rev. Michael Bray and the attendees of the White Rose Banquet, circulated by Bray.

39. Paul Hill, quoted in Henry Chu and Mike Clary, "Doctor, Volunteer Slain Outside Abortion Clinic," *Los Angeles Times*, July 30, 1994, A1.

40. Interview with Takeshi Nakamura, Tokyo, January 12, 1996.

41. "Israel Orders Deportation of 11 Cult Members," *Los Angeles Times*, January 5, 1999, A4. See also Tracy Wilkinson, "Israel Has Eye on Christians Who Have Their Eyes on 2000," *Los Angeles Times*, January 10, 1999, A1.

42. Clifford Geertz, "Centers, Kings, and Charisma: Reflections on the Symbolics of Power," in Joseph Ben-David and Terry Nichols Clark, eds., *Culture and Its Creators: Essays in Honor of Edward Shils* (Chicago: University of Chicago Press, 1977). This essay is reprinted in Clifford Geertz, *Local Knowledge: Further Essays in Interpretive Anthropology* (New York: Basic Books, 1983), 121-46.

43. Geertz, "Centers, Kings, and Charisma," 151.

44. DeLillo, *Mao II*, 157.

45. Interview with Bray, March 20, 1998.

46. Interview with Mahmud Abouhalima, August 19, 1997.

47. Jim Dwyer, David Kocieniewski, Deidre Murphy, and Peg Tyre, *Two Seconds under the World: Terror Comes to America—The Conspiracy behind the World Trade Center Bombing* (New York: Crown, 1994).

48. Egawa Shoko's book on the Aum Shinrikyo movement is *Kyuseishu no yabo* (Tokyo: Kyoikushiryo Shuppankai, 1995).

49. Interview with Seth Sutel, correspondent for the Associated Press, Tokyo, January 9, 1996.

50. Aruthur Sulzberger, Jr., quoted in Robert D. McFadden, "Unabomber Manifesto to Be Published," *New York Times News Service* (posted on America Online), September 18, 1995.

51. Jean Baudrillard, "The Mirror of Terrorism," in *The Transparency of Evil: Essays on the Extreme Phenomena* (London: Verso, 1993) (translated from the 1990 French edition by James Benedict), 75.

52. Baudrillard, *Transparency of Evil*, 75.

53. Neal Horsley, quoted in "Internet Provider Shuts Down Anti-Abortion Site," *Los Angeles Times*, February 6, 1999, A17.

54. Interview with Abouhalima, September 30, 1997.

55. Bourdieu, *Language and Symbolic Power*, 117.

Chapter 8. Cosmic War

1. "*Jihad* is an Individual Duty," *Los Angeles Times*, August 13, 1998, B9.

2. Kerry Noble, *Tabernacle of Hate: Why They Bombed Oklahoma City* (Prescott, Ontario: Voyageur, 1998), 206.

3. Noble, *Tabernacle of Hate*, 215.

4. Bob Matthews, quoted in a story aired on ABC's *Turning Point*, October 5, 1995; Journal Graphics Transcript 150, 7.

5. Michael Teague, quoted in Kim Murphy, "Last Stand of an Aging Aryan," *Los Angeles Times*, January 10, 1999, A14.

6. James A. Aho, *The Politics of Righteousness: Idaho Christian Patriotism* (Seattle: University of Washington Press, 1990), 85.

7. *This Is Aryan Nations*, undated, no publisher or place, quoted in Bruce Hoffman, "*Holy Terror*": The Implications of Terrorism Motivated by a Religious Imperative* (Santa Monica, CA: RAND Corporation, 1993), 7. The capitalization of "believe" is in the original.

8. Interview with Rev. Michael Bray, Bowie, Maryland, March 20, 1998.

9. *The Battle Standard: Journal of the European Institute of Protestant Studies* 1:1, October 1997. The editor of the newspaper is listed as Dr. Ian R. K. Paisley MP, MEP.

10. Billy Wright, quoted in Martin Dillon, *God and the Gun: The Church and Irish Terrorism* (New York: Routledge, 1998), 64.

11. Interview with Yochay Ron, guard at the grave of Dr. Baruch Goldstein, Kiryat Arba, Palestine (Israel), August 18, 1995.

12. Interview with Imad Faluji, Hamas journalist, Gaza, August 19, 1995.

13. Interview with Sheik Ahmed Yassin, spiritual leader of Hamas, Gaza, January 14, 1989.

14. Interview with Mahmud Abouhalima, Lompoc, California, August 19, 1997.

15. Richard Behar, "The Secret Life of Mahmud the Red," *Time*, October 4, 1993, 59.

16. Ayatollah Khomeini, *Collection of Speeches, Position Statements*, translated from 'Najaf Min watha 'iq al-Imam al-Khomeyni did al-Quwa al Imbiriyaliyah wa al-Sahyuniyah wa al-Raj'iyah' ("From the Papers of Imam Khomeyni against Imperialist, Zionist, and Reactionist Powers"), Translations on Near East and North Africa, no. 1902, 1977 (Arlington, VA: Joint Publications Research Service, 1979), 6.

17. Bruce B. Lawrence, *Shattering the Myth: Islam beyond Violence* (Princeton, NJ: Princeton University Press, 1998), 181.

18. Jarnail Singh Bhindranwale, "Two Lectures Given on 19 July and 20 September, 1983," transcribed and translated into English from the videotaped originals in Punjab by Ranbir Singh Sandhu and distributed by the Sikh Religious and Educational Trust, Columbus, Ohio, 1986, 2.

19. Shoko Asahara, *Disaster Approaches the Land of the Rising Sun: Shoko Asahara's Apocalyptic Predictions* (Tokyo: Aum Publishing Co., 1995).

20. The literature on conflict resolution is immense. My own ideas about the subject are based on the teachings of Mohandas Gandhi, with whom I nevertheless have some quarrels. See my *Fighting with Gandhi* (San Francisco: Harper, 1984), reprinted as *Gandhi's Way* (Berkeley: University of California Press, forthcoming).

21. Interview with Bray, April 25, 1996.

22. Interview with Bray, April 25, 1996.

23. Asahara, *Disaster Approaches*, 265.

24. Asahara, *Disaster Approaches*, 279.

25. This summary of Christian Identity teachings comes from Michael Barkun, *Religion and the Racist Right: The Origins of the Christian Identity Movement* (Chapel Hill: University of North Carolina Press, 1994); and James Aho, *The Politics of Righteousness: Idaho Christian Patriotism* (Seattle: University of Washington Press, 1990).

26. Aho, *The Politics of Righteousness*, 90.

27. Interview with Yochay Ron, Kiryat Arba settlement, Hebron, August 18, 1995.

28. Sarah Nachshon, quoted in Marjorie Miller, "Hebron's Fifty Jewish Families Unsettle Mideast," *Los Angeles Times*, October 20, 1996, A1.

29. Hamas communique no. 64, September 26, 1990, quoted in Jean-Francois Legrain, "A Defining Moment: Palestinian Islamic Fundamentalism," in James Piscatori, ed., *Islamic Fundamentalisms and the Gulf Crisis* (Chicago: Fundamentalism Project, American Academy of Arts and Sciences, 1991), 75–76.

30. Abolhassan Banisadr, *The Fundamental Principles and Precepts of Islamic Government*, Mohammed R. Ghanoonparvar, trans. (Lexington, KY; Mazda, 1981), 28–35.

31. Interview with Yoel Lerner, March 2, 1998.

32. Interview with Rantisi, March 2, 1998.

33. Bruce Pierce, member of Aryan Nations' The Order, quoted in ABC's *Turning Point*, October 5, 1995; Journal Graphics Transcript no. 150, 8.

34. Nathuram Godse, deposition, appeals court, government of India, 1948. Godse's court testimony has been made into a controversial play, *Mee*

Nathuram Godse Boltoy ("I Am Nathuram Godse Speaking"), banned by the Maharashtra state government under pressure by the BJP-led federal government in 1998.

35. Kim Murphy, "Last Stand of an Aging Aryan," *Los Angeles Times*, January 10, 1999, A15.

36. Denver Parmenter, member of the Aryan Nations accused of conspiring to kill radio commentator Alan Berg, quoted in ABC's *Turning Point*, October 5, 1995; Journal Graphics Transcript no. 150, 2.

37. Natalie Zemon Davis, "The Rites of Violence: Religious Riots in Sixteenth-Century France," *Past and Present* 59, May 1973, 52–53.

38. Davis, "Rites of Violence," 81–82.

39. Stanley Tambiah, *Leveling Crowds: Ethnonationalist Conflicts and Collective Violence in South Asia* (Berkeley: University of California Press, 1996) 310–11.

40. Tambiah, *Leveling Crowds*, 311.

41. In this section I repeat some of the arguments about the relationship of violence and religion first stated in my book *The New Cold War?*, 153–70.

42. For an analysis of "Onward Christian Soldiers" and other hymns of America's frontier revival movements, see Sandra Sizer, *Gospel Hymns and Social Religion: The Rhetoric of Nineteenth-Century Revivalism* (Philadelphia: Temple University Press, 1978).

43. Harriet Crabtree, *The Christian Life: Traditional Metaphors and Contemporary Theologies* (Minneapolis: Fortress Press, Harvard Dissertations in Religion, 1991). Her findings with regard to warfare are summarized in her article, "Onward Christian Soldiers? The Fortunes of a Traditional Christian Symbol in the Modern Age," *Bulletin of the Center for the Study of World Religion, Harvard University*, 16:2, 1989/90, 6–27.

44. Arthur Wallis, *Into Battle: A Manual of Christian Life* (New York: Harper, 1973), 10. The italics are in the original.

45. Crabtree, "Onward Christian Soldiers," 7.

46. *Bhagavad Gita*, 1:45. The cousins were not quite morally equal, however. One set, the Pandavas, were more wicked than the other.

47. *Bhagavad Gita*, 2:19–34.

48. Ernest Becker, *The Denial of Death* (New York: Free Press, 1973). See also his *Escape from Evil* (New York: Free Press, 1975).

49. Mark Juergensmeyer, "The Logic of Religious Violence," in David C. Rapoport, ed., *Inside Terrorist Organizations* (London: Frank Cass, and New York: Columbia University Press, 1988), 185–90.

50. Weston LaBarre, *The Ghost Dance: Origins of Religion* (London: Allen and Unwin, 1972).

Chapter 9. Martyrs and Demons

1. Timothy McVeigh, quoted in Richard A. Serrano, "McVeigh Speaks Out, Receives Death Sentence," *Los Angeles Times*, August 15, 1997, A1.

2. Interview with Dr. Abdul Aziz Rantisi, Khan Yunis, Gaza, March 1, 1998.

3. Interview with Yochay Ron, Kiryat Arba settlement, Hebron, August 18, 1995.

4. Interview with Jasvinder Singh, member of the Delhi branch of the All-India Sikh Students Federation (Mehta-Chawla group), Rakabganj Gurdwara, New Delhi, January 13, 1991.

5. Interview with Harjap Singh, Sultanwind village, Amritsar district, India, January 21, 1998, with translation assistance from Harish Puri, Raminder Bir Singh, and Harbhajan Singh.

6. Michael Bray, "The Impending Execution of Paul Hill," *Capitol Area Christian News* 25, Summer 1997, 1.

7. Billy Wright, quoted in Martin Dillon, *God and the Gun: The Church and Irish Terrorism* (New York: Routledge, 1998), 65.

8. Osama bin Laden, quoted in *"Jihad* Is an Individual Duty," *Los Angeles Times*, August 13, 1998, B9.

9. J. Frits Staal, *Agni: The Vedic Ritual of the Fire Altar* (Berkeley: Asian Humanities Press, 1983).

10. Maurice Bloch, *Prey into Hunter* (Cambridge: Cambridge University Press, 1992); René Girard, *Violence and the Sacred*, Patrick Gregory, trans. (Baltimore: Johns Hopkins University Press, 1977); René Girard, *The Scapegoat*, Yvonne Freccero, trans. (Baltimore: Johns Hopkins University Press, 1986); Walter Burkert, *Homo Necans: The Anthropology of Ancient Greek Sacrificial Ritual and Myth*, Peter Bing, trans. (Berkeley: University of California Press, 1972); Walter Burkhert, René Girard, and Jonathan Z. Smith, *Violent Origins: Ritual Killing and Cultural Formation*, Robert G. Hamerton-Kelly, ed. (Stanford, CA: Stanford University Press, 1987); Eli Sagan, *The Lust to Annihilate: A Psychoanalytic Study of Violence in Ancient Greek Culture* (New York: Psychohistory Press, 1972); Eli Sagan, *Cannibalism: Human Aggression and Cultural Form* (New York: Psychohistory Press, 1974). For a review of these and other studies, see Richard D. Hecht, "Studies on Sacrifice, 1970–1980," *Religious Studies Review* 8:3, 1982, 13–19.

11. Girard, *Violence and the Sacred*, 36.

12. Girard, *Violence and the Sacred*, 36.

13. René Girard, "Disorder and Order in Mythology," in *Disorder and Order: Proceedings of the Stanford International Symposium* (Stanford, CA: Anma Libri, 1984), 97.

14. For a discussion of Girard's theories, and an alternative to certain aspects of it, see my article "Sacrifice and Cosmic War" in Mark Juergensmeyer, ed., *Violence and the Sacred in the Modern World* (London: Frank Cass, 1991), 101–17, and the concluding reply from Girard in the same volume.

15. See the essays in John Stratton Hawley, ed., *Sati, the Blessing and the Curse: The Burning of Wives in India* (New York: Oxford University Press, 1994).

16. Anthony F. C. Wallace, *The Death and Rebirth of the Seneca* (New York: Random House, 1969) 102–7.

17. For a summary of the project, see John Stratton Hawley, "Introduction: Saints and Virtues," in J. S. Hawley, ed., *Saints and Virtues* (Berkeley: University of California Press, 1987), xi–xxiv.

18. Martin Kramer, "Sacrifice and Fratricide in Shiite Lebanon," in Juergensmeyer, ed., *Violence and the Sacred*, 38–40.

19. James Aho, *This Thing of Darkness: A Sociology of the Enemy* (Seattle: University of Washington Press, 1994), 6.

20. Stanley Tambiah, *Leveling Crowds: Ethnonationalist Conflicts and Collective Violence in South Asia* (Berkeley: University of California Press, 1996), 310–11.

21. Shoko Asahara, *Disaster Approaches the Land of the Rising Sun: Shoko Asahara's Apocalyptic Predictions*, Aum Translation Committee, trans., ed. (Tokyo: Aum Publishing Co., Shizuoka Japan, 1995), 281.

22. See, for example, Hirose Takashi and Akama Takashi, *The Structure of Japan and the Jewish Conspiracy* (Tokyo: Tokuma Press, n.d.); Uno Magami, *If You Understand the Jewish Situation, You Can Understand the World Situation* (Tokyo: Tokuma Press, n.d.).

23. Matthew Hale, quoted in Stephanie Simon, "Leader of Hate's Church Mourns 'One White Man,'" *Los Angeles Times,* July 6, 1999, A1.

24. Robert Matthews, quoted in "Views of a Racist Anti-Government Leader," *Washington Post*, December 26, 1984, 3.

25. Richard Butler, quoted in Kim Murphy, "Last Stand of an Aging Aryan," *Los Angeles Times*, January 10, 1999, A15.

26. Denver Parmenter, interviewed on ABC's *Turning Point*, October 5, 1995; Journal Graphics Transcript no. 150, 2.

27. Rabbi Yitzhak Ginsburgh, quoted in Yossi Klein Halevi, "Kahane's Murderous Legacy," *Jerusalem Report*, March 24, 1994, 17.

28. Halevi, "Kahane's Murderous Legacy," 17.

29. Interview with Yochay Ron, Kiryat Arba settlement, Hebron, August 18, 1995.

30. Interview with Imad Faluji, August 19, 1995.

31. Andrew Macdonald [William Pierce], *The Turner Diaries* (New York: Barricade Books, 1996) (orig. published by National Alliance Vanguard Books, Arlington, VA, in 1978), 42.

32. Jarnail Singh Bhindranwale, "Address to the Sikh Congregation," sermon given in the Golden Temple in November 1983 (transcribed and translated from the audiotape original in Punjab by Ranbir Singh Sandhu, distributed by the Sikh Religious and Educational Trust, Dublin, Ohio, 1985), 1.

33. Bhindranwale, "Two Lectures," July 19, 1983, and September 20, 1983 (translated from the videotaped originals by R. S. Sandhu and distributed by the Sikh Religious and Educational Trust, Dublin, Ohio), 22.

34. Ehud Sprinzak, "Right-Wing Terrorism in a Comparative Perspective: The Case of Split Delegitimization," in Tore Bjørgo, ed., *Terror from the Extreme Right* (London: Frank Cass, 1995), 20.

35. Ian Paisley, editorial in *The Revivalist*, January 1983, 10.

36. Bhindranwale, "Address to the Sikh Congregation," 1.

37. Richard Butler, quoted in Murphy, "Last Stand of an Aging Aryan," A15.

38. Interview with Rabbi Meir Kahane, Jerusalem, January 18, 1989.

39. Interview with Mahmud Abouhalima, August 19, 1997.

40. Ian Paisley, *The Preaching of Ian Paisley* (Belfast: Martyrs' Memorial Recordings, 17 November 1985), cited in Dennis Cooke, *Persecuting Zeal: A Portrait of Ian Paisley* (Kerry, Ireland: Brandon Book Publishers, 1996), 1.

41. Halevi, "Kahane's Murderous Legacy," 18.

42. RAND Chronicle of International Terrorism, reported in Bruce Hoffman, *Terrorism Targeting* (Santa Monica, CA: RAND Corporation, 1992), 17.

43. Robin Wright, "Prophetic 'Terror 2000' Mapped Evolving Threat," *Los Angeles Times*, August 9, 1998, A16.

44. Interview with Abouhalima, September 30, 1997.

45. John J. Goldman, "Defendants Given 25 years to Life in New York Terror Plot," *Los Angeles Times*, January 18, 1996, A1.

46. Osama bin Laden, interviewed on an ABC News report rebroadcast on August 9, 1998.

47. Samel Berger, quoted in *"Jihad* Is an Individual Duty," B9.

48. *"Jihad* Is an Individual Duty," B9.

49. *"Jihad* Is an Individual Duty," B9.

50. Sheik Omar Abdul Rahman, quoted in Kim Murphy, "Have the Islamic Militants Turned to a New Battlefront in the US?" *Los Angeles Times*, March 3, 1993, A20.

51. Ayatollah Khomeini, *Collection of Speeches, Position Statements* (Arlington, VA: Joint Publications Research Service, 1979), 24.

52. Khomeini, *Collection*, 30.

53. Interview with Rabbi Manachem Fruman, Tuqua settlement, West Bank, Israel, August 14, 1995.

54. Interview with Abouhalima, September 30, 1997.

55. Imam [Ayatollah] Khomeini, *Islam and Revolution: Writings and Declarations*, Hamid Algar, trans., annot. (London: Routledge and Kegan Paul, 1985) (orig. published by Mizan Press, Berkeley, in 1981), 27–28.

56. Khomeini, *Collection*, 3.

57. Khomeini, *Collection*, 25.

58. Interview with Rantisi, March 2, 1989.

59. Ehud Sprinzak, "The Process of Delegitimization: Towards a Linkage Theory of Political Terrorism," *Terrorism and Political Violence* 3:1, Spring 1991, 50–68. See also his essay, "Right-Wing Terrorism," in Bjørgo, ed., *Terror from the Extreme Right;* and a forthcoming book in which these ideas are set within a general theory of terrorism.

60. Sprinzak, "Process of Delegitimation," 55.

61. Sprinzak, "Process of Delegitimation," 56.

62. Sprinzak, "Process of Delegitimation," 56.

63. Rabbi Meir Kahane, speech on the announcement of the creation of the independent state of Judaea, Jerusalem, January 18, 1989 (from my notes).

64. Interview with Yoel Lerner, Jerusalem, January 20, 1989.

Chapter 10. Warriors' Power

1. Interview with Dr. Abdul Aziz Rantisi, Khan Yunis, Gaza, March 1, 1998.

2. Interview with Rantisi, March 1, 1998.

3. Robin Wright, "Global Warrior Defends Himself in Court," *Los Angeles Times*, May 12, 1996, A1.

4. Daoud Salahuddin [David Belfield], in an interview on ABC's *20/20*, January 20, 1996; Journal Graphics Transcript no. 1603, 4.

5. Cynthia Keppley Mahmood, *Fighting for Faith and Nation: Dialogues with Sikh Militants* (Philadelphia: University of Pennsylvania Press, 1996), 188.

6. Interview with Takeshi Nakamura, Tokyo, January 12, 1996.

7. Sheik Omar Abdul Rahman, quoted in Kim Murphy, "Have the Islamic Militants Turned to a New Battlefield in the US?" *Los Angeles Times*, March 5, 1993, A20.

8. Interview with Rev. Michael Bray, pastor, Reformation Lutheran Church, March 20, 1998.

9. Floyd Cochran, quoted in Kim Murphy, "Last Stand of an Aging Aryan," *Los Angeles Times*, January 10, 1999, A15.

10. Jonathan Franklin, "Timothy McVeigh, Soldier," *Playboy*, October 1995, 78ff.

11. Reported on NBC's *Dateline*, July 28, 1995, transcript by Burrelle's Information Services, Livingston, New Jersey, 15.

12. Jim Dwyer, David Kocieniewski, Deidre Murphy, and Peg Tyre, *Two Seconds under the World: Terror Comes to America — The Conspiracy behind the World Trade Center Bombing* (New York: Crown, 1994), 148.

13. Interview with Abouhalima, August 19, 1997.

14. Unnamed leader in the mosque that Mahmud Abouhalima attended, quoted in Richard Behar, "The Secret Life of Mahmud the Red," *Time*, October 4, 1993, 60.

15. Interview with Narinder Singh, Punjab University, Chandigarh, India, August 3, 1996.

16. See Ritu Sarin, *The Assassination of Indira Gandhi* (New Delhi: Penguin, 1990), 125ff.

17. Testimony of Sharif Zahde, who was worshiping at the site, reported in Joel Greenberg, "Sounds of Chanting and Gunfire Echo in a Town Awash in Blood," *New York Times*, February 26, 1994, A1.

18. From figures compiled by Prof. Gurinder Singh Mann from twenty obituaries printed in the *World Sikh News* during 1988.

19. Emmanuel Sivan, "Why Radical Muslims Aren't Taking over Governments," *Middle East Quarterly*; reprinted in *Middle East Review of International Affairs* 2:2, May 1998, 2.

20. Kim Murphy, "Islamic Party Wins Power in Algeria," *Los Angeles Times*, December 28, 1991, A15.

21. Kerry Noble, *Tabernacle of Hate: Why They Bombed Oklahoma City* (Prescott, Ontario: Voyageur, 1998), 91.

22. For background on Punjab untouchables, see Mark Juergensmeyer, *Religion as Social Vision: The Movement against Untouchability in 20th Century Punjab* (Berkeley: University of California Press, 1982), 11–21.

23. Ramesh Vinayak, "Striking Terror," *India Today*, September 30, 1995, 27.

24. I do not know who coined the phrase "e-mail ethnicities." I first heard it in comments made by the anthropologist Benedict Anderson, at a conference on nationalism held by the Center for German and European Studies, University of California, Berkeley, March 15, 1992.

25. I discuss further this notion of the global diaspora of religious cultures in my essay "Thinking Globally about Religion," in Mark Juergensmeyer, ed., *Global Religion: A Handbook* (New York: Oxford, forthcoming).

26. Dwyer, et al., *Two Seconds under the World*, 89–101.

27. Martin Dillon, *God and the Gun: The Church and Irish Terrorism* (New York: Routledge, 1998), 138, 143–57.

28. Mahmood, *Fighting for Faith and Nation*, 215.

29. Mahmood, *Fighting for Faith and Nation*, 218.

30. Mahmood, *Fighting for Faith and Nation*, 218.

31. Martin Riesebrodt, *Pious Passion: The Emergence of Modern Fundamentalism in the United States and Iran* (Berkeley: University of California Press, 1993), 176. See also the essays in John Stratton Hawley, ed., *Fundamentalism and Gender* (New York: Oxford University Press, 1994).

32. Kim Murphy, "Algerian Election to Test Strength of Radical Islam," *Los Angeles Times*, December 26, 1991, 19.

33. Kim Murphy, "Islamic Party Wins Power in Algeria," *Los Angeles Times*, December 28, 1991, A1.

34. Sivan, "Why Radical Muslims Aren't Taking over Governments," 2.

35. Rashid Sakher, an Islamic Jihad suicide bomber, interviewed by Dan Setton in the documentary film *Shaheed*; the interview was transcribed and published as "A Terrorist Moves the Goalposts," *Harper's*, August 1997, 19–22.

36. Andrew Macdonald [William Pierce], *The Turner Diaries* (Arlington, VA: National Vanguard Alliance Books, 1978), 45.

37. Darrin McMahon, *Enemies of the Enlightenment: Anti-Philosophes in Eighteenth Century France* (New York: Oxford University Press, forthcoming). For the history of varying Christian attitudes toward homosexuality, see John Boswell, *Christianity, Social Tolerance, and Homosexuality: Gay People in Western Europe from the Beginning of the Christian Era to the Fourteenth Century* (Chicago: University of Chicago Press, 1980).

38. Macdonald [Pierce], *Turner Diaries*, 45.

39. David Lane, "Race, Reason, Religion," unpublished manuscript, 1984, cited in James Aho, *The Politics of Righteousness: Idaho Christian Patriotism* (Seattle: University of Washington Press, 1990), 86.

40. Interview with Avigdor Eskin, writer and activist for right-wing Jewish causes, Jerusalem, March 3, 1998.

41. Ian Paisley, "Swearing Allegiance to King Jesus," sermon of March 24, 1991, Belfast; reprinted in Ian Paisley, *Sermons on Special Occasions* (Belfast: Ambassador Productions, 1996), 124.

42. Paisley, "Swearing Allegiance to King Jesus," 120.

43. Noble, *Tabernacle of Hate*, 216.

44. Interviews with Michael Bray, pastor, Reformation Lutheran Church, Bowie, Maryland, April 25, 1996, and March 20, 1998.

45. Macdonald [Pierce], *Turner Diaries*, 203. Italics in the original.

46. Murphy, "Last Stand of an Aging Aryan," A15.

47. Hamas videotape from the collection of Anne Marie Oliver and Paul Steinberg.

48. Mahmood, *Fighting for Faith and Nation*, 200.

49. Mahmood, *Fighting for Faith and Nation*, 201.

50. Sant Jarnail Singh Bhindranwale, quoted in Shekhar Gupta, "Temple Intrigue," *India Today*, May 15, 1984, 56–57.

51. Gupta, "Temple Intrigue," 56–57. Sodhi was accused of the murders of H. S. Manchanda in Delhi and Harbans Lal Khanna in Amritsar, and of various robberies.

52. Bhindranwale, quoted in Gupta, "Temple Intrigue," 56. Sodhi had been shot as he sat at a tea stall outside the temple compound by a lower-caste woman, Baljit Kaur, who worked for Surinder Singh, alias Chhinda. Sodhi had allegedly previously collaborated in a series of crimes with Chhinda, but the two had a falling out. Bhindranwale claimed that Chhinda and Baljit Kaur were hired as a hit team by the Akali leaders. Both were tortured and murdered hours after Sodhi's killing, as was the owner of the tea stall where Sodhi was shot.

53. Jeffrey J. Kripal, *Kali's Child: The Mystical and the Erotic in the Life and Teachings of Ramakrishna* (Chicago: University of Chicago Press, 1995).

54. Narasingha Sil, "Re: Vahbharambhe Laghurkriya," *Religion in South Asia*, an Internet listserv, May 10, 1998; quoted with the permission of Prof. Sil.

55. Sarah Lee Caldwell, "Re: Kali's Child—Reply," *Religion in South Asia*, an Internet listserv, May 5, 1998; quoted with the permission of Prof. Caldwell.

56. See Kripal, *Kali's Child*, 301–2.

57. See Ashis Nandy, *The Intimate Enemy: Loss and Recovery of Self under Colonialism* (Oxford: Oxford University Press, 1983); Joseph Alter, *The Wrestler's Body* (Berkeley: University of California Press, 1992); Mrinalini Sinha, *Colonial Masculinity: The "Manly Englishman" and the "Effeminate Bengali" in the Late Nineteenth Century* (Manchester: Manchester University Press, 1995); Indira Chowdhury, *Frail Hero and Virile History: Gender and the Politics of Culture in Colonial Bengal* (Delhi: Oxford University Press, 1998).

58. Nandy, *Intimate Enemy*.

59. Vinay Lal, "The Cultural Politics of Indian Nuclearism," op-ed article, *Los Angeles Times*, May 18, 1998.

60. Macdonald [Pierce], *Turner Diaries*, 42.

61. Interview with Eskin, March 3, 1998.

62. Paul Hill, "Why I Shot an Abortionist," letter to the White Rose Banquet, December 22, 1997; posted on the Web site of the Reformation Lutheran Church: www.christiangallery.com/hill3b.html.

63. Erik Erikson, *Identity and the Life Cycle* (New York: Norton, 1980), 55.

64. Erikson, *Identity and the Life Cycle*, 65.

65. Martha Crenshaw, "Theories of Terrorism: Instrumental and Organizational Approaches," in David C. Rapoport, ed., *Inside Terrorist Organizations* (London: Frank Cass, and New York: Columbia University Press, 1988), 13–31.

66. Interview with Harjap Singh, with translation assistance from Harish Puri, Raminder Bir Singh, and Harbhajan Singh, Sultanwind village, Amritsar district, Punjab, India, January 21, 1998.

67. Ian Paisley, *This Is My Life* (Belfast: Martyrs' Memorial Church Recordings, undated), tape 5, quoted in Dennis Cooke, *Persecuting Zeal: A Portrait of Ian Paisley* (Kerry, Ireland: Brandon Book Publishers, 1996), 77.

68. Michel Wieviorka, *The Making of Terrorism* (translated by David Gordon White from the French *Sociétés et terrorisme*) (Chicago: University of Chicago Press, 1993).

69. Wieviorka, *Making of Terrorism*, 291.

70. Interview with Bray, March 20, 1998.

71. Interview with Bray, April 25, 1996.

72. Paul Hill, quoted in Mike Clary, "Suspect in Abortion Slayings Acts as Own Attorney at Trial, *Los Angeles Times*, October 5, 1994, A5.

73. Interview with Imad Faluji, journalist and member of the political wing of Hamas, Gaza, August 19, 1995.

74. Pierre Bourdieu and Loïc J. D. Wacquant, *An Invitation to Reflexive Sociology* (Chicago: University of Chicago Press, 1992), 131.

75. Interview with Bray, March 20, 1998.

76. Dr. Baruch Goldstein, letter to the editor, *New York Times*, June 30, 1981.

77. Interview with Yochay Ron, Kiryat Arba, Israel, August 18, 1995.

78. Interview with Yoel Lerner, director of the Sannhedrin Institute, Jerusalem, August 17, 1995.

79. Leonard Zeskind, *The "Christian Identity" Movement: Analyzing Its Theological Rationalization for Racist and Anti-Semitic Violence* (New York: Division of Church and Society of the National Council of Churches of Christ in the U.S.A., 1986), 35–42.

80. Reported in *Arkansas Gazette*, April 27, 1987; quoted in Bruce Hoffman, *"Holy Terror": The Implications of Terrorism Motivated by a Religious Imperative* (Santa Monica, CA: RAND Corporation, 1993), 8.

81. Interview with Bray, March 20, 1998.

82. Interview with Bray, March 20, 1998.

83. Interview with Abouhalima, August 19, 1997.

84. Interview with Dr. Muhammad Ibraheem el-Geyoushi, dean of the faculty of Dawah, Al-Azhar University, Cairo, May 30, 1990.

85. Interview with Darshan Singh Ragi, former Jatedar, Akal Takhat, Bhai Vir Singh Sadan, New Delhi, January 13, 1991.

86. Interview with Ragi, January 13, 1991.

87. Interview with Sohan Singh, Mohalli, Punjab, August 3, 1996.

88. Interview with Rantisi, March 1, 1998.

89. Frantz Fanon, *The Wretched of the Earth* (New York: Grove Press, 1963).

Chapter 11. The Mind of God

1. From a videotape of Hamas suicide bombers in the collection of Anne Marie Oliver and Paul Steinberg.

2. Interview with Abdul Aziz Rantisi, cofounder and political leader of Hamas, Khan Yunis, Gaza, March 1, 1998.

3. Interview with Rev. Michael Bray, pastor, Reformation Lutheran Church, Bowie, Maryland, March 20, 1998.

4. Interview with Setsufumi Kamuro, secretary general, Tokyo office, and Chieko Haniu, public affairs officer, Kanto Main Tokyo office, Agonshu religious movement, Tokyo, January 10, 1996.

5. Andrew Macdonald [William L. Pierce], *The Turner Diaries* (Arlington, VA: National Alliance Vanguard Books, 1978), 64.

6. Macdonald [Pierce], *Turner Diaries*, 63.

7. Macdonald [Pierce], *Turner Diaries*, 64.

8. Interview with Yoel Lerner, director of the Sannhedrin Institute, Jerusalem, March 2, 1998.

9. For an account of the Abu Bakr takeover, see Jim Dwyer, David Kocieniewski, Deidre Murphy, and Peg Tyre, *Two Seconds under the World: Terror Comes to America—The Conspiracy behind the World Trade Center Bombing* (New York: Crown Publishers, 1994), 140–56.

10. Interview with Ashraf Yaghi, Gaza, August 19, 1995.

11. Interview with Mahmud Abouhalima, convicted codefendant in the bombing of the World Trade Center, federal penitentiary, Lompoc, California, August 19, 1997.

12. Interview with Abouhalima, August 19, 1997.

13. Interview with Abouhalima, September 30, 1997.

14. Macdonald [Pierce], *Turner Diaries*, 42.

15. Macdonald [Pierce], *Turner Diaries*, 73.

16. Macdonald [Pierce], *Turner Diaries*, 74.

17. Pierre Bourdieu, *Language and Symbolic Power*, Gino Raymond and Matthew Adamson, trans. (Cambridge, MA: Harvard University Press, 1991), 72–76. See also Pierre Bourdieu, *Outline of a Theory of Practice*, Richard Nice, trans. (Cambridge: Cambridge University Press, 1977) 171–83.

18. Jürgen Habermas, *Legitimation Crisis*, Thomas McCarthy, trans. (Boston: Beacon Press, 1975).

19. Darrin McMahon, *Enemies of the Enlightenment: Anti-Philosophes and the Birth of the French Far Right, 1778–1830* (New York: Oxford University Press, forthcoming).

20. Bourdieu, *Language and Symbolic Power*, 116.

21. Bourdieu, *Language and Symbolic Power*, 116.

22. Margot Dudkevitch, "Settlers: Netanyahu No Longer Our Leader," *Jerusalem Post* (Internet edition), October 26, 1998.

23. Some scholars have also called for the creation of a postcolonial culture. See Partha Chatterjee, *The Nation and Its Fragments: Colonial and Postcolonial Histories* (Princeton, NJ: Princeton University Press, 1993).

24. Mark Juergensmeyer, *The New Cold War? Religious Nationalism Confronts the Secular State* (Berkeley: University of California Press, 1993), 11–25.

25. Jürgen Habermas, "Modernity—An Incomplete Project," in Paul Rabinow and William M. Sullivan, eds., *Interpretive Social Science: A Second Look* (Berkeley: University of California Press, 1987), 148.

26. For the distinction between postmodernity as a social phenomenon and as a mode of analysis, see David Lyon, *Postmodernity* (Minneapolis: University of Minnesota Press, 1994).

27. See, for instance, Roger Friedland, "When God Walks in History: The Institutional Politics of Religious Nationalism," in *International Sociology* (forthcoming).

28. José Casanova, *Public Religions in the Modern World* (Chicago: University of Chicago Press, 1994), 211.

29. Ehud Sprinzak, "The Process of Delegitimization: Towards a Linkage Theory of Political Terrorism," *Terrorism and Political Violence* 3:1, Spring 1991, 50–68; Ehud Sprinzak, "Right-Wing Terrorism in a Comparative Perspective: The Case of Split Delegitimization," in Tore Bjørgo, ed., *Terror from the Extreme Right* (London: Frank Cass, 1995), 17–43.

30. Press conference with U.S. Secretary of State Madeleine Albright, reported on ABC's *Nightline*, August 21, 1998.

31. George Tenet, ABC News, February 2, 1999.

32. Shoko Asahara, speech of April, 1994, cited in Ian Reader, *A Poisonous Cocktail? Aum Shinrikyo's Path to Violence* (Copenhagen: Nordic Institute of Asian Studies, 1996), 69.

33. Cited in Bruce Hoffman, *Inside Terrorism* (New York: Columbia University Press, 1998), 192.

34. Douglas Jehl, "Despite Bluster Qaddafi Weighs Deal," *New York Times*, November 1, 1998, A8.

35. Kerry Noble, *Tabernacle of Hate: Why They Bombed Oklahoma City* (Prescott, Ontario: Voyageur, 1998), 146.

36. Interview with Rantisi, March 1, 1998.

37. Interview with Rantisi, March 1, 1998.

38. Casanova, *Public Religions in the Modern World*, 40ff.

39. Robin Wright, "Islamist's Theory of Relativity," *Los Angeles Times*, January 27, 1995, A1.

40. Behrooz Ghamari-Tabrizi, "From Liberation Theology to State Ideology—Modern Conceptions of Islam in Revolutionary Iran: Ali Shari'ati and Abdolkarim Soroush," unpublished article, 1997. See also a book on Soroush by Prof. Ghamari-Tabrizi to be published jointly by I. B. Tauris and St. Martin's Press, and an article by Robin Wright, "Iran Moves to Stifle Exchange of Reformist Views," *Los Angeles Times*, December 30, 1995, A6.

41. René Girard, *Violence and the Sacred*, Patrick Gregory, trans. (Baltimore: Johns Hopkins University Press, 1977) (originally published in French as *La Violence et le sacré*, 1972).

42. Mark Anspach, "Violence against Violence: Islam in Comparative Context," in Mark Juergensmeyer, ed., *Religion and the Sacred in the Modern World* (London: Frank Cass, 1991), 25.

43. Interview with the Venerable Palipana Chandananda, Mahanayake, Asigiriya chapter, Sinhalese Buddhist Sangha, Kandy, Sri Lanka, January 4, 1991.

44. Jean-Jacques Rousseau, "On Civil Religion," Chapter 8, Book IV of *On the Social Contract* [see *Basic Political Writings*, Donald A. Cress, ed., trans., (Indianapolis: Hackett, 1987), 226].

45. McMahon, *Enemies of Enlightenment*, Chapter 1.

46. Interview with Abouhalima, September 30, 1997.

47. Robert N. Bellah, "Is There a Common American Culture?" *Journal of the American Academy of Religion* 66:3, Fall 1998, 614, 616.

48. Marcel Gauchet, *The Disenchantment of the World: A Political History of Religion*, Oscar Burge, trans. (Princeton, NJ: Princeton University Press, 1998).

49. Reinhold Niebuhr, *Moral Man and Immoral Society* (New York: Charles Scribner's Sons, 1932), 255.

50. Interview with Imad Faluji, journalist and member of the policy wing of Hamas, Gaza, August 19, 1995.

51. Rashid Sakher, Islamic jihad suicide bomber, interviewed by Dan Setton in the documentary film *Shaheed* (transcribed and published as "A Terrorist Moves the Goalposts," *Harper's*, August 1997, 19–22).

Interviews and Correspondence

Abdullah, Dr. Farooq (conversation). Chief Minister, State of Jummu and Kashmir, India. Jummu, India, January 20, 1998.

Abe, Yoshiya. Professor of Religion, Kokugakuin University. Tokyo, January 9, 1996.

Abouhalima, Mahmud. Political activist, convicted coconspirator of World Trade Center bombing. Federal penitentiary, Lompoc, California, August 19, 1997; September 30, 1997.

———. Correspondence from Lompoc, September 25, 1996; October 21, 1996; January 3, 1997; June 15, 1997; July 20, 1997; August 28, 1997; January 7, 1998. From Leavenworth, Kansas, May 20, 1999.

Abu-Amr, Zaid. Professor of Philosophy and Cultural Studies, Bir Zeit University. Jerusalem, August 15, 1995.

Ahmed, Showkat. Student, Aligarh Muslim University. Pathankot, India, January 18, 1998.

el Arian, Essam. Medical doctor, member of the Assembly, and member of the Muslim Brotherhood. Cairo, January 11, 1989.

Asafi, Muhammad. Medical doctor. Jabaliya camp, Gaza, January 14, 1989.

Asfour, Gaber. Professor of Arabic Literature, Cairo University. Cairo, May 26, 1990.

Ashur, Prof. A. K. Dean of the Faculty of Education, Al Azhar University. Cairo, May 27, 1990.

Auda, Gehad. Research scholar, Al Ahram Institute. Cairo, May 31, 1990.

Ayako (no last name given). Comanager, Satian Bookstore, Aum Shinrikyo. Shibuya, Tokyo, January 11, 1996.

bar Nathan, Arie. Settler in Mitzpeh Jericho. Jerusalem, January 16, 1989.

ben Horin, Michael. Manager of Kach office. Jerusalem, January 15, 1989.

Bray, Rev. Michael. Pastor, Reformation Lutheran Church, and editor, *Capitol Area Christian News*. Bowie, Maryland, April 25, 1996; March 20, 1998.

——. Correspondence from Bowie, Maryland, July 20, 1997; March 9, 1999.
Burns, Bertha Mae (conversation). Staff member, Martyrs Memorial Free Presbyterian Church. Belfast, Northern Ireland, July 30, 1998.
Chandananda, Venerable Palipana. Mahanayake, Asigiriya chapter, Sinhalese Buddhist Sangha. Kandy, Sri Lanka, January 4, 1991.
Chandra, Ram. Office worker in Bharatiya Janata Party. Delhi, January 10, 1991.
Desouki, Ali. Member of Muslim Brotherhood. Cairo, January 11, 1989.
Dhaman, Kuldip Kumar. Student at Guru Nanak Dev University. Amritsar, Punjab, January 11, 1991; January 12, 1991.
Dignan, Stuart. Office staff, Democratic Unionist Party. Belfast, Northern Ireland, July 30, 1998.
Eskin, Avigdor. Writer and political activist. Jerusalem, March 3, 1998.
Faluji, Imad. Writer and political activist. Gaza, August 19, 1995.
Falwell, Jerry (conversation). Pastor, Thomas Road Baptist Church. Lynchburg, Virginia, February 23, 1997.
Fruman, Manachem. Rabbi at Tuqua settlement. West Bank, Israel, August 14, 1995.
Gibney, Jim (conversation). Sinn Féin Public Affairs Officer. Belfast, Northern Ireland, July 30, 1998.
el-Geyoushi, Muhammad Ibraheem. Dean of the Faculty of Dawah, Al Azhar University. Cairo, May 30, 1990.
el-Hamamsy, Leila. Director, Social Research Center, American University. Cairo, January 10, 1989.
Hanafi, Hasan. Student leader of Muslim Brotherhood, Cairo University. Cairo, May 30, 1990.
Haniu, Chieko. Public Affairs Officer, Tokyo office of Agonshu. Tokyo, January 10, 1996.
Hartley, Tom. Councillor and leader of Sinn Féin in Belfast City Council. Belfast, Northern Ireland, July 31, 1998.
Hassan, Ali. Student at Islamic University of Gaza and supporter of Hamas. Gaza, March 1, 1998.
Hiramatsu, Yasuo. Public Affairs Officer, Tokyo office of Aum Shinrikyo. Aoyama, Tokyo, January 13, 1996.
Kahane, Rabbi Meir. Former member of the Knesset and leader of Israel's Kach party. Jerusalem, January 18, 1989.
Kamal, Muhammad. Student at Islamic University of Gaza and supporter of Hamas. Gaza, March 1, 1998.
Kamuro, Setsufumi. Secretary General of Tokyo office of Agonshu. Tokyo, January 10, 1996.
Kaur, Surjit, President of Delhi branch of Women's Akali Dal (Mann group). Rakabganj Gurdwara, New Delhi, January 13, 1991.
Khalifa, Muhammad. Professor of Comparative Religion, Department of Oriental Languages, Cairo University. Cairo, January 9, 1989.
Lamba, Navneet. Librarian, Bhai Vir Singh Sadan. New Delhi, January 9, 1991.
Lerner, Yoel. Director of Sannhedrin Institute. Jerusalem, January 20, 1989; August 17, 1995; March 2, 1998; March 3, 1998.

Levinger, Rabbi Moshe. Leader of Gush Emunim. Jerusalem, January 16, 1989.
Mann, Simranjit Singh. Former Member of Parliament and leader of Akali Dal (Mann faction). Chandigarh, Punjab, August 4, 1996.
Marzel, Baruch. Settler in Kalpat Arba, Hebron. Jerusalem, January 17, 1989.
Miller, Davy (conversation). Sinn Féin supporter. Belfast, Northern Ireland, July 30, 1998.
Muraoka, Tatsuko. Secretary General of Tokyo office, Aum Shinrikyo. Aoyama, Tokyo, January 13, 1996.
Nakamura, Takeshi (pseudonym for a former member of Aum Shinrikyo). Tokyo, January 12, 1996. (In English and Japanese; translation assistance provided by Prof. Susumu Shimazono and Amy Arakane).
Narang, Surjit Singh. Professor of Political Science, Guru Nanak Dev University. Amritsar, Punjab, January 11, 1991.
Pandher, Sarabjit. Principal correspondent, *The Hindu.* Jummu, India, January 19, 1998.
Puri, Harish. Professor of Political Science, Guru Nanak Dev University, Amritsar. Delhi, January 10, 1991. Amritsar, Punjab, January 11, 1991; May 20, 1993; January 20, 1998.
Rabin, Leah (conversation). Widow of former prime minister Yitzhak Rabin. Tel Aviv, March 2, 1998.
Ragi, Darshan Singh. Former Jatedar, Akal Takhat. Bhai Vir Singh Sadan, New Delhi, January 13, 1991.
Rajagopal, Hari. Office worker in Bharatiya Janata Party. Delhi, January 9, 1991.
Rantisi, Dr. Abdul Aziz. Cofounder and political leader of Hamas. Khan Unis, Gaza, March 1, 1998.
Rey, Roy (conversation). Staff member, Martyrs Memorial Free Presbyterian Church. Belfast, Northern Ireland, July 30, 1998.
Ron, Yochay. Guard, Goldstein shrine, Kiryat Arba settlement. Hebron, August 18, 1995.
Salameh, Sheikh. Spiritual teacher at al-Nur mosque. Cairo, May 28, 1990.
Salem, Mohamed Elmisilhi. Professor of Educational Psychology, Al Azhar University. Cairo, May 27, 1990.
Salomon, Gershom. Head of "Faithful of Temple Mount." Jerusalem, May 25, 1990.
Schleiffer, Abdullah. Director of Communications Center, American University. Cairo, January 7, 1989.
Sekhon, Kuldip Singh. Lawyer for Sikh immigration cases. Berkeley, June 1, 1996.
Shiha, Abdul Hamid. Professor of dar el Alum, Cairo University. Cairo, May 27, 1990.
Shimada, Hiromi. Former professor of religion. Tokyo, January 10, 1996.
Shitta, Ibrahim Dasuqi. Professor of Persian Literature, Cairo University. Cairo, January 10, 1989; January 11, 1989.
Shohdy, Nancy A. Director of Public and Ecumenical Relations, Coptic Orthodox Church. Cairo, May 28, 1990.
Singh, Dr. Amrik. Member of All-India Sikh Student's Federation (Mehta-Chawla group). Rakabganj Gurdwara, New Delhi, January 13, 1991.

Singh, Bhagwan. Mulgranthi (chief worship leader), Golden Temple. Amritsar, Punjab, January 11, 1991.

Singh, Darshan. Professor and Head, Department of Guru Nanak Studies, Punjab University. Chandigarh, Punjab, August 2, 1996.

Singh, Gurmit. President of the Delhi branch of the All-India Sikh Students Federation (Mehta-Chawla group). Rakabganj Gurdwara, New Delhi, January 13, 1991. (In English and Punjabi.)

Singh, Gurnam. Professor of Political Science, Guru Nanak Dev University. Amritsar, Punjab, January 11, 1991.

Singh, Harbinder. General Secretary, Delhi branch of All-India Sikh Students Federation (Mehta-Chawla group). Rakabganj Gurdwara, New Delhi, January 13, 1991. (In English and Punjabi.)

Singh, Harcharand. Former Jatedar of the Golden Temple. Rakabganj Gurdwara, New Delhi, January 13, 1991.

Singh, Harjap. Council Member of Amritsar Municipal Corporation and brother of Kanwarjit Singh, leader of Khalistan Commando Force, 1987–1989. Sultanwind village, Amritsar, Punjab, January 20, 1998. (In English and Punjabi. Interview conducted with the assistance of Harish Puri, Harbhajan Singh, and Raminder Bir Singh.)

Singh, Jasvinder. Member of the Delhi branch of the All-India Sikh Students Federation (Mehta-Chawla group). Rakabganj Gurdwara, New Delhi, January 13, 1991.

Singh, Mohinder. Director, National Institute for Punjab Studies. Bhai Vir Singh Sadan, New Delhi, January 9, 1991.

Singh, Narinder. Retired major general, Indian army. Chandigarh, Punjab, August 3, 1996.

Singh, Ramander Bir. Junior research fellow, Guru Nanak Dev University. Amritsar, Punjab, January 20, 1998.

Singh, Sohan. Leader of Sohan Singh Panthic Committee. Mohalli, Punjab, August 3, 1996.

Singh, Yashwant Pal. Manager of Delhi office, All-India Sikh Students Federation (Mehta-Chawla group). Rakabganj Gurdwara, New Delhi, January 13, 1991. (In English and Punjabi.)

Sutel, Seth. Correspondent for Associated Press. Tokyo, January 9, 1996.

Tomoko (no last name given). Comanager of Satian Bookstore, Aum Shinrikyo. Shibuya, Tokyo, January 11, 1996.

Yaghi, Ashraf. Hamas supporter. Gaza City, August 19, 1995.

Yassin, Sheik Ahmed. Founder and leader of Hamas. Gaza, January 14, 1989.

Yokoyama, Minoru. Sociologist and Professor of Criminology, Kokugakuin University. Tokyo, January 10, 1996.

Zamlot, Saleh. Student leader of Fateh, Palestianian Liberation Organization. Al Azhar University, Cairo, May 27, 1990.

Zilberman, Ifrah. Research scholar, Hebrew University. Jerusalem, January 18, 1989; May 25, 1990.

Bibliography

Religion and Violence

Aho, James. *This Thing of Darkness: A Sociology of the Enemy.* Seattle: University of Washington Press, 1994.

Audi, Robert, and Nicholas Wolterstorff. *Religion in the Public Square: The Place of Religious Convictions in Political Debate.* New York: Rowman and Littlefield, 1997.

Barkun, Michael, ed. *Millenialism and Violence.* London: Frank Cass, 1996.

Bataille, Georges. *Erotism: Death and Sensuality.* San Francisco: City Light Books, 1986. (Translated from the 1957 French edition by Mary Dalwood.)

——. Theory of Religion. New York: Zone Books, 1992. (Translated from the 1973 French edition by Robert Hurley.)

Baudrillard, Jean. *The Transparency of Evil: Essays on the Extreme Phenomena.* London: Verso, 1993. (Translated from the 1990 French edition by James Benedict.)

Bell, Catherine M. *Ritual Theory, Ritual Practice.* New York: Oxford University Press, 1993.

Bloch, Maurice. *Prey into Hunter: The Politics of Religious Experience.* Cambridge: Cambridge University Press, 1992.

Bourdieu, Pierre. *Language and Symbolic Power.* Cambridge, MA: Harvard University Press, 1991. (Translated from the 1982 French edition by Gino Raymond and Matthew Adamson; edited by John B. Thompson.)

——. *Outline of a Theory of Practice.* New York: Cambridge University Press, 1977. (Translated from the 1972 French edition by Richard Nice.)

Bourdieu, Pierre and Loïc J. D. Wacquant. *An Invitation to Reflexive Sociology.* Chicago: University of Chicago Press, 1992.

Brass, Paul R. *Theft of an Idol: Text and Context in the Representation of Collective Violence.* Princeton, NJ: Princeton University Press, 1997

Brown, Robert McAfee. *Religion and Violence.* 2nd ed. Philadelphia: Westminster Press, 1987.

Burkert, Walter. *Homo Necans: The Anthropology of Ancient Greek Sacrificial Ritual and Myth.* Berkeley: University of California Press, 1983. (Translated from the 1972 German edition by Peter Bing.)

Burkert, Walter, René Girard, and Jonathan Z. Smith. *Violent Origins: Ritual Killing and Cultural Formation.* Edited by Robert G. Hamerton-Kelly. Stanford, CA: Stanford University Press, 1987.

Candland, Christopher, comp. *The Spirit of Violence: An Annotated Bibliography on Religious Violence.* New York: Harry Frank Guggenheim Foundation, 1993.

Caplan, Lionel, ed. *Studies in Religious Fundamentalism.* Albany: State University of New York Press, 1987.

Casanova, José. *Public Religions in the Modern World.* Chicago: University of Chicago Press, 1994.

Chilton, Bruce. *The Temple of Jesus: His Sacrificial Program within a Cultural History of Sacrifice.* University Park: Pennsylvania State University Press, 1992.

Davis, Natalie Zemon. "The Rites of Violence: Religious Riots in Sixteenth Century France." *Past and Present* 59 (May 1973), 51–91.

Detienne, Marcel, and Jean-Pierre Vernant. *The Cuisine of Sacrifice among the Greeks.* Chicago and London: University of Chicago Press, 1989. (Translated from the 1979 French edition by Paula Wissing.)

Dumouchel, Paul, ed. *Violence and Truth: On the Work of René Girard.* Stanford, CA: Stanford University Press, 1988.

Dupuy, Jean-Pierre. *Ordres et désordres: Enquêtes sur un nouveau paradigme.* Paris: Editions du Seuil, 1982.

Ferguson, John. *War and Peace in the World's Religions.* New York: Oxford University Press, 1977.

Ferguson, R. Brian, with Leslie E. Farragher. *The Anthropology of War: A Bibliography.* Occasional Papers no. 1. New York: Harry Frank Guggenheim Foundation, 1988.

Firestone, Rueven. "Conceptions of Holy War in Biblical and Qur'anic Tradition." *Journal of Religious Ethics* 24:1 (Spring 1996), 99–123.

Foucault, Michel. *The Archaeology of Knowledge.* New York: Pantheon Books, 1972. (Translated from the French by A. M. Sheridan Smith.)

———. *Power/Knowledge: Selected Interviews and Other Writings 1972-1977.* New York: Pantheon Books, 1980.

Gauchet, Marcel. *The Disenchantment of the World: A Political History of Religion.* Princeton, NJ: Princeton University Press, 1997. (Translated by Oscar Burge.)

Gelven, Michael. *War and Existence: A Philosophical Inquiry.* University Park: Pennsylvania State University Press, 1994.

Girard, René. "Disorder and Order in Mythology." In Paisley Livingston, ed. *Disorder and Order: Proceedings of the Stanford International Symposium.* Saratoga, CA: Anma Libri, 1984, 80–97.

———. *The Scapegoat.* Baltimore: Johns Hopkins University Press, 1986. (Translated from the 1982 French edition by Yvonne Freccero.)

——. *Violence and the Sacred*. Baltimore: Johns Hopkins University Press, 1977. (Translated from the 1972 French edition by Patrick Gregory.)

Girard, René, and Mark Anspach. "Reflections from the Perspective of Mimetic Theory." In Mark Juergensmeyer, ed. *Violence and the Sacred in the Modern World*. London: Frank Cass, 1992, 141–48.

Hammoudi, Abellah. *The Victim and Its Masks: An Essay on Sacrifice and Masquerade in the Maghred*. Chicago: University of Chicago Press, 1994. (Translation by Paula Wissing.)

Hawley, John Stratton, ed. *Fundamentalism and the Ideology of Gender*. Boston: Beacon Press, 1995.

Haynes, Jeff. *Religion in Third World Politics*. Boulder, CO: L. Rienner, 1994.

Hecht, Richard. "Studies on Sacrifice, 1970–1980." *Religious Studies Review* 8:3, 1982, 13–19.

Hecht, Richard, and Roger Friedland. "The Bodies of Nations: A Comparative Study of Religious Violence in Jerusalem and Ayodhya." *History of Religion* November 1998, 101–49.

Hoffman, Bruce. *"Holy Terror": The Implications of Terrorism Motivated by a Religious Imperative*. Santa Monica, CA: RAND Corporation, 1993.

Hubert, Henri, and Marcel Mauss. *Sacrifice: Its Nature and Function*. Chicago: University of Chicago Press, 1964. (Translated from the French "Essai sur la nature et la function du sacrifice" in M. Mauss, *Oevres*, vol 1, Paris: Editions de Minuit, 1968, by W. D. Halls.)

Hughes-Freeland, Felicia, ed. *Ritual, Performance, Media*. London: Routledge, 1998.

Ingebretsen, Edward J. *Maps of Heaven, Maps of Hell: Religious Terror as Memory from the Puritans to Stephen King*. New York: Continuum, 1994.

James, E. O. *Origins of Sacrifice: A Study in Comparative Religion* (1933). Port Washington, NY: Kennikat Press, 1971.

Johnson, James Turner. *Ideology, Reason, and the Limitation of War: Religious and Secular Concepts, 1200–1740*. Princeton, NJ: Princeton University Press, 1975.

Juergensmeyer, Mark. *The New Cold War? Religious Nationalism Confronts the Secular State*. Berkeley: University of California Press, 1993.

——. "Sacrifice and Cosmic War." In Mark Juergensmeyer, ed. *Violence and the Sacred in the Modern World*. London: Frank Cass, 1991, 101–17.

——. "Violence and Religion." In Jonathan Z. Smith, ed. *The Harper Dictionary of Religion*. New York: HarperCollins, 1995.

——, ed. *Violence and the Sacred in the Modern World*. London: Frank Cass, 1991.

Kelsay, John, and James Turner Johnson, eds. *Cross, Crescent and Sword: The Justification and Limitation of War in Western and Islamic Tradition*. New York: Greenwood Press, 1991.

——, eds. *Just War and Jihad: Historical and Theoretical Perspectives on War and Peace in Western and Islamic Traditions*. New York: Greenwood Press, 1991.

Lawrence, Bruce. *Defenders of God: The Fundamentalist Revolt against the Modern Age*. San Francisco: Harper & Row, 1989.

Lewy, Guenter. *Religion and Revolution*. New York: Oxford University Press, 1974.

Lincoln, Bruce. *Death, War, and Sacrifice: Studies in Ideology and Practice*. Chicago: University of Chicago Press, 1991.

——, ed. *Religion, Rebellion, Revolution: An Interdisciplinary and Cross-cultural Collection of Essays*. New York: St. Martin's Press, 1985.

Livingston, Paisley, ed. *Disorder and Order: Proceedings of the Stanford International Symposium*. Saratoga, CA: Anma Libri, 1984.

Maddy-Weitzman, Bruce, and Efraim Inbar, eds. *Religious Radicalism in the Greater Middle East*. London: Frank Cass, 1997.

Marty, Martin E., and R. Scott Appleby, eds. *Accounting for Fundamentalisms: The Dynamic Character of Movements*. Chicago: University of Chicago Press, 1994.

——, eds. *Fundamentalisms and Society*. Chicago: University of Chicago Press, 1993.

——, eds. *Fundamentalisms and the State*. Chicago: University of Chicago Press, 1993.

——, eds. *Fundamentalisms Comprehended*. Chicago: University of Chicago Press, 1995.

——, eds. *Fundamentalisms Observed*. Chicago: University of Chicago Press, 1991.

McMahon, Darrin. *Enemies of the Enlightenment: Anti-Philosophes and the Birth of the French Far Right, 1778–1830*. New York: Oxford University Press, forthcoming.

Mestrovic, Stjepan. *The Barbarian Temperament: Toward a Postmodern Critical Theory*. London: Routledge, 1993.

——. *The Coming Fin de Siecle: An Application of Durkheim's Sociology to Modernity and Postmodernism*. London: Routledge, 1991.

Nandy, Ashis. *The Savage Freud and Other Essays on Possible Retrievable Selves*. Princeton, NJ: Princeton University Press, 1995.

Nardin, Terry, ed. *The Ethics of War and Peace: Religious and Secular Perspectives*. Ethikon Series in Comparative Ethics, vol. 1. Princeton, NJ: Princeton University Press, 1996.

Parkin, David, Lionel Caplan, and Humphrey Fisher, eds. *The Politics of Cultural Performance*. Providence: Berghahn Books, 1996.

Robbins, Thomas. "Religious Movements and Violence: A Friendly Critique of the Interpretive Approach." *Nova Religio: The Journal of Alternative and Emergent Religions* 1:1 (Fall 1997), 13–29.

Rapoport, David C. "Observations on the Importance of Space in Violent Ethno-Religious Strife." Unpublished paper.

Reeder, John P., Jr. *Killing and Saving: Abortion, Hunger, and War*. University Park: Pennsylvania State University Press, 1996.

Riesebrodt, Martin. *Pious Passion: The Emergence of Modern Fundamentalism in the United States and Iran*. Berkeley: University of California Press, 1990.

Rudolph, Susanne Hoeber, and James Piscatori, eds. *Transnational Religion and Fading States*. Boulder, CO: Westview Press, 1997.

Sagan, Eli. *Cannibalism: Human Aggression and Cultural Form.* New York: Psychohistory Press, 1974.

———. *The Lust to Annihilate: A Psychoanalytic Study of Violence in Ancient Greek Culture.* New York: Psychohistory Press, 1972.

Sells, Michael A. *The Bridge Betrayed: Religion and Genocide in Bosnia.* Berkeley: University of California Press, 1996.

Sproxton, Judy. *Violence and Religion: Attitudes towards Militancy in the French Civil Wars and the English Revolution.* London: Routledege, 1995.

Tambiah, Stanley. *Leveling Crowds: Ethnonationalist Conflicts and Collective Violence in South Asia.* Berkeley: University of California Press, 1996.

Villa-Vicencio, Charles, ed. *Theology and Violence: The South African Debate.* Johannesburg: Skotaville, 1987.

Walzer, Michael. *Just and Unjust Wars.* New York: Basic Books, 1977.

Westerlund, David, ed. *Questioning the Secular State: The Worldwide Resurgence of Religion in Politics.* London: Hurst, 1996.

Williams, James G. *The Bible, Violence, and the Sacred: Liberation from the Myth of Sanctioned Violence.* San Francisco: Harper, 1991.

Terrorism

Alexander, Yonah, David Carlton, and Paul Wilkinson. *Terrorism: Theory and Practice.* Boulder, CO: Westview Press, 1979.

Alexander, Yonah, and Dennis A. Pluchinsky, eds. *European Terrorism: Today and Tomorrow.* New York: Brassey's, 1992.

Appleby, R. Scott, ed. *Spokesman for the Despised: Fundamentalist Leaders of the Middle East.* Chicago: University of Chicago Press, 1997.

Arnold, Terrel E. *The Violence Formula: Why People Lend Sympathy and Support to Terrorism.* Lexington, MA: Lexington Books, 1988.

Bassiouni, M. C., ed. *International Terrorism and Political Crimes.* Springfield, IL: Thomas, 1974.

Bauhn, Per. *Ethical Aspects of Political Terrorism: The Sacrificing of the Innocent.* Lund, Sweden: Lund University Press, 1989.

Bell, J. Bowyer. *On Revolt: Strategies of National Liberation.* Cambridge, MA: Harvard University Press, 1976.

———. *Transnational Terror.* Washington, DC: AEI-Hoover, 1975.

Billington, James H. *Fire in the Minds of Men: Origins of the Revolutionary Faith.* New York: Basic Books, 1980.

Bjørgo, Tore, ed. *Terror from the Extreme Right.* London: Frank Cass, 1995.

Bodansky, Yossef. *Target America and the West: Terrorism Today.* New York: SPI Books, 1993.

Brown, D. J., and R. Merrill, eds. *Violent Persuasions: The Politics and Imagery of Terrorism.* Seattle: Bay Press, 1993.

Colvard, Karen. "What We Already Know about Terrorism: Violent Challenges to the State and State Response." *HFG Review: A Publication of the Harry Frank Guggenheim Foundation* 1:1 (Fall 1996) (special issue, "The Politics of Violence").

Combs, Cindy C. *Terrorism in the Twenty-first Century*. Upper Saddle River, NJ: Prentice Hall, 1997.

Crelinsten, D. Ronald, Danielle Laberge-Altmejd, and Denis Szabo. *Terrorism and Criminal Justice: An International Perspective*. Lexington, MA: Lexington Books, 1978.

Crelinsten, D. Ronald, and Denis Szabo. *Hostage Taking*. Lexington, MA: Lexington Books, 1979.

Crelinsten, D. Ronald, and Alex P. Schmid, eds. *The Politics of Pain: Torturers and Their Masters*. Boulder, CO: Westview Press, 1994.

Crenshaw, Martha. "How Terrorists Think: Psychological Contributions to Understanding Terrorism." In Lawrence Howard, ed. *Terrorism: Roots, Impact, Response*. New York: Praeger, 1992.

———. *Terrorism and International Cooperation*. New York: Institute For East-West Security Studies, 1989; distributed by Westview Press.

———. ed. *Terrorism in Context*. University Park: Pennsylvania State University Press, 1995.

Crenshaw, Martha, and John Pimlott, eds. *Encyclopedia of World Terrorism*. Armonk, NY: Sharpe Reference, 1997.

della Porta, Donatella, ed. *Social Movements, Political Violence, and the State*. Cambridge: Cambridge University Press, 1995.

———. *Social Movements and Violence: Participation in Underground Organizations*. Greenwich, CT: JAI Press, 1992.

Erikson, Richard J. *Legitimate Use of Military Force against State-Sponsored International Terrorism*. Maxwell Air Force Base: Air University Press, 1989.

Guelke, Adrian. *The Age of Terrorism and the International Political System*. London: I. B. Tauris, 1995.

Gutteridge, William, ed. *The New Terrorism*. London: Mansell, 1986.

Hoffman, Bruce. *An Agenda for Research on Terrorism and LIC [Low-Intensity Conflict] in the 1990s*. Santa Monica, CA: RAND Corporation, 1991.

———. *Inside Terrorism*. New York: Columbia University Press, 1998.

———. *Terrorism Targeting: Tactics, Trends, and Potentialities*. Santa Monica, CA: RAND Corporation, 1992.

Howard, Lawrence, ed. *Terrorism: Roots, Impact, Response*. New York: Praeger, 1992.

Jenkins, Brian. *International Terrorism: A New Kind of Warfare*. Santa Monica, CA: RAND Corporation, 1974.

———. *International Terrorism: Trends and Potentialities*. Santa Monica, CA: RAND Corporation, 1978.

Kurz, Anat, and Ariel Merari. *ASALA—Irrational Terror or Political Tool*. Boulder, CO: Westview Press, 1985.

Laqueur, Walter. *The Age of Terrorism*. Boston: Little, Brown, 1987.

———. "Postmodern Terrorism." *Foreign Affairs* 75:5 (September 1996), 24–36.

Levitt, Geoffrey M. *Democracies against Terror: The Western Response to State-Supported Terrorism*. New York: Praeger and Center for Strategic and International Studies, 1988.

Livingston, M. H., ed. *International Terrorism in the Contemporary World*. Westport, CT: Greenwood Press, 1978.

Lodge, Juliet, ed. *The Threat of Terrorism*. Brighton, MA: Wheatsheaf Books, 1988.

McCauley, Clark, ed. *Terrorism and Public Policy*. London: Frank Cass, 1991.

Merari, Ariel, and Anat Kurz. *International Terrorism in 1987*. Jerusalem: Jerusalem Post and Jaffee Center for Strategic Studies, 1987.

Merkl, Peter, ed. *Political Violence and Terror*. Berkeley: University of California Press, 1986.

Merkl, Peter H., and Leonard Weinberg, eds. *Encounters with the Contemporary Radical Right*. Boulder, CO: Westview Press, 1993.

Nasr, Kameel B. *Arab and Israeli Terrorism: The Causes and Effects of Political Violence, 1936–1993*. Jefferson, NC: McFarland, 1997.

Netanyahu, Benjamin, ed. *Terrorism: How the West Can Win*. New York: Farrar, Straus & Giroux, 1980.

Olson-Raymer, Gayle, with Judith Ann Ryder. *Terrorism: A Historical and Contemporary Perspective*. New York: American Heritage, Custom Publishing Group, 1996.

Rapoport, David C. *Assassination and Terrorism*. Toronto: Canadian Broadcast Corporation, 1971.

——. "Comparing Militant Fundamentalist Movements and Groups." In Martin Marty and Scott Appleby, eds. *Fundamentalisms and the State*. Chicago: University of Chicago Press, 1993.

——, ed. *Inside Terrorist Organizations*. New York: Columbia University Press, 1988.

——. "The Politics of Atrocity." In Y. Alexander and S. Finger, eds. *Terrorism: Interdisciplinary Perspectives*. New York: John Day, 1977.

Rapoport, David C., and Yonah Alexander, eds. *The Morality of Terrorism: Religious and Secular Justifications*. New York: Pergamon Press, 1982.

Reich, Walter. *Origins of Terrorism: Psychologies, Ideologies, Theologies, States of Mind*. Cambridge: Woodrow Wilson International Center for Scholars and Cambridge University Press, 1990.

Robins, Robert S., and Jerold Post. *Political Paranoia: The Psychopolitics of Hatred*. New Haven, CT: Yale University Press, 1997.

Snow, Donald M. *Distant Thunder: Patterns of Conflict in the Developing World*. Armonk, NY: M.E. Sharpe, 1997.

Sprinzak, Ehud. "The Process of Delegitimization: Towards a Linkage Theory of Political Terrorism." In Clark McCauley, ed. *Terrorism and Public Policy*. London: Frank Cass, 1991.

Sterling, Claire. *The Terror Network: The Secret of International Terrorism*. New York: Holt, Rinehart & Winston, 1981.

Stern, Jessica. *The Ultimate Terrorists*. Cambridge, MA: Harvard University Press, 1999.

Sutherland, Charles W. *Disciples of Destruction: The Religious Origins of War and Terrorism.* Buffalo, NY: Prometheus Press, 1987.

Taylor, Maxwell. *The Terrorist.* London: Brassey's Defence, 1988.

Thornton, Thomas Perry. "Terrorism as a Weapon of Political Agitation." In Harry Eckstein, ed. *Internal War: Problems and Approaches.* New York: Free Press, 1964.

Warner, Martin, and Roger Crisp. *Terrorism, Protest, and Power.* Brookfield, VT: Grower, 1990.

Wieviorka, Michel. *The Making of Terrorism.* Chicago: University of Chicago Press, 1993. (Translated from the 1988 French edition by David Gordon White.)

Wilkinson, Paul. "The Media and Terrorism." *Terrorism and Political Violence* 9:2 (summer 1997), 51–64.

——. *Political Terrorism.* London: Macmillan, 1974.

——. *Terror and the Liberal State.* London: Macmillan, 1977.

Wilkinson, Paul, and A. M. Stewart, eds. *Contemporary Research on Terrorism.* Aberdeen: Aberdeen University Press, 1987.

Zulaika, Joseph, and William A. Douglass. *Terror and Taboo.* London: Routledge, 1996.

Christian Movements in the United States and Ireland

Abanes, Richard. *American Militias: Rebellion, Racism and Religion.* Downers Grove, IL: InterVarsity Press, 1996.

Adams, Gerry. *Before the Dawn.* London: Mandarin Paperbacks, 1997.

Aho, James. *The Politics of Righteousness: Idaho Christian Patriotism.* Seattle: University of Washington Press, 1990.

Alexander, Yonah, and Dennis A. Pluehinsky, eds. *European Terrorism Today and Tomorrow.* Washington, DC: Brassey's (U.S.), 1992.

Ammerman, Nancy T. *Bible Believers: Fundamentalists in the Modern World.* New Brunswick, NJ: Rutgers University Press, 1987.

——. "North American Protestant Fundamentalism." In Martin E. Marty and R. Scott Appleby, eds. *Fundamentalisms Observed.* Chicago: University of Chicago Press, 1991, 1–65.

Anti-Defamation League. *The Skinhead International: A Worldwide Survey of Neo-Nazi Skinheads.* New York: Anti-Defamation League, 1995.

Balmer, Randall. *Mine Eyes Have Seen the Glory: A Journey into the Evangelical Subculture in America.* New York: Oxford University Press, 1989.

Barkun, Michael. *Religion and the Racist Right: The Origins of the Christian Identity Movement.* Chapel Hill: University of North Carolina Press, 1994.

——, ed. *Millennialism and Violence.* London: Frank Cass, 1996.

Barron, Bruce. *Heaven on Earth?: The Social and Political Agendas on Dominion Theology.* Grand Rapids, MI: Zondervan, 1992.

Baumgarten, Gerald. *Paranoia as Patriotism: Far-Right Influences on the Militia Movement.* New York: Anti-Defamation League, 1995.

Bennett, David H. *The Party of Fear: The American Far Right from Nativism to the Militia Movement*. New York: Vintage Books, 1995.

Berlet, Chip. *The Increasing Popularity of Right Wing Conspiracy Theories*. Somerville, MA: Political Research Associates, 1996.

——, ed. *Eyes Right: Challenging the Right Wing Backlash*. Boston: South End Press, 1995.

Berlet, Chip, and Matthew N. Lyons. *Too Close for Comfort: Rightwing Populism, Scapegoating, and Fascist Potentials in US Political Traditions*. Boston: South End Press, 1996.

Blanchard, Dallas A., and Terry J. Prewitt. *Religious Violence and Abortion: The Gideon Project*. Gainesville: University Press of Florida, 1993.

Boyer, Paul. *When Time Shall Be No More: Prophetic Belief in Modern American Culture*. Cambridge, MA: Harvard University Press, 1992.

Bray, Michael. *A Time to Kill: A Study Concerning the Use of Force and Abortion*. Portland, OR: Advocates for Life, 1994.

Bruce, Stephen. "The Moral Majority: The Politics of Fundamentalism in Secular Society." In Lionel Caplan, ed. *Studies in Religious Fundamentalism*. Albany: State University of New York Press, 1987.

Bruce, Steve, Peter Kivisto, and William H. Swatos, Jr., eds. *The Rapture of Politics: The Christian Right as the United States Approaches the Year 2000*. New Brunswick, NJ: Transaction, 1995.

Capps, Walter H. *The New Religious Right: Piety, Patriotism, and Politics*. Columbia: University of South Carolina Press, 1990.

Clarke, Sister Sarah. *No Faith in the System*. Cork, Ireland: Mercier Press, 1995.

Coates, James. *Armed and Dangerous: The Rise of the Survivalist Right*. New York: Hill & Wang, 1987.

Cooke, Dennis. *Persecuting Zeal: A Portrait of Ian Paisley*. Kerry, Ireland: Brandon, 1996.

Coppola, Vincent. *Dragons of God: A Journey Through Far-Right America*. Atlanta: Longstreet Press, 1996.

Corcoran, James. *Bitter Harvest: Gordan Kahl and the Posse Comitatus— Murder in the Heartland*. New York: Penguin Books, 1990.

Crabtree, Harriet. *The Christian Life: Traditional Metaphors and Contemporary Theologies*. Minneapolis: Fortress Press, 1991.

——. "Onward Christian Soldiers? The Fortunes of a Traditional Christian Symbol in the Modern Age." *Bulletin of the Center for the Study of World Religion* (Harvard University) 16; 2 (1989/90): 6–27.

Dees, Morris, with James Corcoran. *Gathering Storm: America's Militia Threat*. New York: HarperCollins, 1996.

Diamond, Sara. *Roads to Dominion: Right-Wing Movements and Political Power in the United State*. New York: Guilford, 1995.

——. *Spiritual Warfare: The Politics of the Christian Right*. Boston: South End Press, 1989.

Dillon, Martin. *God and the Gun: The Church and Irish Terrorism*. New York: Routledge, 1997.

Dunlop, John. *A Precarious Belonging: Presbyterians and the Conflict in Ireland*. Belfast: Blackstaff Press, 1995.

Flynn, Kevin, and Gary Gerhardt. *The Silent Brotherhood: Inside America's Racist Underground.* New York: Free Press, 1989.

Griffin, Leslie, ed. *Religion and Politics in the American Milieu.* Notre Dame, IN: Office of Policy Studies, University of Notre Dame, 1989.

Halpern, Thomas. *Beyond the Bombing: The Militia Menace Grows.* New York: Anti-Defamation League, 1995.

———. *The Freemen Network: An Assault on the Rule of Law.* New York: Anti-Defamation League, 1996.

Hammond, Phillip E. "Religion and Nationalism in the United States." In Gustavo Benavides and M. W. Daly, eds. *Religion and Political Power.* Albany: State University of New York Press, 1989.

Haught, James A. *Holy Hatred: Religious Conflicts of the '90s.* Amherst, NY: Prometheus Books, 1995.

Hoffman, David S. *The Oklahoma City Bombing and the Politics of Terror.* Venice, CA: Feral House, 1998.

———. *The Web of Hate: Extremists Exploit the Internet.* New York: Anti-Defamation League, 1996.

Hudson, Winthrop S., ed. *Nationalism and Religion in America: Concepts of American Identity and Mission.* New York: Harper & Row, 1970.

Jarman, Neil. *Material Conflicts: Parades and Visual Displays in Northern Ireland.* Oxford and New York: Berg, 1997.

Kaplan, Jeffrey. "The Context of American Millenarian Revolutionary Theology: The Case of the 'Identity Christian' Church of Israel." *Terrorism and Political Violence* 5:1 (Spring 1993), 30–82.

———. *Radical Religion in America: Millenarian Movements from the Far Right to the Children of Noah.* Syracuse, NY: Syracuse University Press, 1997.

———. "Right Wing Violence in North America." In Tore Bjørgo, ed. *Terror from the Extreme Right.* London: Frank Cass, 1995, 44–95.

Lienesch, Michael. *Redeeming America: Piety and Politics in the New Christian Right.* Chapel Hill: University of North Carolina Press, 1993.

Macdonald, Andrew. *The Turner Diaries.* Hillsboro, WV: National Vanguard Books, 1978. (Reprinted by the National Alliance, Arlington, VA, in 1985, and by Barricade Books, New York, 1996.)

Marsden, George M. *Fundamentalism and American Culture: The Shaping of Twentieth-Century Evangelicalism, 1870–1925.* New York: Oxford University Press, 1980.

McVeigh, Joseph. *A Wounded Church: Religion, Politics and Justice in Ireland.* Dublin: Mercier Press, 1989.

Noble, Kerry. *Tabernacle of Hate: Why They Bombed Oklahoma City.* Prescott, Ontario: Voyageur, 1998.

North, Gary. *Backward Christian Soldiers? An Action Manual for Christian Reconstruction.* Tyler, TX: Institute for Christian Economics, 1984.

———. *Conspiracy: A Biblical View.* Fort Worth, TX: Dominion Press, 1986.

———. *The Dominion Covenant: An Economic Commentary on the Bible.* Tyler, TX: Institute for Christian Economics, 1987.

———. *Is the World Running Down? Crisis in the Christian Worldview.* Tyler, TX: Institute for Christian Economics, 1998.

———. *The Judeo-Christian Tradition: A Guide for the Perplexed*. Tyler, TX: Institute for Christian Economics, 1990.

———. *Lone Gunners for Jesus: Letters to Paul J. Hill*. Tyler, TX: Institute for Christian Economics, 1994.

———. *Millennialism and Social Theory*. Tyler, TX: Institute for Christian Economics, 1990.

North, Gary, and Gary DeMar. *Christian Reconstruction: What It Is, What It Isn't*. Tyler, TX: Institute for Christian Economics, 1991.

O'Brien, Conor Cruise. *Ancestral Voices: Religion and Nationalism In Ireland*. Dublin: Poolbeg Press, 1994.

Paisley, Ian R. K. *Sermons on Special Occasions*. Belfast: Ambassador Productions, 1996.

Paneth, Donald. *The Literature of the Apocalypse: Far-Right Voices of Violence*. New York: Anti-Defamation League, 1996.

Risen, Jim, and Judy L. Thomas. *Wrath of Angels: The American Abortion War*. New York: Basic Books, 1998.

Robinson, Peter. *The Union Under Fire: United Ireland Framework Revealed*. Belfast: Ambassador, 1995.

Rose, Dorothy. *The Jubilee: New Voice of the Far Right*. New York: Anti-Defamation League, 1996.

Roy, Joseph T., ed. *False Patriots: The Threat of Antigovernment Extremists*. Montgomery, AL: Southern Poverty Law Center, Klanwatch Project, 1996.

Rushdoony, Rousas John. *Christianity and the State*. Vallecito, CA: Ross House Books, 1986.

———. *The Institutes of Biblical Law*. Nutley, NJ: Craig Press, 1973.

Shaeffer, Francis. *A Christian Manifesto*. Westchester, IL: Crossway Books, 1982 (published in Association with Nims Communication).

Sizer, Sandra. *Gospel Hymns and Social Religion: The Rhetoric of Nineteenth-Century Revivalism*. Philadelphia: Temple University Press, 1978.

Smith, Brent L. *Terrorism in America: Pipe Bombs and Pipe Dreams*. Albany, NY: State University of New York Press, 1994.

Solnin, Amy C. *William L. Pierce: Novelist of Hate*. New York: Anti-Defamation League, 1995.

Stern, Kenneth S. *A Force Upon the Plain: The American Militia Movement and the Politics of Hate*. New York: Simon & Schuster, 1996.

Strozier, Charles B. *Apocalypse: On the Psychology of Fundamentalism in America*. Boston: Beacon Press, 1995.

Strozier, Charles B., and Michael Flynn. *Two Thousand: Essays on the End*. New York: New York University Press, 1997.

Suall, Irwin. *The Skinhead International: A Worldwide Survey of Neo-Nazi Skinheads*. New York: Anti-Defamation League, 1995.

Tabor, James D., and Eugene V. Gallagher. *Why Waco: Cults and the Battle for Religious Freedom in America*. Berkeley: University of California Press, 1995.

Walter, Jess. *Every Knee Shall Bow: The Truth and Tragedy of Ruby Ridge and the Randy Weaver Family*. New York: HarperCollins, 1995.

Whitsel, Brad. "The Turner Diaries and Cosmotheism: William Pierce's Theology of Revolution." *Nova Religio: The Journal of Alternative and Emergent Religions* 1:2 (April 1998), 183–97.

Wills, Garry. *Under God: Religion and American Politics.* New York: Simon & Schuster, 1990.

Wright, Stuart A., ed. *Armageddon in Waco: Critical Perspectives on the Branch Davidian Conflict.* Chicago: University of Chicago Press, 1995.

Vinz, Warren L. *Pulpit Politics: Faces of American Protestant Nationalism in the Twentieth Century.* Albany: State University of New York Press, 1996.

Zeskind, Leonard. *The "Christian Identity" Movement: Analyzing Its Theological Rationalization for Racist and Anti-Semitic Violence.* New York: Division of Church and Society of the National Council of the Churches of Christ in the U.S.A., 1986.

Jewish Militants

Agus, Jacob B. *Banner of Jerusalem: The Life, Times, and Thought of Rabbi Abraham Isaac Kuk.* New York: Bloch, 1946.

Aran, Gideon. "From Religious Zionism to Zionist Religion: The Roots of Gush Emunim." In Peter Medding, ed. *Studies in Contemporary Jewry,* vol. 2. New York: Oxford University Press, 1986.

———. "Jewish Zionist Fundamentalism: The Bloc of the Faithful in Israel (Gush Emunim)." In Martin E. Marty and R. Scott Appleby, eds. *Fundamentalism Observed.* Chicago: University of Chicago Press, 1991.

Biale, David J. *Power and Powerlessness in Jewish History.* New York: Schocken, 1986.

Cromer, Gerald. *The Debate about Kahanism in Israeli Society, 1984–1988.* Occasional Papers no. 3. New York: Harry Frank Guggenheim Foundation, 1988.

Frankel, Jonathan, ed. *Jews and Messianism in the Modern Era: Metaphor and Meaning,* vol. 7 of *Studies in Contemporary Jewry.* New York: Oxford University Press, and Jerusalem: Institute of Contemporary Jewry, Hebrew University of Jerusalem, 1991.

Friedland, Roger, and Richard Hecht. *To Rule Jerusalem.* Cambridge: Cambridge University Press, 1996.

Friedman, Robert. *The False Prophet: Rabbi Meir Kahane—From FBI Informant to Knesset Member.* London: Faber and Faber, 1990.

———. *Zealots for Zion: Inside Israel's West Bank Movement.* New York: Random House, 1992.

Grossman, David. *The Yellow Wind.* New York: Farrar, Straus & Giroux, 1988. (Translated from the Hebrew by Haim Watzman.)

Halevi, Yossi Klein. "Kahane's Murderous Legacy." *Jerusalem Report,* March 24, 1994, 12–18.

———. "Torn between God and Country." *Jerusalem Report,* August 10, 1995, 12–17.

Kahane, Meir. *Listen World, Listen Jew.* Jerusalem: Institute of the Jewish Idea, 1978.
——. *They Must Go.* Jerusalem: Institute of the Jewish Idea, 1981.
Kotler, Yair. *Heil Kahane.* New York: Adama Books, 1986.
Lustick, Ian S. *For the Land and the Lord: Jewish Fundamentalism in Israel.* New York: Council on Foreign Relations, 1989.
Mergui, Raphael, and Philippe Simonnot. *Israel's Ayatollahs: Meir Kahane and the Far Right in Israel.* London: Saqi Books, 1987 (Originally published as *Meir Kahane: Le rabbin qui fait peur aux juifs.* Lausanne: Editions Pierre-Marcel Favre, 1985.)
Metzger, Alter B. Z. *Rabbi Kook's Philosophy of Repentance: A Translation of "Orot Ha-Teshuvah."* Studies in Torah Judaism, no. 11. New York: Yeshiva University Press, 1968.
Nasr, Kameel B. *Arab and Israeli Terrorism: The Causes and Effects of Political Violence.* Jefferson, NC: McFarland, 1997.
Paz, Reuven. *Ha-'imna ha-islamit umichma'utah 'iyyon rechoni utargum (The Covenant of the Islamicists and Its Significance—Analysis and Translation.)* Tel Aviv: Dayan Center, Tel Aviv University, 1988.
Sprinzak, Ehud. *The Ascendance of Israel's Radical Right.* New York: Oxford University Press, 1991.
——. *Brother against Brother: Violence and Extremism in Israeli Politics from Altalena to the Rabin Assasination.* New York: Free Press, 1999.
——. *Gush Emunim: The Politics of Zionist Fundamentalism in Israel.* New York: American Jewish Committee, 1986.
Weisburd, David. *Jewish Settler Violence: Deviance as Social Reaction.* University Park: Pennsylvania State University Press, 1989.
Zadka, Saul. Blood in Zion: *How Jewish Guerrillas Drove the British out of Palestine.* London: Brassey's, 1995.

Islamic Groups

Abrahamian, Ervand. *Radical Islam: The Iranian Mojahedin.* London: I. B. Tauris, 1989.
Abu-Amr, Ziad. *Islamic Fundamentalism in the West Bank and Gaza: Muslim Brotherhood and Islamic Jihad.* Bloomington: Indiana University Press, 1994.
Adams, Charles. "The Ideology of Mawlana Mawdudi." In Donald Eugene Smith, ed. *South Asian Politics and Religion.* Princeton, NJ: Princeton University Press, 1966.
Ahmad, Mumtaz. "Islamic Fundamentalism in South Asia: The Jamaat-i-Islami and the Tablighi Jamaat." In Martin E. Marty and R. Scott Appleby, eds. *Fundamentalisms Observed.* Chicago: University of Chicago Press, 1991, 457–530.
Arjomand, Said Amir, ed. *From Nationalism to Revolutionary Islam.* Albany: State University of New York Press, 1984.
——, ed. *Political Dimensions of Religion.* Albany: State University of New York Press, 1993.

Dwyer, James, David Kocieniewski, Deidre Murphy, and Peg Tyre. *Two Seconds under the World: Terror Comes to America—The Conspiracy behind the World Trade Center Bombing*. New York: Crown, 1994.

Enayat, Hamid. *Modern Islamic Political Thought: The Response of the Shi'i and Sunni Muslims to the Twentieth Century*. London: Macmillan, 1982.

Esposito, John. *The Islamic Threat?* New York: Oxford University Press, 1983.

——, ed. *Voices of Resurgent Islam*. New York: Oxford University Press, 1983.

Friedman, Robert I. *Sheik Abdel Rahman, the World Trade Center Bombing and the CIA*. Westfield, NJ: Open Media, 1993.

Heikal, Mohammed. *Autumn of Fury: The Assassination of Sadat*. London: Andre Deutsch, 1983.

Hiro, Dilip. *Holy Wars: The Rise of Islamic Fundamentalism*. New York: Routledge, 1989.

Hoffman, Bruce. *The Other Terrorist War: Palestinian versus Palestinian*. Santa Monica, CA: RAND Corporation, 1986.

Humphreys, R. Stephen. *Between Memories and Desire: The Middle East in a Troubled Age*. Berkeley: University of California Press, 1999.

——. "The Contemporary Resurgence in the Context of Modern Islam." In Ali E. Hillal Dessouki, ed. *Islamic Resurgence in the Arab World*. New York: Praeger, 1982.

Hunter, Shireen T., ed. *The Politics of Islamic Revivalism: Diversity and Unity*. Bloomington: Indiana University Press, 1988.

Ibrahim, Saad Eddin. "Islamic Militancy as a Social Movement: The Case of Two Groups in Egypt." In Ali E. Hillal Dessouki, ed. *Islamic Resurgence in the Arab World*. New York: Praeger, 1982, 117–36.

Jansen, Johannes J. G. *The Neglected Duty: The Creed of Sadat's Assassins and Islamic Resurgence in the Middle East*. New York: Macmillan, 1986.

Keddie, Nikki R., ed. *Religion and Politics in Iran: Shi'ism from Quietism to Revolution*. New Haven, CT: Yale University Press, 1983.

Kepel, Gilles. *Muslim Extremism in Egypt: The Prophet and Pharaoh*. Berkeley and Los Angeles: University of California Press, 1986.

——. *The Revenge of God: The Resurgence of Islam, Christianity and Judaism in the Modern World*. University Park: Pennsylvania State University Press, 1994. (Translated by Alan Braley.)

Kelsay, John. *Islam and War: A Study in Comparative Ethics*. Louisville, KY: Westminster/John Knox Press, 1993.

Khomeini, Imam [Ayatollah]. *Collection of Speeches, Position Statements*. Translations on Near East and North Africa no. 1902. Arlington, VA: Joint Publications Research Service, 1979.

——. *Islam and Revolution: Writings and Declarations*. London: Routledge & Kegan Paul, 1985. (Translated and annotated by Hamid Algar.) (Originally published by Berkeley, CA: Mizan Press, 1981.)

Kramer, Martin, ed. *Shi'ism, Resistance and Revolution*. Boulder, CO: Westview Press, 1987.

Lawrence, Bruce B. *Shattering the Myth: Islam beyond Violence*. Princeton, NJ: Princeton University Press, 1998.

Legrain, Jean-Francois. "A Defining Moment: Palestinian Islamic Fundamentalism." In James P. Piscatori, ed. *Islamic Fundamentalisms and the Gulf Crisis*. Chicago: Fundamentalism Project, American Academy of Arts and Sciences, 1991.

———. "The Islamic Movement and the Intifada." In Jamal R. Nassar and Roger Heacock, eds. *Intifada: Palestine at the Crossroads*. New York: Praeger, 1990.

———. "Islamistes et lutte nationale palestinienne dans les territoires occupés par Israel." *Revue Française de Science Politique* 36: 2 (April 1986), 227–47.

Lewis, Bernard. *The Assassins: A Radical Sect in Islam*. New York: Oxford University Press, 1967.

Marsden, Peter. *The Taliban: War, Religion, and the New World Order in Afghanistan*. London: Oxford University Press, 1998.

Martin, Richard C. "Religious Violence in Islam: Towards an Understanding of the Discourse on *Jihad* in Modern Egypt." In Paul Wilkinson and A. M. Stewart, eds. *Contemporary Research on Terrorism*. Aberdeen: Aberdeen University Press, 1987.

Merari, Ariel, and Shlomi Elad. *The International Dimension of Palestinian Terrorism*. Boulder, CO: Westview Press, 1993.

Mitchell, Richard P. *The Society of the Muslim Brothers*. London: Oxford University Press, 1969.

Munson, Henry, Jr. *Islam and Revolution in the Middle East*. New Haven, CT: Yale University Press, 1988.

Nasr, Kameel B. *Arab and Israeli Terrorism: The Causes and Effects of Political Violence*. Jefferson, NC: McFarland, 1997.

Nasr, Seyyed Vali Reza. *The Vanguard of the Islamic Revolution: The Jama'at-i Islami of Pakistan*. Berkeley: University of California Press, 1994.

Nassar, Jamal R., and Roger Heacock. *Intifada: Palestine at the Crossroads*. New York: Praeger, 1990.

Nettler, Ronald L. *Past Trials and Present Tribulations: A Muslim Fundamentalist's View of the Jews*. New York: Pergamon Press, 1987.

O'Balance, Edgar. *Islamic Fundamentalist Terrorism, 1979–95: The Iranian Connection*. New York: New York University Press, 1997.

Oliver, Anne Marie, and Paul Steinberg. *Rehearsals for a Happy Death: Hamas Suicide Bombers in Gaza*. New York: Oxford University Press, forthcoming.

Peters, Rudolph. *Islam and Colonialism: The Doctrine of Jihad in Modern History*. The Hague: Mouton, 1979.

Piscatori, James P., ed. *Islamic Fundamentalisms and the Gulf Crisis*. Chicago: Fundamentalism Project, American Academy of Arts and Sciences, 1991.

———. *Islam in the Political Process*. Cambridge: Cambridge University Press, 1983.

Qutb, Sayyid. *This Religion of Islam (Hadha 'd-Din)*. Palo Alto, CA: Al-Manar Press, 1967. (Translated by Islamdust.)

Rekhess, Elie. "The Iranian Impact on the Islamic Jihad Movement in the Gaza Strip." In David Menashri, ed. *The Iranian Revolution and the Muslim World*. Boulder, CO: Westview Press, 1990.

Roberts, Hugh. "Radical Islamism and the Dilemma of Algerian Nationalism: The Embattled Arians of Algiers." *Third World Quarterly* 10: 2 (April 1988), 567–75.

Sachedina, Abdulaziz Abdulhussein. "Activist Shi'ism in Iran, Iraq, and Lebanon." In Martin E. Marty and R. Scott Appleby, eds. *Fundamentalisms Observed*. Chicago: University of Chicago Press, 1991, 403–56.

———. *The Just Ruler (al-sultan al-'adil) in Shi'ite Islam: The Comprehensive Authority of the Jurist in Imamite Jurisprudence*. New York: Oxford University Press, 1988.

Sivan, Emmanuel. "The Islamic Resurgence: Civil Society Strikes Back." *Journal of Contemporary History* (London) 25 (1990), 353–64.

———. *Radical Islam: Medieval Theology and Modern Politics*. New Haven, CT: Yale University Press, 1985.

———. "Sunni Radicalism in the Middle East and the Iranian Revolution." *International Journal of Middle East Studies* 21 (1989), 1–30.

Sivan, Emmanuel, and Menachem Friedman, eds. *Religious Radicalism and Politics in the Middle East*. Albany: State University of New York Press, 1990.

Steinberg, Matti. "The PLO and Palestinian Islamic Fundamentalism." *Jewish Quarterly* 52 (Fall 1989), 37–54.

Subcommittee on Crime and Criminal Justice, Committee on the Judiciary, United States Congress. *World Trade Center Bombing: Terror Hits Home*. Hearing before the subcommittee. Washington, DC: U.S. Government Printing Office, 1994.

Taheri, Amir. *Holy Terror: Inside the World of Islamic Terrorism*. Bethesda, MD: Alder and Alder, 1987.

Tibi, Bassam. *The Challenge of Fundamentalism: Political Islam and the New World Disorder*. Berkeley: University of California Press, 1998.

Wendell, Charles, trans. *Five Tracts of Hasan al-Banna (1906–1949)*. Berkeley and Los Angeles: University of California Press, 1978.

Wright, Robin. *The Last Great Revolution: Turmoil and Transformation in Iran*. New York: Simon & Schuster, 2000.

———. *Sacred Rage: The Wrath of Militant Islam*. New York: Simon & Schuster, 1985.

Sikh Separatists

Bhindranwale, Jarnail Singh. "Address to the Sikh Congregation." Transcript of a sermon given in the Golden Temple in November 1983. Columbus, OH: Sikh Religious and Educational Trust, 1985. (Translated by Ranbir Singh Sandhu.)

———. "Two Lectures." Given on July 19 and September 20, 1983. Columbus, OH: Sikh Religious and Educational Trust. (Translated from the videotaped originals by R. S. Sandhu.)

Bjørkman, James W., ed. *Fundamentalism, Revivalists and Violence in South Asia*. Riverdale, MD: Riverdale, 1986.

Chopra, V. D., R. K. Mishra, and Nirmal Singh. *Agony of Punjab*. New Delhi: Patriot, 1984.

Citizens for Democracy. *Oppression in Punjab*. Columbus, OH: Sikh Religious and Educational Trust, 1985.

Das, Veena, ed. *Mirrors of Violence: Communities, Riots and Survivors in South Asia*. Delhi: Oxford University Press, 1990.

Embree, Ainslie. *Utopias in Conflict: Religion and Nationalism in Modern India*. Berkeley and Los Angeles: University of California Press, 1990.

Frykenberg, Robert Eric. "Revivalism and Fundamentalism: Some Critical Observations with Special Reference to Politics in South Asia." In James W. Bjørkman, ed. *Fundamentalism, Revivalists and Violence in South Asia*. Riverdale, MD: Riverdale, 1986.

Ganguly, Sumit. *The Crisis in Kashmir: Portraits of War, Hopes of Peace*. Cambridge University Press, 1997.

Gupta, Lina. "Indian Secularism and the Problem of the Sikhs." In Gustavo Benavides and M. W. Daly, eds. *Religion and Political Power*. Albany: State University of New York Press, 1989.

Jalandhary, Surjeet. *Bhindranwale Sant*. Jalandhar, India: Punjab Pocket Books, n.d. [c. 1985].

Jeffrey, Robin. *What's Happening to India? Punjab, Ethnic Conflict, Mrs. Gandhi's Death and the Test for Federalism*. New York: Holmes and Meier, 1986.

Juergensmeyer, Mark. "The Logic of Religious Violence." In David Rapoport, ed. *Inside Terrorist Organizations*. London: Frank Cass, 1988.

Juergensmeyer, Mark, and N. Gerald Barrier, eds. *Sikh Studies: Comparative Perspectives on Changing Tradition*. Berkeley Religious Studies Series no. 1. Berkeley, CA: Graduate Theological Union, 1979.

Kapur, Rajiv A. *Sikh Separatism: The Politics of Faith*. London: Allen & Unwin, 1986.

Kashmeri, Zuhair, and Brian McAndrew. *Soft Target: How the Indian Intelligence Service Penetrated Canada*. Toronto: J. Lorimer, 1989.

Kaur, Amarjit. *The Punjab Story*. New Delhi: Roli Books International, 1984.

Khurshid, Salman. *Beyond Terrorism: New Hope for Kashmir*. New Delhi: UBS, 1994.

McLeod, W. H. *Who Is a Sikh? The Problem of Sikh Identity*. Oxford: Clarendon Press, 1989.

Madan, T. N. "The Double-Edged Sword: Fundamentalism and the Sikh Religious Tradition." In Martin E. Marty and R. Scott Appleby, eds. *Fundamentalisms Observed*. Chicago: University of Chicago Press, 1991.

Mahmood, Cynthia Keppley. *Fighting for Faith and Nation: Dialogues with Sikh Militants*. Philadelphia: University of Pennsylvania Press, 1997.

———. "Sikh Rebellion and the Hindu Concept of Order." *Asian Survey* 29: 3, 1989: 326–40.

Marhwah, Ved. *Uncivil Wars: Pathology of Terrorism in India*. New Delhi: Indus (HarperCollins India), 1995.

Mukherjee, Bharati, and Clark Blaise. *The Sorrow and the Terror: The Haunting Legacy of the Air India Tragedy*. Markham, Ontario: Viking, 1987.

Mulgrew, Ian. *Unholy Terror: The Sikhs and International Terrorism*. Toronto: Key Porter Books, 1988.

Nandy, Ashis. "An Anti-Secularist Manifesto." In John Hick and Lamont C. Hempel, eds. *Gandhi's Significance for Today: The Elusive Legacy.* London: Macmillan, 1989.

Nayar, Kuldip, and Khushwant Singh. *Tragedy of Punjab: Operation Bluestar and After.* New Delhi: Vision Books, 1984.

Oberoi, Harjot Singh. "Sikh Fundamentalism: Translating History into Theory." In Martin E. Marty and R. Scott Appleby, eds, *Fundamentalisms and the State.* Chicago: University of Chicago Press, 1993, 356–85.

O'Brien, Conor Cruise. "Holy War against India." *Atlantic* 262 (August 1988), 78–86.

O'Connell, Joseph T., Milton Israel, and Willard G. Oxtoby, eds. *Sikh History and Religion in the Twentieth Century.* Toronto: Centre for South Asian Studies, University of Toronto, 1988.

People's Union for Democratic Rights and People's Union for Civil Liberties. *Who Are the Guilty? Report of a Joint Inquiry into the Causes and Impact of the Riots in Delhi from 31 October–10 November.* Delhi: Gobinda Mukhoty and Rajni Kothari, 1984.

Pettigrew, Joyce. "In Search of a New Kingdom of Lahore." *Pacific Affairs* 60: 1 (Spring 1987), 78–92.

——. *Martyrdom and Political Resistance: Essays from Asia and Europe.* Amsterdam: VU University Press, 1997.

——. *The Sikhs of the Punjab: Unheard Voice of State and Guerrilla Violence.* Atlantic Highlands, NJ: Zed Books, 1995.

Premdas, Ralph R., S. W. R. de A. Samarasinghe, and Alan B. Anderson, eds. *Secessionist Movements in Comparative Perspective.* London: Pinter, 1990.

Puri, Harish, Paramjit S. Judge, and Jagroop S. Sekhon. "Terrorism in Punjab: Understanding Reality at the Grass-Roots Level." *Guru Nanak Journal of Sociology* 18:1 (1997), 5–12.

Sarin, Ritu. *The Assassination of Indira Gandhi.* New Delhi: Penguin Books, 1990.

Singh, Amrik, ed. *Punjab in Indian Politics: Issues and Trends.* New Delhi: Ajanta Books, 1985.

Singh, Mohinder. "Gandhi, Sikhs and Non-violence." *Khera* 9: 3 (July–September 1990), 72–87.

Tully, Mark, and Satish Jacob. *Amritsar: Mrs. Gandhi's Last Battle.* London: Pan Books, 1985.

van der Veer, Peter. *Religious Nationalism: Hindus and Muslims in India.* Berkeley: University of California Press, 1994.

Wallace, Paul, and Surendra Chopra, eds. *Political Dynamics and Crisis in Punjab.* Amritsar: Guru Nanak Dev University Press, 1988.

Japanese Movements

Abe, Yoshiya. "Violence and Cults: The Case of Aum Shinrikyo." Paper read at the meetings of the International Society for the Study of Religion, Quebec, Canada, June 1995.

Asahara, Shoko. *Beyond Life and Death.* Shizuoka, Japan: Aum, 1992.

———. *The Bodhisattva Sutra: Salvation through Complete Reliance on the Power of the True Victor.* Shizuoka, Japan: Aum, 1994.

———. *Declaring Myself the Christ: Disclosing the True Meanings of Jesus Christ's Gospel.* Shizuoka, Japan: Aum, 1992.

———. *Disaster Approaches the Land of the Rising Sun: Shoko Asahara's Apocalyptic Predictions.* Shizuoka, Japan: Aum, 1995.

———. *Supreme Initiation: An Empirical Spiritual Science for the Supreme Truth.* New York: Aum USA, 1988.

———. *Tathagata Abhidhamma: The Ever-Winning Law of the True Victors.* 2 vols. Shizuoka, Japan: Aum, 1992.

Brackett, D. W. *Holy Terror: Armageddon in Tokyo.* New York: Weatherhill, 1966.

Davis, Winston. "Dealing with Criminal Religions: The Case of Om Supreme Truth." *Christian Century* 112:22 (July 19, 1995), 708–12.

———. "Fundamentalism in Japan: Religious and Political." In Martin E. Marty and R. Scott Appleby, eds. *Fundamentalisms Observed.* Chicago: University of Chicago Press, 1991.

Hardacre, Helen. *Aum Shinrikyo and the Japanese Media: The Pied Piper Meets the Lamb of God.* New York: East Asian Institute Report, Columbia University, 1995.

Haselkorn, Avigdor. "Japan's Poison Gas Apocalyptics." *American Spectator* 28:7 (July 1995), 22–26.

Kitabatake, Kiyoyasu. "Aum Shinrikyo: Society Begets an Aberration." *Japan Quarterly* 42:4 (1995), 376–83.

Mullins, Mark R., Shimazono Susumu, and Paul L. Swanson, eds. *Religion and Society in Modern Japan.* Berkeley: Asian Humanities Press, 1993.

Okawa, Ryuho. *The Challenge of Religion.* Tokyo: Institute for Research into Human Happiness, 1993.

Reader, Ian. *A Poisonous Cocktail? Aum Shinrikyo's Path to Violence.* Copenhagen: Nordic Institute of Asian Studies, 1996.

Sayle, Murray. "Nerve Gas and the Four Noble Truths." *New Yorker* April 1, 1996, 56–71.

Shimazono, Susumu. *Aum Shinrikyo no kiseki.* Booklet no. 379. Tokyo: Iwanami, 1995.

———. "The Expansion of Japan's New Religions into Foreign Cultures." In M. Mullins, S. Shimazono, and P. Swanson, eds. *Religion and Society in Modern Japan.* Berkeley: Asian Humanities Press, 1993, 273–300.

———. "In the Wake of Aum." *Japanese Journal of Religious Studies* 22:3–4, (1995), 381–415. (Condensed version of Shimazono's book *Aum Shinrikyo no kiseki,* translated by Robert Kisala.)

———. "New New Religions and This World: Religious Movements in Japan after the 1970s and Their Beliefs about Salvation." *Social Compass* 42:2 (1995), 193–202.

Yoshino, Kosaku. *Cultural Nationalism in Contemporary Japan.* London: Routledge, 1992.

Index

Compositor: Publication Services
Text: 10/13 Sabon
Display: Akzidenz Grotesk
Printer: Edward Bros.
Binder: Edwards Bros.